MW00834452

"Students, teachers, and the intellectual community generally owe a debt of gratitude to Matthew Minerd for undertaking this translation of the *Le sens commun* of Fr. Reginald Garrigou-Lagrange. This important philosophical work addresses topics as timely now as they were when it was published nearly a century ago: the foundations of human knowledge, the power of human reason to know God, the relationship between faith and reason, the dynamics of the development of doctrine. Readers of this book will understand why the works of this master teacher are lately enjoying a phenomenal revival. Having influenced countless Thomists in the twentieth century, the voice of Garrigou-Lagrange retains its vibrancy and relevance in the twenty-first."

ARCHBISHOP J. AUGUSTINE DI NOIA, O.P.
Vatican City

"Réginald Garrigou-Lagrange enjoys a comeback! This is fitting inasmuch as the Dominican author masterfully exposes the order of things. Fr. Garrigou-Lagrange never ceases to champion a key truth of both philosophy and theology: All contingent being depends upon God's absolute actuality. The latter premoves and perfects the former. In this book, Garrigou-Lagrange shows how God's being, truth, and goodness perfect even the contingencies of human knowing and loving. The author further illuminates how theology reaches beyond dialectical inquiry and historical genealogy. Instead of expounding what others say about God or how they do theology, the author shows us how theology can attain a true knowledge of God and the things that pertain to God. Garrigou-Lagrange restores dignity to the 'Queen of the Sciences.' This volume serves well to introduce students to sound Christian pedagogy. In fact, the recognition that Fr. Garrigou-Lagrange displays the best of *la clarté française* probably accounts for one of the reasons that contemporary young scholars find his work so engrossing and informative."

FR. ROMANUS CESSARIO, O.P.
Adam Cardinal Maida Chair of Theology
Ave Maria University

"It is impossible to understand the twentieth century discussion of the nature of dogma and of dogmatic development, as well as modern magisterial teaching thereon, without Garrigou-Lagrange's *Le sens commun*, and many will be grateful for Matthew Minerd's translation."

FR. GUY MANSINI, O.S.B.
Max Seckler Chair of Theology
Ave Maria University

"Despite being one of the most important Catholic philosophical works of the twentieth century, Garrigou-Lagrange's *Common Sense* has remained unavailable in English for over a century. This remarkable book provided what many considered to be the definitive statement of common sense philosophy in the modern era. It influenced generations of theologians, was read and discussed by the *ressourcement* theologians during their formation in the 1920s, and was the principle behind all of Garrigou-Lagrange's interventions in the *nouvelle theologie* affair in the 1940s, even eventually influencing St. John Paul II's philosophical thought. Published at the height of the Modernist crisis, it served as a preamble and roadmap to virtually all of Garrigou-Lagrange's future philosophical work, which was essentially an extended excursus of common sense and its implications. Natural Theology, the philosophical foundations of Revelation, principles of non-contradiction and final causality, and the immutability of dogma all are treated here in this remarkable synthesis. As we've come to expect from Dr. Matthew Minerd, this volume is a translation of the highest quality, readable and faithful to the original text, always conscientiously providing—and completing, in many cases—the extensive original footnotes."

JON KIRWAN
Assistant Professor of Theology and Director of
Graduate Programs in Theology
University of St. Thomas, Houston

"Why do we trust common sense? Is there an authentic 'common-sense philosophy'? Can common sense grasp the meaning of Christian dogma? In his wide-ranging and luminous exploration of these questions, Garrigou-Lagrange reinvigorates our hope of fulfilling the innate human desire (eloquently stressed by John Paul II in *Fides et Ratio*) for truth that is universal and universally accessible, on both the natural and supernatural planes. We are all in Dr. Minerd's debt for bringing this work to English-speaking readers in such a lucid and insightfully annotated translation."

FRANCIS FEINGOLD
Assistant Professor of Philosophy and Chair of Pre-Theology Program
St. Patrick's Seminary and University, Menlo Park

THOMISTIC
COMMON
SENSE

THOMISTIC COMMON SENSE

The Philosophy of Being and the Development of Doctrine

~~~~~~

RÉGINALD GARRIGOU-LAGRANGE
Translated by MATTHEW K. MINERD

EMMAUS
ACADEMIC

www.emmausacademic.com
Steubenville, Ohio

EMMAUS
ACADEMIC

Steubenville, Ohio
www.emmausacademic.com
A Division of The St. Paul Center for Biblical Theology
Editor-in-Chief: Scott Hahn
1468 Parkview Circle
Steubenville, Ohio 43952

© 2021 St. Paul Center
All rights reserved. 2021
Printed in the United States of America

Original French edition, *Le sens commun: la philosophie de l'être et les formules dogmatiques*, 4th ed., published by Desclée de Brouwer & Cie in 1936.

Library of Congress Cataloging-in-Publication Data applied for
978-1-64585-107-3 hardcover / 978-1-64585-108-0 paperback /
978-1-64585-109-7 ebook

Unless otherwise noted, Scripture quotations are taken from Revised Standard Version of the Bible, copyright 1952 [2nd edition, 1971] by the Division
of Christian Education of the National Council of the Churches of Christ in
the United States of America. Used by permission. All rights reserved.

Cover design by Patty Borgman and Emily Demary
Layout by Emily Demary

"The formal object of the intellect is being, just as color is the formal object of sight."

—Saint Thomas Aquinas, *Summa contra gentiles* II, ch. 83.

TABLE OF CONTENTS

FOREWORD BY
MATTHEW LEVERING

Matthew Minerd's translation of Réginald Garrigou-Lagrange's *Le sens commun: La philosophie de l'être et les formulas dogmatiques* arrives at an auspicious time. Younger theologians and philosophers are inquiring into what Garrigou-Lagrange and his generation had to say. Why did contemporaries such as Jacques Maritain so value Garrigou-Lagrange's *Le sens commun*, and most importantly, have its main insights been confirmed? In this foreword, I hope to explore this question. For me as a Catholic theologian, the importance of Garrigou-Lagrange's work primarily involves what it may offer to current speculative theology. I do not retrieve him as a figure in today's traditionalist battlegrounds, which strike me as fundamentally misguided. I approach Garrigou-Lagrange's work with the goal of learning from it (not replicating it),[1] on the supposition that the best insights of both the Thomist and *ressourcement* streams of thought should be appropriated by Catholic theologians today.

The underlying issue that Garrigou-Lagrange is addressing in *Le sens commun* is the historical contextualization of all truth claims, as understood by the Catholic modernists. Aidan Nichols aptly describes *Le sens commun* as "at once an affirmation of Thomistic ontology against Bergsonian vitalism, for which becoming is more significant than being, and a rebuttal of Modernism's view of dogma."[2] Can the phrase "Jesus is fully

---

[1] See the background provided in Aidan Nichols, O.P., *Reason with Piety: Garrigou-Lagrange in the Service of Catholic Thought* (Naples, FL: Sapientia Press, 2008), 1–8.

[2] Nichols, *Reason with Piety*, 9. Nichols draws attention here to the reading of Catholic modernism found in Pope Pius X's 1907 encyclical *Pascendi Dominici Gregis*, a reading (accurate in my view, if somewhat neglecting the historical and historiographical sources of some exemplars of Catholic modernism) that shapes Garrigou-Lagrange's book. It should go with-

God and fully man" have an enduringly true meaning across diverse languages, cultures, and personal experiences? In response to this question, some may suppose that no enduringly true propositions about divine realities are possible—even if religious experience remains possible. Others may suppose that we have a natural and immediate intuition of the divine that makes dogma superfluous.

By contrast, Garrigou-Lagrange thinks that there are fundamental metaphysical principles constituting the ground of enduring dogmatic truth, that people know without need for study. These principles allow dogmatic propositions to be ontologically understandable by all, so that people are able to affirm the Nicene Creed and to have an adequate sense of what they are affirming. The principles form the foundation of metaphysical realism: that the intellect's object is being; the primacy of being over becoming (the act/potency distinction); the principle of non-contradiction (something cannot be and not be in the same way at the same time); the reality of efficient and final causality; the distinction between person and nature; the substance/accident distinction; and so on.

In making this argument, Garrigou-Lagrange is immersed in conversations that have been forgotten and neglected to the detriment of theology. Post-conciliar Catholic theology has sometimes operated as though the mainstream Catholic theological debates of the late-nineteenth- and early-twentieth centuries can be dismissed as the last gasps of Enlightenment-influenced, rationalistic theology. In fact, the debates to which Garrigou-Lagrange contributes never ceased to be relevant. Reading in *Le sens commun* about the perspectives of such figures as Antonio Rosmini, Anton Günther, Ernst Renan, Édouard Le Roy, and Henri Bergson, one is struck by how contemporary so much of it still is.[3]

---

out saying that I agree with Pius X and Garrigou-Lagrange that Catholic modernism, which "later in the twentieth century . . . acquired an afterlife" (Nichols, 4), is destructive to Catholic faith and life.

[3] As Guy Mansini, O.S.B., says in sketching the influence of Bergson's thought upon the Catholic modernist George Tyrrell: "For Bergson, language exhausts itself in its practical import, the help it gives us to navigate in the world. It speaks of the relations between things, but does not get at things in themselves. For that, there is intuition. Intuition gives us ourselves—our own *durée*—that is, the inmost reality of the person. But intuition gives us also whatever we possess of the reality of *anything*. But once durational reality is cashed out in language—the *morcelage* of the conceptual pieces of thought and language that freeze what is flowing, and stop the motion that is the real—then language abstracts, falsifies, misleads. . . . Access to the true and the real occurs not by language, therefore, but by experience. And if this is true of our knowledge of the self, a religious thinker will infer that it will be true as well of the one in whose image we are made.

While Garrigou-Lagrange affirms doctrinal development and knows that a dogmatic truth cannot be *reduced* to its specific formulation, he sees that the crux of the debate is whether the Church has been given a knowable, *propositionally* enunciable deposit of faith. Regarding the ongoing development of the Church's knowledge of this deposit, he argues that the Church today does not know "more" revealed realities, but rather knows more of what is (and was) present in the revealed realities. At stake is the nature of divine revelation, given that an evolutionary view of ongoing "revelation" would, in the end, amount to not having received a revelation at all.

In *Le sens commun*, originally written in 1909 (the present translation comes from the third edition), the anti-modernist condemnations found in *Lamentabili Sane* and *Pascendi Dominici Gregis* are a significant presence. Less explicitly present, but still visible, are the twenty-two Thomistic theses to which Catholic thinkers of the day were formally required to subscribe as expressing the *philosophia perennis*.[4] As Nichols laments: "Roman neo-Thomism from the pontificate of Pius X onwards, being framed as it was in terms of a response to Modernism, inevitably became associated with the mechanisms of doctrinal control put in pace by the encyclical. This goes a long way towards explaining the *damnatio memoriae* it subsequently suffered."[5] Reading the book in this light, the theologian today may wonder whether the choice is either to do theology and metaphysics exactly as Garrigou-Lagrange does or to fall into modernist error. The impression that these are the only two choices on the table can be bolstered by the fact that Garrigou-Lagrange's robust prose and clear argumentation do not lack for confidence. The result is that theologians who do not belong to Garrigou-Lagrange's school of thought may hasten to condemn *him* before he condemns them; fruitful theological understanding may be cut off before it ever has a chance.

Access to the true and real God will be beyond language, in religious experience" ("Experience and Discourse, Revelation and Dogma in Catholic Modernism," *Nova et Vetera* [English] 17, no. 4 [2019]: 1119–43, at 1132–33). For both critical and, in certain ways, appreciative engagement with Bergson's philosophy—Bergson was his teacher prior to his conversion—see Jacques Maritain, *Bergsonian Philosophy and Thomism*, ed. Ralph McInerny, 2nd ed., vol. 1 of *The Collected Works of Jacques Maritain* (Notre Dame, IN: University of Notre Dame Press, 2007). I note that Garrigou-Lagrange, too, attended Bergson's courses at the Sorbonne as part of his philosophical formation, though unlike Maritain, Garrigou-Lagrange was never attracted by Bergson's philosophy.

[4] Note that "Garrigou did not think that common sense, spontaneous reason, sufficed by itself to found a 'perennial philosophy'" (Nichols, *Reason with Piety*, 13).

[5] Nichols, *Reason with Piety*, 8.

I submit that this atmosphere of fear and condemnation, at least insofar as it involves distinct theological schools that affirm Catholic dogma, needs to be deliberately set to the side in reading *Le sens commun*. After all, *Le sens commun* seeks to defend the claim that non-scholars can know being and can know the truth of the realities attested by historically contextualized dogma. The claim is not that everyone should be Garrigou-Lagrange *in nuce*. Rather, people naturally know basic ontological truths, and therefore, in faith, can understand and affirm the things that the creeds are communicating. This is a refreshingly humble claim for theologians to make.

It is not a matter, then, of being required to do theology as Garrigou-Lagrange does it. To highlight this point, one might examine the approach taken by Pope Francis in his first encyclical, *Lumen Fidei*—largely written by Pope Benedict XVI, an admirer (and exponent) of the *nouvelle théologie*, which Garrigou-Lagrange opposed. Pope Francis emphasizes the role of love in faith, in a manner similar to Pierre Rousselot's *The Eyes of Faith*. This is not the approach that Garrigou-Lagrange would take to theological virtue of faith. At the same time, Pope Francis goes on to say that "love requires truth. Only to the extent that love is grounded in truth can it endure over time, can it transcend the passing moment and be sufficiently solid to sustain a shared journey. . . . Without truth, love is incapable of establishing a firm bond."[6] He has in view truth about God, truth about Jesus Christ, truth about God's covenantal love. Of course, such truth does not mean the reduction of God to propositions; on the contrary, as Garrigou-Lagrange emphasizes, the purpose of propositional knowledge is to unite us to realities, to actual being. According to *Lumen Fidei*, God "is a subject who makes himself known and perceived in an interpersonal relationship," and this relationship takes root through an encounter mediated by words (within the Spirit-guided community of believers): "the word which God speaks to us, the word which God speaks about himself."[7] Receiving this word is possible only if minds, and words, intend and communicate being.

Pope Francis calls the Trinity a communion of love, "an eternal dialogue of communion."[8] In *Le sens commun*, Garrigou-Lagrange say something comparable, arguing that the dogma of the Trinity, though expressed in technical terms indebted to Greek philosophy, resonates with the "common sense" of ordinary believers, with ordinary believers' sense of being, of the real. Garrigou-Lagrange argues that the beings that we see around

---

[6] Pope Francis, *Lumen Fidei* (San Francisco: Ignatius Press, 2013), §27 (p. 48).
[7] Pope Francis, *Lumen Fidei*, §36 (p. 67).
[8] Pope Francis, *Lumen Fidei*, §36 (p. 67).

us show that the higher forms of existence are more able to communicate and to share themselves. Thus it makes sense that God, as infinitely perfect in being, is able to communicate and share himself *perfectly*, so much so as to beget a Son who is utterly identical to God the Father in substance, while differentiated from God the Father in the order of origin.

Any theologian reading Garrigou-Lagrange's *Le sens commun* today will need to attend to the insights of the Benedictine theologian Guy Mansini, especially his recent "The Historicity of Dogma and Common Sense: Ambroise Gardeil, Réginald Garrigou-Lagrange, Yves Congar, and the Modern Magisterium."[9] The author of a dissertation at the Gregorian University in Rome on Édouard Le Roy's understanding of dogma, Mansini has a thorough knowledge of Catholic modernism and its opponents. He writes knowledgeably on the influence of Henri Bergson and Auguste Sabatier, as well as on the views of dogma held by George Tyrrell and Alfred Loisy.[10] He is up to date regarding the contemporary literature about early- to mid-twentieth-century Catholic theology. Among his other contributions, he makes clear that the *nouvelle théologie* movement was not modernist, insofar as figures such as Henri de Lubac insisted upon the indispensable truth of dogma. Based on the evidence, however, Mansini also deems that in the work of some figures associated with the *nouvelle théologie*—he names M.-D. Chenu—the enduring truth of dogmatic propositions was undermined.[11]

A recurring leitmotif of Mansini's work is that "human discourse must be capable of making the intelligibility of realities present to us, and we must be able to appreciate ourselves as creatures whose work it is to be receptive to being, before ever we can hear the word of revelation."[12] This is another way of saying—more phenomenologically, with more attention to language—what Garrigou-Lagrange is saying, by and large, in *Le sens commun*. Mansini emphasizes that the appeal to something like "common sense," which Garrigou-Lagrange worked out in conjunction with his

---

[9] Guy Mansini, O.S.B., "The Historicity of Dogma and Common Sense: Ambroise Gardeil, Réginald Garrigou-Lagrange, Yves Congar, and the Modern Magisterium," *Nova et Vetera* (English) 18, no. 1 (2020): 111–38.

[10] See: Guy Mansini, O.S.B., *What Is a Dogma? The Meaning and Truth of Dogma in Édouard Le Roy and His Scholastic Opponents* (Rome: Gregorian University Press, 1985); Mansini, "Experience and Discourse, Revelation and Dogma in Catholic Modernism."

[11] See Guy Mansini, O.S.B., Review of Jon Kirwan, *An Avant-garde Theological Generation: The* Nouvelle theologie *and the French Crisis of Modernity* (Oxford: Oxford University Press, 2018), in *The Thomist* 83 (2019): 479–82, at 482.

[12] Mansini, "Experience and Discourse, Revelation and Dogma in Catholic Modernism," 1143.

teacher Ambroise Gardeil and others,[13] continues after the Second Vatican Council.

In Pope John Paul II's 1998 encyclical *Fides et Ratio*, for example, the Pope reflects upon the situation of theology, and upon the ability of creedal propositions to communicate enduring truth, in light of contemporary epistemic contexts such as post-modernism and (at another extreme) scientific-technological positivism. At various points in the encyclical, he strongly echoes the perspective of Garrigou-Lagrange's *Le sens commun*. Thus, referencing Pope Pius XII's 1950 *Humani Generis*, John Paul II makes the following claim: "One must reckon seriously with the meaning which words assume in different times and cultures. Nonetheless, the history of thought shows that across the range of cultures and their development certain basic concepts retain their universal epistemological value and thus retain the truth of the propositions in which they are expressed."[14] These basic concepts, found in varying formulations across diverse times and cultures, exhibit the ability of the mind to know being. Among these core philosophical insights, the Pope names "the principles of noncontradiction, finality and causality, as well as the concept of the person as a free and intelligent

---

[13] On Gardeil, see Mansini, "Historicity of Dogma," 112–17, relying largely upon Gardeil's *Le donné révélé et la théologie*, 2nd ed. (Paris: Cerf, 1932). Gardeil's book, like Garrigou-Lagrange's, was originally published in 1909. For further background, see Nichols, *Reason with Piety*, 10–11: "What is 'common sense', and how does it function? Garrigou's use of this term, though it reflects a wider currency than simply among neo-scholastics, seems to have entered contemporary Catholic philosophical parlance through the *Summa philosophica* of the Italian Dominican Cardinal Tommaso Zigliara—whose lectures Leo XIII attended from behind a curtain since it was thought inappropriate for a reigning pope to be seen taking instruction. For Zigliara, the 'inclination of rational nature' to admit certain judgements is *sensus naturae communis*, 'the common sense of nature.' . . . Neo-scholastic use has also to be distinguished from that found in the so-called common sense school in eighteenth-century Scotland. Garrigou considered Thomas Reid and his colleagues to represent a mediocre philosophical response to David Hume's scepticism, vaguely formulated—Reid spoke of a 'natural instinct' for truth—and dependent on an unsatisfactory compromise between metaphysics and empiricism which failed to recongnize that mind is a faculty essentially relative to being. Only *la philosophie de l'être*, 'the philosophy of being,' argues Garrigou, really deserves the title 'common sense philosophy,' since only such an ontology conforms to our most basic judgements and can count as their intellectual development and justification."

[14] Pope John Paul II, *Fides et Ratio*, §96, in *The Encyclicals of John Paul II*, ed. J. Michael Miller, C.S.B. (Huntington, IN: Our Sunday Visitor, 2001), 850–913, at 906. Mansini observes that *Fides et Ratio* exhibits a "recognizable reliance on at least part of what Garrigou-Lagrange called 'common sense'" ("Historicity of Dogma," 133).

subject, with the capacity to know God, truth and goodness."[15] These universally accessible philosophical insights, which John Paul II calls "an *implicit philosophy*" possessed by all persons "in a general and unreflective way," undergird what he describes as "the objectivity of truth," its contact with being rather than simply with appearances or "becoming."[16] The Pope, who wrote his doctoral thesis under Garrigou-Lagrange, observes with regard to the Christian doctrinal significance of metaphysical realism: "A theology without a metaphysical horizon could not move beyond an analysis of religious experience, nor would it allow the *intellectus fidei* to give a coherent account of the universal and transcendent value of revealed truth."[17]

In "Historicity of Dogma and Common Sense," Mansini documents that, between 1965 and 1973, during a time of theological and doctrinal turmoil, the Catholic Church likewise repeatedly invoked something like Garrigou-Lagrange's "common sense." In his encyclical on the Eucharist, *Mysterium Fidei* (1965), Pope Paul VI urges that key dogmatic propositions—such as those regarding the Trinity, the Incarnation, and the Eucharist—are not strictly culture-dependent for their truth, even though they employ culturally grounded language. Paul VI appeals to the way in which these dogmas build upon the foundation of "what the human mind grasps of reality through necessary and universal experience and what it expresses in apt and exact words, whether it be in ordinary or more refined language."[18] The same proposal appears in the International Theological

---

[15] Pope John Paul II, *Fides et Ratio*, §4 (p. 852).

[16] Pope John Paul II, *Fides et Ratio*, §4 (p. 882) and §44 (p. 876).

[17] Pope John Paul II, *Fides et Ratio*, §83 (p. 899–900). John Paul II adds, along lines that resonate with Mansini's emphasis: "The importance of metaphysics becomes still more evident if we consider current developments in hermeneutics and the analysis of language. The results of such studies can be very helpful for the understanding of faith, since they bring to light the structure of our thought and speech and the meaning which language bears. However, some scholars working in these fields tend to stop short at the question of how reality is understood and expressed, without going further to see whether reason can discover its essence. . . . Faith clearly presupposes that human language is capable of expressing divine and transcendent reality in a universal way—analogically, it is true, but no less meaningfully for that. Were this not so, the word of God, which is always a divine word in human language, would not be capable of saying anything about God. The interpretation of this word cannot merely keep referring us to one interpretation after another, without ever leading us to a statement which is simply true; otherwise there would be no Revelation of God, but only the expression of human notions about God and about what God presumably thinks of us" (§84, 900).

[18] Pope Paul VI, *Mysterium Fidei*, §24 (see the Vatican website).

Commission's 1972 *Unity of the Faith and Theological Pluralism*, which argues briefly that dogmas do not require a philosophical education in order to be understood; instead, dogmatic formulations rely upon "the underlying realities of universal human experience" as cognitionally available to everyone, philosopher and non-philosopher.[19] And in 1973 the Congregation for the Doctrine of the Faith, in *Mysterium Ecclesiae*, chimed in by granting, of course, that dogmas are expressed in the philosophical language of particular cultures and can be clarified or more fully expressed. Nevertheless, dogmatic truths are not bound to a particular epoch. Dogmas do more than approximate truth along lines that will be ever-changing; they communicate truth in a determinative way. Put simply, "we can know the true and unchanging meaning of dogmas."[20]

The post-conciliar Church, then, continued to struggle with the same basic issue and to advance the same basic answer as did Garrigou-Lagrange in his critique of Catholic modernism in *Le sens commun*. To give one final example of the post-conciliar ecclesiastical engagement with the issue, let me mention (as Mansini also does) the International Theological Commission's 1990 *The Interpretation of Dogma*, published eight years prior to *Fides et Ratio*. The question, again, is how to "take the hermeneutic circle between subject and object seriously"—thereby avoiding a simplistic realism—"without becoming victims of a relativism which recognizes nothing but interpretations of interpretations, which, in turn, give birth to further interpretations."[21] Fully granting the historicity of dogma, are there grounds for assurance that dogmatic formulations unite us to unchanging realities and thus express enduring truth for all times and places? Or must

---

[19] International Theological Commission, *Unity of the Faith and Theological Pluralism*, reproduced in *International Theological Commission: Texts and Documents, 1969–1985* (San Francisco: Ignatius Press, 1989), 91. Mansini sums up the commission's position, linking it to that of Yves Congar: "Dogma expresses the truth about divine things. Its expressions and conceptuality are worked out historically with what is at hand but are the Church's own creation, a creation enriching the common patrimony of humanity. Still, dogma remains accessible to all. The Commission refuses to let the truth about the historicity of dogma defeat the truth of its accessibility, and vice versa. The Commission does this without any express appeal to already available 'common' or common-sense concepts, although there is a suggestion that there is a production of such a store common to all mankind" ("Historicity of Dogma," 132).

[20] Congregation for the Doctrine of the Faith, *Mysterium Ecclesiae*, §5 (see the Vatican website).

[21] International Theological Commission, *The Interpretation of Dogma*, reproduced in *International Theological Commission: Texts and Documents, 1986–2007*, ed. Michael Sharkey and Thomas Weinandy (San Francisco: Ignatius Press, 2009), 26.

historicism reign? In answering this question, the International Theological Commission appeals to what Garrigou-Lagrange calls "common sense" or to what the commission calls as "certain basic truths (for example, the principle of contradiction)" and "a common pool of human values and, as a consequence, a truth common to all men."[22]

Naturally, Mansini allows that some of Garrigou-Lagrange's arguments in *Le sens commun* can be criticized. Chief among the critics was Étienne Gilson in an essay collected in his 1939 work *Thomist Realism and the Critique of Knowledge.*[23] According to Gilson, Garrigou-Lagrange seeks to ignore the historicity of dogmatic formulations and to avoid studying them in their historical contexts. Gilson thinks that Garrigou-Lagrange is amalgamating Thomas Reid, Aristotle, and Thomas Aquinas. More tellingly, he asks how the knowledge of God's existence, the knowledge of the existence of miracles, and the knowledge of the immortality of the soul can be set up as fundamental principles naturally or easily known to the human intellect (or "common sense") alongside things such as the principle of non-contradiction. Mansini holds that this aspect of Gilson's critique has merit, as does Gilson's concern regarding the need for more than "common sense" to perceive the reasonableness of the contents of divine revelation. As Mansini points out, Yves Congar, in his 1962 *La foi et la théologie*—a work that Mansini identifies as a "vastly under-appreciated" successor to Gardeil's *Le donné révélé et la theologie*—avoids listing the contents of "common sense," even while arguing that the words that the Church borrows from a particular philosophy and culture in order to define a dogma are employed by the Church not in their most technical

---

22 International Theological Commission, *Interpretation of Dogma*, 28. The commission cautions against various inadequate solutions: "At the beginning of this century, Modernism addressed itself to the question [of dogma and history]. It was a poor solution: revelation was improperly conceived and dogmas were given a pragmatic slant. Contemporary theology of the hermeneutical school tries to build a bridge between the dogmatic tradition and modern thought by asking what meaning and what importance dogmas have for man today. But in acting like that, one detaches the dogmatic formulation as such from the *Paradosis* [Tradition] and one isolates it from the living life of the Church. In that way one makes the dogma a substance by itself. What is more, in harping on the practical, existential or social meaning of dogma, the question of truth is lost to sight. A similar objection holds when dogma is held to be a thing of convention, that is a function of ecclesiastical language, necessary as a mark of unity, but ultimately merely provisional and open to further corrections. In that way, dogma is no longer regarded as an inevitable and obligatory mediator of revealed truth" (29–30).

23 See Étienne Gilson, "Realism and Common Sense," in *Thomist Realism and the Critique of Knowledge*, trans. Mark A. Wauck (San Francisco: Ignatius Press, 1986), 27–53.

meaning, but in their "common sense" meaning. Thus Congar does not follow Garrigou-Lagrange fully, but Congar does maintain a central element of Garrigou-Lagrange's viewpoint—namely that the Church expresses divine revelation, which goes beyond what is available to human thought on its own, "in *universally* accessible terms"—thus presupposing that there are basic, universally accessible truths constitutive of human intellection.[24]

In *Le sens commun*, and indeed in his work as a whole, Garrigou-Lagrange does not delve much into the specific historical conditioning of particular dogmatic formulations, although he demonstrates an excellent knowledge of the conciliar texts. With regard to the detailed historical contexts, Congar contributes much more, following in a fruitful Newmanian line.[25] Nevertheless, as Mansini notes, "the appeal to universally accessible notions does not necessarily flatten out the novelty of revelation or make us ignore it."[26] Instead, we are reminded that divine revelation proceeds from within the *created order*, to which pertain certain basic metaphysical and moral principles of human reason. Nichols sums up the main point regarding common sense: "No child needs to be taught the principles of non-contradiction, of substance, sufficient reason, causality, finality, nor the first principles of practical reason that good should be pursued and evil avoided."[27]

In this foreword, my purpose has been to situate the project of *Le sens commun* within post-conciliar Catholic theology, and to do so in conver-

---

[24] Mansini, "Historicity of Dogma," 122.

[25] See Andrew Meszaros, *The Prophetic Church: History and Doctrinal Development in John Henry Newman and Yves Congar* (Oxford: Oxford University Press, 2016). See also, for further discussion of history and dogma, Thomas Joseph White, O.P., "The Precarity of Wisdom: Modern Dominican Theology, Perspectivalism, and the Tasks of Reconstruction," in *Ressourcement Thomism: Sacred Doctrine, the Sacraments, and the Moral Life*, ed. Reinhard Hütter and Matthew Levering (Washington, DC: Catholic University of America Press, 2010), 92–123.

[26] Mansini, "Historicity of Dogma," 136.

[27] Nichols, *Reason with Piety*, 14–15. Nichols adds some further clarifying remarks, summing up Garrigou-Lagrange's position (toward which he is sympathetic): "In effect, these principles give us the structure of reason itself. Together with our first notions of extra-mental reality—the intelligible as found in the sensuous—these are the *prima intelligibilia*, the primary intelligible things. And they are also the proper object of the *sens commun*, along with the great truths which attach themselves to these first notions by way of the first principle: namely, the existence of God, freedom, immortality, and our first natural duties, deduced from applying to human nature the first principles of practical reason" (15).

sation with Church documents and notable contemporary theologians, separated from the context of ecclesiastical crackdown in the debates of theologians faithful to the Church's dogmatic and moral teachings. At present, it is no doubt the question of whether God has spoken his authoritative Word (of mercy, love, holiness, and redemption from sin and death) in Jesus Christ that burns most urgently. Can we know this Word, or is God's speech, if it has been given, locked into—and overwhelmed by—the pastness of events and the hermeneutical circle of interpretations of interpretations? The temptation is to turn Catholicism into another human mode of gesturing more or less articulately toward the ineffable, made concrete in human practices that are sociologically liberative. Reinhard Hütter comments accurately that Catholic theology today is largely "absorbed with various aspects of the [human] subject: its unavoidable construction of religious meaning, its autonomous rationality, its existential authenticity, its prelinguistic primordial religious experience, its unfathomable libertarian freedom, its primordially and inescapably graced nature, and . . . its sociohistorical, cultural, and economic location."[28] All this is interesting enough, but it is not Christ, it is not God, it is not the in-breaking of real salvation from sin and death and the opening up of the Trinitarian life, sending us joyfully forth into the world to proclaim and live the good news. Let Garrigou-Lagrange, therefore, have the last word here: "Our faith has as its object these truths hidden in God, truths that can only be known only if God reveals them and that the Holy Spirit has revealed to us."[29]

---

[28] Reinhard Hütter, *Bound for Beatitude: A Thomistic Study in Eschatology and Ethics* (Washington, DC: Catholic University of America Press, 2019), 200.

[29] Pt. 3, ch, 2, §1 of the present volume.

TRANSLATOR'S INTRODUCTION

Thomistic philosophy is an interesting, if elusive, term. Étienne Gilson and others have done a great deal to draw our attention to the theological character of the Angelic Doctor's thought.[1] Likewise, this fact was not lost on Jacques Maritain, who observed in his well-known jeremiad, *The Peasant of the Garonne*:

---

[1] See Étienne Gilson, *The Christian Philosophy of St. Thomas Aquinas*, trans. L. K. Shook (Notre Dame, IN: University of Notre Dame Press, 2006). Such too was behind the work of Fr. Servais Pinckaers, *The Sources of Christian Ethics*, trans. Sr. Mary Thomas Noble (Washington, DC: Catholic University of America Press, 1995). This also comes to light in Ignatius Eschmann, *The Ethics of Saint Thomas Aquinas: Two Courses*, ed. Edward Synan (Toronto: Pontifical Institute of Mediaeval Studies, 1997). For a general overview, in light of the Aristotelian commentaries, see Jean-Pierre Torrell, *Saint Thomas Aquinas*, vol. 1 *The Person and His Work*, trans. Robert Royal (Washington, DC: Catholic University of America Press, 1996), 236 39. For dissenting voices, see: Ralph McInerny, *Praeambula fidei: Thomism and the God of the Philosophers* (Washington, DC: Catholic University of America Press, 2006); John Wippel, "Thomas Aquinas and the Problem of Christian Philosophy," in *Metaphysical Themes in Thomas Aquinas*, Studies in Philosophy and the History of Philosophy 10 (Washington, DC: Catholic University of America Press, 1984), 1–33.

In addition to these reflections on the relation of philosophy and theology in a broadly construed "Thomism," one can benefit from reading the historical work of Fr. Gerald McCool. Without endorsing every conclusion of his historical studies, one can gain much from his laying out of the vast and differentiated domain of "Thomists" in the nineteenth and twentieth centuries (*The Neo-Thomists* [Milwaukee, WI: Marquette University Press, 1994]; *From Unity to Pluralism: The Internal Evolution of Thomism* [New York: Fordham University Press, 1999]; *Nineteenth Century Scholasticism: The Search for a Unitary Method*, 2nd ed. [New York: Fordham University Press, 1999]).

For a general overview of Thomism and "the Thomists," see the excellent recent volume by Fathers Romanus Cessario and Cajetan Cuddy, *Thomas and the Thomists: The Achievement of Thomas Aquinas and His Interpreters* (Minneapolis, MN: Fortress Press, 2017).

1

St. Thomas's disciples have, to be sure, spoken a good deal about Thomist philosophy, and have taught it, in magisterial commentaries, courses, and textbooks where, more often than not, they were content to pick up, in the theological exposition of St. Thomas, the substance which can be found there—brought there to the light of theology and enveloped in theology: a substance splendidly rich, but all theologized in the use St. Thomas had made of it. Once one had extracted this substance from the theological exposition of the master, one had only to trace off the formulas, often the very order of exposition, to offer in handsome syllogisms some philosophical thesis or other, nay, the "philosophical doctrine" or the Angel of the Schools.[2]

Father Réginald Garrigou-Lagrange is often numbered among those accused of such neat "syllogizing."[3] Certainly, he was not afraid to wield the Scholastic *nego, distinguo*, and *concedo*. Especially in his commentaries on the *Summa* and in *De revelatione*, the Dominican theologian did not fear to express himself in strict syllogistic form in defense of certain conclusions. Nonetheless, even in those works, he dwells at length on the meaning of the content, not merely reducing the theological enterprise to syllogistic chains. Indeed, on various occasions throughout his works, he did not hesitate to speak ill of many philosophical manuals for sacrificing an appropriate sense of mystery to a wrong-headed desire for a superficial form of clarity.[4]

---

[2] Jacques Maritain, *The Peasant of the Garonne: An Old Layman Questions Himself about the Present Time*, trans. Michael Cuddihy and Elizabeth Hughes (New York: Holt, Rinehart, and Winston, 1968), 135–36. For this theme in Maritain's own work, see: "Philosophy and Common Sense," *An Introduction to Philosophy*, trans. E. I. Watkin (London: Sheed and Ward, 1932), 133–43; "Realism and Common Sense," in *The Degrees of Knowledge*, trans. Gerald B. Phelan et al. (Notre Dame, IN: University of Notre Dame, 2002), 86–118.

[3] Most recently, this has been recorded in Tracey Rowland, *Catholic Theology* (London: Bloomsbury T&T Clark, 2017), 58: "This [disputational style] is, of course, quite a different understanding of the theological enterprise from Chenu's notion of the discernment of master-intuitions embodied in historically conditioned conceptual frameworks and from the entire Patristic approach to theology, which was not centered around syllogisms." It should be noted that Rowland is not stating this in a pugilistic fashion, but is only building on the interpretation of Fr. Garrigou-Lagrange's style offered by Richard Peddicord in his *The Sacred Monster of Thomism*.

[4] See Réginald Garrigou-Lagrange: *The Sense of Mystery*, trans. Matthew K. Minerd (Steubenville, OH: Emmaus Academic, 2017), 73–102; *The Order of Things: The Real-*

Many readers will likely suspect that Father Garrigou-Lagrange is one of the "Thomists" maligned by Maritain's aforementioned remark. Their later-life interpersonal difficulties are a matter of common knowledge in Catholic intellectual circles, so one would expect a negative judgment on the "Sacred Monster of Thomism." Nonetheless, the aging Maritain overthrows such assumptions in words of a footnote annexed to the very remark noted above:

> There were certainly, as I have observed, exceptions, although rare to my knowledge. When it comes to overall expositions which have genuine philosophical value, I will name here old Kleutgen, from whom, at one time, I benefited, and in particular two excellent books: Père Garrigou-Lagrange's *La Philosophie de l'être et le sens commun* [sic], and Gilson's *The Spirit of Medieval Philosophy*.[5]

The current volume is thus mentioned by the aging Maritain as having "genuine philosophical value." Father Garrigou-Lagrange's attempt to discuss "common sense" from a Thomistic perspective did not meet with universal agreement. For his part, Gilson did not express himself warmly in referring to Father Garrigou-Lagrange's text. In a lengthy note in *Thomist Realism and the Critique of Knowledge*, Gilson critiques Father Garrigou-Lagrange's *Sens commun*, which he believes to represent "the most sustained effort to integrate a doctrine of common sense into Thomism."[6] In the lengthy footnote, it is not completely clear how Gilson interprets Father Garrigou-Lagrange, for as he closes the footnote, he seems to imply that even Father Garrigou-Lagrange holds "common sense" to be a distinct kind of faculty. This is never the position expressed by Father Garrigou-Lagrange, and Gilson himself does not seem to directly assert that it was either.

In any case, it is not clear that Father Garrigou-Lagrange has committed a grave error in asking the question "What is a Thomist to make of the expression 'common sense?'" Although he discusses the Scottish common-sense philosophy of Thomas Reid and, at times, cites positively Théodore Jouffroy,

---

ism *of the Principle of Finality*, trans. Matthew K. Minerd (Steubenville, OH: Emmaus Academic, 2020), 167, 239–40. Indeed, in these passages, Fr. Garrigou-Lagrange also critiques the tendency of such manuals to reproduce theological reasoning as though it were a kind of pure philosophy. On this, see especially *Order of Things*, 234.

5   Maritain, *Peasant*, 136n7.

6   Étienne Gilson, *Thomistic Realism and the Critique of Knowledge*, trans. Mark A. Wauck (San Francisco: Ignatius Press, 1986), 41n22.

it is clear in what follows that Father Garrigou-Lagrange does not endeavor to take up their terms of the discussion, thus "introducing a dose, no matter how infinitesimal, of Reid" into Thomism, as Gilson claims.[7] As in the case of the temperamental difference between Maritain (the speculative thinker) and Gilson (the historian-philosopher), it seems that here, too, that Minerva and Clio are in dissonance.[8]

The current text does indeed provide a clear overview of important themes in a broadly construed Thomism: opposition to nominalism, the nature of definitions, the nature of knowledge itself, the first metaphysical principles, natural knowledge of God, the nature of analogical predication, individuation, and the nature of personality. Granted, "Thomism" is a slippery term, one appropriated by a number of different approaches to the Angelic Doctor. By not engaging in the lengthy technical polemics of the commentators, to whom he owed much, Father Garrigou-Lagrange presents the reader with a fair account of what is broadly held by any Thomism worthy of the name. To this basic account, he adds the central thesis of the work itself: even when explained in an explicitly metaphysical and philosophical manner, these philosophical positions are wholly conformed to the rudimentary metaphysics contained in the initial insights formed by non-scientific, "common sense" knowledge of the world.

The reader will note, however, that we must make certain attenuations regarding the comments made thus far. *Le sens commun* is indeed quite philosophical in bearing. Nonetheless, its lengthy final section has an overtly theological character. Indeed, it brings to completion the subtitle of the book itself: "The Philosophy of Being *and Dogmatic Formulas*." In this final section, he takes the natural common sense discussed in the first two sections and elevates it to the supernatural order, particularly in relation to the nature of dogmatic formulas that express the content of revelation in an increasingly distinct manner.

---

7 Gilson, *Thomistic Realism*, 42n22.

8 See the remarks in a postscript written in 1972, recorded in Jacques Maritain, "Reflections on Theological Knowledge," in *Untrammeled Approaches*, trans. Bernard Doering (Notre Dame, IN: University of Notre Dame, 1997), 269: "Finally, let me say that what appears to me most significant with regard to my present proposal [concerning Christian philosophy and theology] is the fact that in Gilson's eyes as in mine (and he was following the paths of his cherished lovely Clio, while I preferred those of Minerva, and had the temerity to feel my way along her paths at my own risk and peril) . . ." Likewise, see Kenneth L. Schmitz, *What Has Clio to Do with Athena? Étienne Gilson: Historian and Philosopher* (Toronto: Pontifical Institute of Mediaeval Studies, 1987).

In discussing the nature of dogmatic development, Father Garrigou-Lagrange utilizes a notion that he takes from Aristotle's logic (especially from the *Posterior Analytics*), the process of defining a term. This is an appropriate "model"[9] for discussing the nature of dogmatic *definitions* and their development. As human definitions develop in the individual intellect from vague expression to more distinct expression, so too, he holds, there is an analogous process that occurs in the life of the Church in explicating revealed truths. This is a theme that he takes up elsewhere,[10] noting that this sort of progression is a work of *nous*, of intellectual insight achieved by the first operation of the intellect by means of its "work" of defining.[11]

It is important to remember the centrality of this theological inquiry with which he ends the current edition of the text.[12] The depth of this text's discussions was not lost on a thinker as profound as Monsignor Charles Journet, who cites them when himself treating of the distinction between grace and the Hypostatic Union of the Incarnation in his *Entretiens sur dieu le père*.[13] Likewise, in his *The Mass: The Presence of the Sacrifice of the Cross*, in the subsection entitled "The Dogma of Transubstantiation, Like the Christological and Trinitarian Dogmas, Produces from the Faith a Technical Formulation without, however, Enslaving It to Any One System,"[14] Journet calls to mind the title of the third chapter of the third part of Father Garrigou-Lagrange's work, "Dogmatic Formulas Expressed in Philosophical Language Exceed Common Sense by Their Precision, but They Do Not Make Dogma Subservient to Any System." It is unsurprising that soon thereafter Monsignor Journet cites Father Garrigou-Lagrange precisely on this point.[15] This substantial, theological third section lifts up to the plane of supernatural questions the generally philosophical reflec-

---

[9] See Fr. Garrigou-Lagrange's placement in Réginald-Marie Schultes, *Introductio in Historiam Dogmatum* (Paris: Lethielleux, 1922), 287–96.

[10] See, for example, Garrigou-Lagrange, *Sense of Mystery*, 23. See also, Réginald Garrigou-Lagrange, "On the Search for Definitions According to Aristotle and St. Thomas," *Philosophizing in Faith: Essays on the Beginning and End of Wisdom*, ed. and trans. Matthew K. Minerd (Providence, RI: Cluny Media, 2019), 21–34.

[11] Hence, we have here the *psychological activity* of defining that pertains to the *virtual productivity* presupposed for, but not identified with, the actual act of knowledge.

[12] In his introduction, Fr. Garrigou-Lagrange discusses how he reorganized (and enlarged) the text in the years following the initial upheaval occasioned by the modernist crisis.

[13] Charles Journet, *Entretiens sur dieu le père* (Villars-sur-Glâne, Switzerland: Parole et Silence, 1998), 112–13.

[14] Charles Journet, *The Mass: The Presence of the Sacrifice of the Cross*, trans. Victor Szczurek (South Bend, IN: St. Augustine's Press, 2008), 154.

[15] Journet, *The Mass*, 156.

tions undertaken in the first two sections, and it is brought to a close with the beautiful reflections offered in the closing chapter, which he added to the text for the fourth edition, representing a kind of meditation on the main lines of the arguments made regarding common sense throughout the text.

This translation is being offered to the twenty-first century, a time wherein traditional doctrine and philosophy are by far on the wane in popular consciousness. It has often been the case that various "schools" of thought defending the Church have been vociferously opposed to one another. This is nothing new, of course, but today one is faced with the fractured domain of faithful Catholics variously taking titles for themselves: "*Communio* thinkers," resurgent "Strict Observant Thomists," "Analytic Thomists," those who take Alasdair MacIntyre as *sine qua non* point of departure, "Hildebrandians," more independent phenomenologists such as Monsignor Robert Sokolowski, a strong streak of "Gilsonian" thought among Thomists, academic medievalists, and others. These groups do not always argue among themselves explicitly, but as Matthew Levering has said with poignancy, there is a kind of "circular firing squad" among those who should be allies.

This book is being offered as a voice *among friends*—even if those friends disagree on this or that point. MacIntyre is right: the barbarians are at our doors. Indeed, the destruction that has been wrought in the name of "progress" has been great, and this fact is obvious to any honest observer. In the *Peasant of the Garonne*, this state of affairs was not lost on Maritain, who prophesied in his strong remarks concerning "neo-modernism":

> When one considers the neo-modernist fever (I was bound to mention this sooner or later), very contagious, at least in circles described as "intellectual," compared to which the modernism of Pius X's time was only a modest hayfever, and which finds expression above all in the most advanced thinkers among our Protestant brothers, but is also active in equally advanced Catholic thinkers, this second description gives us the picture of a kind of "immanent" apostasy (that is, which intends to remain Christian at all costs). In preparation for many years, hastened by certain veiled hopes of the repressed regions of the soul which were stirred up here and there on the occasion of the Council, the manifestation of this apostasy is sometimes falsely ascribed to the "spirit of the Council" or even to the "spirit of John XXIII." We know well to whom it is proper to trace the paternity of such lies

(and so much the better if in this way man finds himself a little exonerated).[16]

Therefore, I offer this translation as one small portion of the remedy to this situation. It is not at all a silver bullet—but none of us should look for a "silver bullet" in any author or in any school of thought. All thought is not to be captive to Father Garrigou-Lagrange, nor to Saint Thomas and his so-called "school," nor to any other human reality. No; all thought is to be captive to Christ: "For though we live in the world we are not carrying on a worldly war, for the weapons of our warfare are not worldly but have divine power to destroy strongholds. We destroy arguments and every proud obstacle to the knowledge of God, and take every thought captive to obey Christ" (2 Cor 10:3–5).

On the whole, all lengthy citations from Scripture in this volume are taken from the Revised Standard Version of the Bible. On occasion, it made sense to translate directly from the text at hand, especially when the sense of the Vulgate's Latin was presupposed in an explanation being presented. All citations from Denzinger are amended to follow the numeration and translations from Ignatius Press's 43rd edition of the text. When Father Garrigou-Lagrange translates Latin texts into French, I have generally translated from the original Latin. Notes in the text address any minor concerns that arise occasionally in this regard. Throughout my translation, I have included some pedagogical footnotes. In these, I have tried to provide the reader with remarks concerning points that may well be opaque, often citing the works of Thomists in the same tradition as that of Father Garrigou-Lagrange.

Throughout the text, bibliographical references required expansion, as Father Garrigou-Lagrange often did not provide complete reference information in his citations. Unless otherwise noted, when possible, I have chosen to cite the relevant pages of the English translations of Garrigou-Lagrange's works, as this will be more useful for English readers than would be French citations. I have foregone citing Thomas Joseph Walshe's adaptation and abridgment of *De revelatione*, given that it is not a full translation of the work. Emmaus Academic is planning a translation of this text in the near future.

No work comes about without the involvement of many hands. Special thanks go to Chris Erickson for shepherding this project throughout its process of publication. Being relatively new to this process, I was in need of able

---

[16] Maritain, *Peasant*, 5–6.

guides and gladly had their kind assistance. For help translating an Italian text included in this volume by Father Garrigou-Lagrange, thanks are due to Sister Mary Veronica Sabelli, R.S.M. I owe *immense* gratitude to the two men who spent much labor respectively reviewing my translation and then copyediting it: Dr. Benjamin Heidgerken and Mr. Brett Kendall. Likewise, I express particular thanks to Dr. Scott Hahn, Dr. Matthew Levering, and Father Thomas Joseph White, O.P., for their interest in this project, as well as to the production staff at Emmaus Academic for their design and layout expertise. And let us, together, give thanks to God Almighty for the grace to begin this project and bring it to completion.

This translation is dedicated to my firstborn daughter, Josephine Gaëtane Minerd. My dear, my only goal in doing this kind of translation work is to leave you a world a little bit more wise and beautiful than the world that I inherited as a cradle Catholic during an era when much confusion still reigned. (This volume was long delayed, due to the vagaries involved in publication. My conscience led me to change its dedication, giving it to my daughter, whose birth, in fact, accompanied the completion of the earliest draft of this text. However, I ask that you, reader, also pray for the repose of Father Paulinus Selle, O.S.B., to whom I also considered dedicating this volume. He was a very faithful servant of God, teaching patristics for over sixty years at St. Vincent Seminary. I had the joy of knowing him and was edified by his peaceful and dedicated long suffering during an era of American ecclesiastical history that was a great cross for his soul. Eternal memory! *Vichnaya Pamyat'*!)[17]

---

[17] Father Guy Mansini recently published an important study concerning the relationship between history and the intellectual apprehensions possible for common sense (in the natural order) and Christian common sense (in the supernatural order of faith). See Guy Mansini, O.S.B., "The Historicity of Dogma and Common Sense: Ambroise Gardeil, Réginald Garrigou-Lagrange, Yves Congar, and the Modern Magisterium," *Nova et Vetera* (English) 18, no. 1 (2020): 111–38. In this last-minute footnote, I would merely like to comment that I believe that a path forward is possible *within* the basic overall framework offered by Garrigou-Lagrange, though with important emendations, precisely for the reasons observed by Fathers Mansini, Congar, and others.

I share with Father Mansini a common master, namely, Monsignor Robert Sokolowski. Perhaps a treatment of objective / intentional existence, coupled with an appreciation for history and the phenomenon of "sedimentation" can help to articulate a way forward that avoids the dismissive approach of someone like Gilson in relation to Father Garrigou-Lagrange's Thomistic treatment of common sense. On the phenomenological treatment of sedimentation, see Robert Sokolowski, *Formation of Husserl's Concept of Constitution* (The Hague: Martinus Nijhoff, 1964), 172, 182, 188, 212-213; *Husserlian Meditations* (Evanston, IL: Northwestern University Press, 1974), 42, 66.

Author's Introduction to the Third Edition

This book, which first appeared in 1909,[1] in the midst of the discussions stirred up by modernism concerning the value of the formulas of the Christian faith, has been revised and somewhat enlarged in view of the publication of this edition.

Said controversy, which does not have the same timeliness today, has been placed into the background, leading us to place in sharper relief that which is more positive and of ever-relevant interest in this volume's topics.

The introduction, which is new, poses, from a more strictly philosophical perspective, the problem concerning the nature and value of common sense, which is the subject of the first part of the book. The study concerning "Common Sense and the Traditional Proofs of the Existence of God," which originally was placed in an appendix in the first and second editions of this text, has become the second part of this edition. This new arrangement helps to render the third part more intelligible: "Common Sense and the Understanding [*intelligence*] of theFormulas of the Christian Faith." For the same reason, we have transferred to this third part theological considerations that originally were placed in the introduction in earlier editions. This alteration will enable the reader to readily grasp the sense and scope of these matters.

Two chapters have been added concerning subjective conceptualism and absolute realism inasmuch as they are related to common sense.

We happily express our lively gratitude to Abbé Daniel Lallement, acting professor at the Catholic Institute of Paris, who graciously helped

---

[1] Réginald Garrigou-Lagrange, *Le sens commun: la philosophie de l'être et les formules dogmatiques* (Paris: Beauchesne, 1909).

us make these revisions and corrections. Without his assistance, this third edition likely would not have seen the light of day. Despite its rather abstract character, and notwithstanding the obstacles that its dissemination has encountered, this book, by the grace of God, has already provided light for many sincere, disinterested minds that are desperate not for novelties but for the truth. May it provide light for many others and lead them to see that our intellect, which is made for knowing being, must live, above all, upon knowledge of *Him Who Is*, and that our will, which is made for loving and willing the good, must love, more than ourselves and above all else, the Sovereign Good, the possession of which will be our eternal beatitude. An hour will come—and this is our steadfast hope—the hour of absolute truth, when all forms of illusion and falsehood will no longer be possible, when the false doctrines discussed in this book will no longer exist, when the spirit of opportunism will no longer inspire men to diminish the truth, an hour when the truth will appear forever in all its grandeur, being established at once strongly and sweetly. This will be the immutable hour of God, when we will see the Divine Essence *facie ad faciem*, face to face, as St. Paul says,[2] through an absolutely immediate and inamissible intuitive vision, the hour when all our desires will at last be satisfied. In this beatitude, sin will henceforth no longer exist. We will no longer be able to turn away from God, seen *as He is*,[3] as He sees Himself, and moved by the élan of the purest supernatural love, we will subordinate all things, indeed, even our own happiness, to the glory of Him Who Is, to the brilliant and eternal manifestation of His infinite goodness. *Satiabor cum apparuerit gloria tua* (Ps 16:15). *Ipsi gloria in saecula* ["I will be filled when your glory appears. To Him be glory forever"].

FATHER RÉGINALD GARRIGOU-LAGRANGE
Rome, Angelicum
October 15, 1921, Feast of St. Theresa of Avila

---

[2] 1 Cor. 13:12 (RSV): "For now we see (God) in a mirror dimly, but then face to face. Now I know in part; then I shall understand fully, even as I have been fully understood."

[3] 1 John 3:2: "We know that when He appears we shall be like him, for *we shall see Him as He is*" (RSV).[Trans. note: Fr. Garrigou-Lagrange incorrectly has I John 3:12.]

ANALYTIC TABLE
OF CONTENTS[1]

Introduction: State of the Question

Realist and truth-seeking minds are returning to common sense, both in order to retrieve the primordial and fundamental certainties that constitute it, and also to understand the meaning of the terms from which the formulas of faith are articulated. Hence, there is need to investigate into: the nature of common sense, its object, its limits, its primary and derivative affirmations, and what it is worth in its own sphere.

Part 1: What Is Common Sense?

Ultimately, philosopher's theories of common sense will correlate to their theories of reason. Thus, we here discuss nominalist empiricism and realist conceptualism.

Chapter 1: The Nominalist Theory of Common Sense

A. THE THEORY PROPOSED BY ÉDOUARD LE ROY

§1. *The Particular Prejudices of Common Sense.* Here, we distinguish between, in common sense, on the one hand, particular prejudices specific to each century, arising from the theories in favor in each era, and on the

---

[1]   [Trans. note: This is Fr Garrigou-Largange's original table of contents in the French edition (*Table Analytique*), obviously a more expanded style than done in current Anglophone works.]

other, general prejudices due to the very conditions in which spontaneous knowledge develops. Only the latter are of interest to us. There are those who would also smear Aristotelian philosophy, in whose general outlines Henri Bergson himself recognizes "the natural metaphysics of the human intellect."

§2. *The General Prejudices of Common Sense: (1) the Fragmentation and Dislocation of Matter; (2) the Materialization of Things of the Mind.* (1) Our primordial perception is [supposedly, on this Bergsonian thesis] the perception of a moving and heterogeneous continuity. Into this perceived reality, we introduce convenient, and even necessary, arrangements or simplifications enabling *speech* and *action*. Belief in the existence of bodies that are separate from each other is only the result of the preference given to tactile impressions, which are more common than visual impressions. To the degree that *quality alone is real*, the more does [quantitative] space belong to the mind, not to things. Contrary to common sense, matter can be defined only in terms of the soul: an ocean of qualitative images. (2) *Substance* and *cause* are no more real than is quantity. They are "reifications" fashioned by common sense, which immobilizes everything, even the restless activity of *spirit* itself. To think of the mind as being a *substance* is the greatest error committed by common sense. What does this mean for axioms and categories? In short, they all undergo becoming; they all evolve.

Conclusion: common sense does not have a representation value, but only value in relation to action. The same is true of dogmatic formulas.

B. ABSOLUTE NOMINALISM

§1. *This Theory of Common Sense Represents a Reiterated Form of Absolute Nominalism.* All things that exceed the *factual* object of experience—such as substances, causes, and powers—are only verbal entities. This theory necessary follows for every nominalist who is captive to sense appearances, attending to their perpetual mobility. Domingo de Soto found it among the medieval nominalists. According to Louis Couturat, the old sensualism of Étienne Bonnot de Condillac is easily recognizable in Bergsonian nominalism. In it, Benjamin Jacob sees materialism understood in its deepest meaning.

§2. Refutation of This Nominalism: the Formal Object of the Intellect Is Being (Proof); the Fragmenting of the Sensible Continuum versus That of Being or of the Intelligible. The first of these fragmentations is often utilitarian, whereas the second imposes itself on thinking as true. Ultimate foundation of the proof: the formal object of the intellect is being and not color, nor sound, nor the internal fact of consciousness. This is established by contrasting a mere common image (accompanied by common name) with an idea, associations with judgments, empirical successions with reasoning. In the three operations of the intellect everything is intelligible solely in function of being. The fragmentation of being into subject and object, being and mode of being, and potency and act is necessary under pain of falling into absurdity. The principle of substance is only a determination of the principle of identity implied in the idea of being. If our intelligence "reifies," this is because it has for its object being and not color, nor sound, nor the internal fact of consciousness.

§3. Consequences of Bergsonian Nominalism: the Denial of Reason and of the Objective Value of the Principle of Non-Contradiction [sic].[2] Some go so far as to say: it seems to be the denial of consciousness, which seems to need to sink down in the torrent of vegetative and animal life.

§4. Why Would Common Sense, So Conceived, Preserve an Immutable Practical Value? Émile Boutroux's judgment concerning this pragmatic nominalism: neither the scholar nor the believer can renounce being and objectivity. Reason is the sense for being.

C. Nominalism and Opposed Systems in Relation to Common Sense

§1. Nominalism and Subjective Conceptualism. How does the subjectivist conceptualism of Kant and his followers differ from nominalism? How it resembles it: it too is the destruction of common sense.

§2. Nominalism and Absolute Realism. Nonetheless, it is impossible that

---

[2] [Trans. note: As will be noted in chapters, Fr. Garrigou-Lagrange most often uses "principle of contradiction" for what is now most commonly call the "principle of non-contradiction," but he also sometimes uses the "non-" form for the same thing, and so the practice in this translation has been to mark the latter with "[sic]" for clarity that these are meant as the same that he usually names without the "non-" before, as he does several place below in this table of contents.]

one make recourse to the opposite extreme, namely, the absolute realism of the Platonists and ontologists, who confuse being in general or the being of things with divine being.

Chapter 2: The Realist-Conceptualist Theory of Common Sense

This is the classical theory of common sense. It can be found in the writings of Aristotle and the great Scholastics. It is also found among the intellectualist philosophers of the seventeenth century. It is found in an altered form in the Scottish common-sense philosophers and in Théodore Jouffroy.

§1. *Common Sense Presents Itself de facto as Possessing in a Vague Manner the Certain Solution to the Great Philosophical Problems.* It possesses these solutions in a scattered state, without being able to classify them and subordinate them into a body of doctrine. Hence, it possesses them without being able to justify its own certainty and does not suspect the difficulties and apparent contradictions that will arise when one attempts to reconcile the elementary notions that appear so simple to him.

§2. *The Systems with Which Common Sense Is in Disagreement*: materialism and immaterialism; phenomenalism; pure rationalism and pure empiricism; absolute intellectualism and libertism; morality based solely upon duty and utilitarian morality; pantheism and dualism.

§3. *Traditional Philosophy Justifies Common Sense by Passing from Nominal Definitions to Real Definitions and by Establishing the Relationship of the Certitudes of Spontaneous Reason with Being, the Formal Object of the Intellect.* Why this philosophy is misunderstood. The method of metaphysics; real definitions and reductions to being; only what is attached to being is metaphysically certain.

§4. *The Real Definitions of Inanimate Bodies, Living Being, the Sensing Subject, and Man; How These Different Beings Are Related to Each Other; the Order of the Universe.* The principle for the rebuttal of mechanism and dynamism, as well as for that of the alleged antinomies about the continuum. Living beings are of a higher order than inanimate beings. The animal's sense knowledge; principle for the refutation of idealism and materialism. Man's specific difference; principle for the refutation of empiricism and pure rationalism. The superior is the efficient and final cause with regard to the inferior.

§5. *The Intelligible World in General; What Common Sense Perceives in Being.* The intelligible world is more luminous *quoad se* than is the sensible world; however, it is less so *quoad nos.* The difference between metaphysics, which is science in the perfect sense of the word, and positive sciences, which can only classify laws or general facts by provisional hypotheses. Common sense perceives in being the first speculative and practical principles, as well as the great moral and religious truths that are connected to them: God's existence, freedom, and immortality of the soul. Why is man the only being here alone whose properties can be rendered intelligible?

§6. *The First Principles for Common Sense: The Principles of Identity, Contradiction, Substance,* Raison d'être, *Finality, and Induction; the First Principle of Practical Reason (Duty); Their Connection to the Idea of Being.* In what sense these principles are analytical. Kant did not recognize that any affirmative judgment expresses by means of the verb "to be" an identity that is not logical but real. Affirmative judgments are divided into analytical and synthetic judgments depending on whether the knowledge of this real identity arises merely from the analysis of the notions composing that judgment or from the examination of existing things.

§7. *How Common Sense Raises Itself to God.* The schema for the proofs by movement, contingency, the order of the world, and the multiplicity and degrees of beings. The First Being. The contradiction of dualism and pantheism.

§8. *Why Common Sense Is Aware of Freedom.* Consciousness of free will is, in a vague and implicit state, the *a priori*[3] proof for freedom, which philosophical reason will formulate. Man is conscious of being free insofar as, feeling himself made for the absolute good, the fullness of being, he senses that he holds sway over the choice to respond or not respond to the attraction of a finite good. The reason for the agreement of free will with the principle of sufficient reason: *a sufficient reason that, in fact, is not sufficient, on account of non-being that is—namely, potency.*

§9. *What Is the Source of Common Sense's Belief in the Immortality of the Soul?* The human intellect grasps itself as a relationship to being. Now, being qua being abstracts from space and time, as well as from all matter.

---

3   [Trans. note: See note 51 of pt. 1, ch. 1, in this volume for Fr. Garrigou-Lagrange's meaning of this term.]

---

[4]   [Trans. note: On this distinction, see Réginald Garrigou-Lagrange, *De revelatione per ecclesiam catholicam proposita*, 5th ed. (Rome: Desclée and Socii, 1950), vol. 2, pt. 1, ch. 19.]

[5]   [Trans. note: And, in particular, for the case of the *species expressa intellecta*, it is *id in quo cognoscitur*.]

§16. The Objection against the Objective Value of the Principle of Identity. The ever-changing aspect of sensitive things calls the principle of identity into question for some. This objection is resolved by means of the concept of potency.

§17. If the Principle of Identity Is the Fundamental Law of Reality and if Becoming and Multiplicity Can Be Explained Only by Potency, Then Common Sense and the Philosophy of Being Have Won Their Case against Phenomenalism and the Philosophy of Becoming. Clear on account of the place it gives to act, the philosophy of being is obscure by the place it gives to potency. This relative absence of determination and intelligibility is what leaves room for the divine freedom and human freedom. The value of common sense is the same as that of the principle of identity.

Part 2: Common Sense and the Traditional Proofs of God's Existence

Chapter 1: How the Principle of Raison d'être Is Connected to the Principle of Identity

§1. The Classical Thesis in Its General Formulation.

§2. How Saint Thomas Establishes that There Is an Ultimate Principle. Its subject must be *being* and its predicate that which belongs *per se* [*première-ment*] to being.

§3. What Is the Exact Formulation of the Ultimate Principle? Every being is that which constitutes it properly [*en propre*].

§4. In What Manner Are Principles Connected to the Ultimate Principle? By a *reductio ad absurdum.* The details of this reduction for the case of the principle of *raison d'être.* In what sense is the principle analytical?

§5. An Important Consequence of This Thesis in Natural Theology. The proof of God [of his existence] that contains all the others in short.

existence by movement is applied to volitional movement as well as to local movement.

§5. *The Thomist Proofs Do Not Imply Any Recourse to the Ontological Argument.* Saint Anselm should only have said: "The greatest being that can be conceived necessarily exists by himself and not by another, *if such a being exists.*" We can say reciprocally: "*If such a being exists,* the necessary being must be the Being Itself and, therefore, infinitely perfect." Now, one does prove that a necessary being in fact exists.

§6. *The Thomist Proofs Establish the Existence of a First, Transcendent Cause.* There can be neither multiplicity nor becoming within the Absolute. Now, the world is essentially multiple and changing. Therefore, God is essentially distinct from the world. This is the proof given by the [First] Vatican Council (*Dei Filius*, ch. 1). It is directly connected to the principle of identity. If this principle is the fundamental law of reality, the fundamental reality must be related to being as A is to A. Nonetheless, *Ipsum Esse* is alive and free.

Chapter 3: The Pantheism of the New Philosophy

§1. *Evolutionist Pantheism in Bergson.* In the Bergsonian system, God is "a reality that makes itself," "a continuous flow." He is no longer conceived without the world and is absorbed into it. Bergsonism is an inverted form of Hegelianism.

§2. *The Proof That Le Roy Substitutes for the Traditional Proofs Leads to Pantheism.* This new proof is based on arbitrary and contradictory assumptions. An infinity of becoming remains for us. This is the transcendent God. This God cannot be conceived without the world. He does not yet exist, and he never will. The pragmatic creedal expression of the divine personality ultimately conceals a pantheistic metaphysics that is radically opposed to the [First] Vatican Council no less than to the first principle of reason, the principle of identity.

Chapter 4: The Fundamental Truth of the Philosophy of Being

The fundamental truth in the analytical order (*in via inventionis*) is the principle of identity, implied in our first idea, the idea of being. The fundamental truth in the synthetic order (*in via judicii*), the one that answers our last whys about God and the world, is the same principle realized in all its purity in God: *in solo Deo essentia et esse sunt idem*; in God alone are essence and existence the same; "I am He Who Is."

Appendix 1 [of Part 2]: The Philosophy of Being and Ontologism

Appendix 2 [of Part 2]: The Natural Affirmation of Being Is Not a Postulate

Part 3: Common Sense and the Understanding of Dogmatic Formulas

In order to suppose that, even when expressed in philosophical language, dogmatic formulas have no other meaning than that which common sense can give them, it is important to know what its scope is. If common sense is only a utilitarian organization of thought in view of practical life, dogmas have only a practical meaning, defined by the attitude or conduct required of us. This position is condemned in the twenty-sixth proposition in the decree *Lamentabili Sane Exitu*.

Chapter 1: How Dogmatic Formulas Are Given Precision in Philosophical Terms

§1. *The Progressive Precision of Dogmatic Formulas.* If the primitive formula of common sense needs to be given precision, will this not be through recourse to this philosophy of being, which is, in reality, nothing other than the extension and justification of common sense? The best analogy for the development of fundamental dogmas: the explicitation of the first principles.

§2. *The Dogmatic Formula of the Trinity.* The appearance of the terms "nature," "person," "subsistence," and "relation." Anton Günther destroys the dogma of the Trinity by means of his "modern" notion of personality defined by self-consciousness.

§3. *Dogmatic Formulas of the Mystery of the Incarnation.* The terminus of the Hypostatic Union, the two natures, and the two wills. The error of Günther, who by means of his notion of the personality returns to Nestorius.

§4. *The Council of Vienne's Definition Concerning the Soul, the Form of the Body.* What is the meaning of the word "form" in this definition? The position held by Matteo Liberatore, Tomasso Zigliara, and Domenico Palmieri. This definition at least affirms that the rational soul is the principle of the human body's life.

Chapter 2: Do Dogmatic Formulas, Thus Given Precision,
Remain Accessible to Common Sense?

§1. *Dogmatic Formulas Thus Given Precision Are Inaccessible to Common Sense if the Latter Is Only a Utilitarian Organization of Thought in View of Practical Life.* The twenty-sixth proposition of the decree *Lamentabili Sane Exitu.* The verb "to be" in these formulas retains its objective meaning. For the preservation of metaphysical terms, the Church has resigned herself to experiencing the most painful of schisms. The condemnation of Pope Honorius I. The goal of the Fathers' treaties against Sabellius. The concept of relationship. The condemnations of Gilbert de la Porrée and of Anton Günther. According to the [First] Vatican Council, the object of faith is the same as that of the Beatific Vision, the *profunda Dei*, the depths of God. How could the teaching of Christ, who had the Beatific Vision, be devoid of ontological value? Intellectual visions of the Trinity.

§2. *Why Le Roy's Objections against the Thomist Doctrine of Analogy Do Not Hold; the Foundation of This Doctrine.* The foundation for this doctrine is found in Aristotle: *being* and *the transcendentals* (unity, truth, goodness) are not genera, but rather analogues. The concept of *being*, through the first principle it implies, postulates by itself and necessarily Self-Subsistent *Esse*, and therefore applies analogously to the latter. God exists in his way, and creatures in their way. *Simpliciter simplices* perfections are those that are defined by an immediate relation to *being* or to one of the transcendentals (namely, intelligence and will, and the properties that derive from them). Therefore, they must be analogous like *being*, and like it, susceptible to being purified of all potentiality, without losing anything of their formal notion. They are found in a *pure state* only in God. There are not two unknowns involved in the proportions thus established. What separates Saint Thomas from Moses Maimonides. In a sense, we know God by reason alone better than we know our most intimate friends, the divine nature better than human nature and, above all, better than animal, vegetable, or mineral nature.

§3. *Dogmatic Formulas Expressed in Philosophical Language Remain to a Degree Accessible to Common Sense if the Latter Is a Rudimentary Ontology.* They are irreconcilable with a philosophy of *phenomena* or of *becoming*.

A. Phenomenalist or purely dynamist notions of personality are irreconcilable with the dogma of the Incarnation. (In Christ, there are two consciences and two freedoms. One cannot be satisfied, like Günther, with a psychological or moral definition of personality.)

B. Common sense possesses an ontological notion of personality, the foundation of psychological personality and moral personality.

C. This ontological notion of personality enables common sense to understand the mysteries of the Hypostatic Union and of the Trinity.

D. By [the preaching of] "elevations," the profound meaning of the mysteries of the Incarnation and the Trinity can be made accessible to common sense.

Chapter 3: Dogmatic Formulas Expressed in Philosophical Language Exceed Common Sense by Their Precision, but They Do Not Render Dogma Subservient to Any System

§1. *These Formulas Exceed Common Sense by Their Precision.* The notion of subsistence is the explicitation of a vague datum of common sense. Common sense makes use of this notion (*in actu exercito*); the Councils clarified it (*in actu signato*) after long discussions between Greeks and Latins. The same may be said of "substance" in transubstantiation.

§2. *Dogmatic Formula Expressed in Philosophical Language Remains within the Prolongation of Common Sense and Does Not Render Dogma Subservient to Any System, Properly Speaking; Theological Systems.* Example: the notion of "subsistence" or "personhood" as it is used by the Councils is not taken with its systematic value, which arises from the relations it has with the first principle of a philosophical body of doctrine. In the Thomist system, this notion is connected to being by way of analysis: a study of what is required *a parte rei* in order to verify the affirmative judgments of common sense that oppose the *self* to everything that is attributable to it; an analysis of the real element thus obtained, its relation to essence and existence, the first divisions of being. Consequences of this Thomistic notion of personality in the theological treatise on the Incarnation. The Suarézian and Scotist conceptions of personality, and the danger that they involve.

§3. *Far from Being Rendered Subservient to Our Concepts, Revelation Judges Them and Utilizes Them.*

§4. *The Principle of the Autonomy of the Mind.* The agent must assimilate the patient and not be assimilated by it. This enslavement frees us. The fear of God. Intellectual sin [*Le péché de l'esprit*] and its theological formulation.

§5. *Dogma Is Known More Explicitly in the Church by the* Maiores *Charged with Teaching Others, but It Is Penetrated More Profoundly by Those Whose Souls Are Purer.* Saint Teresa's Judgment on the theologians. Christianity is not only a [way of] *life*; it is also a *doctrine*. The two wisdoms according to Saint Thomas: doctrinal wisdom *secundum perfectum usum rationis* and experiential wisdom *per modum inclinationis*. True pragmatism makes a mockery of pragmatism.

§6. *The Church Has Her Own Sense of Things, as well as Her Own Philosophy.* It is related to the primitive creed in a way akin to how "the natural metaphysics of human intellect" is related to common sense.

Chapter 4: The Intellect's First Glance and Contemplation

The First Intellectual Apprehension of Intelligible Being.

The First Glance of the Intellect on the Good.

The Supernatural First Glance.

The Darkening of the First Glance.

The Superior Simplicity Retrieved with Greater Experience.

INTRODUCTION

§1. The Problem at Hand

In recent days, the problem concerning the nature and scope of *common sense* (or, of *natural understanding*) has been posed anew with regard to the most serious questions concerning *the value of our primordial and fundamental forms of knowledge*: knowledge of the first rational principles, common to all men, and of the moral law, something necessary for the life of individuals and of peoples; natural knowledge of the existence of God, the Principle and End of all things; knowledge of supernatural mysteries, which revelation expresses in terms drawn from common sense so as to be accessible to all intellects in all countries and in all eras.

Many realist minds, hungering and thirsting for truth, wearied by interminable, supposedly philosophical discussions concerning the value of these primordial and fundamental forms of knowledge, wish to free themselves from the individuality of this or that thinker, from the particularism of schools of thought, and to return to common sense, to the first certitudes of natural reason.

Many philosophers themselves, despite everything that divides them, are inclined to admit that all the kinds of knowledge needed for the intellectual, moral, and religious life of humanity as a whole must be interpreted in accord with the same language in which they are expressed, the language of common sense, and not in accord with the technical terminology of this or that philosophy. From this perspective, the meaning and value of these fundamental assertions would be the very same ones as what common sense generally recognizes them to be.

On this point, even some Catholic theologians are in agreement with the modernists when it comes to determining the sense in which we must understand dogmatic formulas, which express the mysteries of

25

the Christian faith.[1]

Without a doubt, this position deserves deep consideration by all; we need not insist upon its advantages. Nonetheless, even if it is accepted in view of these very advantages, it goes without saying that a great number of questions still will need to be answered: *What is common sense?* What is its *object?* What are its *limits?* What are its *first affirmations* and its *derivative affirmations?* What affirmations are sometimes attributed to it undeservedly? Finally, what is its *value* in its own, proper sphere?

Once the question is posed in this manner, whose job is it to resolve it? Does it fall to the common man, who is incapable of distinguishing the fundamental assertions of natural reason from what has adventitiously come to be attached to them, the residue of the prejudices of a given race or a given civilization? Obviously not. In order to resolve this problem, will we need to address our inquiry to a particular science such as physics, mathematics, biology, or philology? Each of these particular sciences can indeed inform us about its proper object, its method, and its special problems and certitudes; however, none of them can be elevated to the generalities with which we are occupied at this moment.

It belongs to philosophy to treat of the loftiest generalities, and by addressing the problem concerning the nature and value of *natural understanding* (or, of common sense), it already touches upon the problem concerning its proper value. Obviously, here the concern is to avoid a *petitio principii* or a vicious circle so that we may stick to an attentive examination of *reality* as it is immediately *given* and of the intellect itself.

This is indeed a weighty question! Here the differences between various philosophers will more or less reappear.

The agnostic (who holds that we can know only phenomena and that, even if God does exist, He would be absolutely unknowable) will claim that common sense is only a first, vague knowledge of this phenomenal order. He would like to see in it only a rudimentary philosophy of *phenomena* and will fail to provide an acceptable sense for the commonly admitted notions of being and of substance.

The absolute evolutionist[2] (who holds that the fundamental reality and source of all appearances is becoming, forever unstable with its in-

---

[1] See *Revue du clergé français* 52 (October, 15, 1907). [Trans. note: Fr. Garrigou-Lagrange cites only this date. He perhaps has in mind J. Bricourt, "Ce qui n'est pas du modernism" (129–45), and Édouard Le Roy and F. Dubois, "Dogme et vérité" (210–25).]

[2] [Trans. note: See note 63 in chapter 1 of this first part of this text for an explanation for what Fr. Garrigou-Lagrange means when he uses this term.]

cessantly renewed forms) will seek to find in common sense a rudimentary philosophy of *becoming*. If we object to him that common sense is, at bottom, immutable, by the fact that it exists in all times and in all places, he will respond that this immutability is only superficial, only the immutability of a *utilitarian kind of knowledge, formed in view of action*, and not that of a profound knowledge of reality, which is forever changing. The evolutionist will thus concede a certain immutability belonging to the practical order, and if he acknowledges the dogmas of Christianity, he will hold them to be immutable only from the utilitarian perspective, in view of moral and religious action.

At the opposite extreme, the absolute realism of the ontologists (who claim that the first act of our natural understanding is a vague intuition of God, the first, absolutely immutable Being) will seek to find this intuition in common sense, at the risk of confusing being in general (the being of all things) with the Divine Being and our intellect with the Divine Intellect.

Finally, differing profoundly from all these opposing conceptions, traditional philosophy, which acknowledges the absolute immutability of the first principles of reason and of reality (or of *being*), also recognizing the existence of God, the First Being, forever identical to Himself (and, by that fact, essentially distinct from the ever-changing world), must see in common sense—as we will show—a rudimentary philosophy of *being* opposed to agnostic or atheistic philosophies of phenomena and of becoming, as well as to pantheistic ontologism.

* * *

As our adversaries themselves indeed confess, such is the problem at hand. The point can become even clearer if we consider what a well-known Bergsonian, Éduouard Le Roy, wrote concerning the value of the first notions and that of the formulas of faith, which imply these notions:

> The formulas of faith must be understood in their *obvious* sense and not in a *learned* one. We agree with all of this, and it is certainly not a negligible affair. But, all this, however, to a certain extent—here is what should be noted—constitutes perhaps less a solution to the problem than the statement thereof. Indeed, what is the precise scope of common language? To what level of thought does it belong? In what specific way and in which aspects can the affirmations of common sense be said to be wholly independent from theoretical philosophy? . . . Here, we have a funda-

mental problem whose resolution is not as simple as one might think at first glance. . . . Let us not forget that, as soon as we look at things from the perspective of theoretical representations, the obvious sense [of such formulas] does not remain absolutely the same in all ages. In particular, it would not be difficult to note more than one difference between antiquity and the Middle Ages, as well as between the thirteenth century and our own era, in this regard. . . . And if, in order to discover what in common sense is really independent from every system, we forever remain attached to an intellectualist perspective, that is, to the perspective of *a theoretical representation*, then we will expose ourselves, almost inevitably, to the danger of gravely misunderstanding things. . . . Common sense contains, in an unformed and vague state, who knows what residues of all the philosophical opinions and of all the systems having had some fashionableness. It resembles a rich and diverse alluvial soil, of such a character that *nearly any metaphysics can come to be recognized in it.* Thus, each person will be naturally inclined to hold that the primary foundation of common sense is that of his own theoretical tendencies, with which he effortlessly sympathizes. . . . *Therefore, will we need to assign the task of defining the "system" of common sense to uncritical minds [esprits], to those unlearned people who are incapable of disentangling the influences that they undergo?*

Be that as it may, eager to escape, to the degree this is possible, from a delusion of this kind, I have striven to define common sense in itself and for itself, not as a first approximation of this or that metaphysics. It has thus appeared to me not as being a rudimentary philosophy or science but as a *utilitarian organization of thought from the practical point of view.* In this way, apart from every speculative opinion, *even from those that he himself professes,*[3] it is *experientially really lived* by all. And this is likewise how this matter has been conceived by him who, among all philosophers, has most profoundly reached its original and specific nature, namely, by Henri Bergson. We can say that the proper language of common sense is the language of habitual perception, therefore, a *language relative to action*, made for expressing action, modeled upon action, . . . an action that obviously enough implies thought, since we are speaking of the action of a rational being, though one

---

3   It is unnecessary to note that, on this point, we will profoundly distinguish ourselves from Le Roy.

that thus encapsulates only a *wholly practical thought* itself.[4]

Le Roy concludes from this that the dogmas of the Catholic faith have only a practical meaning: "The reality that constitutes the object of faith is defined for us by the attitude and conduct that it requires of us."[5] It is well known that this doctrine was condemned by the Church in the twenty-sixth proposition of the decree *Lamentabili* on July 3, 1907.[6] Indeed, from this perspective, the dogma "Jesus is God" would mean only: "Behave toward Jesus as you would toward God, without, nonetheless, affirming that He actually is God."

We have permitted ourselves to cite him at such length because—all while giving a nominalist and pragmatist solution that is much more unacceptable to our eyes than is the absolute realism (be it Platonic or ontologist) that is radically opposed to it—the citation poses quite well the problem that must, at all costs, be resolved. Le Roy faults "the theologians of our days" for no longer truly being philosophers in their claims. He takes up against them anew the critique that is generally registered against the opinion held by the Scottish school that is called the school of common sense: "Therefore, will we need to assign the task of defining the 'system' of common sense to uncritical minds [*esprits*], to those unlearned people who are incapable of disentangling the influences that they undergo?"

Would traditional philosophy—prepared by Socrates and Plato, systematized in its general lines by Aristotle, developed in part by the Church Fathers and more perfectly by Saint Thomas and his successors—be nothing but a pure and simple codification of the truths of common sense, a fashionable codification made by truly thinking minds, like that of the Scottish school of common sense or that of the Eclectics, though without intellectual vigor, without profound originality, without a dominating principle, without a guiding idea, which by its own development organizes all of its parts? Is traditional philosophy nothing more than a *mid-point* between obviously erroneous extreme systems, between materialism and absolute idealism, between atheism (the radical denial of God) and acos-

---

4   Le Roy and Dubois, "Dogme et vérité," 212–14. I have added emphasis to a number of phrases of capital importance in this citation.

5   Le Roy and Dubois, "Dogme et vérité," 212–14.

6   "The dogmas of faith are to be held only according to their practical sense; that is to say, as preceptive norms of conduct and not as norms of believing" (Denzinger, no. 3426). The Holy Office here condemns a pragmatism that actually exists, and not a chimerical pragmatism that would give no part to the intellect in this *sensum practicum* rule of action.

mism (the radical denial of the world, absorbed into God)? Was traditional philosophy formed by neutralizing these extreme systems by one another, so that it might itself remain in a veritable mediocrity? Rather, is it not a summit that is elevated, not only above these extreme, mutually opposed systems but also above eclectic and opportunist mediocrity, which forever only manages to reach the half-way point on the road toward its destination, given that it does not glimpse the superior principles that reconcile all things? Is it not the case that the apparent contradictions presented by the various aspects of reality find their resolution only when their terms, pushed to their loftiest degree, find true equilibrium? Harmony is found at the summit of the pyramid, at the pinnacle of thought, in a unique principle that virtually contains the various aspects of the reality that, at first glance, are irreconcilable.

This is what we would like to show in the present work: above a pragmatic or utilitarian nominalism (which leads one to declare that reality is unknowable) and above a naïve realism (which believes that it already experiences, here-below, an immediate intuition of God), and likewise above a vague philosophy of common sense (a kind of compromise that is content with neutralizing extreme systems with one another without providing us with any vigorous, precise, and comprehensive affirmation)—above all these is elevated the true, traditional metaphysics, *the philosophy of being*, which alone is truly conformed to common sense because it alone is the development and justification of this common sense.

* * *

Therefore, we will examine the principal theories proposed concerning the nature and value of common sense, particularly the pragmatist theories recently set forth by Bergson and Le Roy, whom we cited above. In them we will see, under the obscurities and the verbiage in which it is shrouded, a somewhat novel application of the most radical sort of empiricist nominalism. This nominalism, which ultimately reduces intellectual knowledge to sense knowledge, must inevitably lead to the denial of the ontological value of dogmas, as much as (and more than) does Kantian conceptualism.

By contrast, we will briefly see what can be said about this same subject by obviously excessive realism, after the manner of the Platonists and the ontologists, who tend to confuse the Divine Being and the being of things, God and the world.

Above these mutually opposed conceptions and above a vague eclecticism that forever oscillates back and forth, we will set forth the classical theory concerning the nature and value of common sense such as it is found in the works of Aristotle and of St. Thomas. Spontaneous reason will manifest itself to us as being a rudimentary philosophy of *being*, already dominating, from on high, the philosophy of *phenomena* and that of *becoming*.

We have been led to this conclusion by studying the three operations of the intellect: conception, judgment, and reasoning.

We have seen this assertion of Aristotle and of St. Thomas verified forever more fully: *the formal object of the intellect is being*, as the formal object of sight is color, that of awareness the subjective fact, and that of the will the good. Indeed, from this perspective of the formal object, the distinction between the image and the idea, that between judgment and association, and that between reasoning and empirical successions become all the more striking, and rational principles are hierarchized more easily under the *principle of raison d'être*,[7] which is itself attached by a *reductio ad absurdum* argument to the *principle of identity*, which states what is befitting in the first place to *being*. The problem concerning the objectivity of knowledge, that concerning substance, and that concerning God, like those concerning freedom and the spirituality of the soul, are illuminated in a new light and find their resolution through a constant reduction to *being*. "Being is that which the intellect first conceives, as it were, as what is most known and in which it resolves all of its conceptions."[8] In this necessary process of the mind judging all things through a reduction to being, its formal object, we have been led to see a mere precision of the natural movement of spontaneous intelligence. "The intellect *naturally* knows being and those things that belong *per se* to being as such, upon which its knowledge of the first principles is founded."[9] From this comes the theory of common sense that above all sees in it (in a rudimentary state) the

---

[7] [Trans. note: After long meditation on Fr. Garrigou-Lagrange's language, this has been my manner of translating his expression *principe de raison d'être*. Sometimes, it is translated as the principle of "sufficient reason," which can be misleading. In English, the expression should maintain the sense of "reason for being" expressed by the French *raison d'être*. Indeed, when writing in Latin, Fr. Garrigou-Lagrange will translate this as *principium rationis essendi*. Moreover, see his own remarks in *De revelatione*, 5th ed. (Rome: Desclée and Socii, 1950), 238n2. Note, however, that Dom Bede Rose, in his admirable translations, renders *principe de raison d'être* as "the principle of sufficient reason." Likewise see Réginald Garrigou-Lagrange, "On the Search for Definitions According to Aristotle and St. Thomas," in *Philosophizing in Faith*, trans. and ed. Matthew K. Minerd (Providence, RI: Cluny Media, 2019), 24n6.]

[8] Aquinas, *De veritate*, q. 1, a. 1.

[9] *Summa contra gentiles* II, ch. 83.

supreme science defined by Aristotle: *epistēmē tis ē theōrei to ē hon kai ta toutō hyparchonta kath' auto* ["scientia quae speculatur ens, prout ens est et quae ei per se insunt"; "the science that speculates about being, inasmuch as it is being and those things that belong to it *per se*"].[10]

This theory is, in reality, only a schema of a general systematization of the philosophy of being that we shall attempt to develop.

Thus, we have already been led to conclude that dogmatic formulas themselves, even those which are expressed in philosophical language, are accessible, to a degree, to common sense. If they exceed it on account of their precision, they remain within the ambit of its natural prolongation and do not make dogma subservient to any system, properly so-called.[11]

In our study of Saint Thomas's thought, we have been particularly inspired by the works of Father Ambroise Gardeil published in *Revue thomiste*, in particular an article that appeared in January of 1904 on the "Relativity of Dogmatic Formulas."[12]

We have also been aided by the synthesis outlined by Father Norbert Del Prado, O.P., in his work *De veritate fundamenti philosophiae christianae*,[13] in which Saint Thomas's treatises on God and creation are connected to this ultimate truth: in God alone are essence and existence identical.[14]

---

[10] Aristotle, *Metaphysica* 3.1.

[11] Faith, founded upon revelation, requires an infused supernatural light, but not new ideas or notions, unknown by common sense.

[12] [Trans. note: He is referring to Ambroise Gardeil, "La réforme de la théologie catholique: La relativité des formules dogmatiques," *Revue thomiste* 12 (1904): 48–76.]

[13] Norbert del Prado, *De veritate fundamentali philosophiae christianae* (Fribourg, Switzerland: Imprimerie S. Paul, 1911).

[14] Finally, we are in debt to the work of Afrikan Spir, *Pensée et réalité*, translated from German by Auguste Penjon, for certain clarifications concerning the relations between the principle of *raison d'être* and the principle of identity, enabling us to understand better the thought of Aristotle and St. Thomas. In his attempt to reform critical philosophy, Spir has striven to give the principle of identity its rightful place in philosophy. His originality is to have understood that this principle is like the sun that illuminates all things in the domain of knowledge, denouncing the contingency and relative unintelligibility of the world and leading us to the affirmation of God, the only being who is wholly and entirely identical to himself. Persuaded that he had at last found the true foundation and the veritable method of philosophy, Spir thus returned to the profound thought of Aristotle, who attaches all science to the principle of contradiction and all reality to Pure Act.

In the midst of the nearly universal philosophical skepticism born from Descartes, Hume, and Kant, we are happy to find a philosopher who, despite a number of errors, knew how to arrive at, and preserve himself in, this conviction, which has forever been that of the School, that in philosophy there are a great number of partial truths and that it is, above all, important to order them under a supreme principle, the principle of iden-

§2. Division of the Work

The division of the present work comes from the very nature of the problem posed.

In the first part, we will examine "What Is Common Sense?": its object, its limits, its fundamental affirmations, and its value. We will study the response given to this question by different, mutually opposed schools and, finally, the answer given by traditional realism (or the philosophy of being). We will see the merits of this doctrine that develops and justifies the spontaneous certitudes of natural understanding by showing their relationship with "being," the formal object of the intellect, and with the principle of identity (or, of non-contradiction [*sic*][15]).

In the second part, we will see what the philosophy of being, itself the development and justification of common sense, tells us about *the existence of God*, as well as what is the worth of the traditional proofs of this existence, doing so in relation to recent objections from agnosticism and evolutionism. This study will supplement the first by emphasizing the principle of identity (or of non-contradiction) as the fundamental law of thought and of reality.

Finally, in the third part we will inquire into whether it is true to say that *the dogmatic formulas of Christian faith*, even when expressed in philosophical language, have no other meaning than what common sense

---

tity, under a single idea, the idea of being. Forming a whole, these partial truths at last take on their true meaning and all their value. As Spir's French translator interprets his thought: "Thus, one will perceive the differences and interrelations existing between philosophy and the sciences. Philosophy goes all the way to the foundation of things; it begins where the sciences, unable to go beyond the domain of appearance, are constrained to halt. Philosophy gives them their principles and assures the validity of their inductions. If we understand this aright, we would avoid the confusion in which, still in our own days, philosophy is struggling; we would cease to enslave it— thus reversing their roles—to the sciences, and would stop limiting its task to vain generalizations that are forever rendered insufficient by new progress in the endless study of the empirical world. We would see in it, finally, what it is: the *most positive of the sciences, the only one that can reach, right now, a definitive truth*" (Afrikan Spir, *Pensée et réalité*, trans. Auguste Penjon [Paris: Félix Alcan, 1896], ix–x).

[15] [Trans. note: Fr. Garrigou-Lagrange most often uses "principle of contradiction" for what is most commonly referred to now as the "principle of non-contradiction" (in a sense, he labels it by the topic, whether there can be contratdiction, while it is now most commonly labeled by the verdict on that matter, that there cannot be). But he does on occassion use "non-contradiction" for the same, and I mark those instances with "[*sic*]" to signal that he means the same thing as in most places he means by "principle of contradiction" (and we now commonly mean by "principle of non-contradiction")].

can give for them. We are not very convinced of the truth of the thesis [holding that their meaning is limited to common sense *tout court*], a thesis that is thought to be in agreement with our own; we do not accept it without reservations. However, supposing that it be true, we can ask what value the first notions of common sense must have in order to be capable of expressing the divine reality that God reveals to us. In this third part, we will, in particular, study the notion of the person from the ontological, psychological, and moral perspectives as involved in the mystery of the Incarnation (or of the Hypostatic Union).

Part 1

----------- ∽∝⋙∾ -----------

WHAT IS COMMON SENSE?

Given that, by universal admission, common sense is nothing other than spontaneous (or primordial) reason, it is to be expected that we will find philosophers expressing as many theories of common sense as there are theories of reason. Empiricism, like rationalism, must be represented. It would even not be impossible to find here the four great, general [philosophical] theories: (1) empiricism; (2) innate rationalism (Plato) or ontologism (Malebranche) with a pure intuition of the intelligible; (3) innate rationalism without intuition of the intelligible (Immauel Kant); (4) empirical rationalism with an abstractive intuition of the intelligible in the sensible (Aristotle). Or, metaphysically speaking: (1) nominalism; (2) Platonic realism; (3) pure conceptualism; (4) realist conceptualism (or, moderate realism).

In truth, common sense is recognized only in the most comprehensive of these four theories, in empirical rationalism (or, realist conceptualism), which, in Henri Bergson's own opinion, represents precisely "the natural metaphysics of the human intellect."[1] The nominalist theory of common sense is much rather a kind of *litigation against common sense* [*procès du sens commun*], as would also be, to varying degrees, a realist theory along Platonic lines or a purely conceptualist theory along Kantian lines.

Note that, to characterize the doctrine of Aristotle and of Saint Thomas, we just used the expression "*abstractive intuition* of the intelligible in the sensible," and we will employ this expression often in the pages that follow. It is an abridged manner of translating what Saint Thomas calls the *intellectual apprehension* of intelligible being in the sensible, as well as the *intellectual intuition* of the first principles or laws of being, an

---

[1] Henri Bergson, *L'évolution créatrice*, 352. [Trans. note: Fr. Garrigou-Lagrange does not mention the edition. In other books, his pagination slightly differs.]

35

intuition united to the abstraction that extracts from the sensible individual what essentially constitutes it, what is most real in it, its foundational law (see *Summa theologiae* [*ST*] I, q. 85, a. 1).

Very often, Saint Thomas speaks of *simple intellectual apprehension*, the first operation of the intellect [*esprit*], prior to judgment and to reasoning. He also calls it *understanding of indivisibles*, and in *De veritate*, q. 15, a. 1, ad 7, he says, "The *gaze* [*intuitus*] of our intellect is fixed first upon the *natures* of sensible things," and in *ST* II-II, q. 8, a. 1: "*To understand* [*intelligere*] is called a kind of *reading into the interior* [*intus legere*]. . . . For sense knowledge is occupied with sensible, exterior qualities, whereas intellective knowledge *penetrates* all the way to the essence of the thing, for as is said in *De anima* 3.4, the object of the intellect is *that which is*." On the intuitive character of this first intellectual knowledge, see one of the most profound Thomists, John of St. Thomas, *Cursus philosophicus*, volume 1, part 2 (*Logica materialis*), and vol. 2 (*Philosophia naturalis*), q. 1, a. 3.[2]

---

[2] [Trans. note: On this subject, Fr. Garrigou-Lagrange elsewhere cites M. R. Jolivet, "L'intuition intellectuelle," *Revue thomiste* 15 (January 1932): 52–71.]

Chapter 1

THE NOMINALIST THEORY
OF COMMON SENSE

In order to show how nominalism is led to conceive of common sense: (1) we will recount a theory recently proposed by Édouard Le Roy; (2) we will thus be led to see what absolute nominalism entails; and (3) we will compare nominalism with opposed systems, in relation to the question of common sense.

A. THE THEORY PROPOSED BY ÉDOUARD LE ROY

This theory is set forth in an article that appeared in July of 1899 in *Revue de métaphysique et de morale* under the title "Science et philosophie."[1] We will attempt to draw its principal lineaments to the fore.

§1. The Particular Prejudices of Common Sense

Let us first clear up a critique made by Le Roy concerning the immutability of common sense. This critique is not, we believe, necessarily integrally connected to his theory. "[Common sense] does not remain absolutely the same in all ages as soon as we look at things from the perspective of a theoretical representation. In particular, it would not be difficult to note more than one difference between antiquity and the middle ages, as well as between the thirteenth century and our own, in this regard." Le Roy must distinguish, I imagine, two spheres for common sense: one corresponding

---

[1] Édouard Le Roy, "Science et philosophie," *Revue de métaphysique et de morale* 7 (1899): 375–425 and 708–31.

to the order of the positive sciences (what Aristotle called the first degree of abstraction), and the other corresponding to the metaphysical, moral, and religious order (what Aristotle called the third degree of abstraction).[2] In this latter sphere, Bergson recognizes the immutability of common sense, even if one takes up the perspective of a theoretical representation. Did he not write, as regards the philosophy of Plato and Aristotle: "A solid frame of this immense edifice remains, and this frame sketches out the broad lines of a metaphysics that is, we believe, the natural metaphysics of the human intellect"?[3] "An irresistible attraction brings the intellect back to its natural movement, the metaphysics of the moderns to Greek metaphysics."[4] "Everything is obscure in the idea of creation if one thinks of *things* that would be created and of a *thing* that creates, as one usually does, indeed, as our understanding cannot resist doing." This represents an illusion that is "natural to our intellect."[5]

Elsewhere, Le Roy himself acknowledges, on the subject of common sense, *"particular prejudices* proper to each century and to each temperament, as well as *the general prejudices* related to the very conditions in which spontaneous knowledge develops."[6] Into the first group, he places "the systematic errors—various, depending upon person, circumstance, country, and era—arising from the fashionable theories of each age, besmirching ordinary knowledge."[7] Indeed, if one holds that common sense is the ensemble of opinions generally received in the age in which one lives, it is easy to show that it falls into error and changes. One will say, "Common sense, holding to first appearances and, furthermore, mixing its imaginations in with them, often admits as being true things that are

---

[2] See Aristotle, *Metaphysica* 10.3. The natural sciences abstract only from individual sensible matter, while still considering common sensible matter; the chemist abstracts from the particularities of a given molecule of water in order to study the sensible properties of water (first degree of abstraction). The mathematical sciences abstract from common sensible matter so as to consider now only continuous or discrete quantity (second degree of abstraction). Metaphysics, logic, and moral philosophy [*morale*] abstract from all matter [reading *matière* for *manière*] in order to no longer consider anything but being inasmuch as it is being and its properties, or beings that are defined by a relation to being inasmuch as it is being, namely, intellectual beings and their intellectual and voluntary activity (third degree of abstraction).

[3] Bergson, *L'évolution créatrice*, 352. [Trans. note: Again, Fr. Garrigou-Lagrange does not mention the edition, and his pagination slightly differs in other books.]

[4] Bergson, *L'évolution créatrice*, 355.

[5] Bergson, *L'évolution créatrice*, 270.

[6] Le Roy, "Science et philosophie," 379.

[7] Le Roy, "Science et philosophie," 379.

THE PARTICULAR PREJUDICES OF COMMON SENSE

false. There is no single, great scientific truth that common sense did not at first misconceive and reject. To their own eras, Christopher Columbus, Galileo, and William Harvey all seemed devoid of all common sense."[8] Likewise, if by this word one refers to the habitual and somewhat down-to-earth manner of judging found among the common men, one will not delay to add:

> In the very order of moral truths, it suspects everything that departs from the ordinary and the common. Socratic virtue disturbs it; Stoic virtue startles it; Christian virtue itself has been called the folly of the cross. The good sense of the excellent Pliny cannot understand it at all. When the Apostles, animated by the new spirit, speak to the crowd, the crowd judges them to be "full of sweet wine"; and the enthusiasm of St. Paul drew from Festus this curious reprimand: "Paul, you do not have common sense. *Insanis Paule!*"[9]

Based on all this, it is easy to conclude that to appeal to common sense is, in fact, to appeal to ignorance and to prejudice.

Le Roy was obviously thinking of these "particular and variable prejudices of common sense" when he wrote: "The obvious sense [of such formulas] does not remain absolutely the same in all ages as soon as we look at things from the perspective of a theoretical representation. . . . Common sense contains, in an unformed and vague state, who knows what residues of all the philosophical opinions and of all the systems having had some fashionableness."[10]

"However, alongside these particular prejudices proper to each century and to each temperament, there exist general prejudices related to the very conditions in which spontaneous human knowledge develops."[11] And given that these general prejudices are, for Le Roy, the very same ones that besmirch the metaphysics of Aristotle and of Saint Thomas, it is no longer true to say that, in this sphere, common sense "resembles a rich and diverse alluvial soil, of such a character that nearly any metaphysics can come to be recognized in it."

---

[8] Élie Rabier, *Leçons de philosophie*, vol. 2, *Logique*, 2nd ed. (Paris: Librarie Hachette et Cie, 1886), 375.

[9] Rabier, *Leçons de philosophie*, 2:375.

[10] Le Roy, "Dogme et vérité," 212–14. [Trans. note: This most likely cites Édouard Le Roy and F. Dubois, "Dogme et vérité," *Revue du clergé français* 52 (October, 15, 1907): 210–25.]

[11] Le Roy, "Science et philosophie," 379.

§2. The General Prejudices of Common Sense

Therefore, let us see what these general prejudices are. It is here that we arrive at the nominalist theory of common sense.

These prejudices or postulates of common thought are: (1) the fragmentation and dislocation of matter; (2) the materialization of the things of the mind.

Le Roy rejects the [Kantian] theory of the noumena, as well as the vulgar empiricism that would lead one to hold as reality itself what our mind sees in experience: "Let us declare quite simply that we are plunged in an ocean of *images* that constitute, by definition, what we call reality, and let us propose to examine the value of the organization that we have spontaneously imposed upon this immense mass."[12]

He first establishes, without great difficulty, that our primitive perception is that of a moving and heterogeneous continuity, *continuum sensibile*. In certain regards, this is equivalent to what Saint Thomas, following Aristotle, says in *ST* I, q. 85, a. 3: "Sense knowledge, like intellectual knowledge, is at first a vague form of knowledge; our primitive perception is that of an amorphous, indistinct, and moving mass, in which a multitude of still-undistinguished qualities appear and disappear."[13] However, from the point of departure of knowledge, Aristotle and Saint Thomas part ways with empiricism by simultaneously assigning this first abstractive intuition of the intellect its proper object, one that is distinct from that of sensation: *being* in the concrete, the something that is *to on* [Gk.]. For them, this is what renders man's primitive perception different from that had by animals: "As much for sense as for the intellect, more common knowledge is prior than less common knowledge." At the beginning of his commentary on the *De ente et essentia*, Thomas de Vio Cajetan extensively analyzed this very first form of knowledge: "Concrete being in a sensible quiddity is first known by our intellect through an actual, confused knowledge."[14]

Alongside the Bergsonian continuum or within this continuum, which according to us is the *primum cognitum sensibile*, there is a *primum*

---

[12] Le Roy, "Science et philosophie," 382.
[13] [Trans. note: The text appears to be an interpretation of the Latin translated below. I am following Fr. Garrigou-Lagrange's French.]
[14] [Trans. note: See Thomas de Vio Cajetan, *Commentary on Being and Essence*, proem. q. 1, trans. Lottie H. Kendzierski and Francis C. Wade (Milwaukee, WI: Marquette University Press, 1964), 44. Kendzierski and Wade translate the famed *ens concretum quidditati sensibili* as "being embodied in an essence able to be sensed."]

cognitum intelligibile. We admit that, in a certain manner, by fragmenting the amorphous, indistinct, and moving *continuum*, sense knowledge can become intellectual knowledge by fragmenting *being*; gradually we will divide being into object and subject, into substance and accident (being and manner of being), into act and potency, and so on, and nothing will be intelligible except in function of undergoing such fragmentation. And if we must indeed acknowledge that the fragmenting of the sensible continuum is often utilitarian, artificial, and practical, we will need to maintain that the fragmenting of that which is intelligible is a requirement of thought, something necessarily true to the degree that this thought grasps, in one notion, the *raison d'être* of another notion.

From this first difference separating empiricism from realist conceptualism, a second follows: to admit the abstractive intuition of *being* in the first perception of the sensible, amorphous continuum is to admit the duality of the object, the being existing independently from the representation, and the representation that is essentially relative to the being. Henceforth, knowledge is conceived, by Aristotle and by Saint Thomas, as a form of contact between the subject and the object, between the sense and the phenomena of the exterior world, between the intellect and being. The indistinct perception of the infant in the cradle is, therefore, only a first and very imperfect form of contact with things. It is simultaneously sense and intellectual knowledge, both beginning to pass from their state of indetermination or pure potency. By this first perception, the infant vaguely knows the entire external world, as by its first abstractive intuition of being it vaguely knows metaphysics (or, the science of being inasmuch as it is being). By contrast, for Le Roy, this primitive perception is the ideal toward which pure knowledge must strive to return: is not reality "this ocean of images into which we are plunged"? Our primitive perception revealed it to us without deforming it. Following that, "we introduced into perceived reality *arrangements and simplifications* that are convenient and even necessary for speech and for action. We have lived: it would be quite strange if, stirring about in the midst of things without yet knowing them, we would not have jostled them about in some manner."[15] Would you like a proof for how we have fragmented and dislocated the heterogeneous and fleeting continuum that we first perceived: "From one solid to another, there is discontinuity for touch, continuity for sight; why prefer the former of these indications to the latter if not because the latter is less *convenient* and less *useful* than the former, or, if one wishes, because the former ex-

---

[15] Le Roy, "Science et philosophie," 381.

presses better than the latter a property of how we act?"[16]

Though we may be disposed to admit the often-utilitarian character of the fragmentation of the sensible continuum, we cannot here follow Le Roy. No one can deny the influence of practical convenience on the organization of our knowledge of sensible things. Quite clearly, we neglect many unusable and cumbersome data. However, does not action itself presuppose knowledge: "nihil volitum nisi praecognitum ut conveniens"? And is not action all the more certain, efficacious, and better when we have a better grasp concerning what must be done? In the present case, we had always thought that it was fitting to prefer the indications of touch to those of sight because sight has for its proper object color (or, the colored surface), whereas touch has for its proper object extended resistance and, by that fact, extension in three dimensions, which precisely constitutes the solid form.

Furthermore, the data provided by touch are not the only ones that enable us to establish the individuality of bodies. A being's quantitative unity in space is not the criterion for its substantial unity. This quantitative unity presumes only an accidental union (an aggregate of molecules). The sole criterion [for substantial unity] is activity, and the action that reveals *the unity of a whole* must be produced by *only one part* and not by the association of parts; however, it is necessary that the influence of other parts emerge in this action.[17] It is with the help of this principle, which is vaguely known by the common man, that one establishes the individuality of superior animals. When, in reality, we distinguish two animals from each other or an animal from its surrounding environment, is this only an "arrangement, a simplification that is convenient for speech and for action?" Bergson, in *Creative Evolution*, recognizes that the living body is isolated by its very nature, although its individuality is not perfect. It is all too simple for one to establish this artificial character of fragmentation by the simple comparison of tactile and visual impressions, concluding: "The existence of separated bodies is not given to us immediately; it is the result

---

[16] Le Roy, "Science et philosophie," 383.

[17] Marc de Munnynck, "L'individualité des animaux supérieurs," *Revue thomiste* (1901): 644. The author cites as an example the following fact: "A mare breaks its cannon bone [i.e., the large metatarsal bone on the front of the lower leg of the horse]. After recovering, it was made to reproduce. One of its foals, which had to be killed, presented a weld in its cannon bone as though it had been fractured. One has found a similar weld in the kneecap of child whose mother had violently fallen upon her knees." [Trans. note: The citation is taken from p. 645. Obviously, this dated physiology is problematic today.]

of the preference given to tactile impressions."[18]

Le Roy continues:

> What remains for us in order to believe in the reality of bodies that are independent from each other? Perhaps one will say that each of these is a region of homogeneity in the sense that two points of the same solid differ less from each other than does a point on this solid and a point in the surrounding environment. But what does this *less* mean? We must understand well that *quality alone is real*. Quantity exists only where measurement is possible, where there is a relation of container to content, in a word, a spatial character. Now, inasmuch as it is the principle of measure, space is the object of intuition, not of experience. It belongs to the mind [*l'esprit*], not to things; the latter are purely qualitative."[19]

The *extensive* character of sensations of touch and of sight does not permit one easily to admit what Le Roy claims here.

Father Marc de Munnynck recently said, while speaking of Ostwald,[20] who also sacrifices quantity in order to explain all things by energy:

> If one browses through all the characteristics that he attributes to energy, all the functions that it must satisfy, one arrives at the fatal conclusion that it possesses all the properties and implies all the requirements of *local movement*. . . . Now, it has not yet been possible to extricate the notion of "local movement" from that of "place." Logic could well establish *a priori* that this enterprise of *purification* is condemned in advance, and a *real* place is *real* and *actual* only when it is occupied in some manner. But then, by what is it occupied? And let it not be said that such "presence" is still only a manifestation of energy. One can and ought to recognize that a deployment of energy is indispensable in order for a presence to be made known to us. However, we are not here concerned with the conditions of our knowledge. Rather, we are determining the logical requirements on the objective side of our representations. In short, we see reemerging here this so-abhorred "subject," and once we commit ourselves to taking this path, it is

---

[18] Le Roy, "Science et philosophie," 385.
[19] Le Roy, "Science et philosophie," 387.
[20] [Trans. note: Likely the chemist Wilhelm Ostwald (1853–1932).]

not impossible that we will travel all the way to material, quantitative substance, which the dynamists have relinquished since Leibniz.[21]

The kind of space that belongs to the mind and not to things is absolute, homogeneous, indefinite space, the possibility of unlimited extension in length, width, and depth. However, this very notion of absolute space can arise only from real and finite space—that is, place occupied by extended or quantitative bodies.

Let us suppose that, without committing any paralogism, Le Roy has eliminated quantity. We see that he is led to conclude: *"Contrary to common sense*, which fashions an indispensable and primordial support out of matter, the latter can be defined only in relation to the mind, its essence expressed only in terms of the soul, and its reality suspended only to the interior life and to moral action."[22] Indeed, what is the material world? It is an ocean of qualitative images, "a plastic and malleable paste where living activity traces figures and arranges systems of relations" following upon what is expedient in practical life.[23]

Beyond independent bodies, real quantity, must we say the same concerning substance, about causes? Obviously. Heterogeneous and fleeting, qualitative continuity alone is real:

> However, we must schematize in order to understand, and we do so spontaneously. Such is the origin and the immediate meaning of the notions of *substance, cause, relation, subject,* and so forth. Obsessed with practical preoccupations, common sense imagines bodily existence in the form of invariance, which it symbolizes by means of a position in space. As we have seen, this already involves the activity of abstracting and simplifying. However, when it then comes to the mind [*esprit*], its tendencies do not abandon it; it therefore buries the mind—this activity that never rests—in a dead permanence without which, quite wrongly, it no longer sees true existence: behold, its gravest error. . . . A fragmentation is practiced in its own turn upon the moving continuity of interior intuition. . . . We form separated ideas upon the image of indepen-

---

[21] A. Blanche and Marc de Munnynck, "Bulletin philosphique," *Revue des sciences philosophiques et théologiques* 2 (1908): 137.

[22] Le Roy, "Science et philosophie," 390.

[23] Le Roy, "Science et philosophie," 390.

dent bodies (and think of the mind as we do of substance).[24]

By contrast, in the eyes of the philosopher, *"axioms and categories, forms of understanding and of sensibility, all such things become, all such things evolve*; the human mind [*esprit*] is plastic and can change its most intimate desires."[25]

Such are the general prejudices of common sense: the fragmentation and dislocation of matter, and the materialization of the things of the mind. The conclusion: "Common sense, when it speculates, produces *verbal entities.* . . . On the other hand, it is inclined to consider only what is seen and is touched. It spatializes and materializes. It reifies and quantifies all things."[26]

Despite this, Le Roy affirms: *"The foundation is sure of this*, the form able to be critiqued."[27] What is this foundation? It is something which is really *lived* by all, a utilitarian organization of thought in view of practical life. Common sense does not have a *representation value* but does have a *signification value* inasmuch as it gives notice of the existence of a reality, inasmuch as it determines the attitude and conduct what we ought to take and follow in order to orient ourselves toward the object in question. Consequently, in regard to dogmatic formulas, we must distinguish between their signification value and their representation value. The irreformable and absolute adherence of faith is addressed only to the former.

B. ABSOLUTE NOMINALISM

§1. This Theory of Common Sense Represents a Reiterated Form of Absolute Nominalism

This theory of common sense is not absolutely new. It would not be impossible to find its first lineaments in Heraclitus. It is (and forever will be) imposed upon every nominalist captive to sensible appearances and responsive to their perpetual mobility. For such a person, *substances* and *things* can be only verbal entities (*flatus vocis*), by which common sense

---

[24] Le Roy, "Science et philosophie," 392. [Trans. note: The parentheses are Fr. Garrigou-Lagrange's own closing of the quote.]

[25] Édouard Le Roy, "Sur quelques objections adressées a la nouvelle philosophie," *Revue de métaphysique et de morale* 9 (1901): 305.

[26] Le Roy, "Dogme et vérité," 213.

[27] Le Roy, "Dogme et vérité," 213.

reifies and immobilizes the universal flux. All of this has been quite clear from the time of Hume onward. Thomists were already cognizant of this, saying of the medieval nominalists: "The nominalists' opinion falls in with the opinion of Heraclitus and Cratylus who (as book 4 of Aristotle's *Metaphysics* records) believed that nothing exists other than the sensible things that they saw, and since they experienced such things as being in continuous flux, constantly and fully lacking certitude, they inferred that nobody can have science concerning things."[28]

We can apply to Le Roy the words written by Gottfried Wilhelm Leibniz concerning Thomas Hobbes: "more than a nominalist [*plus quam nominalis*]." The preceding pages concerning the fragmenting of reality basically reproduce what had already been expressed quite clearly in John Stuart Mill's *Logic*, the *summa* of nominalism. In the third book of that work, in no. 4 of chapter 5, it is established that the distinction between agent and patient is illusory. The thesis is clear and is necessary following upon exposition of the sensualist principles from which it is derived.[29]

---

[28] Domingo de Soto, *Dialectica Aristotelis, De universalibus*, q. 1. Medieval nominalism consisted in *denying the objective reality of relations* of likeness, the foundation for the objective value of our concepts. This denial is found again in Bergson (see *L'évolution créatrice*, 385). Modern sensualist nominalism goes further; it reduces the *idea* to a *common image accompanied by a name* (327). On the basis of these principles, Le Roy should end up at the conclusions drawn by Ockham, who believed himself also to have definitively ruined the traditional proofs for the existence of the unique and infinite God who is distinct from the world, as well as those for the spirituality of the soul and for the distinction between good and evil, likewise declaring that everything that exceeds experience is an object of individual supernatural faith. [Trans. note: Fr. Garrigou-Lagrange does not cite the printed edition of Soto's work cited. Regarding the importance of relation for epistemological realism, see interesting similar observations made in John Deely, *Four Ages of Understanding* (Toronto: University of Toronto Press, 2001).]

[29] John Stuart Mill, *A System of Logic Ratiocinative and Inductive, Being a Connected View of the Principles of Evidence and the Methods of Scientific Investigation (Books I-III)* , ed. John M. Robson, Collected Works of John Stuart Mill 7 (Toronto: University of Toronto Press, London: Routledge and Kegan Paul, 1974), 334–35 (bk. 3, ch. 5, no. 4): "In most cases of causation a distinction is commonly drawn between something which acts, and some other thing which is acted upon; between an agent and a patient. Both of these, it would be universally allowed, are conditions of the phenomenon; but it would be thought absurd to call the latter the cause, that title being reserved for the former. The distinction, however, vanishes on examination, or rather is found to be only verbal; arising from an incident of mere expression, namely, that the object said to be acted upon, and which is considered as the scene in which the effect takes place, is commonly included in the phrase by which the effect is spoken of, so that if it were also reckoned as part of the cause, the seeming incongruity would arise of its being supposed to cause itself. . . . Those who have contended for a radical distinction between agent and patient,

Louis Couturat does not exaggerate in anyway when he writes with regard to the Bergsonian system: "Under the subtle and refined metaphysics that disguises it, we quite readily find the old sensualism of Condillac, whose characteristic aphorism Le Roy adopts as his own: the sciences are only well-constructed languages."[30] The same opinion is found in Benjamin Jacob in his remarkable study concerning "the philosophy of yesterday and that of today." He says:

> The new philosophy is, quite precisely, something wholly the opposite of the rationalism of Plato, Aristotle, Descartes, and of Leibniz. . . . Fundamental contingency, unlimited becoming, an interior life prior to intelligence and to intelligibility, indeed creating both of them. . . . What rises up to the surface is ancient matter, suppressing the idea. . . . Here (much more than in Spencer) every intellectual norm disappears, truth no longer maintains any meaning that is elevated above pure and simple experience. . . . Behold the office of philosophy: to retrieve the sensible under the deceitful intelligible that covers and masks it, and not, as was said in past days, to retrieve the intelligible under the sensible that hides it. . . . This is to overthrow the legislation of the understanding, though this does not thereby prove that one can be dispensed of it. . . . Behold the terms that best express the new philosophy: a becoming without fixed points and without laws where thought, properly so called, arises only denying reality. Indeed, does this not precisely define materialism, understood in its most profound sense?[31]

By contrast, Le Roy wishes to reserve the name of "materialism" for immobilists. To this end, we would need to use the term "materialist" for all the partisans of conceptualist philosophy—Socrates, Plato, Aristotle,

---

have generally conceived the agent as that which causes some state of, or some change in the state of, another object which is called the patient. But a little reflection will show that the license we assume of speaking of phenomena as states of the various objects which take part in them . . . is simply a sort of logical fiction, useful sometimes as one among several modes of expression, but which should never be supposed to be the enunciation of a scientific truth."

30 Louis Couturat, "Contre le nominalisme de M. Le Roy," *Revue de métaphysique et de morale* 8 (1900): 93.

31 Benjamin Jacob, "La philosophie d'hier et celle d'aujourd'hui," *Revue de métaphysique et de morale* 6 (1898): 170–201, 177.

Plotinus, Saint Augustine, Saint Thomas, Descartes, Spinoza, Leibniz, and Kant—whereas, the term "spiritualism" should henceforth be accorded to the ancient hylozoists: Heraclitus, the Stoics, the medieval nominalists, and the English empiricists. However atomistic these latter may be, according to the representatives of the new philosophy, they are, all things considered, less immobilist (and thus, according to Le Roy, less materialist) than the partisans of conceptualist philosophy who acknowledge the immutability of God, that of the immortal soul, and that of the moral law. In reality, Le Roy is an idealist in the sense that he reduces *reality* to the *image*; however, this reduction is precisely the denial of the *idea*, so that this sensualist or nominalist idealism is very closely related to what the superior form of spiritualism has always called materialism.

§2. Refutation of This Nominalism: The Formal Object of the Intellect Is Being (Proof); the Fragmenting of the Sensible Continuum versus That of Being or of the Intelligible

Here, we will content ourselves with sketching out a refutation of nominalism. As we have said, from the starting point of our knowledge's genesis, we part ways with Bergson by admitting, on the side of the *indistinct and moving continuum* (which, for us, is the first object vaguely known by the senses), a *primum cognitum intelligibile*, which is *being* in the concrete, *to on* [Gk.], the something that is. Just as nothing is visible except by *color* (the formal object of sight) and nothing perceivable by hearing except by *sound* (the formal object of hearing), so too is nothing intelligible except by *being*, on account of its relationship with being (the formal object of the intellect). Above all, the intellect is intelligible to itself only as something that is relative to being (or to the *raison d'être*), which is the intelligible center of all its ideas, the bond of all its judgments and of all its reasonings. Sight can be defined only in relation to light and to color, hearing in relation to sonorous body, consciousness in relation to a known fact, and the intellect in relation to being.[32] To affirm with Le Roy that the

---

[32] Saint Thomas, [*SCG*] II, ch. 83: "Since nature is always ordered to one thing, it will be necessary and naturally the case that there be one object for a given power: just as *color* for sight and *sound* for hearing. Therefore, since the intellect is one power, it has one natural object of which it essentially [*per se*] and naturally has knowledge. Now, this must be that under which is included all that is known by the intellect, just as all colors which are essentially [*per se*] visible are included under color. Now, this is nothing other than *being*. Therefore, our intellect naturally knows *being* and *those things that are es-*

notions of substance, cause, relation, subject, and so forth, as well as those of potency and act, are not first divisions of being, but instead the result of a utilitarian fragmentation of the *sensible continuum*, obviously would require us to adopt, as Couturat notes, the most radical sensualism that ever has existed.

This sensualism is refuted by emphasizing the distinction that separates man from the animals. Jean-Jacques Rousseau said, "According to me (reproducing, perhaps unwittingly, Aristotle's thought),[33] the distinctive faculty of the intelligent being is the power to give a sense to this little word, 'is,'"[34] which it pronounces every time that it judges. Aristotle said equivalently, though in a more precise manner, that the formal object of the intellect is being. The proof of this is that, in each of its three operations (conception, judgment, and reasoning), the intellect attains nothing except from the perspective of being.

Let us examine, in detail, these three operations of the intellect [*esprit*].

The idea differs from the image because it contains the *raison d'être* of what it represents ("quod quid est, seu ratio intima proprietatum," that which is, or the intimate reason for the properties), whereas the common image spoken of by the nominalists,[35] accompanied by a common name,

---

sential [*per se*] *with regard to being, inasmuch as it is being*; in this knowledge is founded the knowledge of the first principles, such as [that] something cannot at the same time be affirmed and denied, and other such things. Therefore, our intellect naturally knows only these [first] principles [reading *principia* for *prima*], whereas conclusions are known through them, just as through color sight knows all sensible things, as much common sensibles as those that are sensible *per accidens*."

[33] [Trans. note: The comment is added by Fr. Garrigou-Lagrange.]

[34] Jean-Jacques Rousseau, "Profession de foi du vicaire savoyard," in *Émile*. [Trans. note: He does not provide an edition, though the text is from the French original. It is likely that he took it from p. 248 of Rabier's aforementioned *Leçons de philosophie*.]

[35] For Bergson and Le Roy, as for Hobbes, nearly all English [philosophers], Condillac, and Taine, the abstract concept is only a residue that is poorer than the concrete and living images from which it arises. It is only an *averaged-out image* accompanied by a *name* or by a tendency to name. "When the successive images do not differ much from one another, we consider them all as being an increase or decrease of a single *averaged-out image*, or as the distortion of this image in different ways. And this average is what we think of when we speak about the *essence* of a thing or about the thing itself" (Bergson, *L'évolution créatrice*, 327). "I have only verbal knowledge of becoming itself" (332). In *Matière et mémoire: essai sur la relation du corps a l'esprit* (Paris: Ancienne librairie Germer Bailliere et Cie, 1903), 167–76, Bergson indicates the whole utilitarian origin of the general idea: the same kind of reaction to superficially different actions whose differences do not interest us is the germ that human awareness develops into general ideas. This is explained by the constitution of our nervous system: the quite-diverse ap-

contains only, in a state of juxtaposition, the notes it makes known, without however rendering these notes intelligible.

Often, the idea is contrasted with the image by saying that the idea is abstract and universal, whereas the image is concrete and particular. The opposition between them is less clear if we are here speaking of the common or composite image mechanically formed by the association of particular, similar images (by strengthening resemblances and eliminating differences), above all if we consider this common image accompanied by a common name. Moreover, the character of abstraction is only a property of the idea and, indeed, even a property of the human idea precisely inasmuch as it is human, being drawn from sensible things. Universality is likewise only a property of the idea,[36] a property following upon its abstract character; it does not designate its essence. The essence of the idea inasmuch as it is an idea, whether we are speaking of human ideas, angelic ideas, or the Divine Idea, is to contain the formal object of the intellect inasmuch as it is an intellect (human, angelic, or divine)—that is, being or the *raison d'être*.

An example cited by Jean-Michel-Alfred Vacant will help us grasp this difference in the most elementary kind of intellectual knowledge:

Place a savage in the presence of a locomotive. Force him to walk in front of it. Give him the leisure to examine it and to examine

---

paratuses of perception, all connected by the intermediary of the [neural] centers to the very apparatuses of motion. *Therefore, abstraction is an emphasis due to a motor phenomenon.* Here, we find ourselves far from the agent intellect spoken of by Aristotle. The essence of the general idea thus abstracted must, of itself, move ceaselessly between the sphere of action (a bodily behavior to perform or a word to pronounce) and the sphere of memory, which contains thousands of individual images. The general idea escapes us as soon as we claim to fix it to either of these two extremities: "It consists in the double current that passes from the one to the other, forever ready either to be crystallized in pronounced words or to evaporate into memories." The general idea is thus due to the constitution of our brain. We find an equally materialistic explanation of freedom in *L'évolution créatrice*, 284–87. [Trans. note: I have added the edition of *Matière et memoire* that appears to match Fr. Garrigou-Lagrange's pagination. The quoted remark comes from p. 177, though he does not cite it.]

[36] [Trans. note: That is, of the objective concept (the thing as a known, precisely as intentional or, in similarly classical terminology, "objectively existing"). Concerning the distinction between the subjective (or, formal) concept from the objective concept, see John Frederick Peifer, *The Concept in Thomism* (New York: Bookman, 1952), 132–212 . For a discussion of the way that logical second intentions accrue to known things, see Matthew K. Minerd, "Thomism and the Formal Object of Logic," *American Catholic Philosophical Quarterly* 93, no. 3 (2019): 411–44.

other similar machines. So long as he only sees them run, so long as he is content with considering their various parts, he will have only a sensible and particular knowledge of it (or, if you wish, a common image, accompanied by a name, like what a parrot could have).[37] However, if he is intelligent, one day, he will understand that a motive force must necessarily be here, a force that the locomotive produces or that it applies. . . . If he comes to understand that this motive force is obtained by the expansion of imprisoned vapor, he will understand *what* a locomotive is (*quod quid est*)[38] and will form a specific concept of it. . . . The senses see only the material elements, a mass of black iron, arranged in a particular manner. The idea shows something that is *immaterial: the raison d'être* of this arrangement and of the configuration of these various pieces. The idea gives a character of *necessity*. Through it, we see that every locomotive must act in accordance with the conditions which heretofore had been unseen. Finally, the idea is *universal*. Through it, we understand that all machines so fabricated will have the same ability and will arrive at the same result.[39]

The common image of the locomotive contained only the common sensible elements in a state of juxtaposition; it did not contain its *raison d'être* and did not render those elements intelligible.

Let us now take the idea of man such as is given to us by the full account provided in rational psychology.[40] This idea does not contain, in a mechanically juxtaposed and associated manner, the characteristics that are common to all men: rational, free, moral, religious, social, endowed with speech, and so on. Rather, it renders all these characteristics *intelligible* by showing that their *raison d'être* is found in the first among them [i.e., rational]; it expresses the *quod quid est* of man [i.e., *what* he is *essen-*

---

[37] [Trans. note: The parenthetical remark is added by Fr. Garrigou-Lagrange.]

[38] [Trans. note: Again, the parenthetical remark is added by Fr. Garrigou-Lagrange.]

[39] J. M. A. Vacant, *Études comparées sur la philosophie de S. Thomas d'Aquin et cur celle de Duns Scot*, vol. 1 (Paris: Delhomme et Briguet, 1891), 134.

[40] [Trans. note: By this, Fr. Garrigou-Lagrange is referring to the natural philosophy studied in the tradition that developed the discussions undertaken in the *De anima*, with particular focus on those elements pertaining to man. His use of "rational psychology" shows the marks of the ecclesial curriculum of his day, but it is unfair to claim that he viewed the philosophical disciplines according to the Wolffian schema. On this, see the fourth chapter of the second part of Reginald Garrigou-Lagrange, *The Order of Things: The Realism of the Principle of Finality*, trans. Matthew Minerd (Steubenville, OH: Emmaus Academic Press, 2020), 225–50.]

tially]. What makes man a man is not freedom, morality, religion, sociability, or speech. It is reason, for all the other notes are deduced from reason. Rationality is itself rendered intelligible when we establish, as we are doing right now, that the *raison d'être* of the three operations of the intellect [*esprit*] is found in the intellect's essential relation to *being*.

In fact, we must concede to the nominalists that few ideas are likely to become fully intelligible, that few manage to be connected [directly] to being, the formal object of the intellect. These are the ideas of the third degree of abstraction (abstraction from all matter), those of the metaphysical, spiritual, and moral order (the ideas of being, unity, truth, goodness; the idea of the intellect defined in relation to being; the idea of will defined in relation to the good; the idea of the first divisions of being into potency and act, the four causes; etc.). From the start, the second degree of abstraction (mathematics) has less intelligibility, although the study of these sciences is easier for man because the objects of said sciences is closer to the senses. Finally, at the first degree of abstraction, in the natural sciences, we no longer have anything but empirical or descriptive definitions; we do not succeed at rendering the properties *intelligible* by finding their *raison d'être* in a specific difference.[41] "We are unaware of a great number of properties of sensible things, and in most cases we cannot perfectly discover the essence [*ratio*] of the properties of the things that we do grasp by our senses."[42] This is the domain of *doxa* [Gk.], opinion, as Plato said. It is the domain of those things that are accessible to our senses but are of little intelligibility in themselves, as Aristotle said, for they are essentially material and variable (*in materia et in motu*). On this point, the recent critique of the sciences is plainly in agreement with Plato and Aristotle;[43] it recognizes

---

[41] [Trans. note: See the aforementioned chapter in *The Realism of the Principle of Finality* for some added nuance to this position. The philosophy of nature, itself at the first degree of abstraction, does not fall completely under these strictures according to Fr. Garrigou-Lagrange's position here. He himself notes this elsewhere, remarking on how the philosophy of nature functions as the first discipline in which we grasp some of the basic divisions of causality and being, which then must be raised to the level of metaphysical intellection.]

[42] Aquinas, *SCG* I, ch. 3. See also *De potentia*, q. 9, a. 2, ad 5: "The essential differences of things are frequently unknown and unnamed." Likewise: *In* I *analyt. post.*, lec. 41; *In* II *phys.*, lec. 3; *In* II *metaphys.*, lec. 1; *In* IV *metaphys.*, lec. 1 . [Trans. note: *sensu*, "by our senses" was missing from Fr. Garrigou-Lagrange's Latin but has been reinserted here.]

[43] In his *Essai sur la notion de la théorie physique de Platon à Galilée* (Paris: A. Hermann, 1908), taken from *Annales de philosophie chrétienne* that same year, Pierre Duhem made clear that St. Thomas, and after him, the University of Paris "from the beginning of the fourteenth century up to the beginning of the sixteenth century, as regards physical

that positive science can only note facts, their relatively constant relationships or their approximate laws, classifying these laws or general facts by means of provisional hypotheses that cannot hope to be connected to being.

This comes down to saying, contrary to Kant and to the positivists, that hardly anything other than metaphysics (general metaphysics, as well as special metaphysics concerning God and the soul),[44] along with logic, moral philosophy [*morale*], general cosmology,[45] and mathematics, is truly a *science* in the full sense of the word, if by "science" one means knowledge that assigns the *why* or the *necessary raison d'être* of what it affirms.[46] Positive science does not know this *propter quid* but only the *quia*, the general facts.[47] It knows *that* heat expands iron but not *why* heat expands iron, for

---

methodologies, set forth teachings whose accuracy and depth surpass much of what the world will hear said on this subject up to the middle of the 19th century."

The classical passage from St. Thomas is well known: "However, the suppositions of the astronomers have devised need not necessarily be true: for although by granting such suppositions the appearances may preserved [*apparentia salvarentur*], we nevertheless do not need to say that these suppositions are true, for perhaps the appearances concerning the stars may be saved in some other manner, which man does not yet know" (*In* II *de caelo*, lec. 17). See also *In* I *de caelo*, lec. 3, and *ST* I, q. 32, a. 1, ad 2. [Trans. note: The passage from the *De caelo* commentary is taken from the original Latin, though it does not differ significantly from Fr. Garrigou-Lagrange's French.]

Duhem equally shows that "Bellarmine and he who came to be Urban VIII responded to Galileo with the very logical remarks that had been so clearly formulated previously by St. Thomas Aquinas, Osiander, and many others; however, they did not succeed, it seems, to convince him and divert him from his exaggerated confidence in the scope of the experimental method" ... "Against the impenitent realism of Galileo, the Pope gave free rein to (what had become) the intransigent realism of the Peripatetics of the Holy Office." [Trans. note: Fr. Garrigou-Lagrange cites the portion of Duhem's work found on pages 352–76 of the July 1908 edition of "Annales de philosophie chrétienne." For last two quotes, he cites the September edition. He has altered them, but the original can be found on 586–87 of that edition.]

[44] [Trans. note: Again, one must read this in light of the aforementioned treatment of the Wolffian schema. Presumably, he means here "the spiritual soul."]

[45] [Trans. note: i.e., The natural philosophy akin to what is undertaken in Aristotle's *Physics*.]

[46] See *In* I *analyt. post.*, lec. 4: "To know, without qualification, is to know the cause on account of which a thing is and cannot otherwise be."

[47] [Trans. note: For some of the implications of this perspective on the sciences, one that is not necessarily accepted by all Thomist schools (especially those owing much to Laval and the so-called "River Forest" school of Thomism), see Jacques Maritain, *The Degrees of Knowledge*, trans. Gerald Phelan et al. (Notre Dame, IN: University of Notre Dame Press, 1997), 23–73, 145–214. Maritain's remarks are slightly more nuanced and have much greater philosophical attention to the matters at hand. See also Jacques Maritain, *The Philosophy of Nature*, trans. Imelda C. Byrne (New York: Philosophical Library, 1951).]

it does not know the specific *raison d'être* of both heat and of iron. What intelligibility it has comes from the application that it makes of the metaphysical principles of causality, induction, and finality. Because it is essentially material and unstable, its object is at the lower frontiers of being and, consequently, of intelligibility.

The second operation of the intellect [*esprit*], judgment, shows even better, if such is possible, that the formal object of the intellect is *being*. The soul of every judgment is the verb "to be": "this man walks" means "this man *is* walking." In judgment, the verb "to be" affirms the real identity of a subject and predicate which are only logically distinct: this man is (the same being that is) walking.[48] In other words, the verb "to be" affirms that what is designated by the subject and what is designated by the predicate is, in reality, *one and the same* (possible or actual) *being*. Judgment recomposes and restores to being what abstraction has separated.[49] "Those things that we know separately must be rendered one for us by way of composition or division, by forming an enunciation."[50] This presence of being in judgment is radically different from the association that is only a mechanical juxtaposition of two images.

Finally, by reasoning, we perceive in what is more known the (extrinsic) *raison d'être* of what is less known, whereas the empirical successions ruled by the laws of association are, again, only juxtapositions of images. Demonstration *a priori* makes us know the extrinsic *raison d'être* of the thing affirmed by the conclusion; demonstration *a posteriori* makes us know the extrinsic *raison d'être* of the affirmation of the thing. An example of demonstration *a priori*: every being whose nature is absolutely simple is incorruptible; now, the human soul has an absolutely simple nature; therefore, it is incorruptible. This reasoning shows us the extrinsic *raison d'être* for the soul's incorruptibility. This presupposes that one has in the major premise the intellectual intuition of simplicity, considered both in itself

---

48 [Trans. note: To understand this *very* important remark aright, see John C. Cahalan, "The Problem of Thing and Object in Maritain," *The Thomist* 59, no. 1 (1995): 21–46. See also: Maritain, *Degrees of Knowledge*, 96–107; Yves R. Simon, *Introduction to Metaphysics of Knowledge*, trans. Vukan Kuic and Richard J. Thompson (New York: Fordham University Press, 1990), 136–49.]

49 Neither God nor the angels perform this mental synthesis, an expression of a real identity, for they do not abstract the intelligible from the sensible; by understanding an intelligible, they penetrate, by a single intuition, its nature and its properties.

50 *ST* I, q. 14, a. 14. See also *ST* I, q. 85, a. 5, and *SCG* I, ch. 57. [Trans. note: On the Thomistic distinction between the enunciation and the judgment, see: Jacques Maritain, *An Introduction to Logic*, trans. Imelda Choquette (London: Sheed & Ward, 1946), 84–98; Simon, *Introduction to Metaphysics of Knowledge*, 136–58.]

and as the *raison d'être* of incorruptibility. If, on the contrary, as the nominalists wish, the terms of the premises are only common images accompanied by a name, this ultimately means that the syllogism is an empty
tautology, as was held by Sextus Empiricus, John Stuart Mill, and Herbert
Spencer. The major premise, Sextus said, assumes that one has verified all
of the particular cases, including the one aimed at in the conclusion. Indeed, for the nominalist, the common name does not express the universal
that is foundational in things, but instead only designates a collection of
individuals. Demonstration *a posteriori* gives us the extrinsic *raison d'être*
for the affirmation of the thing. For example: the mode of operation follows
the mode of being; now, the human soul has an operation intrinsically independent from every organ; therefore, in its being, the human soul is intrinsically independent of every organ; that is, it is spiritual. Thus, we see the
reason why we must necessarily affirm the spirituality of the soul.[51]

If we now consider the principles upon which the consequence
of demonstrations rests, we will again see that this consequence can be
grasped only if I have a faculty that has *being* as its formal object. Direct
(or, ostensive) demonstrations are founded on the principle of identity, immediately implied in the idea of *being*: indeed, they rest upon the principle
that "what is said of all the things is said of each thing contained under it
[dictum de omni dicitur de singulis contentis sub illo]," or from the point

---

[51] [Trans. note: The senses of *a posteriori* and *a priori* here are not the same as what is
received from Kant's *Critique of Pure Reason*. Although Kant is the inheritor of much
medieval, Renaissance, and baroque Scholasticism, his sense of the terms is quite different from the developed Scholastic position within the Thomist school. Although
Fr. Garrigou-Lagrange, may be using the terms a little bit loosely, he was well aware
of how these terms were used by Thomist logicians in his day. Indeed, he approved of
Éduoard Hugon's *Cursus Philosophicus Thomisticae*, vol. 1, *Logica* (Paris: Lethielleux,
1927), in which see 384: "Demonstration *a priori* does not coincide with demonstration
propter quid, nor does demonstration *a posteriori* coincide with demonstration *quia*.
For demonstration *a priori* proceeds through causes of any sort, whether proximate or
remote; however, demonstration *propter quid* . . . through proper, immediate, and adequate causes. Hence, every demonstration *propter quid* is *a priori*; however, not every
demonstration *a priori* is *propter quid*. Demonstration *a posteriori* is only through an effect; however, demonstration *quia* is through an effect or [lit. *et*] through remote causes.
Therefore, every *a posteriori* demonstration is *quia*, while it is not the case that every
quia demonstration is *a posteriori*" (translation mine). Although the immediate context
justifies reading *et* as "or," see also his remarks from 383: "Demonstration *quia*, taking
the word *quia* not as causal [i.e., meaning "because"] but meaning 'that the thing is,'
proceeds either through a sign and effect or through remote, common, and inadequate
causes."]

of view of comprehension,[52] that "what is predicated of the predicate is predicated of the subject [praedicatum praedicati est praedicatum subiecti]," which comes down to saying, "those things that are the same as some third thing are the same as each other [quae sunt eadem uni tertio sunt eadem inter se]," a principle that derives immediately from the principle of identity: "Being of its self is one and the same."[53] Indirect demonstrations (or,

---

[52] [Trans. note: That is, the breadth of an objective concept in comparison to the *intelligible notes* that pertain to it. This is contrasted to its extension, which is the breadth of an objective concept in comparison to the objects contained "under" it. On this distinction, see Maritain, *Introduction to Logic*, 20–30.]

[53] [Trans. note: Here, some light will be shed by considering the following explanation from Hugon, *Cursus Philosophicus Thomisticae*, vol. 1 (*Logica*), pt. 1 (*Logica Minor*), tract. 3, q. 1, a. 2, no. 7:

Based on what has been explained up to this point, it is clear, therefore, that the foundation for syllogisms, in which two extremes are compared with a middle term, is the principle of identity ("those things that are one and the same with a third term are the same as each other") and the principle of discrepancy ("when two things are compared to a third and one is the same as that thing and the other is not, then those two things are themselves diverse"). Whence, the termini in a syllogism have this sort of relationship: *spiritual substance = immortal*; *the human soul = spiritual*; *therefore, the human soul = immortal*. And, by way of contrast: *material substance ≠ immortal*; *the souls of brute animals = material*; *therefore, the soul of brute animals ≠ immortal*. However, already, a comparison with a middle term cannot be brought about unless the middle term has *suppositio* universally [*generaliter*] and distributively, in accord with the rule that will soon discuss: "The middle term must be general [*generaliter esto*] in at least one premise."

Now, the comparison with the middle term is made by virtue of the principle *dictum de omni, dictum de nullo.* (In French, Euler expresses this principle thus: "*Everything* that is in the containing is in that which is contained. Everything that is outside of the containing is outside of the content.") The sense of the principle, *dictum de omni* is: "whatever is affirmed universally [*generaliter*] and distributively of a given subject must be affirmed of all those things contained under it." For example, we may say: "every animal is sensate; every man is an animal; therefore, every man is sensate." "Man," the less universal subject, is contained under "animal," which is more universal. Therefore, if "sensate" is said of "animal," it must also be said of "man," which is contained under "animal." In this respect, a syllogism is defined [as] "an argument in which the conclusion is reached that all the predicates that belong under the more universal subject belong to all the particular [subjects] contained under it."

The sense of the principle *dictum de nullo* is: "whatever is universally [*generaliter*] and distributively denied of a given subject must be denied of all those that are contained under it. For example, we may say: "no living thing is a stone; every plant is a living thing; therefore, no plant is a stone." "Plant" is contained

---

demonstrations by *reductio ad absurdum*) are founded on the principle of contradiction,[54] which is nothing other than a negative form of the principle of identity: "One and the same being cannot at the same time and in the same respect be what it is and not be what it is." Given that, despite whatever the nominalists may say about it, the principle of induction is itself derived from the principle of *raison d'être*,[55] we can see that reasoning (whether deductive or inductive) can only be the act of a faculty that has *being* as its object.

Therefore, the examination of the three operations of the intellect [*esprit*] shows us that, if the *proper object* of the human intellect inasmuch as it is human (inasmuch as it is united to the body) is the *essence of sensible things*, in function of which, here below, it knows all things, nonetheless, the *formal and adequate object* that belongs to it inasmuch as it is an intellect (thus, dominating bodies) is *being* without restriction, which will enable it to know, in a certain manner, all beings, everything that has a *raison d'être*.[56] The being in question here is not precisely being that in fact exists. Rather, it is being as it abstracts both from the state of mere possibility and from the state of actual existence. It is that which is or can be. This is how we can see *what* man *is*. Similarly, we judge that man is free and we prove it:

---

under "living thing" as something inferior under something more universal. Therefore, whatever is opposed to "living thing" is opposed to "plant." In this case, a syllogism is defined [as] "an argument in which the conclusion is reached that all the predicates which are opposed to the more universal subject are opposed to all the particulars contained under it."

Therefore, there are four principles. Affirmative syllogisms are founded upon the principle of identity and the principle *dictum de omni*. The negative syllogism is founded upon the principle of discrepancy and the principle *dictum de nullo*. Indeed, the structure of the syllogism is founded upon the principles of identity and of discrepancy, whereas the rectitude of the syllogism is founded upon the principles *dictum de omni, dictum de nullo*.

Regarding the nature of *suppositio*, see Jacques Maritain, *Formal Logic*, trans. Imelda Choquette (New York: Sheed and Ward, 1946), 57–76.]

[54] [Trans. note: As noted in the introduction to the 3rd edition, Fr. Garrigou-Lagrange most often uses "principle of contradiction" for what is most commonly referred to now as the "principle of non-contradiction." Thus, on the rarer occasions when he does use "principle of non-contradiction" for the same, I mark those instances with "[*sic*]" to signal that he means the same thing as in most places he means by "principle of contradiction" (and we now commonly mean by "principle of non-contradiction").]

[55] If the same natural cause in the same circumstances would not produce the same effect, the change with regard to effect (without a prior change in the cause and the circumstances) would be without a *raison d'être*.

[56] See *ST* I, q. 12, a. 4.

because he is rational. The object of the intellect is real being divided into the possible and the actual, for the possible already belongs to reality,[57] *quid capax existendi*, distinct from rationate being [*ens rationis*] (*something that is merely thinkable*)[58] and from the pure nothingness that cannot even be the object of thought. When I say, "if the thing is, it is impossible that it not be," I affirm a real impossibility and not only a logical impossibility (or unthinkability).

Therefore, *being* emerges as the objective light of the intellect, the principle of universal intelligibility: "The intellect naturally knows *being* and *those things that are essential* [*per se*] *with regard to being,* as such; in this knowledge is founded the knowledge of the first principles."[59] The principles of finality and of causality, like the principle of induction, are derived from the *principle of raison d'être*. And, as we will show below,[60] this last principle is linked *to the principle of identity* by the principle of contradiction. As regards the *principle of substance,* as we will see, it is merely a simple determination of the principle of identity.

Therefore, if our intellect reifies, this is not in the least because it is "obsessed with practical preoccupations." Rather, it is because it is an intellect, because it has for its object this transcendental that perfuses all things: *being,* and not color, nor sound, nor the internal fact [of consciousness].

Far from being "a position in space," the result of the fragmentation of the sensible continuum, *substance* is a formal principle belonging to an order beyond quantity and sensible qualities. A whole entirely in the whole

---

[57] See: St. Thomas, *Quodlibet* VIII, q. 1, a. 1; Cajetan, *In I de ente et essentia,* c. 4, q. 6. See also, Tommasso Maria Zigliara, *De la lumière intellectuelle,* vol. 3, p. 209. [Trans. note: The text by Zigliara appears to be an unnamed printing of the French edition of his *Della luce intellettuale e dell' ontologismo secondo la dottrina di S. Bonaventura e Tommaso d'Aquino.* He may be referring to the edition translated by a Fr. Murgue and published by Vitte et Perrussel in Lyon in 1880 and 1881.]

[58] [Trans. note: *Entia rationis* include negations, privations, and *relationes rationis* that exist only with thinking intellects. The most important of these for the Thomist school are the *relationes rationis* that are called second intentions, the sorts of relations that are studied in logic. The domain of *ens rationis,* however, plays a very large role in human experience, though it rarely receives the attention owed to it. On this topic, see Matthew K. Minerd: "Beyond Non-Being: Thomistic Metaphysics on Thomistic Metaphysics on Second Intentions, *Ens morale,* and *Ens artificiale,*" *American Catholic Philosophical Quarterly* 91, no. 3 (Summer 2017): 353–79; "Thomism and the Formal Object of Logic," *American Catholic Philosophical Quarterly* 93, no. 3 (Summer 2019): 411–44. See also the lucid intellectual history in Daniel D. Novotný, *Ens Rationis from Suárez to Caramuel: A Study in Scholasticism of the Baroque Era* (New York: Fordham University Press, 2003).]

[59] [Trans. note: The text is taken from *SCG* II, ch. 83.]

[60] See pt. 1, ch. 2, §6.

and entirely in each part, this formal principle assures the unity of the whole. The senses cannot grasp it. The intellect alone reaches it. To the eyes of the intellect, substance is only the first determination of being, necessary for rendering intelligible, in function of being, a group of phenomena presenting themselves as being independent. At the time of the first presentation of any sensible object, like the blankets in which the infant is wrapped, whereas sight grasps the color of this object and touch its form and resistance, the intellect vaguely grasps *being*, "something that is." This first object known by the intellect will become, in a precise manner, a subject that is one and permanent (substance) when the intellect notes the multiplicity of its phenomena and their changes. Indeed, the multiple is intelligible only in function of the one, and the transitory only in function of the permanent or the identical, for according to one of the formulations of the principle of identity, "being, of itself, is one and the same," of which the principle of substance is only a determination. In the genesis of its various forms of knowledge [*connaissances*], the intellect passes from the idea of being, which already implicitly contains the idea of substance, to the vague ideas of the mode [*manière*] of being, of multiplicity, and of change; it seeks to render these new ideas intelligible in light of the idea of being. It is then that it knows the "something that is," as a subject that is one and permanent, as *being* in the full sense of the word, *as that which exists or subsists* (*substance*). From here, it is led to give precision to the idea of the mode [*manière*] of being, which can be defined only in function of that which exists in itself: a mode [*manière*] of being, *ens entis*, is not that which exists or subsists (*id quod est*), but rather, that by which something is modified in this or that manner [*manière*] (*id quo aliquid est tale*).[61]

---

[61] St. Thomas has set forth this progress in intellectual knowledge very well, passing like sense knowledge from the vague to the distinct. This is the profound reason for why our intellect must unite or separate notions in its affirmative or negative judgments and in its reasonings. See *ST* I, q. 85, a. 5: "The human intellect does not immediately, in its first apprehension, grasp a perfect cognition of the thing. Instead, it first grasps something concerning the thing, for example, the quiddity of the thing itself, which is the first and proper object of the intellect (vague knowledge of the real definition, *quid rei*, implied in the nominal definition, *quid nominis*); then, it understands the properties, accidents, and relations that surround the essence of the things. (This is vague knowledge of the properties giving precision to the knowledge of the definition and enabling one to extract the specific difference, the distinct *quid rei*, which in turn *a priori* explains the properties). And for this reason, it must compose and divide one understood thing with another and from one composition and division proceed to another, which is the process of reasoning."

Such is the fragmentation of the intelligible, parallel to the fragmentation of the

"Modifications presuppose what is modified. The latter alone can account for the permanence and continuity of reality under the evolutive flux of the cosmos."[62]

Bergson and Le Roy seek to explain the human intellect by the hypothesis of evolution linking man to animal;[63] if the animal deprived of

---

sensible, but in another order. [Trans. note: In the text above, I am reading "mais ce par quoi quelque chose est modifié de telle ou telle façon" for "mais ce par quoi quelque chose qui est modifié de telle ou telle façon." The remarks in parentheses above are Fr. Garrigou-Lagrange's additions. Also see Reginald Garrigou-Lagrange, "On the Search for Definitions According to Aristotle and St. Thomas," in *Philosophizing in Faith: Essays on the Beginning and End of Wisdom*, ed. and trans. Matthew K. Minerd (Providence, RI: Cluny Media, 2019), 21–34.]

62 De Munnynck, "L'individualité des animaux supérieurs," 137.
63 Bergson, *L'évolution créatrice*, 1: "Our intellect, in the narrow sense of the word, is destined to assure the perfect insertion of our body into its environment, to represent the relations of exterior things with each other, and, at last, to think [upon] matter. The intellect feels at home inasmuch as it is left among inert objects, more especially among solids, where our action finds its fulcrum and our industry its instruments for work."
[Trans. note: Garrigou-Lagrange did not devote lengthy reflection to the topic of the contemporary theory of evolution. His primary concern seems to be with evolutionism as a metaphysical doctrine which would have that which is *more* come forth from what is *less*, without some elevation by God. When he discusses the topic, he is quite brief, though he explicitly makes room for forms of "moderate evolutionism."
See Reginald Garrigou-Lagrange, "Verité et immutabilité du dogme," *Angelicum* 24, no. 2/3 (1947): 124–39, at 136–37:

As regards the problem of evolution, it is important to clearly distinguish the domain of scientific hypotheses proposed for examination (i.e., that of sensible appearances) and the domain of being, which is that of metaphysics, where we must hold that God specially intervened in the production of vegetative life, sense life, and intellectual life and *a fortiori* in a wholly special way in order to produce the life of grace in man.

Finally, we absolutely cannot admit that the Incarnation of the Word and the Redemption would be moments in evolution. And if this evolution were explained along the lines of Hegelian metaphysics, which was condemned by the [First] Vatican Council, this would properly speaking be a heresy. Indeed, it would be even more than a heresy. It would complete apostasy, for the absolute and pantheistic evolutionism of Hegel does not allow *any* Christian dogmas to survive. In denying the True God, who is really and essentially distinct from the world, he denies *all* the revealed mysteries and can preserve only their verbal forms.

Also, see Garrigou-Lagrange, *De Revelatione*, 5th ed., vol. 1 (Rome: Desclée, 1950), 220–21.
Early in his career, his beloved teacher, Fr. Ambroise Gardeil, took great interest in working out the conditions for a reconciliation between evolution and the strict principles of Thomist metaphysics, writing a lengthy series of articles on the topic. See Gardeil,

intelligence could speak, then substance, *that which is*, would be for it only a verbal entity, a *flatus vocis*. "The distinctive faculty of the intelligent being is the power to give a sense to this little word, 'is.'" But, for the same reason, Bergson and Le Roy ought to refuse to say that man, just as much as animals, has self-awareness. Would man have awareness of himself as opposed to the non-self if his intellect, by reflection upon itself, did not divide being (*primum cognitum*) into a subject relative to being and an object conceived henceforth as non-self, and if it did not conceive the subject as one and identical under its multiple and transitory phenomena—that is, as a substance?

We will show at length below[64] that potency and act, matter and form, and efficient and final causality are not divisions of the sensible continuum, but instead are divisions of being that the intellect alone perceives in this continuum that the senses apprehend. Potency and act, along with the four causes, are divisions of being that are necessary for rendering *multiplicity* and *becoming* intelligible, in function of *being* and the principle of identity.

Substances, causes, potency and act—all verbal entities, says Le Roy, a utilitarian fragmentation to which we have recourse because it facilitates the speech and action of practical life. Let us, however, go further and say: an absolutely necessary fragmentation, let us say, on pain of falling into absurdities, denying the principle of identity as the fundamental law of reality, and placing contradiction at the principle of all things.

§3. Consequences of Begsonian Nominalism: The Denial of Reason and of the Objective Value of the Principle of Non-Contradiction [*sic*]

Indeed, this represents the last word of Bergsonism: the theory of common sense presented to us here presupposes the truth of empiricist nominalism, though it is a nominalism of such a sort as to be the absolute denial of reason and perhaps even of consciousness.

It is a denial of reason because it holds that there are no "natures" corresponding to rigid concepts. For it, the first notions and very first principles are, themselves, only superficial outlooks concerning becoming. The

---

"L'évolutionisme et les principes de S. Thomas," *Revue thomiste* 1 (1893): 27–45, 316–27, and 725–37; 2 (1894): 29–42; 3 (1895): 61–84 and 607–33; 4 (1896): 64–86 and 215–47.]

[64] See pt, 1, ch. 2, §§6–7; and in the study following upon the proofs of God's existence in pt 2, see ch. 2, §§4–5.

principle of identity (or, of non-contradiction) is deceptive. Though it is the first law of discursive reason [*raison raisonnante*], [we are told that] it cannot be the first law of reality, for the fundamental reality is becoming. In proof, there is this testimony of the *senses*: "There is *more* in movement than in the successive positions attributed to the mobile, more in becoming than in the forms traversed in turn, more in the evolution of the form than in the forms realized one after another."[65] This claim would be incontestable if we were speaking only about an immobility grasped by the senses concerning becoming, but when it comes to be erected into an absolute principle, this proposition becomes: "*There is more in movement than in the immobile*; therefore, in order to explain the mobile, speculation must take its point of departure from movement."[66] The fundamental reality is becoming.

Such is the argument upon which the entire Bergsonian system rests. It is easy to see that it represents the denial of the objective value of the principle of identity. What is the source of Bergson's contention that there is *more* in movement than in the immobile? It is the fact that he, like Heraclitus, considers matters from the perspective of the senses (both the external senses and internal experience). Therefore, for him, *the immobile* is *that which is in rest*, and we can never make movement come about from rest, as Zeno's arguments proved. For Plato and Aristotle and for traditional philosophy in general, there is *more* in the immobile than in movement, for, looking at things from the perspective of the intellect, they hold that *the immobile* is *that which is* most of all, in opposition to that which does not yet exist but, instead, is becoming, just as the immutable is that which is and cannot not be, in opposition to that which, not having the sufficient reason for its existence in itself, can cease to exist. Therefore, the sensualist principle that "there is more in movement than in the immobile" becomes, if one transposes it into the terms of the intellect, "there is more in that which becomes and does not yet exist than in that which is." Therefore, becoming cannot have its [explanatory] reason in being. It is self-explanatory, a *ratio sui*. Thus, one is led to deny the objective value of the principle of identity (or, of non-contradiction). Indeed, becoming is a successive union of diverse things (e.g., a violet object becomes red). To say that *the uncaused union of diverse things is possible* is to say that *the diverse, of itself, is one and the same, at least with a unity of union.*[67] For example, that which is violet

---

65 Bergson, *L'évolution créatrice*, 341.
66 Bergson, *L'évolution créatrice*, 341.
67 [Trans. note: This expression "unity of union" might also be translated as "unity of

of itself and as such (unconditionally) becomes red, although inasmuch as it is violet, it is non-red. This is to deny a formula immediately derived from the principle of identity (or, of non-contradiction) and to hold that the absurd is only *unthinkable*, though not *impossible*. The intimate nature

composition." The basic distinction here is between a unity of simplicity and a unity of composition (see *ST* I, q. 11, a. 1). At the time of this translation (in late 2020), it is not clear when the distinction between *unitas unitatis / unitas compositionis* and *unitas simplicitatis* sedimented terminologically in Western Scholasticism. One can find echoes of it in texts like the aforementioned text from Aquinas, as well as in *ST* I-II, q. 17, a. 4 ("Quae vero sunt diversa secundum substantiam, et unum secundum accidens, sunt diversa simpliciter, et unum secundum quid, sicut multi homines sunt unus populus, et multi lapides sunt unus acervus; quae est *unitas compositionis, aut ordinis*. Similiter etiam multa individua, quae sunt unum genere vel specie, sunt simpliciter multa, et secundum quid unum, nam esse unum genere vel specie, est esse unum secundum rationem") and *In divinis nominibus*, ch. 9, lec. 4 ("Sic igitur, *unitas simplicitatis* et immobilitatis pertinet ad rationem identitatis divinae; unitas autem operationis in effectus pertinet ad rationem iustitiae, et ideo dixerat quod in aequalitate intelligitur Dei nominatio et eiusdem et iustitiae"). The terminology "unity of union" and "unity of simplicity" are clearly crystalized in Bl. Duns Scotus by the time of the writing of the *Ordinatio*. See Richard Cross, "Duns Scotus on Essence and Existence," in *Oxford Studies in Medieval Philosophy*, vol. 1, ed. Robert Pasnau (Oxford: Oxford University Press, 2013), 176.

An account of this distinction likely close to that of Fr. Garrigou-Lagrange's understanding can be found in Éduoard Hugon, *Cursus Philosohpiae Thomisticae*, vol. 3, *Metaphysica* (Paris: Lethielleux, 1935), 330–40. Likewise see Austin Woodbury, *Ontology*, ch. 43, a. 1 (no. 864): "Accordingly, TRANSCENDENTAL UNITY is either unity OF SIMPLICITY (namely, unity of a being lacking parts, v.g, the unity of God) or unity OF COMPOSITION (namely, unity of a being having parts). Now, the latter sort of unity is either PER SE or PER ACCIDENS. In the former case, it is unity of that WHEREOF THE BE [*esse*] IS ONE, such as is the unity of the compound from matter and form (e.g., the unity of a body). In the latter case, it is unity of that WHEREOF THERE IS NOT ONE SOLE BE [*esse*]. It is the unity of that which consists of many complete essences and many be-s, accidentally united. Now, this accidental union can take place in a number of ways: (a) by juxtaposition, in which case there is AGGREGATIONAL unity (v.g., the unity of a heap); (b) by extrinsic causality, in which case there is CAUSATIONAL UNITY, namely, either by EFFICIENT causality (v.g., the unity of a litter [of kittens]) or by FINAL causality (v.g., the unity of a society); (c) or by information, in which case there is INHERENTIAL unity, which is had either (1) through information of a substance by an accident (v.g., the unity of he compound of water and heat, namely, of hot water) or (2) through information of an accident by an accident (v.g., the unity of the compound made up of intellect and wisdom, namely, [the unity] of wise intellect" (slightly edited; the use of all capitals is a convention particular to Fr. Woodbury; quotations of Woodbury are from holdings of his work in The John N. Deely and Anthony F. Russell Collection, Latimer Family Library, St. Vincent College, Latrobe, PA). The reader should consult the whole of this article.]

of things is, as Hegel said, a realized contradiction. Consequently, God is not related to being as A is to A. He is not the *Ipsum Esse*, completely and utterly self-identical. He is not absolutely simple and immutable Pure Act and, by that, essentially distinct from the multiple and changing world. God is a "reality that makes itself,"[68] "a continuous gushing forth"[69] *who can no longer be conceived without the world that gushes forth from Him.* Thus, we return to evolutionist pantheism.[70] In reality, God becomes and does not yet exist. Truth be told, he will never exist.[71]

---

[68] Bergson, *L'évolution créatrice*, 341, 269.

[69] Bergson, *L'évolution créatrice*, 341, 270.

[70] See below in pt. 2, ch. 3, §§1– 2: "Pantheism for the new philosophy."

[71] For Bergson, all immobility is the inertia of being that is fixed, crystallized, and deprived of life. He has no difficulty showing that the living being is superior to this inert, inanimate being. However, he forgets that above the instability of this living being, always in search of what it does not have, there is the immutability of that being who is immediately in possession of the fullness that it ought to have (see pt. 2, ch. 2, §6, of the present volume).

   In all orders, there are two species of immutability. First, there is that of the "glutted," as St. Paul says, the immutability of narrow minds and tight hearts, the immutability of the obstinate who see only one side of things and wish to make it absolute. This is what made Renan say [that] the convinced are fools, unilateral and simplistic people. This is the immutability of the fanatic and the sectarian. From the perspective of the heart, this is the egoist, who is full of himself and satiated. This is the immobility of the pleasure of repose dreamed of by Epicurus, a form of non-trouble, *ataraxia*, that is obtained by the suppression of desire. Above this cadaverous immobility that arises from narrowness of receptive capacities and of desire, there is something superior, found only in natures capable of seeing the multiple aspects of things, without, however, being able to bring this multiplicity back to a superior unity. This is the instability of the dilettante, too demanding ever to be satisfied with what he has; it is the instability of a Goethe, a Sainte-Beuve, a Renan. Here, we have inconstancy and agitation, a seeking that does not arrive at a result. This is the state of mind of those who prefer, as Pascal says, the search for the truth to truth itself, for they do not have the strength to stop and contemplate it when they possess it, for they fear is requirements: "When I knew the truth, I believed that it was a friend; When I understood and felt it, I was already disgusted with it."

   Above this, there is the immutability that arises not from the narrowness of capacities, nor from the poverty of desire, but rather from the perfection of what one possesses, from the value of the realized end. This is no longer the immutability of the simplistic person, of the closed mind; it is that of the synthetic thinker who knows how to extricate himself from details, to pass beyond the multiple, to give a unity to his science, in a way akin to someone like Plato, Aristotle, Thomas Aquinas, or Leibniz. From the perspective of the will, this superior immutability is that by which holiness is defined (*ST* II-II, q. 81, a. 8). The saint is a being who is immutably fixed in God by [the Beatific] Vision and charity; this is the immutability of beings who have passed beyond

Reason continues to call out, but what is it? [For Bergson, it is] an immobile system of forms and of categories, a dead residue of action. Moreover, why would these fundamental axioms not change: "Axioms and categories, forms of the understanding and of the sensibility, all such things undergo becoming, all such things evolve; the human mind [*esprit*] is plastic and can change its most intimate desires."[72] Above reason there is instinct, the free inspiration that innovates and creates. We must admit that Bergson and his disciples have admirably placed in relief these facts *in the order of discovery*;[73] but the conclusions that they draw from them against intellectualism are manifestly excessive. Why not explain these facts as Henri Poincaré did, by referring to the special aesthetic sensibility that only the true inventor possesses: "Useful combinations are precisely the most beautiful ones, by which I mean those that can best charm this special sensibility had by mathematicians, though the uninitiated are so unaware of it that they are often tempted to smirk at it."[74] Obviously, these facts of inspiration do not suffice for establishing that mind [*esprit*] at its root retains [utter] freedom [here], freely giving itself its first principles. Nonetheless, such is the Bergsonian doctrine: mind [*esprit*] is the highest manifestation of this *élan vitale*, the profound reality that, "lacking a better word, we have called *consciousness*,"[75] though one should instead call it, *The Unconscious*.[76] The absolute

---

the relative and who have truly found the Absolute. (See *ST* I, q. 9, aa. 1 and 2: Whether God is entirely immutable.) God himself is immutable, as ever-actual Thought thinking Thought, or the Act of eternally subsistent Good. [Trans. note: For a discussion of the way the blessed experience *participated eternity*, see Carl J. Peter, *Participated Eternity in the Vision of God: A Study of the Opinion of Thomas Aquinas and his Commentators on the Duration of the Acts of Glory* (Rome: Gregorian University Press, 1964).

This is so so evident that Heraclitus himself recognized the immutability superior to the universal flux, superior like a law that is imposed upon it, the law of movement, the union of contraries, their reconciliation, their harmony: "the fatal law," "armed justice." If the sun were to transgress the law of its course, the Furies would come to the aid of Justice and there would be an eternal night. Despite everything, Heraclitus preserved the name of this armed justice, considered as governing: it is God.

Bergson claims to identify the divine reality with a becoming that has no fixed points and no laws. To speak with Benjamin Jacob, "What rises up to the surface is ancient matter, suppressing the idea." St. Thomas would say: "And this falls into the error of David of Dinant, who most foolishly held that God is prime matter" (*ST* I, q. 3, a. 8).

[72] Le Roy, "Sur quelques objections," 305.

[73] [Trans. note: *D'invention* likely is meant to call to mind the *via inventionis*.]

[74] Henri Poincaré "L'invention mathématique, conférance faite a l'institut générale psychologique le 23 Mai 1908," *Revue générale des sciences pure et appliquées*19 (1908): 525.

[75] Bergson, *L'évolution créatrice*, 258.

[76] The creative impulse, blind and without intelligence, similar enough to the obscure will

anti-intellectualism of Bergson thus appears as being an upside-down form of Hegelianism. Hegel reduced the real to the rational, fact to right, freedom to intellectual necessity, and success to morality. The anti-intellectualists do the opposite, reducing the rational to the real (understood to mean the *fact*), right to the accomplished fact, necessity to a freedom without understanding (pure spontaneity),[77] and morality to success. The two extreme systems touch each other and inevitably had to meet, since each of them, being the offspring of Heraclitus, wishes to be a philosophy of becoming and of the fusion of contraries.

Bergsonian nominalism is not only the denial of reason, which it subordinates to consciousness. It also seems to be the denial of this consciousness, which would be subordinated in its own turn to animal and vegetative life, thereby wholly reduced to biology. This is what Couturat and Jacob claimed, something that Poincaré also says, indeed, something that certain most faithful disciples of Bergson recognize. As Couturat remarks:

According to this new method, in order to know things such as they are, one need not use the intellect, which can only denature them. Rather, one must draw closer to brute experience, plunge

---

of Schopenhauer, as is noted by [Antonio] Aliotta in *La cultura filosofica*, September 15, 1907.

[77] According to Bergson, the general idea of human freedom is due to the constitution of the human brain: "The universal consciousness falls asleep when life is condemned to automatism; it awakens as soon as the possibility of a choice is reborn. And in animals with a nervous system, it is proportionate to the complication of the junction where the so-called sensorial and motorial ways cross, i.e. that of the brain. . . . The human brain differs from other brains inasmuch as it can set up an indefinite number of mechanisms, and consequently, an indefinite number of triggering points for its choices. . . . Man not only maintains his machine; he comes to use it as he pleases. He owes this to the superiority of his brain" (*L'évolution créatrice*, 284–87).

This freedom is not the freedom required by the Church so that there may be merit or demerit, i.e., the ability to decide between two possible things. According to Bergson, "If our action has seemed free to us, this is because the relation of this action to the state from which it emerged could not be expressed by a law, given that this psychic state is unique in its kind and unable ever to occur again" (*Essai sur les données immédiates de la conscience*, ch. 3 ["De l'organisation des états de conscience: La liberté"]). "One never bathes two times in the same river." Behold freedom: why would it not exist just as well in the dog as in man? At bottom, this is to return to the empiricism of Hume, who held that neither "necessity" nor "freedom" had a proper meaning. [Trans. note: Fr. Garrigou-Lagrange's passage is taken from the end of the text. He cites pages 127–38. After consulting several editions from between 1889 and 1908, this pagination appears to be approximate, though close to the content on free will.]

down into the whirlwind of sensations, and finally, crash into the torrent of animal and vegetative life, losing oneself in unconsciousness and drowning in things. This psychological realism leads to *de facto* idolatry in metaphysics and in morality. However, it destroys itself, for by attaching itself to immediate data and wishing to free them from intellectual forms, it succeeds at dissolving consciousness itself and at making the self evaporate in the midst of nature.[78]

Indeed, according to Le Roy, should not pure consciousness strive to return, as much as is possible, to the primitive perception had by the infant in the crib? This perception alone reveals reality without deforming it. Such a return is not absolutely impossible, and:

We can suspect this based on certain experiences. Indeed, let us imagine circumstances in which our habits are disoriented. For example, here we are lying in the countryside, half-sheltered from the sun, under moving foliage, on a hot summer's day, in that languid and retired state of mind wherein *our consciousness seems to dissolve under the soft weight of the universal flux of life*. We are dazzled, overwhelmed, broken up, and drowned under the incessant flux of brilliant images, and at the same time, we feel the precise limits that fragment Nature for our ordinary outlook vanish, along with the desire for any activity.[79]

Elsewhere, it is a question of the "sincerity" of a bicyclist who "surrenders himself to the peculiar charm of change, to the delightful intoxication of becoming."[80] This is what Le Roy calls "allowing oneself the intelligent pleasure of receiving, without reacting, impressions as revelations of Being."[81] Couturat prefers to say: "It is to crash into the torrent of animal and vegetative life, losing oneself in unconsciousness and drowning in things." In the same place, he describes this process of knowledge as being "*a priori* absurd mystical sensualism." I do not see what can be said in response to him. Indeed, he has never been responded to, any more than a response

---

[78] Louis Couturat, "Sur l'hypothèse des atoms," *Revue de métaphysique et de morale* 5 (1897): 241–42.

[79] Le Roy, "Science et philosophie," 383. I have added emphasis in the text. [Trans. note: Fr. Garrigou-Lagrange wrongly has 384 instead of 383.]

[80] Le Roy, "Science et philosophie," 414.

[81] Le Roy, "Science et philosophie," 414.

has been given to Jacob, whose objections remain so strongly substantiated.[82] It goes without saying that, by his *intuition*, Le Roy is above all the critiques that a logician can present to him.

Nonetheless, he has sought to legitimate his position by making use of scientific criticism. Yet, Poincaré's difficulty remains:

> We see you have written lengthy articles, and to do this you had need of words. And were you not thereby much more "discursive" and, consequently, much further from life and truth than are animals, which quite simply live their philosophy? *Would it not be that this animal is the true philosopher?* . . . Perhaps we must conclude that action has "primacy." Still, our intellect is what draws this conclusion. Thus, even while the footfall of action pushes onward, the intellect will thereby preserve the superiority of the thinking reed.[83]

However, even more embarrassing, the same objection is registered by certain wholly convinced Bergsonians who are most docile to the master's voice. Georges-Henri Luquet, who has no other pretension than to be "an orthodox Bergsonian" and of "making Bergson available to candidates for the baccalaureate," ends up concluding his exposition of Bergsonism with these words:

> Thus, it is through vital utility, *through an immanent finality that, moreover, does not in any way imply a directive intelligence, be it Providence or nature, a finality which can very well be reconciled with mechanism, that an explanation is given, in the last analysis, for the existence of consciousness,* its modalities and its development, its real characteristics and the apparent characteristics that it presents to a superficial observation.[84]

Hence, one sees [some] Catholic theologians converting to Bergsonism in the wake of Le Roy. Nonetheless, this is what the author of *Dogma and Criticism* invites us to do. If ever Catholic theologians do convert to

---

[82] Jacob, "La philosophie d'hier et celle d'aujourd'hui."

[83] Henri Poincaré, *La valeur de la science*, 216. [Trans. note: Fr. Garrigou-Lagrange gives no edition.]

[84] Luquet (a former student of the *École normale supérieure*, a professor *agrégé* of philosophy), *Idées générales de psychologie* (Paris: Alcan, 1906), 288.

Bergsonism, there would not be a great difference between their theology and that of Albrecht Ritschl.[85] For over half a century, German thinkers have proposed time and again the course of reflection proposed today to us by Le Roy.

§4. Why Would Common Sense, So Conceived, Preserve an Immutable Practical Value?

Finally, there is one last difficulty: why would "common sense, inasmuch as it is a utilitarian organization of thought in view of practical life," be something stable? Why would *its signification value* deserve an irreformable and absolute adherence that its representation value does not have? Here, Le Roy becomes quite timid. Why should one have this conservative, practical instinct if "axioms and categories, forms of the understanding and of the sensibility, all such things undergo becoming, all such things evolve; the human mind [*esprit*] is plastic and can change its most intimate desires"? Why not speak about the principles of morality along the same lines as does Jean Weber, drawing the rigorous consequences of Bergsonism and ending up at *de facto amoralism*: success justifies all?[86] If we must

---

[85] See Ernest Bertrand, *Une nouvelle conception de la redemption: la doctrine de la justification et de la réconciliation dans le système théologique de Ritschl* (Paris: Fischbacher, 1891). The author shows very well how "the empiricist or nominalist theory of knowledge is the key to Ritschl's theological system," and how "it explains and implies the whole of this theologian's dogmatic theology" (29ff and 149ff). Also, it has been shown very exactly how this theological system presents the synthesis expected from a whole stream of philosophical and moral ideas that have Kant as their source. See Henri Schoen, *Les origins historiques de la théologie de Ritschl* (Paris: Fischbacher, 1893).

[86] As is written in Jean Weber, "Une étude réaliste de l'acte et ses conséquences morale," *Revue de métaphysique et de morale* 2 (1894): 549–60: "By planting itself on the terrain where ceaseless invention gushes forth, immediately and full of life, by posing itself as *the most insolent encroachment of the world of the intellect upon spontaneity*, morality was destined to receive the continual denials of this undeniable reality of dynamism and creation that is our activity. . . . Faced with *these moral ideas*, we outline morality, or rather *de facto amoralism.* . . . We call 'good' that which has triumphed. . . . *Success*—provided it be implacable and fierce, provided that the vanquished be greatly vanquished, destroyed, abolished without hope—*justifies everything.* . . . The man of genius is profoundly immoral, but it does not belong to just anyone whatsoever to be immoral. In this world of egoisms, foreign to one another, 'duty' is nowhere and it is everywhere, *for all actions equal each other in absolute value.* The act is its own law. . . . The sinner who repents deserves the torments of his contrite soul, for he was not strong enough to transgress the Law; he was unworthy of sinning. The unpunished criminal, tortured

arrive at this challenge raised against common sense in the practical order, why would the practical meaning of dogma be immutable? Indeed, if God is a "reality that is made," an incessant becoming, what prevents one's profound sense for God from changing? We will say, rather: *a fortiori*, if the utterly primary principles of speculative reason are called to change, then nothing remains stable from the practical perspective. If the fundamental reality is essentially becoming and freedom, why would the conveniences that dictated for us the fragmentation of reality not themselves be modified from one day to the next?

Will common sense ever recognize itself in the portrait that Le Roy has drawn of it? It is better to confess, with Bergson himself, that this nominalist philosophy of becoming is utterly opposed to "the natural metaphysics of the human intellect." Bergson says: "Speculation must take movement as its foundation. However—note well this fact[87]—the intellect reverses the order of these two termini, and on this point ancient philosophy proceeds along the same lines as does the intellect."[88] It explains movement by the immobile. This is why it acknowledges an immutable God, Pure Act, as well as created things (or, substances). Bergson should say: it explains becoming by being and the phenomena by substance in order to remain faithful to the principle of identity, which must be the fundamental law of reality, just as it is the fundamental law of the intellect, which has being itself as its formal object.

Common sense will never recognize itself in a *philosophy of becoming*, any more than in a *philosophy of phenomena*. As we will see, it is a *rudimentary philosophy of being*.

Drawing this section to a close, we were happy to find nearly the same sort of conclusion drawn by Émile Boutroux in his latest book, *Science and Religion*, in a section entitled "Critical Remarks Concerning the Philosophy of Action":

> The philosophy of action may well present multiple ingenious analyses and arguments. With difficulty, it persuades scientists that science not only invents all its concepts, all the measures into which it encloses the phenomena, but also that it fabricates the

---

by remorse, giving way and confessing his crime, deserves chastisement, for he was not strong enough to bear its terrible weight with a stolid soul." Henceforth, there is no difference between Ravachol [a French anarchist bomber] and the Christian martyr.

[87] [Trans. note: This aside is added by Fr. Garrigou-Lagrange.]

[88] Bergson, *L'évolution créatrice*, 342.

phenomena themselves. . . . On the other hand, in what concerns the work that the mind accomplishes in creating scientific symbols, the scientist cannot admit that all that is involved here are purely arbitrary operations, leading to the formulation of mere conventions. . . . These operations are ruled by certain intellectual principles. They tend to introduce *intelligibility* into our knowledge of things. They respond to an ideal that we propose to ourselves. In a word, they imply what one calls *reason*, the *sense for being*, order, harmony. . . .

Does religion, at least such as it is developed by the philosophy of action, remain intact? One posits as a principle that everything that is addressed to the understanding is an expression, a symbol, a vehicle of religion, but not religion itself. The domain of religion would be, in this sense, exclusively practical, life. However, in reality, every sentiment, every religious action, envelops ideas, concepts, theoretical forms of knowledge. What will remain when, religions being such as they are given to us, one literally eliminates every intellectual element from them? Action, for [the sake of] action, by action, pure practice, perhaps begetting concepts, but itself independent of every concept—does this abstract pragmatism still deserve to be called religion?[89]

The scientist cannot settle for scientific pragmatism, nor the believer for religious pragmatism, nor can either of them renounce the idea of *being* and that of *objectivity*.

C. NOMINALISM AND OPPOSED SYSTEMS IN RELATION TO COMMON SENSE

To complete this study concerning nominalism, it is not useless to devote some words to opposed systems that are less in favor today, systems that, in certain regards, like nominalism, do violence to common sense. We thus find ourselves led to speak briefly about subjective conceptualism along the lines of Kant and his disciples, as well as about a doctrine that is truly

---

[89] Émile Boutroux, *Science et religion dans la philosophie contemporaine* (Paris: Flammarion, 1919), 293ff. These remarks by Boutroux had made us hope that he would himself arrive at views more conformed to Catholic theology. [Trans. note: This volume seems to be following the same pagination as the unnamed edition cited by Fr. Garrigou-Lagrange in the original French.]

the extreme opposed to nominalism, which is the absolute realism of the Platonists and the ontologists.

§1. Nominalism and Subjectivist Conceptualism

Kant's subjectivist conceptualism differs from nominalism (in other words, from empiricism and positivism) because it claims to preserve a kind of *necessity* for the first rational principles, a necessity rejected by empiricism. In particular, Kant could not place in doubt the necessity of the moral law, nor even the necessity of the first principles of Newton's physics.

On the other hand, he conceded to empiricism that our intellect can have no intuition of intelligible being, that it consequently cannot elevate itself scientifically to the existence of *causes* and of *substances*, holding that, in fact, when it wishes to pose these problems, it gets tied up in antinomies. Henceforth, for him, as for empirical nominalism, metaphysics is impossible, and only science of the phenomenal order exists; Newtonian physics is imposed, he believes, as being necessary.

How are we to explain this *necessity* involved in scientific knowledge? Experience manifests quite well the relations that exist between facts (e.g., heat expands iron), but it does not show us the necessity of these relations. Thus, Kant drew the conclusion that the mind is what establishes these necessary connections between phenomena, through the application of its *categories* of substance, causality, reciprocal action, and so on. These categories are the *a priori forms* of our understanding, the *subjective necessities* of thought without which our intellect cannot function, which enable us to form *a priori* connections between phenomena or to form synthetic *a priori* judgments. The necessity of science is thus explained, as well as that of physics and of the moral law. However, it is only a *subjective necessity*, holding solely for the nature of our mind and in no way for the nature of things in themselves. The latter are unknowable noumena. We conceive of their existence without being able to say what they are. We never know if the necessary laws of our mind are the very laws of reality or of being.

Understandably, Johann Gottlieb Fichte responded to this: if this is how matters stand, *then the application of the subjective categories to external phenomena remains arbitrary.* Indeed, why do some phenomena come to be ranked under the category of substance and others under that of causality? Why does not every phenomenal succession, like that of day and night, for example, appear as being a case of causality? If, in order to avoid arbitrariness, we were to acknowledge the recognition of the relations of accident to substance and of effect to cause in external objects themselves, then we would return to an intellectual apprehension of the intelligible in the sensible thing, as was held by traditional philosophy.

Moreover, as the empiricists say, and from a perspective opposed to Fichte, nothing proves that the phenomena, if they come from without, always docilely settle in under the subjective categories. What guarantees the fact that the world of sensations will always be susceptible to becoming an object of thought and will not someday appear as chaos and chance?

To avoid this last difficulty while remaining a subjectivist, one will need to maintain, with Fichte, that the phenomena themselves, like the categories, proceed from the self and that our knowledge [*science*], like God's, is the measure of all things. However, in that case, we could not be unaware of anything. There would no longer be mysteries for us—a claim contradicted by the most certain facts of our experience.

Subjectivist conceptualism encounters many other difficulties as well. It is obliged to admit, using the term "synthetic a priori judgments," blind judgments without any objective motive, in which one affirms, *without seeing* either *a priori* or *a posteriori* what one affirms, judgments that are not motivated by any evidence. In other words, it must admit intellectual acts without a sufficient reason, thus placing irrationality at the very heart of what is rational.

Finally, to nearly the same degree as empirical nominalism, subjective conceptualism does violence to common sense, instead of explaining it. Without a doubt, it seeks to maintain the universality and necessity of the first rational principles, though it does so by sacrificing their objectivity, their real (or, ontological) value as laws of being. Now, this objectivity is affirmed *naturally* by all men's intellects with no less certitude than are the two preceding characteristics of universality and necessity. When philosophical reflection explains this, the former should rejoin *nature*, not contradict it. If it were possible to show that there is a "natural illusion," that our intellectual nature deceives us—and how would it come to do this without, at the same instant, contradicting itself?—one would still need to explain this illusion.

Now, not only does Kant not explain it, but moreover, by doing violence to the fundamental affirmation of common sense (or, of natural understanding), he renders all the elements of knowledge absurd. In his system, it is no longer true to speak of the known object. The only things known are our ideas. No longer do we know real causality, but instead only the idea of a cause, as though the *idea* or representation were, in direct knowledge, *the terminus* of knowledge and not, instead, a *means* that is essentially relative to that which is represented. An idea that would not be essentially relative to an actual (or, at least, possible) being would be the idea of nothing. It would at once be an idea and not an idea—an absurdity. For the same reason, it is equally absurd to doubt the real value of the principle of non-contradiction, to suppose that an *inconceivable* and *contradictory* thing, like a square circle, is perhaps, nevertheless, *realizable* or possible.[90]

In other words, when deprived of its essential relation to being, the intellect is no longer conceivable. It becomes absolutely unintelligible and absurd. Therefore, it is not without immense disadvantages that one does violence to nature and, above all, to the very nature of the intellect. One would do just as well to construct a mathematics by staring out with a denial of [its] first definitions and fundamental axioms.

Therefore, in order avoid all these insoluble difficulties and all these contradictions, would it be necessary to return to absolute realism such as it was conceived in antiquity by Plato and in modern times by the ontologists? This is what remains for us to examine, by comparing this system with the preceding ones.

§2. Nominalism and Absolute Realism

Standing in direct opposition to the nominalists or empiricists, Plato, in his defense of the value of the intellect, maintained the most absolute realism, which has also been called, in opposition to materialist empiricism, "idealism"—an objective idealism, one that, it goes without saying, is radically opposed to the subjective idealism of Kant and his disciples.

According to Plato, the universal conceived by the intellect exists in the manner in which it is conceived—that is to say, it exists formally as universal (*universale existit formaliter a parte rei, seu extra animam* ["the universal formally exists, from the perspective of reality, that is, outside the soul"]). Above the individuals of different species, in an intelligible order of reality, separated from matter, there is gold-in-itself, wheat-in-itself, lion-in-itself, man-in-itself, being-in-itself, good-in-itself.

Aristotle objected, with common sense: man-in-itself cannot exist separately from matter, since the latter is implied in its definition (if not

---

[90] We have developed this critique of subjectivist conceptualism at length in another work. See Reginald Garrigou-Lagrange, *God: His Existence and His Nature*, trans. Bede Rose, vol. 1 (St. Louis: Herder, 1949), ch. 2 (61ff), and especially 111ff.

this flesh and *these* bones, at least *some* flesh and *some* bones, a common matter that can be conceived [so] but cannot exist separately from individuating conditions).[91]

The Platonists responded: man-in-itself exists at least as a Divine Idea, and this Divine Idea is what our intellect vaguely knows when we think, not about this or that man, but rather about man in general. This Divine Idea is the immediate object of our intellect, which emerges above the senses and the imagination.

Moreover, they add that, if man-in-itself cannot exist without matter, deprived of flesh and bones, nonetheless, the same is not the case for Being-in-itself, for Good-in-itself, or for the True-in-itself, nor for Wisdom and Love, for their definitions contain no matter. Being-in-itself subsisting from all eternity, or the Good-in-itself [as] the fullness of being, is God himself, and such is the object of our intellectual knowledge when we think not about a given being in particular or about a given particular good, but rather about being in general or about the good in general.

This conception seems to lead necessarily to the confusion of the Divine Being with the being of things, which is, in the final analysis, absorbed into God. Indeed, if man's essence is not *in* individual humans, but rather outside of them, in a superior intelligible world, what therefore, in themselves, are these individuals without an essence? In them there is neither a specific difference, nor a proximate genus, nor a supreme genus. In themselves, they have neither humanity, nor life, nor substance, nor being.[92] In the end, they are not anything at all, and all that exists is God, the First Being and Sovereign Good, though he finds himself thus deprived of omnipotence, since he cannot produce anything outside of himself.

Thus is one led to a kind of mirror image of atheism, namely, to the denial of the world, a form of acosmism. These are the two extremes between which pantheism is forever tossed back and forth. Unable, without obvious contradiction, to identify God and the creature, the Infinite and the finite, it must either absorb God into the world or absorb the world into God. In the latter case, almost as much as in the first, it does violence to common sense. As Aristotle showed in the seventh book of the *Metaphysics*, this is where a doctrine that confuses being in general and the Divine Being must ultimately end up.

---

[91] See Aristotle, *Metaphysica* 1 (lec. 14–15 of St. Thomas's commentary), *Metaphysica* 7 (lec. 9–10), and *ST* I, q. 84, a. 7.

[92] See Aristotle, *Metaphysica* 7, where he critiques Plato's absolute realism.

* * *

This absolute intellectual realism reappeared among modern thinkers in Spinoza, at least for so-called simple, clear, distinct, and adequate notions—notions of substance, of thought, and of extension. According to Spinoza, substance exists in a universal manner just as it is conceived. It can be only God himself, and universal thought and extension are his infinite attributes.[93] Individual thoughts and particular forms of extension are only phenomena that succeed one another, and the series of these phenomena have no beginning. The succession advances from all eternity, in accord with absolutely necessary laws. This represents a radical denial of both creative freedom and human freedom, affirmed by common sense.[94]

In other words, according to this system, our intellect's first known object is *the First Being* (or, the Divine Being), just as the first object of sight is color, and all our intellectual knowledge depends upon this first intuition of the First Intelligible Being. Whence it is given the name "ontologism" *to on* ([Gk.]; being), the doctrine holding that the First Being is what is first known. And here, in Spinoza, we have pantheistic ontologism, which, contrary to common sense, identifies the substantial being of things—that of rocks, plants, animals, men—with the being of God, or which denies the existence of individual substances.[95]

---

[93] See Spinoza, *Ethica*, p. 2, pr. 44. On the other hand, Spinoza is a *nominalist* for the notions that he calls vague [*confuses*], and that designate, according to him, collections of phenomena, like the notions of animality, humanity, and of the intellectual faculty. In any case, this nominalism is a consequence of the absolute realism applied to the simple notion of substance, since, in virtue of this absolute realism, there can be only one substance. The others, along with their faculties, are henceforth only verbal entities, *flatus vocis*. Thus, the two extremes touch each other, or rather error forever oscillates from one to the other in its wanderings. The truth is elevated like a summit above these wanderings, and only it reconciles what is true in each of these contrary errors.

[94] [Trans. note: The sentence is rendered in such a way that "affirmed" appears like it modifies only human freedom, though perhaps it was meant to refer to both.]

[95] Only the distinction between *natura naturans* and *natura naturata* remains, which Spinoza explains by saying in *Ethicia*, p. 1 pr. 29, scol.: "By *natura naturans* one must understand what is in itself and is conceived by itself, i.e., God. And by *natura naturata*, I understand everything that *necessarily* follows upon the divine nature." [Trans. note: Fr. Garrigou-Lagrange's citation is a slight condensation of the text but maintains the original on the whole.]

By this, we can see that (despite what may have been recently said [about this]), in this system, the relation between *natura naturans* and *natura naturata* has no resemblance to that which, according to Catholic faith, exists in Christ between his divine nature and his human nature, which was *freely created* and *freely assumed* by the Word.

* * *

Something similar can be found in the ontologism of Nicolas Malebranche and in that of Antonio Rosmini.[96]

Malebranche believed that universal and necessary truths, like the first rational principles or natural laws of being, are seen intuitively by us in God himself, the First Being. Thus, we would have a pure intellectual intuition of the intelligible in God, naturally present in us as he is in all things. Without seeing the Divine Essence such as it is in itself, we would see the Divine Ideas, the archetypes and exemplars of things—the ideas of substance, of mind [esprit], and of extension. Indeed, according to Malebranche, the universal or intelligible cannot not be abstracted from singular things by our intellect, which amounts to saying that it does not exist in them, but instead exists only in God. This represents an attenuated form of Plato's own absolute realism.

However, the system thus modified must necessarily run into the same difficulties and is scarcely more in conformity with common sense.

Malebranche in no way proves that our intellect cannot discover the common characteristics of singular things of the same species, that it cannot *abstract* the intelligible from the sensible. As the light of the sun actualizes the colors of bodies that it illuminates, why could our intellect not

---

Consequently, pantheism would not be completely realized if the Word were united personally (or hypostatically) to all individual human natures, or even to all created substances. Moreover, it is certain that this is not the case, for the Word made flesh is necessarily sinless [impeccable], not only in his divine nature but in his human nature; now, it is, alas, a very clear fact of experience that we sin against the law of our conscience.

The *Dictionnaire apologétique*, in its article on pantheism establishes a rapprochement, one that truly seems quite forced, between the relation of *natura naturans* and *natura naturata* according to Spinoza and the relation between the divine nature and the human nature in Christ (see cols. 1326–31). The author of the article thus no longer sees all the power of the traditional refutation of Spinozism according to the principles of St. Thomas, and he is drawn into a very complicated, subtle refutation, which seems unconvincing.

[96] [Trans. note: Bl. Antonio Rosmini-Serbati (1797–855) had his work *Delle Cinque Piaghe della Santa Chiesa* placed on the Index during his lifetime. After his death, forty propositions taken from his works were condemned. He was later rehabilitated and beatified for his heroic virtue in 2007. Details on his rehabilitation should be interpreted in light of the 2001 decree by then-Cardinal Ratzinger, "Note on the Force of the Doctrinal Decrees concerning the Thought and Work of Fr. Antonio Rosmini Serbati," promulgated July 1, 2001. *Rosmini* was rehabilitated, not the conclusions that might be drawn from his works by those who are not careful.]

make intelligibility appear—that is, the intelligibility that exists in things, as Aristotle and Saint Thomas say?[97]

Everything leads us to think that the *first* object known by our intellect, which is naturally united to the senses, is, as Saint Thomas shows,[98] not God, pure spirit, but rather, *the intelligible being of sensible things.* This is not our *adequate* object, for we could know God in himself. However, it is the first known and *proportionate* objet, that which is proportioned to the weakness of our intellect, whereas the essence of the pure created spirit is the proportionate object of the angelic intellect, and the Divine Essence the proportionate object of the Divine Intellect.[99] God alone *naturally* sees

---

[97] See *ST* I, q. 85, a.1.

[98] See *ST* I, q. 88, a.3.

[99] See *ST* I, q. 12, a. 1–4. [Trans. note: On these points, a summary statement from Fr. Garrigou-Lagrange's student Fr. Austin Woodbury is likely helpful, as in *Natural Philosophy: Treatise 3, Psychology*, no. 920 : "'The proper object of the human intellect, in state of union with the body, is the quiddity or nature existing in corporeal matter' of a thing represented by an image of the imagination, but as it is universal." See also no. 904:

The adequate object of [the] human intellect is at least material being and whatsoever other being according as it has analogical community therewith. For a power that apprehends essences is a power that knows things under the reason or character of being, as said above (no. 895C); for essence and being are convertible; for being is nothing else than essence having being [i.e., existence] (actually or potentially). But [the] human intellect, as said above (nos. 646–48; nos. 650–51; no. 889; no. 895), apprehends the essences of things.

But the reason why [the] human intellect apprehends the essences of things is: that the human intellect receives forms immaterially: not as they are the forms of this individual matter, but as they are forms; and therefore receives forms immaterially: not merely as that whereby something manifests itself exteriorly—as sense receives forms—but as they are determinative of the quiddity of a thing, as said above (no. 648; no. 889Ad2b).

But from this, that our intellect knows things under the reason or character of being, it follows that our intellect is cognoscitive of whatsoever has the character or reason of being at least according as it is manifestable whether immediately or mediately by the formal reason whereunder our intellect understands. But the formal reason whereunder our intellect naturally understands is that degree of immateriality that is immateriality through abstraction from individual matter, as said above (nos. 653–56).

But: what is immediately manifested by this degree of immateriality is the entity of material things (cf. nos. 653–56), as will be shown more copiously in the following chapter; *however, what are mediately manifested by this degree of immateriality are other beings inasmuch as they have (at least analogical) community with material beings.* Therefore, our intellect is cognoscitive of material being and of whatsoever else has the reason or character of being at least according

all things in himself as in the cause upon which all things depend. For us, the vision of the Divine Essence and of all things in God can be only supernatural.

Besides, if matters were otherwise, if our intellect knew all truth immediately in God, why would we have the senses? What use would they be for us? They would in no way be an aid for our intellect, but much rather an obstacle. If we perceived every intelligible in God, why would our ideas always be accompanied by a sensible image? Why would the blind not have knowledge [*science*] of colors? Why would our intellect not also see angelic substances?

There are so many insoluble questions involved in Malebranche's ontologism.

Moreover, merely because God is intimately present in us and in all things, as our conserving *cause*, it does not follow that he would be present in us as an *object*.[100] To see Him, we would need to have received, like the blessed, the light of glory, which supernaturalizes the human intellect in order to give it the power of perceiving the infinite splendor of the Light Itself. Without this supernatural elevation, our intellect would be, before God, like the eye of the owl before the sun; it would not be able to bear the light of his radiance.[101]

Finally, to say that the being of things is intelligible only in God is to say that intelligible being does not exist in things. In that case, what are they if not *pure nothingness* [*un pur néant*]? This is the conclusion ultimately led to by the three ontologist propositions condemned by the Holy Office.[102] Malebranche's occasionalism leads to the same conclusion.

---

as it has analogical community with material being (emphasis added).

Strictly speaking, the adequate object includes the proper and common objects of the intellect, the latter including in itself the mediate and extensive objects. The mediate object is whatever is manifested mediately by the proper object. The extensive object is "that towards which the power is only not repugnant by virtue of its order towards its proper object (i.e., by virtue of its nature).

See no. 902 for a schematic summary. Woodbury's complete treatment deserves consultation by the interested reader.]

[100] See *ST* I, q. 84, a. 5.

[101] *ST* I, q. 12 a. 1.

[102] Indeed, in 1861, the Holy Office condemned, with the annotation *tuto tradi non possunt* ["cannot be handed on without risk"], the following ontologist propositions: "The immediate knowledge of God, habitual at least, is essential to the human intellect, so much so that, without it, it [the intellect] can know nothing, since indeed it is itself the light of understanding. That being which we know in all things and without which [we know] nothing is the divine being. Universals, considered in their reality, are not really

Indeed, if *God alone acts* in all things—if things cannot themselves act under the Divine motion—*God alone exists*, for action follows being, and the mode of action follows the mode of being.[103]

Thus, we can see that absolute realism leads, contrary to common sense, to the identification of God and the world. However, instead of absorbing God into the world, as do atheistic evolutionism and, generally speaking, empirical nominalism, absolute realism tends to absorb the world into God.

Rosmini even held that being, the first object known by our intellect, is something of God.[104]

This always involved confusing being in general and the Divine Being. It was what led Rosmini to say: "There is no finite reality, but God causes it to exist by adding limitation to infinite reality. Initial being (which is something of God) becomes the essence of every real being."[105] Forgetting that there can only be an analogical likeness between God and creatures, and not a univocal one, Rosmini said: "Being that actuates finite natures and is joined with them is cut off from God."[106] One forever here recognizes, as in Malebranche, the same tendency as that which is found in Plato's own absolute realism.[107]

Conclusion

Where will we find the truth? On the one hand, nominalism and subjectivist conceptualism renounce the knowledge of *being* in order to hang onto the knowledge of phenomena; on the other hand, absolute realism naively believes itself to have, already here-below, intuitive knowledge of God, the First Being, with whom it confuses, contrary to common sense, being in general (or, the being of things).

Will the truth be found in an opportunist eclecticism that neutralizes,

---

distinct from God" (see Denzinger, nos. 2841–47).

[103] "Operari sequitur esse et modus operandi modum essendi."

[104] Indeed, the following claim can be read among the condemned Rosminian propositions: "Being, which man contemplates, must be something of the necessary and eternal being, the creating cause, the determining and final cause of all contingent beings; and this is God" (Denzinger, no. 3205).

[105] Denzinger, no. 3212. [Trans. note: The text presented above is taken from Denzinger, not from the French translation offered by Fr. Garrigou-Lagrange. However, the text in parentheses is added by him and is here translated from his French.]

[106] Denzinger, no. 3212.

[107] Concerning Rosmini, see the appendix that is found at the end of the second part of this work: "The Philosophy of Being and Ontologism."

as well as it can, the opposed systems by means of each other, so as hang onto an veritable mediocrity, forever bound to oscillate to the right and to the left without ever arriving at a vigorous, precise, and comprehensive affirmation? We will see that this is not the position held by traditional philosophy, which found its most perfect formulation among the ancients in Aristotle and in the Middle Ages in Saint Thomas Aquinas and his successors. It elevates itself above extreme systems and above a characterless eclecticism, so as to place in full relief the fundamental law of thought and of being, the principle of identity (or, of non-contradiction), a law realized in all beings, though in the loftiest and purest manner in the First Being, in whom essence and existence are identical: "I am He who is."

This doctrine, which is above all a metaphysics, can be called a philosophy of being, one that is wholly different from a philosophy of phenomena or that of becoming. By this very fact, it is highly superior to empirical nominalism and to subjectivist conceptualism. However it may seem it at first glance, it is also superior to the absolute and naïve realism of Plato and of his disciples, who believe themselves to have already here-below and naturally the intuition of God. It can be called a conceptualism (for it gives superiority to the concept over the sensible image), though it is a realist conceptualism or a moderate realism. This is what we must now examine.

Chapter 2

———————— ⟡⟨⟨⟨⟨⟩⟩ ————————

THE REALIST-CONCEPTUALIST
THEORY OF COMMON SENSE

We still must establish the classical or realist-conceptualist theory of common sense, a theory that will show us that common sense contains a rudimentary philosophy of being and will determine its object, fix its limits, and justify its spontaneous certitudes by establishing their relationship with *being*, the intellect's formal object as well as with the principle of identity. In this way, we will be led to conclude that common sense is, in a rudimentary state, not *a* philosophy but *the* philosophy, for the philosophy of *being*, in opposition to the philosophy of *phenomena* and of *becoming*, is alone true, for it alone respects the principle of identity and refuses to admit the possibility of absurdity.

This realist-conceptualist theory of common sense is what we find in the host of philosophers whose thought represents what Gottfried Wilhelm Leibniz called *quaedam perrenis philosophia*, ["a kind of perennial philosophy"]. Édouard Le Roy implicitly recognizes it himself when he writes, "The great philosophical current, up to these recent days (up to Henri Bergson, whose admirable *oeuvre* is the point of departure for a profound revolution in traditional ideas), flowed with the full force of rationalism, in conformity with the original impulse given to it by the Greeks."[1]

This theory can easily be drawn from the writings of Aristotle and of the great Scholastics. It is found again in the intellectualist philosophers of the seventeeth century, in particular in François Fénelon.[2] In the eigh-

---

[1] Édouard Le Roy, "Science et philosophie," *Revue de métaphysique et de morale* 7 (1899): 375–425 and 708–31, at 727. As Louis Couturat has noted, Le Roy could not say anything more strongly so as to discredit Bergsonism.

[2] François Fénelon, *De l'existence de Dieu*, pt. 2, ch. 2. [Trans. note, given the differences

teenth and nineteenth centuries, it took on an altered form in the writ-ings of the Scottish [common sense "school"], who exaggerated the role of common sense, striving in vain to thereby escape the skepticism of David Hume. The theory retrieves a less-inexact expression in Théodore Jouffroy in his *Mélanges philosophiques* ("On Common Sense and Philosophy").[3] However, Jouffroy remains still very close to Thomas Reid, no more him-self managing to escape skepticism.

Before critiquing common sense and classifying its particular and general prejudices, traditional philosophy first asks itself what everyone means by the word, "common sense." In other words, it asks: What does common sense think of itself? How does it *de facto* present itself? Follow-ing this, traditional philosophy then asks whether such common sense is right or wrong, if the certitudes on which it relies are well-founded.

§1. Common Sense Presents Itself *de facto* as *Possessing in a Vague Manner the Certain Solution to the Great Philosophical Problems*

Jouffroy says:

Everyone understands by "common sense" a certain number of principles or notions that are self-evident, from which all men draw the motives for their judgments and the rules for their con-duct. Indeed, nothing is truer than this idea. However, what is not well-enough known is that these principles are, quite simply, positive solutions to all the great problems that philosophy stirs up. How would we direct our conduct, of what judgments would we be capable, if we could not distinguish the good from the bad, the true from the false, the beautiful from the ugly, one being from another being, or reality from nothingness? If we did not know what to hold concerning what we see with our eyes, feel with our consciousness, and conceive with our reason? If we had

---

in reference style, I will translate directly from Fénelon's French text instead of taking it from the English edition of 1888. I correlate Fr. Garrigou-Lagrange's French selections to François Fénelon, *Traité de l'existence et des attributs de Dieu*, new ed. with notes, ed. A. Aulard (Paris: Librairie Classique d'Eugène Belin, 1878).]

3   [Trans. note, he appears to be referring to the essay "On Common Sense and Philoso-phy" in Théodore Jouffroy, *Mélanges philosophiques*, 7th ed. (Paris: Librarie Hachette et cie, 1901), 105–20.]

no idea concerning what the end of this life is, as well as its consequences? No idea of the Author of all things and of His nature? What would be the torch of the intellect and how would human society proceed if there were even the shadow of doubt in the notions that we possess concerning most of these points?[4]

Therefore, common sense would provide solutions, ones that are vague but nonetheless certain and strictly sufficient for the common run of men, for the common metaphysical, moral, and religious questions: What is being, the true, the good, the beautiful, along with their contraries, nothingness, the false, the bad, the ugly? Does God exist? What is God in Himself and for us? Does man belong to an order superior to the animal order? Is he free? What is his destiny?

Jouffroy says, moreover, "Common sense is a philosophy prior to philosophy properly speaking, since it is found spontaneously at the foundation of every act of awareness, independent of scientific research." His words are in profound agreement with those of the Scholastics:

Nobody who has the slightest experience of his own human nature will deny that man has within himself a certain judgment, the truth of which is upheld *always, everywhere*, and *by all*. Such things include judgments like: *God exists; parents are to be honored; parents by nature love their children*; and other like things. The principle of such judgments is neither study, nor reflection, nor experience of life itself (from which *proverbs* are derived), for these means are not common to all. Rather, it must be designated as being rational nature itself, something found in each person. This inclination of the rational nature to certain judgments that are to be recognized is called *the common sense of nature*. . . . (And just as the instinct of animals lacking reason is determined to the necessities of life and to those that are easily attained, so too) we must say concerning our sense of nature: certainly, that sense is exclusively concerned with the necessities leading to, or at least initiating, animal and rational life; and above all it is exercised concerning easier matters, for things that are lofty and difficult to know are neither necessary nor accessible to every man.[5]

---

4   Jouffroy, "On Common Sense and Philosophy," 110–11.

5   Tommaso Maria Zigliara, *Summa philosophica in usum scholarum*, 12th ed., vol. 1 (Paris: Delhomme et Briguet, 1900), 257–58.

In order to draw up a list of the truths of common sense, one could make use of works like those of Archbishop Alexandre le Roy on the religion of indigeonous peoples [*Primitifs*]. After having lived for many years with such people [*les sauvages*], he compared all non-Christian religions and eliminated those elements which distinguished them from another; he thus obtained a residue of common elements that corresponds nearly to what traditional philosophy holds is the object of common sense.[6]

As has often been noted, common sense, according to the word itself, is a quality *common* to all men, equal in each, and nearly invariable. "Good sense," on the contrary, is a quality susceptible to various degrees, more or less developed in different minds. It is the aptitude to judge well in particular cases, to apply the principles of common sense to them as is necessary.

Therefore, common sense is present as possessing, in a vague manner,

---

[6] This is how he summarizes these elements: (1) the distinction between the visible world and the invisible world; (2) the feeling of man's dependence upon this superior world, particularly in the use of nature; (3) belief in a Supreme Being who is the creator, organizer, and master of the world and, at the same time, the father of men; (4) belief in independent spirits, some tutelary and others hostile; (5) belief in the human soul, distinct from the body, aware, surviving death; (6) belief in a world beyond, where the spirits live and souls survive; (7) universal moral sense based on the distinction of good from evil and the feelings of modesty, of justice, of responsibility, of freedom, of duty; explicit or implicit recognition of conscience; (8) prescriptions or proscriptions in view of a moral or some reputed end, the notion of sin with sanction applied by the world's invisible authority or its representatives; (9) cultic organization, prayers, sacrifice; (10) priesthood charged with sacred functions; (11) the distinction between the profane and the sacred; (12) the establishment of the family as the religious and social center. See Alexandre le Roy, *La religion des primitifs* (Paris: Beauchesne, 1909), 464ff. [Trans. note: The summary list may be found in Alexandre le Roy, *The Religion of the Primitives*, trans. Newton Thompson (New York: Macmillan, 1922), 306.]

Moreover, we cannot accept what has recently been held, namely, that in all likelihood most men *are invincibly ignorant* of the existence of God and of the first precepts of the natural law if they did not learn them in the family or in school. This would represent the destruction of common sense and of natural remorse. Pius IX said that, "the precepts of the natural law are impressed by God in the heart of *all* men" (Denzinger, no. 2866). We have refuted this hypothesis elsewhere; see Reginald Garrigou-Lagrange, "Le principe de finalité et l'ignorance invincible," *Revue thomiste* 26 (1921): 405–24. [Trans. note: He cites *Études*, 1920, p.317 and 535 for the view with which he disagrees. The text from Pius IX is here taken from Fr. Garrigou-Lagrange's French. The official text reads, "We know as well as you that those who suffer from invincible ignorance with regard to our most holy religion, by carefully keeping the natural law and its precepts, which have been written by God in the hearts of all, by being disposed to obey God and to lead a virtuous and correct life, can, by the power of divine light and grace, attain eternal life."]

the certain solution to the great problems of philosophy. However, if it possesses these solutions, it does so in a scattered state without being able to determine their relations, without being able to classify and subordinate them into a doctrinal body—hence, without being able to justify its own certitude. It does not suspect the difficulties and apparent contradictions that will arise when one attempts to reconcile these elementary notions, which seem so simple to it. It does not know that wonder that is, as Plato and Aristotle noted, the beginning of philosophy and of science. Jouffroy says: "If you ask the first-comer what idea he has formed concerning the good or what he thinks about the nature of things, he will not know what you are talking about. . . . However, attempt to place in question, with the Stoics, that pleasure is a good or to deny, with the spiritualists, the existence of bodies, and he will laugh at your folly and bear witness to the most unwavering conviction concerning these two points."[7]

§2. The Systems with Which Common Sense Is in Disagreement

Common sense acknowledges matter and mind [*esprit*] without reflecting too deeply on how matter can act upon mind and mind upon matter; the philosopher, if he does not find a satisfying explanation, will deny one or the other of these terms. Common sense acknowledges that the soul and the body are substances without seeking to determine the relationship between substance and the phenomena by which it is manifested; the phenomenalism born of the need for an explanation cannot be satisfied by our spontaneous understanding. Common sense discerns the immutable and universal reason for contingent and particular experience without posing to itself the problem of the origin of the first notions, and it could recognize itself neither in pure rationalism, nor in pure empiricism, nor in Platonic realism, nor in sensualist nominalism. Common sense acknowledges the subordination of the will to the intellect ("nihil volitum nisi praecognitum [nothing is willed unless it is first known]") and also acknowledges the existence of freedom, without perceiving the difficulty involved in reconciling these two terms. It will never be either a determinist-intellectualism in the manner of someone like Leibniz or a libertinist in the manner of Charles Secrétan (1815–1895). Common sense respects obligation and holds that the search for goodness is legitimate. It can accept neither utilitarian positivism nor Kant's moral rationalism, for the former denies the very existence of duty, while the latter

---

7 Jouffroy, "On Common Sense and Philosophy," 113–14.

banishes every other [moral] sentiment than respect for the law. Common sense holds that God is absolutely one and immutable but, nevertheless, is living and free; it will condemn philosophers who, like Parmenides, sacrifice life and freedom to unity and immutability, as well as those who, like Heraclitus and Hegel, make becoming the fundamental reality and deny the objective value of the principle of identity (or, of non-contradiction [*sic*][8]).

Le Roy critiques common sense, taken as a theoretical representation, for fragmenting reality. Indeed, this is because, in opposition to the Bergsonian system, common sense is, in a rudimentary state, a philosophy of the discontinuous. It holds that there is a distinction of orders between brute matter and living matter, between the simple living thing like the plant and the living thing endowed with sensation, between the senses and the intellect, between animal and man, between the world and God. It is neither mechanist nor hylozoist, neither realist-materialist nor idealist; neither empiricist nor rationalist, neither nominalist nor realist-Platonist, neither intellectualist nor libertinist, neither pantheistic nor dualistic. It sees distinctions everywhere, and our innate need for unity remains, in spite of everything, satisfied by the mysterious relations that it recognizes to exist between distinct elements—between brute matter and life, between life and sensation, between sensation and the external bodies that it represents, between the image and the idea, between the will and the intellect, between God and the world.

Do we not here have the solution that common sense *de facto* provides to the great problems, the only ones that are truly interesting for us? Is it wrong; is it right? If this question is posed, does it not fall to the philosopher to respond to it?

§3. Traditional Philosophy Justifies Common Sense by Passing from Nominal Definitions to Real Definitions and by Establishing the Relationship of the Certitudes of Spontaneous Reason to Being, the Formal Object of the Intellect

There is a philosophy that, without difficulty, remains in accord with common sense solely by the fact that it refuses, so to speak, to go beyond it.

---

[8]   [Trans. note: As noted in previous chapters, Fr. Garrigou-Lagrange most often uses "principle of contradiction" for what is most commonly referred to now as the "principle of non-contradiction." Thus, on the rarer occasions when he does use "principle of non-contradiction" for the same, I mark those instances with "[*sic*]" to signal that he means the same thing as in most places he means by "principle of contradiction" (and we now commonly mean by "principle of non-contradiction").]

It is the Scottish ["school" of common-sense] philosophy. However, there is also a learned speculation, much too abstract even for our contemporaries, nearly all of whom are positivists, a speculation that, despite this abstract character (or, rather, in virtue of the very effort of abstraction that it presupposes) succeeds at rejoining common sense, as true art exceeds the artificial and rejoins to nature. If this philosophy exists, why is it so misunderstood today? One could pose the same question on the subject of God. The responses would not be unrelated.

This speculation is none other than the traditional philosophy constituted through the ages by the ensemble of intellects that are more enamored with truth than with novelty. The essential lineaments of this philosophy, as Bergson himself has told us recently, is found in Plato and Aristotle: "Of this immense edifice, a solid frame remains, and this frame sketches out the broad lines of a metaphysics that is, we believe, the natural metaphysics of the human intellect."[9] What would have become of this philosophy without Christianity? After many eclipses, it would have always reappeared, since it is reason itself. However, would it have received the development and precision that it has found in the School?[10]

Can the study of true philosophical problems—of metaphysical, moral, and religious problems—be at one and the same time serious, durable, and fruitful outside the true religion?[11] In order to be interested for a long time in the soul and in God, one must seek God with all one's soul. The philosopher who is not religious does not remain indifferent: "He who is not with me is against me" (Matt 12:30). Laboring first against the God of faith, he then comes to strive against the God of reason, for one and the same denunciation ends up involving one's philosophical position, given the manifold relations revealed dogma has with natural theology and the metaphysics of the soul. One comes, at last, to attack the absolute character of the moral law, and absolutely nothing remains of philosophy as a science distinct from the positive sciences. Our age of positivism indicates this eloquently enough: more than one Kantian who ten years ago

---

[9] Henri Bergson, *L'évolution créatrice*, 352. [Trans. note: Fr. Garrigou-Lagrange does not mention the edition. In other books, his pagination slightly differs.]

[10] [Trans. note: Though one may refer here to any of the major Scholastic *scholae*, one rightly infers that he means above all the developments in the Thomist School developed within the Dominican order.]

[11] [Trans. note: On this topic, the reader will likely benefit from consulting the opinion discussed in Reginald Garrigou-Lagrange, "On the Relationship between Philosophy and Religion," in *Philosophizing in Faith: Essays on the Beginning and End of Wisdom*, ed. and trans. Matthew K. Minerd (Providence, RI: Cluny Media, 2019), 36–98.]

still spoke of the categorical imperative now rallies to the most outrageous ideas of the positivists and no longer recognizes the moral law except in name alone. Thus is the word of the Gospel verified: "For to everyone who has will more be given, and he will have abundance; but from him who has not, even what he has will be taken away" (Matt 25:29). God takes away both reason and morality from those who resist the motives of credibility and the grace of faith so as to pride themselves in their reason and in their natural morality; man ends by confessing that his knowledge, like that had by animals, does not exceed the sensible order. No longer God, nor the soul, nor duty remain as the motivation for man's activity; all that remains is self-love and the calculation of pleasure. How many times, after leaving the courses of the Sorbonne, did the judgment of Saint Paul concerning the philosophers of his times come back to our own mind: "For what can be known about God is plain to them. . . . So they are without excuse; for although they knew God they did not honor him as God or give thanks to him, but they became futile in their thinking and their senseless minds were darkened. Claiming to be wise, they became fools, and exchanged the glory of the immortal God for images resembling mortal man" (Rom 1:19–23). To the eyes of faith and of simple good sense, this is the history of philosophy in France these past thirty years; despite the desperate efforts of certain Kantians,[12] it today sinks down into the most radical utilitarian positivism. Outside of Catholicism, there is no longer much more left in France today than an official philosophy, which is the denial of metaphysics and of morality—that is to say, the denial of philosophy, just as it is the denial of religion. Philosophy, as a science distinct from the positive sciences, cannot live for long without religion. On this point, we are in agreement with the positivists.

Hence, it need not be surprising if "the natural metaphysics of the human intellect" cannot be preserved for long except in the Church. The faithful guardian of reason, the Church has received, baptized, and developed Greek philosophy and, indeed, *philosophy* itself. The Platonism of the Fathers, of Saint Augustine, of the Augustinians, and of Saint Anselm continued on in Scholastic Aristotelianism, just as Plato continued on in Aristotle. Boutroux was able to write, "Indisputably, the most considerable work of Aristotle is the organization of this Christian philosophy, which is so complete, so precise, so logical, and so firmly established in the least

---

[12] See Lionel Dauriac, "Crépuscule de la morale kantienne," *Année philosophique* 16 (1906): 126.

of its details that it seems to be established for Eternity."[13] The same historian added, "Once more, Aristotle is today one of the masters of human thought; his system can be placed without disadvantage into competition with two doctrines that today hold the greatest place in the philosophical world: Kantian idealism and evolutionism. It even seems that Aristotelianism responds in particular to the preoccupations of our age."[14] This was written in 1893, if I am not mistaken. Since then, Kantianism has considerably declined, while positivist evolutionism has triumphed. We find ourselves in the midst of a doctrinal and moral nihilism that does not fail to raise concerns for the great leaders of the university. For a number of Bergsonians, morality is a dance by which we play through all the forms of becoming without ever stopping at any.[15] For Émile Durkheim, the only form of morality is an external one that is fashioned by the decisions of the collectivity. Nothing, or nearly nothing, remains from philosophical tradition. Scripture speaks of "the fascination of foolishness"[16] exercised over us by the sensible appearances and their incessant becoming; their very inconsistency becomes, at times, a sign of life for us. This is the very evil from which we suffer. However, the excess will itself cure us. Perhaps, we will finish by feeling the void and the nothingness of what is happening and will return to what is lasting. We will once again seek God. In Germany at the present hour, many are returning, in a sense, through Leibniz by way of the metaphysics of Hermann Lotze. The native masters of human thought will again become our masters. Plato, Aristotle, Augustine,

---

[13] Émile Boutroux, *Études d'histoire de la philosophie*, 3rd ed. (Paris: Felix Alcan, 1908), 200.

[14] Boutroux, *Études d'histoire de la philosophie*, 202.

[15] [Trans. note: This expression may well be taken from Jacques Maritain when he was a young Bergsonian before his dual conversion to Catholicism and then to Thomism. Citing a letter from Fr. Garrigou-Lagrange to Fr. Ambroise Gardeil, Jean-Luc Barré writes in *Jacques and Raïssa Maritain: Beggars for Heaven*, trans. Bernard E. Doering (Notre Dame, IN: University of Notre Dame Press, 2005), 57: "[Maritain] stood out at the Sorbonne with his ardent Bergsonism, often not without irony and an air of provocation. A Dominican, Father Garrigou-Lagrange, who was attending the courses of Gabriel Séalilles in May 1904, took note of the public questioning by 'a tall young man with a very gentle countenance, a Slav, it would seem, from all his hair, almost always accompanied . . . by a young woman who looks almost like she could be his younger sister,' holding forth in a vigorous attack on the formalism of Kant and defining morality as a kind of dance 'which is performed through all the different forms of becoming, without ever stopping at any single one.'"]

[16] Wis 4:12: "The fascination of wickedness obscures what is good."

Saint Thomas, and Leibniz[17] will help us once more to pass beyond our senses and to overcome appearances, phenomena, and becoming in order to discover the reason for them in "He Who Is." The *perennis philosophia* cannot die, any more than human reason can or more than the Church of Christ can.

This traditional philosophy, the work of centuries, is at its foundation nothing other than a perpetual justification of the solutions offered by common sense. It gradually draws forth from *nominal definitions* (or common definitions) the *real definitions*[18] that were implicitly contained in the former. After thus specifying the comprehension of the ideas of common sense, it subordinates them to one another, ranking them in a body of doctrine that is wholly dominated by the idea of *being*, the formal object of the intellect, the proper object of metaphysics, the supreme science. In this body of doctrine, all that is connected to being by the principle of iden-

---

[17] We only consider here in Leibniz those of the great traditional theses that he victoriously defends, whether against the empiricists or against Descartes and Spinoza.

[18] Real definitions are determined by the process indicated in the *Analytica posteriora* 2 (cf. Aquinas's commentary, lec., nos. 13–17). We must, Aristotle says: (1) begin with the nominal definition, or, the definition of common sense (the proto-thesis as we would say today), the point of departure for the examination and discussion; (2) examine the beings or facts that correspond to this nominal definition so as to discover their constant characteristics; (3) among these characteristics, seek what is *the first, dominating, raison d'être* for the others; (4) compare these beings with those that most resemble them, to seek the constant characteristics of these latter, and see whether or not they are irreducible to the constant characteristics of the first group to be defined.

For example, Aristotle takes magnanimity. We can take, for example, life. We begin with the nominal definition, or, that of common sense. For everyone, what makes living things differ from non-living things is spontaneous movement. If we examine the beings and facts that correspond to this nominal definition, we will discover as constant characteristics, in the cell: nutrition, growth, reproduction. And in differentiated organisms: nutrition, digestion, absorption, circulation, respiration. Among these characteristics, one of them is the *raison d'être* for all the others: nutrition. A living thing is a being that nourishes itself, or, refashions itself. Finally, we compare this vital fact with those that most resemble it (the crystal also refashions itself) and note its irreducibility: in the living being there is an assimilation; in the crystal, mere juxtaposition. Thus, we arrive at the real definition of the *living thing*: a bodily being that nourishes itself and refashions itself. By means of the same procedure, we arrive at the real definition of *animal*: a bodily, living being endowed with sensation. Sensation is, indeed, in it, the *raison d'être* for desire and movement. Equally, we thus can arrive at the real definition of *man*: a rational animal; reason is, in it, the *raison d'être* for its interior and exterior voluntary activity. See also Aristotle, *De anima* 2.1.

[Trans. note: See Reginald Garrigou-Lagrange, "On the Search for Definitions according to Aristotle and St. Thomas," in Minerd, *Philosophizing in Faith*, 21–34.]

tity and its derivatives is rendered metaphysically certain. In short, this is the analytico-synthetic method of metaphysics.[19] Instead of relying solely upon common sense, like the Scottish school, the philosophy of Aristotle explains, by the formal object of the intellect, the absolute certitudes of common sense in its proper sphere: spontaneous understanding, which is a living relation to being, cannot be deceived concerning the first principles and the great truths to which they are linked, because it perceives them as immediately implied in being, its formal and adequate object, an absolutely simple formal object that it cannot distort, an adequate object outside of whose limits it cannot pass.[20]

It is this justification of common sense whose essential traits we must recall.

§4 The Real Definitions of Inanimate Bodies, of Living Being, of the Sensing Subject, and of Man; How These Different Beings are Related to Each Other; the Order of the Universe

Aristotelian philosophy, by determining real definitions, recognizes the distinction of orders that common sense acknowledges between brute matter, life, sensation, and intelligence, as well as between the world and God. It then attempts to explain how these different orders are related to each other, in order to thereby satisfy the intellect's innate desire for unity, a desire that derives from the intellect's ordination to its formal object, being, which has unity as a transcendental property. In a general manner, the multiple relations of beings of different orders are explained by the very first division of being into act and potency; this division, necessary for rendering *multiplicity* and *becoming* intelligible in function of being, one and identical, must at the same time render intelligible *the dynamic union of the various orders of the universe.*

Instead of reducing the superior to the inferior, as does materialist monism, or the inferior to the superior, as does idealistic monism, Aristo-

---

[19] [Trans. note: To understand this aright, and not in the Kantian sense of these terms, which are not those of the Thomist school that Fr. Garrigou-Lagrange is following, see Reginald Garrigou-Lagrange, "On the Twofold *Via inventionis* and the Twofold *Via iudicii* according to St. Thomas," in Minerd, *Philosophizing in Faith*, 11–20.]

[20] *Being* is *the formal and adequate object* of our intellect as an intellect. The *proper object* of the human intellect, inasmuch as it is *human* and united to the senses, is *the being or the essence of sensible things* in the mirror of which we here below know purely spiritual realities, our soul, and God.

telianism always considers the inferior as potency and the superior as act. And merely by the fact that potency designates essentially a relation to act (*as to something more perfect, or as to an end*) and can be actuated only by an act, the inferior always has the character of being an actualizable matter, and the superior always has the character of being the efficient and final cause. In this way, we have an explanation for the universe, unity in diversity.[21]

Let us recall the real definitions that, by their gradation, constitute the ladder of beings, briefly indicating how the various orders are related to each other.

Brute matter itself cannot be defined by extension alone. It is obviously endowed with activity, meaning that deterministic mechanism is ruled out. Nor can it be defined solely by force, thereby sacrificing the reality of extension. Dynamism is no less false than deterministic mechanism. Rather, we must acknowledge two elements in it: matter, the principle of quantity and of passivity, and form, the principle of quality and of activity. A body is not just one of them, for by itself, matter is undetermined and receives every determination from form, which is at one and the same time the efficient and final cause. Chemical combinations are explained by substantial mutation: the permanence of matter and the substitution of form. By this, we also have a resolution for the supposed antinomies posed with regard to the continuum: extension is [potentially] divisible, not [actually] divided, *ad infinitum*. An extended substance is something other than a collection of indivisible unextended things. Its unity is assured by a principle that is superior to the spatial order: the form, which is wholly in the whole and wholly in each part, requiring such an extended *minima* as the material condition for the substance of the composite. By this, again, we have a resolution for the difficulties concerning the transitive action of bodies upon one another. In each of them there is a principle of activity and a principle of passivity. The convergence of these two principles gives birth to movement.

The simple living thing, like a plant, is in its own turn explained by a composition of matter and form, but here the form is a principle of superior activity, an immanent and not solely transitive activity; the plant not only acts and undergoes, but also *rebuilds itself*.[22] This living thing, com-

---

[21] *Summa theologia* [*ST*] I, q. 47.
[22] [Trans. note: On the issue of immanent activity in plants, see the critical remarks by Yves Simon in *An Introduction to Metaphysics of Knowledge*, trans. Vukan Kuic and Richard J. Thompson (New York: Fordham University Pres, 1990), 82n46. However,

posed in part of matter, can receive the brute matter into it and assimilate it by its form, which is at one and the same time the efficient and final cause. Here we have neither deterministic mechanism nor hylozoism.

With animals, an incontestably superior form appears: the principle of knowledge. The animal not only can act and undergo action like the body, and not only rebuild itself like the plant, but moreover, through sensation, it can in a certain manner *become the other beings* that surround it (*fieri aliud*), for to see and to hear these beings is, in a manner, to become them.[23] Whereas the plant is closed within itself, the animal, by its senses, is open to the entire sensible world; it, so to speak, passes out of itself, out of the limits that its body occupies. This quasi-infinite amplitude of the animal form presupposes a kind of independence with regard to the extended matter that it informs; in other words, it presupposes a certain spirituality. The representation existing in the animal is of an order superior to that of the material bodies that it represents. Thus is materialism ruled out, and nevertheless idealism too is avoided: the sensing subject can immediately receive an impression from the external bodies precisely because sensation is not an act of the soul alone, but rather is a combined act of the soul and the body at one and the same time, an act of an *animated organ* (matter

---

for something closer to Fr. Garrigou-Lagrange's line of thought, see Jacques Maritain, "Philosophie de l'organisme: Notes sur la fonction de nutrition," *Oeuvres complètes*, vol. 6 (Fribourg, Switzerland: Éditions Universitaires, 1984), 981–1000. Also see Maritain, "Philosophie de l'organisme: Notes sur la fonction de nutrition," *Revue thomiste* 37 (1937): 263–75. A translation of the latter is to be published in the near future in *Nova et Vetera*.]

[23] *ST* I, q. 14, a. 1. See also *De anima* 2.12 (Aquinas's commentary, lec. 24) and 3.8 (Aquinas's commentary, lec. 13). We are very surprised to see a neo-Scholastic like Nicolas Balthasar misunderstand this great Aristotelian and Thomist thesis: "cognoscens fit aliud a se [the knower becomes that which is other than itself]." (See Nicolas Balthasar, "Travaux récents de métaphysique," *Revue néo-scolastique de philosophie* 23 [1921]: 85.) Refer to the commentaries of Cajetan and John of St. Thomas on *ST* I, q. 14, a. 1. There are uniformly accelerated philosophical ascents and others that are uniformly slowed. This is particularly apparent if one follows from the time of Aristotle up to our days the interpretations that are given for this profound formula: "cognoscens quodammodo fit cognitum, anima est quodammodo omnia" (*De anima*, 3.8; Aquinas's commentary, lec. 13). Scotus and Suarez differ notably from St. Thomas on this point. See J. M. A. Vacant, *Études comparées sur la philosophie de S. Thomas d'Aquin et cur celle de Duns Scot*, vol. 1 (Paris: Delhomme et Briguet, 1891), 88–107. [Trans. note: For Fr. Garrigou-Lagrange's response to Balthasar; also see Reginald Garrigou-Lagrange, "Cognoscens quodammodo fit vel est aliud a se (On the Nature of Knowledge as Union with the Other as Other)," in Minerd, *Philosophizing in Faith*, 63–78.]

and form). Composed in part of matter, the animal can be impressed by external bodies; then, thanks to its superior form, it represents them to itself and can, in consequence, act upon them and appropriate them to itself. With man, a form of an incomparably more elevated order appears: not only the principle of knowledge, but the principle of rational knowledge, which seeks the *raison d'être* of that which it grasps. Man does not perceive only the beings that surround him; he also conceives *what they are* (*quid sint*). He is not content only with associating sensations and images; he judges—that is to say, he affirms that a given thing *is* or *is not* (*an sit*). Finally, his representations are not linked together in a mechanical fashion, as is the case for the animal, but instead, he reasons, giving the *raison d'être* for what he affirms (*propter quid*). Therefore, in each of these three operations, the object of his intellect is *being*, and not color, sound, or the facts that internal experience reveals. Man is not only, like the animal, open to the whole sensible world standing at the door of the senses. He is open upon all that which has a *raison d'être*. Thus is empiricism ruled out. The idea is distinct from the image, judgment from association, reasoning from empirical successions. However, so too is pure rationalism avoided: the intelligible was in potency in the sensible, the intellect needed to extract the intelligible from it. Moreover, it is always conceived in the sensible. Here below, there is no pure intuition of the intelligible, and the idea remains united to the image as the intellective soul remains united to the body of which it is the form.[24] Because of this intellectual knowledge, man

---

[24] [Trans. note: On the necessity of conversion to a phantasm in all knowledge, the following summarization by Austin Woodbury will likely be helpful for the reader to understand this point aright. Slight editorial changes were necessary for readability, given the schematization in which the summary is presented. See Austin Woodbury, *Natural Philosophy: Treatise 3, Psychology*, no. 1063: "Our intellect knows nothing without conversion to an image. This is so whether it be understanding MATERIAL things, or it be apprehending IMMATERIAL things. The necessity for understanding material things is manifested by several indications, namely, from the connection between intellection and lesions of organs and from internal experience. It is proven as regards both perfect and imperfect knowledge. Perfect is singular and therefore is not without sense and imagination. This objective dependence on matter *a fortiori* must be found in imperfect intellection; in the apprehension of a quiddity in common, we cannot totally abstract from (singular) existence. As regards the apprehension of immaterial things, this dependence upon the image is necessary because nothing is known save by the mediacy of the proper object of the human intellect in state of union with the body, which is not known without an image" (*Natural Philosophy: Treatise 3, Psychology*, The John N. Deely and Anthony F. Russell Collection, St. Vincent College, Latrobe, PA, p. 901; the use of all-caps is a convention original to Fr. Woodbury).]

can, in a sense, embrace the universe as well as himself. In consequence, he can govern himself and make inferior beings serve his ends.

Thus far, all such beings are composed of potency and act (matter and form). In this, we have an explanation for how they are related to each other: every body, being composed of these two principles, can act and undergo action. The living thing composed of matter can receive brute matter into itself and assimilate it by its form, which has the notion of being the efficient and final cause. The sensing subject ([with its] animated organ) composed of matter can be impressed by external bodies, can represent them in virtue of its superior form, consequently acting upon them, being served by them, and thus becoming, in its own turn, an efficient and final cause. Finally, man, through the knowledge that he has concerning the notions of things, can govern himself and use all beings that are inferior to him.

§5 The Intelligible World in General; What Common Sense Perceives in Being

Can we elevate ourselves higher? Can human reason transcend the limits of experience and affirm the existence of a being superior to man? Can it determine what man's destiny is, if he also has an end, if he is truly the master in attaining or not attaining this end, if his soul is immortal? These are the great metaphysical, moral, and religious problems. Is the solution provided for them by common sense the true solution? It is here *above all* that the philosophy of being, divided into potency and act, justifies common sense, by showing that what it affirms *is seen in being itself*, the formal object of the intellect. The preceding questions concerning brute matter, life, and sensation are clearer *for us*, said Aristotle,[25] because they belong to the sensible order and because our ideas come from the senses; however, these metaphysical, moral, and religious questions are clearer *in themselves* because they belong to the intelligible order and are susceptible to being attached directly to being, the principle of all intelligibility. Indeed, in them, we make abstraction from all matter (third degree of abstraction; *Metaphysics* 10.3).

In contrast to the positive sciences, which can never can do anything but classify general facts through provisional hypotheses (representative and not explanatory hypotheses), without giving the *raison d'être*, the *propter quid* for these facts, metaphysics, the supreme science, appears here

---

[25] See *Metaphysica* 1 (Aquinas's commentary, lec. 2).

as a science in the full sense of the word, as a *form of knowledge that assigns the reason why*, the necessary *raison d'être* of what it affirms.[26] As we will show, this *propter quid* is nothing other than the explanation of what common sense sees in being without coming to precisely formulate it.

In being, common sense first perceives the first speculative and practical principles (the principles of identity, non-contradiction, substance, *raison d'être*, and finality, as well as the first principle of morality: the good must be done and evil avoided). Next, by means of a process of reasoning which is very simple, it likewise sees therein the existence of God, the efficient and final Cause of all things, the Sovereign Good and Sovereign Law-Giver. It also sees therein the distinction of the intellect from the senses, the existence of free choice, and in a certain way, the spirituality of the soul and its immortality (in a word, the properties of an intelligent being, properties which derive wholly from its specific difference, i.e., from its intellectual relation to being). Here below, man is the only being whose specific difference belongs to the purely intelligible world and not only to the sensible world. This is what enables us to deduce his different properties. Inferior beings do not become truly intelligible except in their transcendental notes (i.e., those common to all beings) and their generic notes.[27]

---

[26] *In* I *analyt. post.*, lec. 4: "*To know scientifically* [*scire*], *without qualification*, is *to know* [*cognoscere*] *the cause on account of which a thing is and cannot otherwise be*." The positive sciences never come to give this *propter quid,* this *raison d'être* that renders the general facts to be intelligible; they remain sciences of *quia,* that is to say, they find *that* the fact is without being able to explain it, without being able to say why the fact happens thus and not otherwise. A recent article by Pierre Duhem wholly affirms these views of Aristotle concerning the relations of metaphysics, the supreme science, with the positive sciences. See Pierre Duhem, "La valeur de la théorie physique a propos d'un livre récent," *Revue génerale des sciences pures et appliquées,* January 1908. This article has been reproduced in an appendix in the second edition of his *Théorie physique* (Paris: Rivière, 1914). [Trans. note: See note 43 in ch. 1 of pt. 1 of the present volume.]

[27] For example, we know that mercury is a bodily substance, a liquid metal; however, we do not know its specific difference. When we must give precision to these generic notions, we have only an empirical, descriptive definition that does not arrive at rendering *intelligible* the properties of this body. We content ourselves with saying: mercury is a liquid metal at an ordinary temperature, having a silver-white color, solidifiable at -40 degrees, able to be boiled at 360 degrees, and very dense; its salts are very active, but also very toxic, antiseptics. We find the facts without being able to say *why.* Likewise for the plant and the animal. Who will assign the specific difference of a given species in such a way that one will then be able to deduce its properties? In the case of man, on the contrary, among all the notes common to all men: rationality, freedom, morality, sociability, speech, religion, etc., one among them, rationality, appears as the *raison d'être* of

§6 The First Principles for Common Sense: The Principles of Identity, Contradiction, Substance, *Raison d'être*, Finality, and Induction; the First Principle of Practical Reason (Duty); Their Connection to the Idea of Being

And first of all, our intellect perceives the first principles. Adherence to these first principles is, in some way, natural.[28] A child does not need a master to teach him the principles of contradiction, substance, *raison d'être*, causality, and finality. He seeks the cause and end for all things, tiring us with his repeated questioning: "why?" If he did not possess these principles, a teacher's own action upon him would be impossible, according to the expression of Aristotle: "Every teaching and every discipline comes from knowledge that already preexists."[29]

Why is our adherence to these first principles natural? Because their truth is immediately perceived in the light of being, the natural and first object of the intellect:

What first falls into apprehension is being, the understanding of which is included in all things whatsoever one apprehends. And therefore, the first indemonstrable principle is that "something is not affirmed and denied at the same time," which is founded on the notion of being and non-being; and all the other principles are founded on this principle, as the

---

all the others. . . . All these notes can be rendered intelligible, that is, attached to being by the intermediary of rationality; this is the whole task of rational psychology. [Trans. note: See note 40 in ch. 1 of pt. 1 of the present volume.]

[28] *Summa contra gentiles* [*SCG*] II, ch. 83: "The intellect naturally knows *being* and those *things that belong per se to being as such*, upon which its knowledge of the first principles is founded." See also *ST* I-II, q. 51, a. 1: "The *habitus* of first principles is partly from nature and partly from an external principle; it is natural as regards its beginning. For, based on the very nature of the intellectual soul, it is fitting to man that, immediately upon knowing what a whole is and what a part is, he know that every whole is greater than its part; and similarly in other cases. However, he cannot know what a whole is and what a part is except through intelligible species drawn from the phantasms. For this reason, the Philosopher, at the end of the *Posterior Analytics* (bk. 2, final chapter), shows that knowledge of principles arises for us from the senses."

[29] Aristotle, *Analytica posteriora* 1.1. See also *ST* I, q. 117, a. 1: "There is in each man a kind of principle of science, namely the light of the agent intellect, through which we naturally know, *immediately from the start*, certain universal principles of all the sciences." Also, see *De veritate*, q. 11, a. 1.

Philosopher says in *Metaphysics* 4.[30]

Common sense first perceives in being the truth of the *principle of identity:* "every being is itself," "every being is something determined," "every being is one and the same," and so on; for example, "flesh is flesh," "spirit is spirit", and *est est, non non.* The *principle of non-contradiction* is only a negative form of the preceding: "One and the same being cannot at one and the same time and in the same respect be and not be what it is." *The principle of substance* is immediately grasped as a determination of the principle of identity: "That which is is one and the same under its multiple and transitory manners of being"; the multiple is only intelligible in function of the one, and the transitory only in function of what is permanent and identical, if being of itself is one and the same. This is why Saint Thomas says, following Aristotle, that substance is a sensible *per accidens*—that is, a reality that *per se* is of the intelligible order but that is immediately grasped by the intellect at the simple presentation of a sensible object.[31] As soon as the data of each of the external senses are centralized by the first of the internal senses,[32] the intellect grasps in this sensible object its proper object, being, and that which is *being in itself,* substance, even before grasping the manner of being: the phenomenon or accident.

Common sense next perceives, in the light of being, the truth of the *principle of raison d'être:* "Everything that is has its *raison d'être*"; "everything is intelligible." In an implicit manner and without being able to formulate it, it connects this principle to the principle of identity by a *reductio ad absurdum*: every being has its *raison d'être,* that which is necessary for it to be; to deny this would be to identify that which is with that which is not. Every being has in itself or in another the *raison d'être* of that which is fitting for it: *in itself,* if this belongs to it with regard to what constitutes it in what is proper to it (to deny this would be to deny the principle of identity); *in another,* if this does not belong to it with regard to what constitutes it in what is proper to it, if a union of diverse things are found in it. To deny this relation of *dependence* would be to identify what does not exist through itself with what does. It would be to say that the *uncaused* union of diverse things is possible, that the diverse through itself and as

---

[30] *ST* I-II, q. 94, a. 2. See also lec. 6 of St. Thomas's commentary on *Metaphysica* 4.

[31] See St. Thomas, *In* II *De anima,* lec. 13: "Not everything that can be grasped by the intellect in the sensible thing can be called *sensible per accidens,* but only *what is apprehended by the intellect immediately upon experiencing the sensed thing."*

[32] [Trans. note: i.e., the common sense.]

such is one and the same, which would be the denial of the principle of identity.[33] "Everything that belongs to something not according to what that thing is belongs to it through some cause, for that which does not have a cause is primary and immediate."[34]

In this way, we arrive *at the principles of causality and of finality*. Change is precisely the union of the diverse; therefore, it requires an extrinsic *raison d'être*. This extrinsic *raison d'être* is twofold: efficient and final. Proof: becoming is the union of diverse things; indeed, it includes two elements: potency and act. On the one hand, that which already is does not become ("ex ente non fit ens, quia iam est ens"); on the other hand, nothing can come from nothingness ("ex nihilo nihil fit"). Therefore, what becomes can arise only from an intermediary between determined being and pure nothingness; this intermediary is undetermined being, or, potency.[35] Thus, for being, becoming is the passage from indetermination to determination, from potency to act; and given that, of itself, potency is not act, it needs an extrinsic principle that determines or actualizes it (*ens in potentia non reducitur in actum nisi per aliquod ens in actu*). This determining or active principle is called the *efficient cause*. However, this cause itself must have a reason for acting, as well as for doing this rather than that; the potency upon which it acts must likewise be susceptible to receiving a given determination and not some other. Without this, the cause would produce everything or nothing, and not a given particular effect. If everything has its *raison d'être*, the effect must be predetermined. Therefore, the active potency of the agent and the passive potency of the patient (e.g., the nutritive power and food) must pre-contain the determination of their effect (nutrition). However, potency cannot pre-contain in act [*actuellement*] the determination of its effect; it can pre-contain it only inasmuch as it is *ordered* to a given act and not to some other as to its perfection and its fulfillment, only inasmuch as it has *its raison d'être* in it ("potentia dici-

---

33 For the development of this *reductio ad absurdum*, see pt. 2, ch. 1, §4, of the present volume. Concerning the various senses of the word *reason* and the expression *raison d'être*, see the word *ratio* in the general index of the works of St. Thomas. *In us*, the word *ratio* designates our intellectual faculty and the arguments that it proposes; *outside of us* in things, it designates either their essence (the *raison d'être* of their properties) or their cause.

34 *SCG* II, ch. 15.

35 This proof of the *reality of potency*, which is necessary in order for us to render *multiplicity* and *becoming* intelligible in function of being, is developed below in our examination of the criticism of the Thomist proofs of God's existence made by Le Roy (pt. 2, ch. 2 §4, of the present volume).

tur ad actum"). Let it not be said that this act is a pure *terminus*, a pure result, [for then] it would not be predetermined. And how would it be a pure *terminus*? Being more perfect than the potency, the principle of operation, it is necessarily *that for the sake of which* (*to hou heneka* [Gk.]; *id cuius gratia*) the potency is made, as the imperfect is necessarily *for* the perfect and the relative *for* the absolute. Indeed, only the Absolute has its *raison d'être* in itself. This act, the *raison d'être* of the potency, for which it is made, in view of which the agent acts, is called *the end*. And the principle of finality is formulated: "Every agent acts on account of an end; otherwise, from the agent's action this would not follow rather than that, except by chance";[36] or, again, "potency is *for* act," "potentia dicitur ad actum [potency is designated in relation to act]."[37]

Therefore, becoming has a twofold extrinsic *raison d'être*: efficient (order of exercise) and final (order of specification). It is thus rendered intelligible in function of being by the division of being into potency and act. "Being does not come from being, for it already is being; from nothing, nothing comes; and nevertheless, being comes about. From what does it come about? From a kind of middle between nothingness and being, or from undetermined being, which is called potency."[38] Potency is undetermined being; act, depending on the perspective under consideration, is the formal, efficient, or final determination. And the two principles of causality and finality are combined into one: "All that becomes requires an efficient and final cause."

However, there is another formulation of these two principles, one that is closer to the principle of *raison d'être*: "Every multiplicity or every composite requires a cause." Not only is becoming thus rendered intelligible in function of being by potency and act and the four causes; in the static order, and in the furthest depths of being, which movement does not reach, multiplicity or diversity is likewise rendered intelligible by this formulation. Like becoming, multiplicity (a plurality of beings possessing a common element, or a number of parts of one and the same being) is a union of diverse things and by that very fact requires a twofold extrinsic

---

[36] *ST* I, q. 44, a. 4.
[37] Aristotle, *Physica* 2, ch. 3. See alo *SCG* III, ch. 2, and *ST* I-II, q. 1, a. 2: "For if the agent were not determined to a given effect, it would not do this rather than that." There can be the fortuitous encounter of two agents, but each of these agent acts necessarily for an end. In virtue of this principle, all things, even the most particular, must be preordained by the supreme agent if it is true that its action reaches all beings. See also *ST* I, q. 22, a. 2.
[38] This is the summary of Aristotle's demonstration. See *Physicsa* 1, ch. 8 (St. Thomas's commentary, lec. 14).

raison d'être: efficient and final. Indeed, like the preceding, this union of diverse things first presupposes two elements that constitute multiplicity intrinsically: *potency and act*. The existence of a number of individuals possessing the same determination, the same *form*, is explained only by the presence in them of an element that is susceptible to being determined by this form: *matter*. The multiplicity of beings possessing the same *act of existing* is explained only by the presence in them of an element susceptible to receiving existence: *essence*. (Act is multiplied and limited through potency.)[39] Each of these beings, since they are composite, is itself a union of diverse things. Since this union cannot be *uncaused*, each of these beings calls for an efficient and final cause, and we have a formulation of the principle of causality: no longer "all that becomes requires a cause," but "every multiplicity or every composite required a cause," "every composite has a cause, for those things that are, of themselves, diverse, do not come together in some one thing except through some cause uniting them."[40]

As regards *the principle of induction*—"The same natural cause in the same circumstances necessarily produces the same effect (for example, heat expands iron)"—it is obvious that it is connected to the principle of *raison d'être*. If a natural cause A in particular, determinate circumstances were to produce at one time the effect B and at another time the effect B′ in utterly akin circumstances, the change in the effect would lack a *raison d'être*. We will see below that this principle does not constitute, however, an insoluble objection against free will, for the latter is not a natural cause determined by nature to a single effect.

By means of the idea of the end, we are led to the *first principle of practical reason*: "The good must be done and evil avoided; "Do what you must, come what may." The perfect actuality to which the operation that has its principle in an operative potency leads merits, as we have said, the name of "end," and not only that of "terminus" or "result," for it is predetermined like a perfection in relation to the operative potency, a perfection that increases the agent's being, filling a void in it. Potency does not simply lead to act; it exists *for* the act, as the relative is *for* the absolute. Therefore, the end must have the character of the good, for goodness is nothing other than *the perfection of being* that provides the foundation for desirability [*appétibilité*] or provokes love.[41] The end is the good in view of which the agent acts, the perfection capable of perfecting it, that which it desires for

---

[39] See *ST* I, q. 7, a. 1.
[40] See *ST* I, q. 3, a. 7.
[41] See *ST* I, q. 5, a. 1.

this: "The good is what all things desire." Common sense is led by this to the first principle of morality. It distinguishes three species of good: the sensible (or simply delightful) good; the good that is useful in view of an end; and the fitting [*honnête*] good. The animal takes rests in the first, and by instinct utilizes the second without seeing the *raison d'être* in the end for which it employs it. Man alone, by his reason, knows *utility* or the *raison d'être* of the means found in the end; also, he alone knows and can love the fitting good. The latter appears to him as being *good in itself*, *desirable in itself*, independent of the enjoyment that accompanies its possession and independent of all usefulness; it is good and desirable solely by the fact that it is conformed to right reason and appears as the normal perfection and achievement of man as man (as rational and not as an animal). It is good in itself, independent from the pleasure that one finds in it and from the advantages that one draws from it: to know the truth, to love it above all, to always act in accord with right reason, to be prudent, just, courageous, and temperate. Moreover, this fitting or rational good appears as being an *end that is intrinsically obligatory*: every man understands that a rational being *must* have a conduct conformed to right reason, as right reason is itself conformed to the absolute principles of being.[42] Here is the rational origin of the notion of duty: "Do what you must, come what may." The just man who is beaten black and blue by a rascal proves the existence of an intelligible world superior to the sensible world when he cries out to him, "You are stronger than I, but this does not prove that you are right."

Indeed, reason justifies its command by the principle of finality (or, what comes to the same thing, by the division of being into potency and act): the will of the rational being *must* tend toward the fitting (or, rational) good, in relation to which it has the character of potency, for the entire *raison d'être* of potency is found in [its correlative] act ("potentia dicitur ad actum"). And as the efficient cause coincides with the final cause, it is necessary to add: the will of the rational being *must* tend toward the fitting (or rational) good, for this good is the *end for which* it has been *made* by a superior efficient cause who himself had this rational good in view (for, the end of the agent and of the patient, each considered as such, is the same, although each in different respects[43]). This is why, to the eyes

---

[42] This is at least the *proximate foundation of moral obligation*. Its *ultimate foundation* is found in the *Eternal Law* of God who made us to live in accord with right reason. See *ST* I-II, q. 19.

[43] *ST* I, q. 44, a. 4.

of common sense, duty is ultimately founded on the being, intellect, and will of God; this is its ultimate foundation.

The first principle of practical reason is immediately perceived, Saint Thomas says, in the idea of the good (act or perfection of being), just as the principle of identity is perceived in the idea of being.[44] Common sense respects duty and holds the search for happiness to be legitimate. At once, it rejects utilitarian morality and Kantian morality. The philosophy of being continues it and justifies it, founding duty upon the idea of the rational good that is for man, at once, the end in itself, for which he is made, as well as the source of true happiness.

All these speculative and practical principles are *analytic* in the Aristotelian sense of the word:[45] in them, the predicate and the subject *a priori*[46] show themselves to be necessarily linked by the verb *being*, which affirms, under their *logical diversity, their real identity in one and the*

---

[44] *ST* I-II, q. 94, a. 2: "Just as being is the first thing that falls into apprehension, speaking without qualification, so too the good is the first thing that falls into the apprehension of practical reason, which is ordered to a given deed. For every agent acts for the sake of an end, which has the character [*rationem*] of the good. And therefore, the first principle in practical reason is that which is founded on the notion [*rationem*] of the good, namely: 'The good is what all things desire.' Therefore, this is the first precept of the law: the good is to be done and evil avoided; and all the other precepts of the natural law are founded on this."

[45] [Trans. note: The words being used here are loose. Given Fr. Garrigou-Lagrange's training and the general character of his writings, he does not mean the expression "analytical" in the sense used by many authors today. It is evident that he only means that the proposition "Every agent acts for an end" is *per se nota*—known of itself without objective inference through a middle term. He would most certainly agree with the summary notes made by Jacques Maritain in his unfinished text in material logic: "There are neither *analytic* judgments nor *a priori* judgments in the Kantian sense. Every judgment is a synthesis. [i.e., inasmuch as the enunciation formed by the intellect's second operation involves the formation of a complex of two notions.] The authentic *a priori* is born of the evidence of the object"; see Jacques Maritain, *Grand Logique ou Logique de la raison vraie (Logica major)* in *Oevres Complètes*, vol. 2, ed. Jean-Marie Allion et al. (Fribourg, Switzerland: Éditions Universitaires, 1987), 758 (my trans.). One can, however, speak of *analysis* as pertaining to syllogistic analysis (whence, one speaks of the "analytics" of Aristotle). On the distinction between assent and analytical resolution, see John of St. Thomas, *The Gifts of the Holy Spirit*, trans. Dominic Hughes (London: Sheed and Ward, 1950), 132–34 (*Cursus theologicus* I-II, q. 70, disp. 18, nos. 21–25).]

[46] [Trans. note: By this, Fr. Garrigou-Lagrange means they are *per se nota* propositions; he does not use *a priori* in the sense that would indicate that such things are known in a manner wholly disconnected from human experience. The sense of *a priori* here is slightly different than that used to describe demonstration *a priori*.]

same being, whether possible or actual.[47] (e.g.: Every being *is* having its *raison d'être*. The potency ordered to the rational good *is* before achieving [*réaliser*] it.) Because "Kant did not understand that all knowledge is expressed exactly by the verb *to be*, the copula of every judgment," the principle of *raison d'être*[48] and its derivatives became for him wholly subjective *a priori syntheses* without a bearing upon being. Having misunderstood the formal object that gives unity to the intellect, he no longer could find in it anything but a plurality of scattered principles that still are imposed as necessary, though with a necessity whose reason is no longer grasped.[49]

---

[47] [Trans. note: On this, one should also consult the works of Cahalan and Maritain cited in note 48 of the pt. 1, ch. 1 of the present volume.]

[48] [Trans. note: Adding "d'être" to "principe de raison."]

[49] See Charles Sentroul's thesis "L'objet de la métaphysique selon Kant et Aristote" (Institut supérieur de philosophie [Louvain, Belgium], 1905), edited and expanded in 1913 under the title *Kant et Aristotle* (Louvain and Paris: Alcan). We draw our references below from the second edition of the text. In it, the author shows how Kant misunderstood the fundamental truth of traditional philosophy, along with the profound meaning that Plato and Aristotle gave to the definition of the intellect: "The object of the intellect is being." It is well known that an adaptation of this thesis was awarded a prize of four hundred marks by the *Kantgesellschaft* of Halle, presided over by Hans Vaihinger.

"Kant," the author says, "Contrary to Aristotle, did not understand that all knowledge is expressed exactly by the verb *to be*, the copula of every judgment . . . that all judgments have as their formal character the fact that they are the union of a predicate and a subject by means of the verb *to be* employed as the sign of the identity of the termini. . . . Knowledge of a thing consists precisely in seeing it is identical to itself under two different aspects (*Metphysica* 4.7). To have knowledge of a triangle is to say that it *is* a given figure; to have knowledge of what a cause is to say that it *is* that which contains the effect; to have knowledge of man is to say that he *is* endowed with imagination. And in order to give a judgment that is wholly accidental, to say that a wall *is* white is to say: this wall *is* this white wall (p. 303). If the subject and the predicate agree in being connected by the verb *to be*, this is because the predicate and the subject express one (and the same) reality" (p. 187).

Kant recognized identity only in what he calls analytic judgments, pure tautologies to his eyes, and not in the extensive judgments that alone can advance knowledge and that he calls synthetic *a priori* or *a posteriori*, because they are formed, according to him, by the juxtaposition of distinct notions. He thus misunderstood the fundamental law of every judgment: "A judgment formed by the juxtaposition or the convergence of several notions would be a false judgment, since it would express as identical two terms that would not have any identity with each other but, rather, simply some other relation. . . . The principle of the Aristotelian division of propositions is not the identification or non-identification of the predicate and the subject. Aristotle distinguishes them depending on whether the knowledge of this identity arises solely from the analysis of notions or from the examination of existing things" (p. 304).

The reason for all this is that Kant, beginning with the subject, holds that "the cat-

Equally true for all and know by all,[50] these principles are immutable in themselves and in us. They are *immutable in themselves*: the absolute necessity that they express in the order of the possible and the impossible can have neither a beginning nor an ending; the contingent act of our intellect feels itself to be conditioned and measured by these eternal truths that can have their foundation only in the Absolute. From the start, common sense understands Scripture when it affirms that the first principle of the moral law is like a participation in the Divine Intellect in us:

> *Many say, "Who shows unto us good things?"* To this question, the Psalmist responds saying: "The light of Your face, O Lord, is signed upon us," as it were, the light of natural reason by which we discern what is good and what is bad, which pertains to the natural law; it is nothing other than an impression of the Divine Light upon us.[51]

These principles are also *immutable in us*, inscribed in an indelible manner upon human reason; they are, in some way, identical with it, since, after all, reason is nothing other than a transcendental relation[52] to being inasmuch as it is being, which implies in itself all these very first truths.

§7 How Common Sense Raises Itself to God

With the aid of these principles, by means of a process of reasoning that is

---

egories are purely logical," whereas for Aristotle, beginning with being, holds that "the categories are half-logical, half-ontological" (p. 187), and that the affirmative judgment recomposes and restores to reality that which abstraction separated. The whole life of the intellect is explained by its order to being. Not only can he who begins with the subject never rejoin being, but the intellect itself will also become incomprehensible for him. He will either deny it, like the empiricists or will see in it, like Kant, only a multitude of *a priori* syntheses, blind syntheses that he no longer can manage to legitimate and link to a superior principle that is intelligible of itself.—These multiple principles can be connected to the principle of identity only by the division of being into potency and act, the division that here, as everywhere else, alone explains the multiple in function of the one.

50 See *ST* I-II, q. 94, a. 4.

51 *ST* I-II, q. 91, a. 2.

52 [Trans. note: On the distinction between transcendental relation and predicamental relation see Reginald Garrigou-Lagrange, "There Cannot Be Genuine Sensation without a Real Sensed Thing," trans. Thomas DePauw and E. M. Macierowski in Minderd, *Philosophizing in Faith*, 116–19.]

very simple, common sense raises itself to God. Philosophical reason only provides a more precise formulation for this reasoning: if everything has its *raison d'être*, if what becomes requires an extrinsic *raison d'être* which is at once the efficient and final cause, must we not say that everything that changes, ourselves and everything surrounding us, has an efficient and final cause that does not change (first, second, and third ways)?[53] If the intellect alone can grasp the relations between things, the *raison d'être* of the means in the end, must we not say that the first cause of this world, the system of means and ends, is an intelligent cause? The intellect, a living transcendental relation to being, does not intrinsically imply any more imperfection than does being itself (fifth way).[54] Finally, if multiplicity (a plurality of beings possessing a common element, or a plurality of parts in one and the same being), no more than becoming, does not have its *raison d'être* in itself, if the diverse cannot of itself be one and the same (the principle of identity), then must we not conclude that the first cause is one, just as it is immutable, simple, wholly and entirely self-identical, pure act, that it is related to being as A is to A, *Ipsum Esse subsistens*, absolute perfection (fourth way)?[55]

Dualism is thus ruled out: every being must arise from him who alone is Being-through-himself, in whom essence and existence are identical, and who admits besides himself only composites of potency and act, of non-being and being, of essence (susceptible to existing) and existence. Pantheism is no less absurd, for at the heart of *Self-Subsistent Being*, wholly and entirely self-identical, there can be neither multiplicity or becoming. Therefore, God is distinct from the essentially diverse and changing universe.

---

[53] *ST* I, q. 2, a. 3.

[54] We will be able to attribute *analogically* to God all *simply simple perfections*, but them alone—this has not been noted well enough in recent controversies. These perfections, the formal meaning of which intrinsically implies no imperfection, are precisely *those that have an immediate relation to being* and to the transcendentals: intelligence and the properties of an intelligent being (free will, with the moral and intellectual virtues, Providence, Justice, and Mercy). No anthropomorphism is involved in this. We do not conceive of God as though he were a man whose proportions would be carried to infinity, but rather conceive of him as *Being Itself, Ipsum Esse*, and we recognize for him only the attributes that necessarily follow from this concept of *Ipsum Esse*. The Thomist doctrine of analogy is the same one elaborated by Aristotle in his doctrine of the transcendental properties of being: Unity, Truth, Goodness and, in parallel, intelligence and will. See pt. 3, ch. 2, §2, in the present volume.

[55] See the explication that we have given of this fourth way in Reginald Garrigou-Lagrange, "Note sur la preuve de Dieu par les degrés des être chez saint Thomas," *Revue Thomiste* 12 (1904): 363–81.

Common sense sees all of this implicitly without being able to formulate it. It does not demonstrate it, but through its *instinct for being*, it feels it. It has the vague intuition that the principle of identity is the fundamental law of reality, just as it is the fundamental law of reason, and that the fundamental or ultimate reality must be related to being as A is to A, absolutely one and immutable and, by that very fact, transcendent.[56]

Is it any wonder if theologians commonly deny the possibility of ignorance or invincible error as regards the subject of the existence of God, the Author of the natural order: "The invisible things of God are clearly seen, having been understood through those things that have been created" (Rom 1:20). If ignorance or invincible error cannot exist with regard to the first precepts of the natural law, there cannot be error with regard to their Author. Therefore, the Church has condemned the distinction "between philosophical sin, which is contrary to reason alone, and theological sin, which would be an offense against God and can exist only in those who arrive at knowledge of God, or who have God in mind at the moment when they sin."[57]

The idea of God, the First Being, the First Intelligence, the Sovereign Good, can no more be erased from the human mind than the first principles of the natural law. Only this or that essential attribute of God can be misunderstood for a given time; thus, the secondary principles of the natural law can be abolished as a result of bad habits, as in those who do not hold that theft is a sin, or even that sins against nature are sins.[58]

§8 Why Common Sense Is Aware of Freedom

Natural reason also has a *sense of our freedom* in relation to the partial goods that attract us. Here again, it perceives this in the light of being, its formal object. Because people do not ponder this formal object of spontaneous intelligence, they often speak quite simplistically about our awareness of the free choice exercised by the will [*libre arbitre*]. To the degree that man distinguishes *the good, the fullness of being*, from this or that particular good, he will feel that he is made for the total, absolute good;[59]

---

[56] See Aquinas, *In Boeth. de trin.*, q. 1, a. 3, ad 6.

[57] See Denzinger, no. 2292. (Decree of the Holy Office, August 24, 1690). [Trans. note: I have rendered the text following Fr. Garrigou-Lagrange's French, which makes the passage in question fit into the flow of his own narrative.]

[58] *ST* I-II, q. 94, a. 6.

[59] See *ST* I-II, q. 2, a. 7 and the commentaries on this by Cajetan and Conrad Koellin, who

he perceives the infinite gulf that separates this absolute good from every partial and limited good and consequently feels himself to exercises a form of *mastery* and is able to respond or not respond to the attraction of a finite good, which he can always judge to be insufficient. The awareness of this dominating indifference, derived from reason itself, is what everyone calls awareness of the free choice exercised by the will [*libre aribitre*]. Jacques-Bénigne Lignel Bossuet put this quite excellently: "Let each of us listen to and consult ourselves; *he who does will feel that he is free, just as he will feel that he is rational.*"[60]

This awareness of free will is, in a vague and implicit state, the *a priori* proof of freedom that philosophical reason will formulate. And here again philosophical reason will justify common sense by eliminating both deterministic intellectualism and libertinist voluntarism. The will is subordinated to the intellect from the perspective of the specification of its acts, but all its advances are not, for all that, necessarily determined by the intellect; it is free when the judgment remains indifferent or undetermined on account of the *potentiality* or the indetermination of its object. Two partial goods, however unequal they may be, are both mixtures of potency and act, and for that reason, are *equally related to infinity*, to the total Good, which alone is Pure Act. When faced with them, freedom remains. *There is no infallibly determining sufficient reason* for passing from infinity to one given finite quantity or quality rather than to another. There is a *relatively sufficient* reason (for motivating a free choice), though not *an absolutely sufficient* one (for necessitating the will). It is a sufficient reason that (in a sense) does not suffice. This apparent restriction made to the principle of *raison d'être* is nothing other than the restriction made to the

---

show well what must be exactly understood regarding this proposition so frequently found in St. Thomas: *the object of the will is the universal good.* It is not the *abstract good, in universali,* for the will is concerned with the good that exists in things or that it wishes to realize; nor is this good immediately *God himself,* who immediately specifies only the theological virtues. Rather, it is the *non-limited good, bonum non coarctatum,* as Cajetan says, and as such, it exists only in God, who can be known and loved either naturally or supernaturally.

[60] Jacques-Bénigne Lignel Bossuet, *Traité du libre arbitre,* ch. 2. Fatalistic religions themselves recognize moral and social responsibility, accept the legitimacy of laws and tribunals, speak of remorse and moral satisfaction—all of which would be absurd if they did not admit free will. In reality, as has often been noted, their fatalism is the denial not of free will, but of physical liberty. "It is in virtue of destiny that Oedipus kills his father; but Oedipus does not will this murder." [Trans. note: The remark by Bossuet is found at the beginning of said chapter, though Fr. Garrigou-Lagrange does not cite the edition he is consulting.]

principle of identity by the affirmation of *potency*, that non-being which is a kind of middle between determined being and pure nothingness. There is indetermination in the will because there is indetermination in the intellect and, in the end, because there is indetermination or potentiality in being. Therefore, the proof of freedom comes back to the distinction between potency and act.[61] Common sense has a vague intuition of all this. And because it rests upon this foundation, our awareness of freedom is not moved by the Spinozist objection: "You do not know all the causes that influence your determination." "Even though I might be unaware of more than one of them," common sense vaguely says to itself, "I see the infinite disproportion between the partial good and the absolute good."

§9 What Is the Source of Common Sense's Belief in the Immortality of the Soul?

Finally, natural reason has a *sense of the spirituality* and *the immortality* of the soul. It is true to say with Spinoza, "we feel that we are eternal," or, at least, "that we are immortal." Saint Thomas affirms, "Everything having an intellect naturally desires to exist forever"; man desires to exists *forever*, and he feels that this natural desire cannot be in vain.[62] This natural desire had by the intelligent being is again founded on its intellect (or, on the sense that it has of being). Spontaneous understanding has this vague intuition that it does not succeed at formulating: being, my formal object,

---

[61] We have developed this *a priori* proof at length in Reginald Garrigou-Lagrange, "L'Intellectualisme et la liberté chez S. Thomas," *Revue des sciences philosophiques et théologiques* 1 (1907): 641–73, and *Revue des sciences philosophiques et théologiques* 2 (1908): 5–32; article reproduced in the work *God: His Existence and His Nature*. [Trans. note: See Reginald Garrigou-Lagrange, *God: His Existence and His Nature: A Thomistic Solution of Certain Agnostic Antinomies*, vol. 2, trans. Bede Rose (St. Louis: B. Herder, 1949), 268–350. An excellent digest of Fr. Garrigou-Lagrange's work in these articles and text can be found in the sixth chapter of Jacques Maritain's *Bergsonian Philosophy and Thomism*, ed. Ralph McInerny, trans. Mabelle L Andison and J. Gordon Andison (Notre Dame, IN: University of Notre Dame Press, 2007).]

[62] See *ST* I, q. 75, a. 6. See also F. Galibert, "La foi du nègre," *Annales de philosophie chrétienne*, October 1907, pp. 66–80. What is found in the African man [*nègre*] in a most particularly striking manner, on account of his primitive state, is inquietude, the expectation of a definitive deliverance and of a fulness that leaves nothing to be desired. Rude prejudices, it goes without saying, alter the idea that he makes concerning the future life. [Trans. note: Obviously, Fr. Garrigou-Lagrange's manner of making this basic point is marked by the vocabulary of his era.]

abstract[63] from all matter, space, and time. Given that I am a pure relation to it, I am similarly of the same order as it: "Desire in thinking things follows upon knowledge. However, sense does not know being except under the conditions of the here and now; however, the intellect grasps being absolutely and in accord with all time. Whence, everything having an intellect naturally desires to exist forever."[64] Hippolyte Taine objected to Jouffroy: the steer that you kill also naturally desires to live. However, this natural desire had by the animal, no more than the sensible knowledge that founds it, does not surpass space and time. The animal naturally desires to live *here and now*, but not *forever* in the full sense of the word. Man's natural desire, like reason, which founds it, is concerned not with a given being or a given particular good, but rather with absolute being and the absolute good. Man naturally conceives and, consequently, naturally desires an absolute beatitude that has the property of being inamissible; to fear losing it would mean one already is no longer fully happy.

This intuition of common sense has been given precision by philosophical reason. This precision was first given by Socrates, Plato, and Saint Augustine: the intellect, they say, sees that its object—necessary, universal, and eternal truths—dominates space and time, *abstrahit ab hic et nunc*. [It abstracts from the conditions of the here and now.] Now, the intellect is necessarily of the same order as its object and superior to time like it. As we ourselves feel, our rational and moral activity belongs to an order that is superior to everything in us that must pass away. Saint Thomas, building on Aristotle's analyses concerning the intellect's object, provides further precision: the human intellect grasps itself as a relation to being. Now, being inasmuch as it is being, *abstracts from all matter*. Essentially relative to such an object, the intellect is therefore absolutely immaterial, *penitus immaterialis*.[65] This traditional proof of the spirituality and immortality of the soul, an extension of common sense's own intuition, is greatly misunderstood by Christian philosophers of today. Some[66] contest its rigor because they do not understand what Aristotle and Saint Thomas mean by the formal object of the intellect. This formal object stands forth in all

---

[63] *Abstract* (*abstrahit*) here means: *being* implies in its formal notion neither matter, nor space, nor time.

[64] *ST* I, q. 75, a. 6.

[65] *ST* I, q. 50, a. 2; q. 75, aa. 5 and 6; *In* I *metaphys.*, lec. 1–3; *In* XI *metaphys.*, lec. 3; and elsewhere.

[66] Clodius Piat, *La personne humaine*, p.78. [Trans. note: Fr. Garrigou-Lagrange does not cite the edition, and the reference is not wholly clear. He is referring to either the first edition (Paris: Alcan, 1897) or the second edition (Paris: Alcan, 1913).]

its purity if one considers it at the third degree of abstraction (that is, at the degree of metaphysical abstraction); indeed, it becomes the proper and exclusive object of the supreme science. There are, Aristotle says,[67] certain sciences, such as the natural sciences, that abstract only from individual sensible matter (first degree of abstraction). They still consider common sensible matter. Thus, the chemist abstracts from the particularities of a given molecule of water so as to study water's sensible properties. The mathematical sciences abstract from common sensible matter in order to consider only continuous or discrete quantity (the second degree of abstraction). Metaphysics, logic, and general moral philosophy *abstract from all matter* (the third degree of abstraction) in order to consider only being insofar as it is being and its properties or the beings that are defined by a relation to being inasmuch as it is being, intellectual beings and their properly intellectual and voluntary activity. There is no longer anything material or quantitative in being and its transcendental properties (unity, truth, and goodness), no more than in the first divisions of being (potency and act, essence and existence, and formal, efficient, and final causality). At this third degree of abstraction, the intellect grasps itself as *essentially relative to [that which is] immaterial*. The inferior sciences (existing at the first and second degrees of abstraction) become intelligible to it only provided that they can be illuminated by the very principles of being, which forever remains the intellect's formal object, the principle of universal intelligibility. Therefore, the intellect is necessarily immaterial as well, like its formal object, like the *raisons d'être* or relations that it perceives. "Immaterial," what does this mean? Intrinsically independent from an organ. It depends on a body only extrinsically inasmuch as it cannot think without images.[68] Now, immaterial intellection can proceed only from an immaterial substance: "Operation follows upon being, and the mode of operating follows upon the mode of being." Therefore, we must conclude that the human soul is immaterial, intrinsically independent of the body that it informs and dominates, and that, consequently, it can *subsist without it*. Moreover, if it is absolutely *simple* (and it must be, just as its object is), it is naturally *incorruptible* and *immortal*.[69] It only remains distinct from its existence, like every creature, and God alone, who was able to create it, could annihilate it. However, God moves beings as befits their natures and

---

[67] See Aristotle, *Metaphysica* 10.3. See also Aquinas, *In IX metaphys.*, lec. 3.
[68] [Trans. note: That is, without the phantasms, which are the objective instrumental causes of human intellectual cognition.]
[69] See *ST* I, q. 75, aa. 5 and 6.

never ceases to preserve in being the creature that by definition can endure forever and that naturally desires such.

This proof, drawn from the intellect's formal object (i.e., being), is only the extension of common sense's intuition: "Everything having an intellect naturally desires to exist forever."

§10. How Common Sense Perceives God's Finger in a Miraculous Fact

According to traditional Thomists, the ascertainment of the miracle is a common-sense intuition of the same kind as that by which it attains a substance under its phenomenon, the freedom of the will, or the immateriality of intellection in our own acts. In a miraculous fact like the resurrection of a dead person, spontaneous reason would vaguely grasp an immediate relation to being, its formal object, as well as to the proper cause of being inasmuch as it is being—that is, to God. This intuition would prevent common sense from being moved by the objection raised by philosophers who are foes of miracles, saying that we do not know all the powers of nature. Doubtlessly, this is true. However, we know the proper effect of God the Creator: being itself. And the miracle (at least a certain miracle) appears to the intuition of spontaneous understanding as an exceptional production of being, comparable to creation.[70] Thus, in order to see the *finger of God* present in a miraculous fact, one does not need faith, as Le Roy claims. It suffices that we have natural reason, this innate sense of being. This is what enabled Thomas de Vio Cajetan to say that the existence of a true miracle is evident *to the senses*,[71] which can be understood only as referring to that which is *per accidens sensible*, as substance is.[72]

---

[70] Thus, the Thomists liken the obediential potency prerequired for miracles to the pure logical possibility prerequired for creation. To the degree that passive potency decreases, active potency must increase; when passive potency is only a pure logical possibility, the active potency must be infinite. However, it is clear that miracles, such as they are defined by the philosophy of being, are "inconceivable or unintelligible" for a partisan of the Bergsonian philosophy of becoming. And Le Roy can see nothing but a [mere] "word" in [the classical notion of] "obediential potency."

[71] See Cajetan, commentary on *ST* II-II, q. 1, a. 4, no. 5.

[72] [Trans. note: On *per accidens sensibles*, see: Reginald Garrigou-Lagrange, *The Sense of Mystery: Clarity and Obscurity in the Intellectual Life*, trans. Matthew K. Minerd (Steubenville, OH: Emmaus Academic, 2017), 9n11; Garrigou-Lagrange, "The Empiricist Skepticism of David Hume: A *Reductio ad absurdum* in Defense of Traditional Realism," in Minerd, *Philosophizing in Faith*, 274–76]

However, this intuition must be explained, just as philosophical reason did for the cases of substance, God, and for the soul's freedom, spirituality, and immortality.[73] We can prove, for example, that the multiplication of loaves or the resurrection of a dead man can have for its cause only the First, Creative, and Conserving Agent. The multiplication of the loaves presupposes a new production of matter; the resurrection or reunion of the soul and the body (substantial parts) presupposes an action that reaches immediately not only accidents but the very substance of the being in question—something that is proper solely to the divine action.[74] Just as one proves that the spiritual soul, which does not depend on matter in its *being*, cannot depend on it in its *becoming*, but instead must be created by God and united to a body,[75] so too one can establish that God alone can reunite it to this body. A man who is really dead cannot naturally return to life; this is so evident for common sense that the unbeliever does not place it in doubt and has no other resources than to deny the reality of the death [in question] or that of the resurrection.[76]

True, the stupendous effect to be explained cannot always appear as being an effect proper to God (e.g., on a crucifix, a heavy body remains in the air without being supported or suspended). Here the certitude that this phenomenon is not due to an unknown natural and invisible agent is analogous to that of all our predictions founded upon the law of gravity. Common sense and philosophical reason are as certain that there is a miracle in this latter case as we are all certain that a stone thrown in the air *will fall back down* and will not stop in the midst of falling because of some unknown and invisible natural agent. This certitude, no longer metaphysical, like the preceding, but physical, is connected indirectly to the first laws of being by the principle of induction.

Finally, the connection of an extraordinary phenomenon with the free, moral, and religious acts that precede it, accompany it, and follow it give common sense a moral certitude concerning God's intervention, a certitude that is connected to being through the intermediary of the moral

---

[73] We have developed this question concerning miracles at length, concerning both its possibility and its discernability from the point of view indicated here in Reginald Garrigou-Lagrange, *De Revelatione*, vol. 2, 35–107 and 325–51. [Trans. note: This citation does not refer to the final edition of the work. A translation of this text is anticipated in the near future by Emmaus Academic.]

[74] See *ST* III, supplement, q. 75, a. 3.

[75] *ST* I, q. 90, a. 2.

[76] We have treated of this question concerning the discernibility of the miracle elsewhere in *De revelatione*, 2:63–106.

principles founded on the idea of the good.

§11. Common Sense Is Thus Justified Only in Its Proper Sphere, That of Truths Susceptible to Being Connected to Being

Such are the genuine "revelations of Being," to use an expression of Le Roy. Those who have transmitted them to us are named Socrates, Plato, Aristotle, Plotinus, Saint Augustine, Saint Anselm, and Saint Thomas Aquinas; next to these intellects, the thought of Bergson is only a fanciful and amusing reverie, and its intuitive proceedings child's play. Recall the little method that, for a Bergsonian, leads one to being. It consists "in abandoning oneself (upon a bicycle) to the foreign charm of change, to the intoxication of becoming,"[77] or even more, "in the countryside, half-sheltered from the sun, under moving foliage, on a hot summer's day, in that languid and retired state of mind . . . (where we will be) dazzled, overwhelmed, broken up, and drowned under the incessant flux of brilliant images, and (where we will) at the same time feel the precise limits that fragment Nature for our ordinary outlook vanish, along with the desire for any activity."[78] Is this truly "to receive the revelations of Being?" Is it not, rather, to lose oneself in that which is not but which becomes, in non-being or in *hylē*? Plato, Aristotle, and Plotinus would say, as today Louis Couturat and Benjamin Jacob say: this is "to crash into the torrent of animal and vegetative life"; it is to say that matter is the terminus of contemplation. Up to now, we had thought that true contemplation consists in seeing all things in the light of the first principles, in their relations with Being Itself, the First Cause and the End of all things.

Therefore, the philosophy of being justifies the immutable certitudes of common sense by illuminating them with the light of the formal object of the intellect: natural reason affirms what it sees in its *formal object*. Universal consent has its reason in the *objective* evidence of the truths to which it adheres. These natural certitudes are justified again to the eyes of the phi-

---

[77] Le Roy, "Science et philosophie," 413. [Trans. note: Fr. Garrigou-Lagrange cites page 414. Also, this quote is slightly reworked to fit into his sentence, though the sentence is mostly maintained.]

[78] Le Roy, "Science et philosophie," 383. The "Midi" of Leconte de Lisle substituted for the twelfth book of the *Metaphysica* or for the *prima pars* of St. Thomas's *Summa theologiae*. [Trans. note: Fr. Garrigou-Lagrange wrongly has 384 instead of 383. Also, he has added the parenthetical remarks to make the quote fit his narrative.]

losopher inasmuch as they proceed from the rational nature that has God as its author: God who is Being Itself and, consequently, Truth Itself could not give to his creature a natural and invincible inclination that might make him to hold error as being the truth. "The teaching," says Bergson, "with regard to the idea of creation, cannot help but to lead one to think of *things* that would be created and of a *thing* that creates."[79] But never will human reason admit, as Bergson wishes, that this would involve, "a *natural illusion for our intellect*, an essentially practical function, made for representing things and states to us rather than changes and acts."[80]

However, it is very important to note that *common sense is thus justified only in its proper sphere*, in the sphere of truths that are admitted by all and necessary for each person's animal and rational life, necessary at least for beginning this life. The proper object of common sense is first and foremost the first notions and principles connected to being (*prima intelligibilia*), which are like the structure of reason. Moreover, its proper object consists in the great truths that are connected to the first notions by the first principles (the existence of God, freedom, the spirituality of the soul, and its immortality, as well as the first natural duties that are deduced from the first moral principle applied to our nature). Finally, its proper object consists in certain truths that are obtained by a spontaneous induction, like those of the physical order needed for animal life and those needed for life in society. *Outside of these limits, common sense no longer has competence*, and what are called "its particular prejudices varying with time and place" are not attributable to it, if we were to speak truly. They are the prejudices common to men of a given time and place, often the residue of certain very particular philosophical systems; they are not the prejudices of common sense. "Common sense" is not what rejected and misunderstood, at the outset, the discoveries of Christopher Columbus, of Galileo, or of William Harvey.

§12. Three Degrees of Certitude in the Judgments of Common Sense

In the second place, we must note that, in its own proper sphere, common sense does not adhere with equal certitude to all the truths that it

---

[79] Bergson, *L'évolution créatrice*, 270.

[80] Bergson, *L'évolution créatrice*, 270. [Trans. note: In both of these texts, Fr. Garrigou-Lagrange has slightly reordered Bergson's text.]

acknowledges. In each of us, the judgments of common sense are meta-physically, physically, or morally certain, depending on the nature of their object. They are metaphysically certain when their object is susceptible to being connected necessarily to being in a direct manner or in an indirect manner by a *reductio ad absurdum*, when we see that the contrary of what we affirm implies a contradiction. Our judgments of common sense have physical certitude when they are concerned with data of experience or with physical laws brought into focus through spontaneous induction. Here, we see that the contrary of what we affirm is not absolutely contradictory, at least in the sense that a supernatural cause (in miracles) can be added to those that we have identified and can change the expected effect. Our judgments of common sense have moral certitude when, in some moral matter, freedom can thwart our forecasting and render the appearances deceptive: the judge who condemns to death an accused man based on the deposition of many trustworthy witnesses is morally certain concerning the culpability of the accused person.[81]

Finally, when one makes appeal to common sense, we must carefully distinguish the common sense of humanity (otherwise called universal consent) from the common sense had by each one of us. Universal consent, invoked as a criterion by Lamennais,[82] can function only as an extrinsic criterion, an argument from authority that begets a moral certitude. In

---

[81] Here, we have a case of *speculative moral certitude*, moral certitude of a thing *that is*. Prac-tical moral certitude is concerned with something *that is to be done*. This practical moral certitude can furthermore be inferior to the preceding when speculative reason has only probabilities which have transformed into practical certitude through their congruence [*convenance*] with right will. . . . "The truth of the speculative intellect is taken through *conformity to the thing*, whereas, the truth of the practical intellect is taken through *con-formity to right appetite*, in contingent things that can be done by us" (*ST* I-II, q. 57, a. 5, ad 3). The *pragmatist* wishes to make this last degree of certitude the exemplar [*type*] of ev-ery type of certitude. [Trans. note: On this, one should also consult: Reginald Garrigou-Lagrange, "Remarks Concerning the Metaphysical Character of St. Thomas's Moral The-ology, in Particular as It Is Related to Prudence and Conscience," trans. Matthew Minerd, *Nova et Vetera* (English) 17, no. 1 (2019): 245–70; Garrigou-Lagrange, "Prudence's Place in the Organism of the Virtues," in Minerd, *Philosophizing in Faith*, 153–70; Garrigou-Lagrange, *The Sense of Mystery*, trans. Matthew Minerd (Steubenville, OH: Emmaus Aca-demic, 2017), 40–44; Garrigou-Lagrange, *The Order of Things: The Realism of the Princi-ple of Finality*, trans. Matthew K. Minerd (Steubenville, OH: Emmaus Academic, 2020), 273–86.]

[82] [Trans. note: Félicité Robert de Lamennais (1782–854), a controversial French cleric whose political and theological views involved him in the controversies surrounding Gregory XVI's encyclical *Mirari Vos* and who ultimately left communion with the Church because of his various theological, philosophical, and political views.]

each of us, on the contrary, the judgments of common sense, inasmuch as they proceed subjectively from our reason's natural inclination and are objectively motivated by the evidence of the truth, are certain with a metaphysical, physical, or moral certitude, depending upon the nature of their object.

§13. What Is the Value of This Justification of Common Sense?

We now know what common sense is, what its object is, what its limits are, and what it is worth in its own sphere. We still must ask *what, in its own turn, this conceptualist-realist theory and the philosophy of being* presented as its justification, are worth.

First, we can see that this philosophy of being does not agree with common sense by having recourse to the procedures used by the Scottish school of common sense or by eclectic thinkers. The Scottish common-sense philosophers, rather than justifying common sense by their supposed philosophy, instead wholly base the latter upon the former. Eclecticism is constituted by we-know-not-what choice of what is least contestable in various systems. The philosophy of being, by contrast, is truly a form of philosophy and proceeds from a unique principle: it is essentially a philosophy of being that explains multiplicity and becoming by real non-being (or, potency). There is its strength, though also its obscurity: fully intelligible when it speculates about being, it inevitably presents a relative absence of intelligibility when potency or non-being is involved: "Each thing is known inasmuch as it is in act, however, not inasmuch as it is in potency. Knowledge [*scientia*] primarily and principally considers being in act."[83] Let us briefly develop these different points.

§14. The Doctrine of Objective Evidence or of Evident Being; the Error of the Scottish Common-Sense Philosophers

Instead of basing itself wholly on common sense, the philosophy of being justifies common sense by means of its doctrine of *objective evidence* (or, of *evident being*). Jouffroy, following Reid, founds the certitude of the first principles on a kind of instinct of the rational nature, a sort of inspi-

---

[83] Aristotle, *Metaphysica* 8.9 (ed. Didot). See also Aquinas, *In IX metaphys.*, lec. 10.

ration or suggestion that each person experiences in himself, something that would precisely be common sense. Jouffroy, like the Scottish, thus misunderstands the nature of knowledge and does not manage to elude skepticism. Knowledge, being the knowledge of something, must be determined by this something and reach it, on pain of not being knowledge thereof. What could a form of knowledge determined by some blind natural spontaneity actually be? Our intellect, when it judges and affirms its conformity with the object, either sees this conformity or does not see it. If it sees it, its certitude no longer is based on the instinct spoken of by Reid and Jouffroy. If it does not see it, its judgment is not knowledge. In reality, evidence is what motivates our adherence, not subjective evidence, such as Descartes conceived it to be, but instead, objective evidence (or, evident being). And again, this can be understood only by means of the distinction between potency [*puissance*] and act, a distinction that is necessarily required if the intellect is a power [*puissance*] that is essentially relative to being and if it grasps it as such. Now, the intellect indeed, by reflecting back upon itself, grasps itself as a power that is *intentional* or relative to being in its absolute character and as being determinable by it. *In its very first apprehension, it knows being, that which is, before knowing itself, and without knowing it precisely as the non-self;*[84] *then, by reflection, it knows itself as relative to intentional being; then, it judges the being as distinct from itself, as the non-self;*[85] this *is the first fragmentation into object and subject.* The idea or representation is also known only through reflection and as being posterior to the represented [thing], which is the object of the direct act. And it also appears to the intellect as being essentially relative to the represented [thing], which is wholly its *raison d'être*, as that by which (*id quo*) we know, and not that which (*id quod*) we know.[86] Idealism, howev-

---

[84] See *De veritate*, q. 1, a.1.

[85] See *De veritate*, q. 1, a.9. [Trans. note: Also, on the topic of self-knowledge, see Reginald Garrigou-Lagrange, "Whether the Mind Knows Itself through Its Essence or through Some Species," in Minerd, *Philosophizing in Faith*, 79–100.]

[86] *ST* I, q. 85, a. 2. [Trans. note: In other texts, Fr. Garrigou-Lagrange more carefully notes the role of the *species intellecta expressa* as *id in quo* the known is grasped, as opposed to the *species intellecta impressa*, which properly speaking plays the role of an *id quo*. See Garrigou-Lagrange, *Order of Things*, 196n36: "Properly speaking, the *verbum mentis* is not *id quod intelligitur*, but *id in quo res concepta intelligitur*. Also, see Garrigou-Lagrange, "Whether the Mind Knows Itself," and *The One God*, trans. Bede Rose (St. Louis, MO: B. Herder, 1946), 340–41. Cf.: John N. Deely, *Intentionality and Semiotics* (Scranton, PA: University of Scranton Press, 2007), 56–71; John Frederick Peifer, *The Concept in Thomism* (New York: Bookman, 2020), 63–96, 162–64; Yves Simon, *An Introduction to the Metaphysics of Knowledge*, trans. Vukan Kuic and Richard J. Thompson

er paradoxical as it may appear, misunderstands what constitutes the idea inasmuch as it is an idea, its relative or intentional being. In this way, it destroys the very concepts of representation, of knowledge, and of the intellect. The representation is conceived of only as a reality that is relative to what is represented, knowledge as relative to the known, the intellect as relative to being. A representation that would be a representation of nothing would be, at the same time and in the same respect, something relative and an absolute. This is not only unthinkable; it is evidently impossible.

Most modern philosophers speak of the natural tendency of every representation to be objectified; this tendency must be explained, and this can be [done] only by the essentially relative character of the representation that, in direct acts of knowledge, makes one know without the representation itself being known, for it is the means of knowledge and not its terminus. If, on the contrary, one holds, with Jouffroy and Reid, that it is a blind tendency, this tendency remains an *unexplained* fact, and by it, non-knowledge is introduced into the very heart of knowledge. No more than Reid do we thereby, in the end, escape from the skepticism of Hume: is this blind tendency of our nature recognized by our mind as a fact having an infallible connection with the truth? If yes, this recognition can take place only in virtue of another criterion. If no, all our certitude rests upon a criterion about which we know not the existence or, at least, the value—which is skepticism itself.

§15. Subjective Evidence; the *Cogito Ergo Sum* Does Not Reach Its Desired Conclusion; the Veritable Opposition between the Philosophy of Being and Idealism; Are We Certain of the Objectivity of the Principle of Contradiction?

Descartes[87] and the modern idealists wish to accept only subjective evidence because, for them, the intellect knows itself before knowing being. It bases its reflection on the *cogito*; however, it could never conclude *ergo sum* without surreptitiously presupposing the ancient axiom "the object of the intellect is being." Kant and the phenomenalists saw this quite clearly.

(New York: Fordham University Press, 1990), 113–36.]

[87] [Trans. note: This section can be profitably read alongside Reginald Garrigou-Lagrange, "The Thomist Critique of the Cartesian Cogito," in Minerd, *Philosophizing in Faith*, 261–72. Moreover, see the whole of part 4 of *Philosophizing in Faith*, titled "*Garrigou pugnans*: Critical Philosophical Essays," as many of the themes taken up here are repeated throughout the chapters in that section.]

Therefore, we would need to content ourselves with saying, "cogito ergo sum cogitans." And again, even this would not be certain. According to its proper principles, idealism does not know *the reality of its action*, but only the representation that it forms of it, and were the idealist to know this reality by means of consciousness, he could not be absolutely certain that it is indeed real, for the idealist doubts the objectivity of the principle of identity, its value as a law of being. If reality can be contradictory at its foundation, nothing can assure such an idealist that the action that it holds as being real is, in fact, real. If being is not the first and formal object of the intellect, the intellect will never attain it in an evident manner. The phenomenalists are right a thousand times over. The case is closed.[88] Finally, one could no longer even say, "I think," for in its depths, the "I" is inevitably ontological. We would need to content ourselves with affirming, along with I-know-not-what German philosopher: "*There is thought*, just

---

[88] Jacques Chevalier recently accused "modern Thomists" of entirely misunderstanding Descartes when they critique him for having posited the first principle of the modern divorce between thought and being. He entirely misunderstands them himself and falls into the fault called *ignoratio elenchi*. This matter has been justly remarked on recently by Jacques Maritain in a profound study concerning Descartes that appeared as "L'esprit de Descartes," in *Les Lettres*, February and March 1922. Never, we believe, has there been a better presentation given concerning what separates Cartesianism (considered not only in its letter but formally in its spirit) from traditional philosophy and theology (especially the Thomist teaching). [Trans. note: The text of Maritain can be found in Jacques Maritain, *The Dream of Descartes*, trans. Mabelle L. Andison (London: Editions Poetry London, 1946), 24–82.]

For the subject that occupies us, Maritain shows that the judgment of the "modern Thomists" concerning the opposition between Cartesian idealism and traditional realism does not differ from that of Boutroux. See Mairtain, "L'esprit de Descartes": "When one speaks of Cartesian idealism 'enclosing thought in itself,' it is clear that one does not mean to attribute to Descartes the doctrine of Berkeley or that of Kant; no more does one claim that Descartes denied the reality of the external world, nor the existence of real objects known thanks to our ideas. Rather, what is meant is that he held that the only object reached *directly and immediately* by the act of knowledge is thought, not things, and thus, although his intentions may be realist, he, in fact, posited *the problem*, and introduced *the principle*, of modern idealism" (February 1922, p. 185).

"Boutroux puts it very well: 'The central problem of Cartesian metaphysics is the passage from thought to existence. Thought alone is indissolubly inherent to itself; therefore, how, by what right and in what sense, can we affirm existences? . . . Existence, which for the ancients was something given and perceived, merely calling for analysis, here is a remote object, which must be reached, if it is indeed possible to reach it'" (see Émile Boutroux, "De l'opportunité d'une édition nouvelle des oeuvres de Descartes," *Revue de métaphysique et de morale* 2 [1984]): 248–49).

as one says, 'It is raining in my attic.'"[89] And still, even this is not certain, for perhaps such impersonal thought is, in itself, identical to non-thought.

This is the well-worn refutation of Cartesianism offered by the Thomists in the seventeenth century.[90] The point of departure for knowledge is not the *cogito*. It is *being* and the first principle that it implies: the principle of identity, or of non-contradiction. All of ancient philosophy is contained within this expression: *the object of the intellect is being*. Nothing is intelligible except in function of being; above all, the intellect itself is not intelligible except in function of being, which it knows directly before knowing itself through reflection. Therefore, the first principles are laws of thought, a relative form of being, only because they first of all are laws of being. It is first and foremost evident that reality cannot, at one and the same time, be and not be. The whole of modern subjectivism is contained within this other expression which does not reach its desired conclusion: *cogito ergo sum*. The *cogito* reaches its conclusion only in God because only the Divine Thought, Pure Actuality, is identical with being itself. In every creature, the intellect is necessarily a power that is relative to being. Therefore, it has being and its laws for its first object, and not a given particular being (i.e., our own self). To deny this is to wish, in a perverse fashion, to imitate God, and as our thought is neither our own being nor creative of being, it is shut up in a solipsism from which nothing will enable us to escape. Modern subjectivism is, in the intellectual order, analogous to what the sin of the angel was in the moral order. The angel placed its ultimate end *in itself* and immobilized itself in evil; Descartes, "the inventor of the philosophy of the Ego [du *Moi*]," has placed the terminus of the intellect within man and has definitively closed off the only route that leads to God. Descartes and Kant, the founders of idealism, are great, fallen intellects; this is why the enemies of the Church have so greatly availed themselves of them. In their school, modern philosophy and modern society have lost the notion

---

[89] [Trans. note: Fr. Garrigou-Lagrange is playing on the impersonal French paralleling *li pense* with *il pleut*.]

[90] See Antoine Goudin, *Philosophia*, pt. 4, disp. 1, q.1 (1860 edition, vol. 4), 254: "However, Descartes is not to be tolerated here when he commands that the mind, for the time being holding every other exposited principle in doubt, begin its knowledge of things with, 'I think,' from which it would immediately infer: 'Therefore, I am.' For, so without arguing about other points [*ut coetera non urgeam*], if the mind were to set aside even our own principle, along with all the others, as something that must remain doubtful, another doubt will remain: *whether he who thinks exists or does not*. For he could think and, nonetheless, not exist, if it were possible that *one and the same thing could be and not be*."

of God. "The fathers have eaten sour grapes, and the children's teeth are set on edge" (Jer 31:29).

Between ancient philosophy and idealism, what we must ask is whether or not we are certain of the objectivity of the principle of identity (or, of non-contradiction) if it is evident for us that the absurd is not only *un-thinkable* but also *impossible*. Would Le Roy and Maurice Blondel like to respond categorically to this question? To our eyes, this involves a form of evidence, the very first evidence. We feel ourselves to be dominated and measured by it—that is, by evident being—and in this very first adherence, our creaturely intellect appears as being potential and conditioned.[91]

---

[91] See Alberto Lepidi, O.P., *Ontologia*, 35. [Trans. note: Edition unnamed.]

We are not unaware of what was written in Charles Renouvier, *Dilemmes de la métaphysique pure* (Paris: Alcan, 1901), 2–3: "For lack of having been able to discover the first truth in the form and denomination of a *subject of existence* at one and the same time independent and defined without possible dispute, one has believed oneself at least to hold a universal and unshakeable *principle of affirmation* in the principle of contradiction, which is only concerned with relations. However, wholly to the contrary, and because it is concerned with relations in a general manner, this principle is what gives way to the most profound division and in its applications, whether accepted or denied, furnishes a matter of irreducible oppositions between metaphysical theories.... Nothing prevents one, after having thought separately about two propositions which the mind is incapable of conceiving as being simultaneously thinkable, from declaring that they are nevertheless both true of their subject taken in itself. However, for discursive thought, discourse and controversy, the reunion of two assertions in a like case is impossible; thus, submission to the principle of contradiction is compulsory."

We are content to oppose against these comments a remark from François Evellin: "Despite a long-lived prejudice, the problem relative to the scope of the principle of [non-]contradiction does not seem to us to be resolved. It may be, and we believe it to be, the case that the principle of principles is more than the essential requirement of thought; we must seek it out as the primitive law, the fundamental law, at the very root of being. Here, we can only indicate our opinion, only a word will suffice to make it understood: the principle of [non]-contradiction requires, for example, that a length cannot be, at the same moment and in the same circumstances, simultaneously one meter and ten meters. What is the meaning of this requirement? Does it mean that thought cannot conceive the fact, though the fact in itself is very possible? If it were, *being would lose precisely what makes it being, that is to say, its self-identity, and consequently, would no longer be.* All would disappear into an elusive flux. Perhaps, therefore, the principle "That which is" has its fulcrum in nature, or rather, we willingly say that *it itself is what constitutes nature by freeing it in its depths from the phenomenon.* (The principle of substance is only a determination of the principle of identity.) The phenomenon does not exist because I think it; rather, it is because it exists, living among things, that my thought, concerned, like all other things, with guarding its self-identity, is defended like all the others against the contradiction that would destroy it. The imagination harasses speculative reason by objecting to it that its affirmations have nothing to do with

And if this is truly so, we have an explanation for the infallibility of common sense's adherence to the very first speculative and practical principles: it sees them immediately in being, its formal object. As Aristotle said, just as vision (setting aside every case of organic lesion) cannot misinform us about its proper object, color, but only on account of errors of associations concerning a common sensible such as extension or concerning a *per accidens* visible such as taste, and just as the will, however perverse it may be, cannot will the evil for its own sake, but instead always wills it under the notion of the good, so too spontaneous understanding cannot err in its knowledge of its first object and in the simple notions that are immediately connected to it.[92] These simple notions are either known or not known, but one cannot know them halfway, distorting them, for the very reason that they are simple. As Saint Thomas explains:

In simple things, in whose definitions composition cannot intervene, we cannot be deceived. Instead, *we fail by wholly not arriving at them*, as is said in *Metaphysics* 9.[93] And for this reason, we cannot err concerning those propositions which are immediately known, once the quiddity of the terms are known, just as is the case for the first principles, which are the source for the infallibility of truth had in our certitude concerning the conclusions had through scientific knowledge.[94]

---

the sensible and that what it proposes cannot be seen, but reason is defended without difficulty: in addition to the fact that for it reality cannot be seen, it can show that at each step its rival's argumentation is at fault. This is the drama of the life of the mind" (*Congrès de Métaphysique* [Paris, 1900], 175). Between Le Roy and us, partisans of the philosophy of the concept, the problem is located here and not elsewhere. At bottom, it is nothing other than the opposition of imagination to reason. With Evellin, we think that "rational thought, which is superior to empirical thought, is established and in some manner seated within the objective reality of the absolute."

Concerning Hegelian arguments, see Zigliara, *Summa philosophica*, 1:243–52 and 1:331. We will summarize this classic defense of the principle of contradiction in the second appendix in ch. 2 of pt. 2 of the present volume.

[92] Even if vision could deceive us as regards color (physical certitude), it would not follow that the intellect could deceive us as regards being and those things that are immediately connected to it (metaphysical certitude).

[93] Aristotle, *Metaphysica* 8.10 (ed. Didot). See also Aquinas, *In* IX *metaphys.*, lec. 11.

[94] *ST* I, q. 85, a. 6.

§16. The Objection against the Objective Value of the Principle of Identity

According to Aristotle,[95] one cannot deny the very first principles without lying, without rendering thought impossible, without falling into self-contradiction and renouncing oneself in the practical life. He who denies them speaks meaningless words. "In what way does such a man differ from a plant?" Like the plant, he is shut up within himself; he cannot go forth from himself. Aristotle recognized, however, that, despite the absurdity of these denials, it can be explained by the fact that the ever-changing appearance of sensible things has given birth to such denials, not in the intellect but, instead, in the imaginations of some people. As François Evellin says today, "The imagination harasses speculative reason by objecting to it that its affirmations have nothing to do with the sensible."[96]

Indeed, such is the origin of the Heraclitian objection raised against the objective value of the principle of identity (or, of non-contradiction). If we look at the sensible world, Heraclitus tells us, we will see that, in reality, *nothing is*; instead, *all becomes*: "We never step into the same river twice."

This is the theme expanded on today by Bergson. If we wish to put the objection in a logical form, we will say like the ancient sophists:[97] "All that becomes, before becoming, is *non-being*, for that which already is cannot become, for it already is (*ex ente non fit ens, quia iam est ens*); however, on the other hand, nothing can arise from non-being or from nothingness (*ex nihilo, nihil fit*). Therefore, at the origin of becoming, we must admit a *non-being* that belongs to *being*. Becoming arises from something that, at one and the same time, *is* and *is not*. Holding that both being and non-being are pure abstractions, words which have no profound meaning (absolute nominalism), the only thing in reality is becoming, which is self-explanatory. At its foundation, reality is not self-identical; it ceaselessly changes. Nothing is, all becomes, and in [such] self-explanatory becoming contradictories are identified with each other." Thus, remarks Aristotle, Heraclitus is said to have denied the principle of contradiction (or, of non-contradiction [*sic*]), since he affirmed that each thing is and is not. However, the Stagirite adds, "We

[95] Aristotle, *Metaphysica* 4.4–5.
[96] Evellin, *Congrès de Métaphysique*, 175.
[97] See this objection, such as it is reported by Aristotle in *Physica* 1.8 (Aquinas commentary, lec. 16).

need not actually think everything we happen to say."[98]

Aristotle himself responds to this objection from Heraclitus by means of his notion of *potency* (or, of undetermined being), a kind of middle between being in act and pure nothingness. Potency, like the seed contained in the acorn from which the oak comes forth, from one perspective *is* and from another *is not*.[99] Potency is non-being in relation to act (or, to determined or developed being). It is non-act. Nevertheless, from another perspective, it is called *being (ens secundum quid)*, in opposition to nothingness, which is not only non-being relative to act, but absolute non-being.

Thus, Aristotle remarks, what becomes, like the tree in its own self-development, arises from a potency that contains it in germ, a middle between determined being and pure nothingness. The same is true for a science that develops in an intellect (or, an intellectual power).

Now, this potency, since by itself it is not act, cannot by itself pass to act. It must be reduced to it by a prior act, by an active potency [*puissance*]; what is heated must be heated by a source of heat. However, for the same reason, this active potency must be pre-moved or actuated, and pre-moved, in the final analysis, by an ultimate active power [*puissance*], which in order to suffice for this must be its own activity and, therefore, Being itself, for action follows being and the mode of acting follows the mode of being. In this way, we have an explanation for becoming, and the principle of identity (or, non-contradiction) is maintained in all beings and is realized in all its purity in the First Being.

* * *

It is not useless to recall here the dialectical objection raised by Hegel against the same principle. It is set forth at length in his [*Science of*] *Logic*.[100] Broadly speaking, it is reduced to this:

> *Being* is the most universal notion. However, by this very fact, it is also the poorest notion. To be white, to be black, to be extended—this is to be something. However, to be without any determination—this is

---

[98] See Aristotle, *Metaphysica* 4.3ff, on the defense of the principle of contradiction and of the value of the notion of being that founds this principle.

[99] See Aristotle: *Physica* 1.8; *Metaphysica* 4(3).3–5; *Metaphysica* 9(8) in whole. In the present volume, see pt. 2 ("Common Sense and the Proofs of God's Existence"), ch. 2, §4.

[100] [Trans. note: He literally says, "It is set forth at length in the *La logique de Hegel*, trans. A. Vera, 2nd ed., vol. 1, p. 399–408." He also cites, in footnote, Georges Nöel, *La Logique de Hégel* (Paris: Alcan, 1897), 24 and 135.]

to be nothing, it is not to be. Therefore, being purely and simply is the same as non-being. It is, at one and the same time, itself and its contrary. If it were only itself, it would remain immobile and sterile; if it were only nothingness, it would be synonymous with nil [*zéro*] and, in this case still perfectly powerless and infertile. The contradiction that it contains requires it to develop itself in the form of becoming in which non-being and being are merged and reconciled.[101]

As Tommaso Maria Zigliara shows, this is a sophistical argument.[102] Put into logical form, it comes down to this: *Pure being is pure indetermination; now, pure indetermination is pure non-being; therefore, pure being is pure non-being.* It is easy to see that the middle term *pure indetermination* is taken in two different senses. In the major premise, it designates only the denial of generic, specific, and individual determinations; in the minor premise, it designates the very denial of the transcendental being-ness [*entité*] that dominates all genera; it denies determinations not only of *such* being-ness, but of being-ness itself.

Moreover, Hegel must confess that, "if it is true to say that being and non-being are the same, it is also wholly true to say that they differ and that one is not what the other is."[103] The denial of the principle of contradiction destroys itself; moreover, it is as much a denial as it is an affirmation, as true as it is false.

Augusto Vera, in his introduction [to his translation of Hegel's *Logic*], claims: "A logic that teaches that the principle of contradiction is the criterion of truth will go against the very nature of things. Indeed, if this principle were true, it would be logical to say: *man is a being endowed with the faculty of laughing*; however, it would be illogical to affirm: *man is a being endowed with the faculty of crying*."[104] The sophism committed here is puerile: the faculty of crying is not the negation of the faculty of laughing in the same way as non-being is the negation of being. These are two positive faculties that are opposed only with regard to the same object considered in the same respect. Man does not have the faculty of laughing and of crying about the same thing considered from the same perspective.

In recent times, it has been claimed that Hegel "never claimed that con-

---

[101] [Trans. note: The text is Fr. Garrigou-Lagrange's own summarization.]
[102] See Zigliara, *Summa philosophica*, 1:246.
[103] [Trans. note: Following the French translation cited by Fr. Garrigou-Lagrange, 1:404.]
[104] *La logique de Hegel*, trans. A. Vera, 2nd ed., 1:41.

tradictories are identical."[105] Nevertheless, he teaches quite clearly that the principle of identity (or, of non-contradiction [sic]) can be only a law of inferior reason, which reasons concerning immobile abstractions; it is not, he says, a law of the intellect, which, like reality, is *pure becoming, a perpetual absence of identity*. And it is clear that every doctrine of pure becoming is the denial of the real (or, ontological) value of the principle of identity (or, of contradiction), as Aristotle has shown[106] against Heraclitus, whose fundamental thesis, which is absolute evolutionism, was taken up anew by Hegel.

Once this doctrine is admitted, it is necessary to say with Bergson: "There is *more* in becoming than in the immobile,"[107] and to add with his disciple Le Roy:

The principle of non-contradiction [sic] is not as universal and necessary as it is believed to be. It has its domain of application and has its restricted, limited meaning. As the ultimate law of *discourse* and not of *thought in general*, it holds only for the *static*, the fragmented, the *immobile*—in brief, it holds for things endowed with an *identity*. However, there is contradiction in the world, just as there is identity. It is made up of fleeting mobilities—becoming, duration, life—which by themselves are not discursive and are transformed by discourse in order to grasp them in contradictory schemata.[108]

And given that, in this doctrine, reality is, at bottom, *pure becoming*, it is

---

[105] See *Le dictionnaire apologétique*, the article on *Pantheism*, col. 1327. Against certain assertions contained in this article (cols. 1326–27), we ought not be surprised that even genial intellects fall into radical absurdity as soon as they deeply alter the first notion of our mind, the notion of *being*, the foundation for the principle of contradiction, and when, in place of God, *Being Itself*, they wish to posit a creative evolution which is self-explanatory. One must not fear seeing the error as it is and saying that the denial of the true God and of his absolutely immutable nature posits a contradiction to the principle of all things. Not to recognize the value of this critique of evolutionist pantheism is, perhaps, to appear to be a very wise historian of philosophy, but to others, it is to show that one has never understood the nature of the essential vice of absolute evolutionism.

We would have liked to have seen this foundational absurdity of pantheism, indeed of all forms of pantheism, placed better in relief in the article dedicated to this subject in the *Dictionnaire apologétique*. We will return to it at the end of the pt. 2 of the present volume.

[106] See Aristotle, *Metaphysica* 4.

[107] Bergson, *L'évolution créatrice*, 341–42.

[108] Éduoard Le Roy, "Sur la logique de l'invention," *Revue de métaphysique et morale* 13 (1905): 200–204.

realized contradiction, radical absurdity, something completely opposed to Self-Subsistent Being, [which is] always self-identical, in eternal immobility. All this presupposes that becoming can exist without a cause, that there is *more* in it than in the immobile, as Bergson holds. However, to hold this is to say that *there is more in what becomes and does not yet exist than in what is*, more in the seed than in the fully developed oak, more in the embryo than in the adult man, more in time than in eternity, more in the continual wanderings of the sophists than in the immutable knowledge that attains all times past and to come in a single intuition.

§17. If the Principle of Identity Is the Fundamental Law of Reality and if Becoming and Multiplicity Can Be Explained Only by Potency, Then Common Sense and the Philosophy of Being Have Won Their Case against Phenomenalism and the Philosophy of Becoming

Thus, we return always to the first division of being into potency and act. This is the essential characteristic of Aristotelianism; it is what gives it its power, as well as its obscurity. A strange philosophy, our neo-positivists say, one that is ready-made, with its *Scholastic entities*, claiming to escape from all antinomies by means of this singular affirmation of the reality of potency, a kind of middle between being and pure nothingness. All the antinomies exchanged for just one: that of a *non-being that is*.

Such is, nevertheless, the only philosophy that is fully in agreement with common sense. It succeeds at rejoining it in virtue of the effort of abstraction that it presupposes, as true art succeeds at exceeding the artificial and rejoins nature. Ready-made, with its Scholastic entities! Obviously, since it presents itself as a philosophy of being: substances and faculties (potencies, proximate principles of operation) are required by the principle of identity. "It itself," say Evellin, "constitutes nature by freeing it, in its depths, from the phenomena."[109] The choice must be made: either the philosophy of being, with its Scholastic entities (substance and potency), or the philosophy of phenomena and of becoming. And the alternative amounts to this other choice: yes or no, is the principle of identity the fundamental law of reality?

(1) If the principle of identity is the fundamental law of reality, the multiple phenomena and becoming (a union of the diverse) presuppose a fun-

---

[109] Evellin, *Congrès de Métaphysique*, 175.

damental reality that is wholly and entirely self-identical, is related to being as A is to A, *Self-Subsistent Being* or *Pure Act*. (2) If the principle of identity is the fundamental law of reality, multiplicity and becoming are intelligible only if one acknowledges that they contain an intermediary between *pure being* and *pure nothingness: potency*. Therefore, there is no multiplicity, no becoming at the heart of the fundamental reality, Pure Being, which is absolutely one and immutable and, by that fact, transcendent and distinct from the essentially composite and changing universe. (3) If the principle of identity is the fundamental law of reality, different groups of relatively autonomous, multiple and transitory phenomena are explained only by a subject that is one and permanent (*substance*). These substances, merely by the fact that they are multiple, each must be composed of potency and act (essence and existence), and in this respect, it is not contradictory to say that they would contain a multiplicity of phenomena and becoming. By contrast, it is necessary that they be endowed with operative powers [*puissances*], for given that they are not pure act, they are not, by themselves, their own activity, any more than they are their own existence; only he who is *Ipsum Esse* is simultaneously he who is *Ipsum agere*.[110] Action presupposes being, and the mode of acting follows upon the mode of being.

If, on the contrary, the principle of identity is not the fundamental law of reality, phenomenalism and the philosophy of becoming have won their case; but, then, one must affirm with Hegel that the fundamental law of reality is absurdity or contradiction. There is no middle, given that the principle of non-contradiction [*sic*] is nothing other than the negative formula of the principle of identity—to deny the objective value of the one is to deny the objective value of the other. At two extreme poles of philosophical thought, Parmenides affirms that being is, that non-being is not, denying, in virtue of this principle, multiplicity and becoming. Heraclitus and Hegel, all the while maintaining the value of the principle of identity as a merely logical law, deny its real value. According to them, at bottom, being is identical to non-being: nothing is; everything becomes. Émile Boutroux asks himself, "Between the Eleatic doctrine and the doctrine of Hegel, which is true?"[111] "In all likelihood, neither the one, nor the other," he responds. We say: "Ob-

---

[110] See *ST* I, q. 54, a. 1: "Whether the angel's understanding is its substance." This question 54 of the treatise of the angels, along with q. 3 of the *prima pars*, contains the fundamental principles of Thomistic metaphysics. The treatise on the angels is particularly important as a treatise on the first creature or on the creature as such.

[111] Émile Boutroux, *De l'idée de loi naturelle dans la science et la philosophie contemporaines: Cours professé à la Sorbonne en 1892–1893*, 2nd ed. (Paris: Lecène, Oudin et Cie), 18.

viously, neither the one nor the other." Against Parmenides: becoming and multiplicity are givens (in brute experience and in conceptual knowledge). Against Heraclitus and Hegel: nothing is intelligible except in function of being and in function of the principle of identity. Only one solution is possible, that of Plato and Aristotle: *non-being is*, undetermined being, potency, which from one perspective is and from another is not. It provides the only reconciliation of experience, which presents us diversity and change, with reason, which forever seeks the one and immutable—the reconciliation of empiricism and rationalism. The philosophy of being, divided into potency and act, thus emerges as the only philosophy that, at one and the same time, takes into account the facts and the principle of non-contradiction. Every other philosophy is driven either to deny, with the Eleatics, the facts, or to deny, with Heraclitus, Hegel, and Bergson, the objectivity of the very first rational principle. A philosophy of phenomena or a philosophy of becoming contains only one part of the truth, for they acknowledge only one part of reality—this surface with multiple changing forms that experience directly reaches. Their error consists in making this surface of reality out to be the Absolute; there is no Absolute except the Absolute. A is A.

This philosophy of being, like common sense itself, is at once clear and obscure: clear by the place that it gives to act, obscure by the place that it gives to potency: "Each thing is known inasmuch as it is in act, however, not inasmuch as it is in potency."[112] Should we be astonished at this obscurity? At bottom, this relative absence of determination and intelligibility is what enables us to make room for divine and human freedom, to conceive of the existence of the created next to the Uncreated, the finite next to the Infinite, the multiple and changing next to the One and Immutable God. God alone is fully intelligible in all that he is, for he is Being Itself, Pure Actuality. The world, by contrast, to the degree it contains multiplicity and becoming, is a *non-being that is*, as Plato says. By this very fact, it is something obscure in itself. Such is the hardiest affirmation of Platonic, Aristotelian, and Thomistic metaphysics: there is a middle between being and pure nothingness, non-being, or, potency. The creature is distinct from God on account of the fact that it is a composite of non-being and being, of potency and act, of real essence and existence, of operative potency [*puissance*] and action. This affirmation, however abstract and paradoxical as it may appear, merely makes explicit an insight of common sense. One does not need to have intensely studied Plato's *Sophist* or Aristotle's *Metaphysics* in order to find a meaning for this utterance by God to Moses: *I*

---

[112] Aquinas, *In IX metaphys.*, lec. 10.

am who am (as though to say, Him in comparison to whom those mutable things that have been made *are not*);[113] or this word of our Savior to Saint Catherine of Siena: "I am He Who Is, you are she who is not."[114]

Common sense, such as we have defined it, has the same value as the principle of identity.[115]

---

[113] See Augustine, *De civate Dei* 8.11.

[114] See Bl. Raymond de Capua, *Vie de saint Catherine de Sienne* (Paris: Poussielgue, 1859). On page 70, see how the Saint made this the rule of her whole life.

[115] It is in part for not having understood well the sense and scope of the notion of *potency* in the Aristotelian doctrine that Jacques Chevalier, in his 1915 thesis on *La notion du nécessaire chez Aristote*, held that this doctrine should lead, from the perspective of knowledge, to panlogism and, from the perspective of reality, to pantheism: only the necessary and the general would exist. On the contrary, Aristotle ceaselessly affirms that the singular alone exists in reality, that contingency, and even chance, has its place next to the necessary, that our will is a free cause of its acts (e.g., see: *De interpretatione* 9; *Physica* 2.4–6; *Metaphysica* 5.30; *Ethica nicomachea* 3.7, etc.). The misunderstanding of one of the cornerstones of the Aristotelian system leads J[ules] Chevalier to declare that, "even in the principles of Aristotle, there is something rotten." On this account, it would be necessary to say the same concerning the principles of St. Thomas's philosophy, although the author defends them very firmly.

Part 2

Common Sense and the Traditional Proofs of God's Existence

The preceding study concerning common sense and the philosophy of being would be incomplete and would fail to reach its ultimate goal if we did not show that it implicitly contains a response—indeed, a decisive one, we believe—to the objections that have been registered recently against the Thomistic proofs for God's existence.

First, we will establish what, for Saint Thomas, is the value of the principle of *raison d'être* upon which all these proofs rest. We will do so by setting forth in detail the connection of this principle with the principle of identity and the idea of being.

Second, we will set forth and examine the criticism presented by Le Roy against the Thomist proofs for God's existence.

Finally, we will see with what proof the new philosophy replaces the traditional proofs and whether it leads to the evolutionist pantheism condemned by the [First] Vatican Council.

Chapter 1

————— ∾⨯⨯⨯⨯∾ —————

HOW THE PRINCIPLE OF *RAISON D'ÊTRE* IS CONNECTED TO THE PRINCIPLE OF IDENTITY (ACCORDING TO SAINT THOMAS)[1]

The classical (or, conceptualist-realist) theory of common sense has shown us a rudimentary philosophy of being contained in it. It has justified the spontaneous certitudes of common sense by establishing their relationship with being, the formal object of the intellect, and with the principle of identity. This reduction to being is brought about by the reduction of the principles of induction, causality, and finality to the principle of *raison d'être*, and by the connection of this last to the principle of identity (immediately implied in the idea of being), of which the principle of substance is only a determination.

Of all these reductions, the principal one is that of the principle of *raison d'être* to the principle of identity. In our preceding study, we were able to provide only a very succinct exposition of this; it requires *ex professo* treatment if one wishes to understand the Thomist proofs for God's existence. The occasion for this discussion is furnished by an article by Amédée Bouyssonie concerning the "reduction of the principles of reason to unity,"[2] wherein the author tries to show the weak points of the thesis

---

1 This chapter appeared originally as Reginald Garrigou-Lagrange, "Comment le principe de la raison d'être se rattache au principe d'identité d'après saint Thomas," *Revue thomiste* 16 (1908): 422–42.

2 Amédée Bouyssonie, "De la réduction à l'unité des principes de la raison," *Revue de philosophie* 13 (1908): 107–22.

that we have set forth[3] and presented as an Aristotelian doctrine received in the School. We are told there is neither a direct and absolute reduction that would consist in connecting all the other principles to a supreme principle to the point of identifying them with it, nor even an indirect reduction that would consist only in showing that one is led to deny an ultimate principle if one denies the other principles. In reality, there would be no ultimate principle. "The value of the principle of identity is not superior to that of sufficient reason [*raison suffisante*],"[4] and "there is no *contradiction* involved, only *unintelligibility*,"[5] in denying the principle of sufficient reason. Here once again, we find ourselves faced with the Kantian thesis.

We can only thank Monsieur Bouyssonie. His often very tight argumentation will require us to give precision to our ideas concerning this question, which is, we believe, one of the most important ones in general metaphysics.

(1) We will state the classical thesis in its general formulation; (2) we will see how Saint Thomas establishes that there is an ultimate principle; (3) we will seek the exact formulation of this principle; (4) we will show how the other principles are connected to it; (5) we will indicate an important consequence of this thesis in natural theology.[6]

§1. The Classical Thesis in Its General Formulation

The thesis that we sustained in our earlier articles is the classical thesis: "Metaphysics explains and defends all the principles, not indeed ostensively [directly],[7] but rather, by reducing [*deducendo*] to impossibility and

---

[3] Above [in pt. 1 of the present volume] and in Reginald Garrigou-Lagrange, "Intellectualisme et liberté chez saint Thomas: Accord du libre arbitre et du principe de raison d'être ou de raison suffisante," *Revue des sciences philosophiques at théologiques* 2 (1908): 5–32.

[4] [Trans. note: From here on, I will translate *raison suffisant* as "sufficient reason" and *raison d'être* by reproducing the French.]

[5] The remarks are those of Bouyssonie.

[6] [Trans. note: The text reads *théodicée*. As Fr. Garrigou-Lagrange shows elsewhere in his *oeuvre*, while his vocabulary is somewhat constrained because of the ecclesiastical system of his day, he is not an adherent of the Wolffian schema of sciences. In particular, see the Reginald Garrigou-Lagrange, "The Order of the Philosophical Sciences," in *The Order of Things: The Realism of the Principle of Finality*, trans. Matthew Minerd (Steubenville, OH: Emmaus Academic, 2020), 225–50.]

[7] [Trans. note: On the distinction between ostensive and non-ostensive demonstration, see Austin Woodbury, *Logic*, ch. 31, 351A : "The types of demonstration we have been

to that supreme principle: *it is impossible for one and the same thing to be and not be.*" This thesis is formulated and defended by Aristotle in the fourth book of his *Metaphysics*.[8] After having explained this in this place in his commentary, Saint Thomas reproduced it many times in his own works. He summarizes the *a priori* reason for it in this passage from the *Summa theologiae [ST]* I-II, q. 94, a. 2: "What first falls into apprehension is being, the understanding of which is included in all things whatsoever one apprehends. And therefore, the first indemonstrable principle is that 'something is not affirmed and denied at the same time,' which is founded on the notion of being and non-being; and all the other principles are founded on this principle, as the Philosopher says in *Metaphysics* 4."[9] It is nearly the same formula that we find in *De veritate*, q. 1, a. 1: "Being is that which the intellect first conceives, as it were, as what is most known and in which it resolves all of its conceptions." [Likewise] in *Summa contra gentiles [SCG]* II, ch. 83: "The intellect naturally knows *being* and those things that belong *per se* to being as such, upon which its knowledge of the first principles is founded." Many other similar texts could be cited.

This thesis is unanimously accepted among Scholastic authors.[10] If there has been a discussion among the Scholastics, it is only concerning this secondary question: is the ultimate principle the principle of contra-

---

discussing heretofore show that the predicate befits the subject, and for that reason they are called OSTENSIVE or DIRECT demonstration. They pertain only to propositions that are NOT SELF-EVIDENT (*non per se notas*). However, if we wish, by some demonstration, to manifest SELF-EVIDENT propositions (*propositiones per se notas*), we must employ INDIRECT or APAGOGIC demonstration, also called demonstration THROUGH THE ABSURD. Such a demonstration shows, through IMPOSSIBLE CAUSES or through IMPOSSIBLE EFFECTS that P befits S" (p. 276; from The John N. Deely and Anthony Russell Collection, Latimer Family Library, St. Vincent College, Latrobe, PA). He then follows with examples. I have slightly edited this for readability; the use of all capitals for certain words is a unique convention original to Woodbury.]

8 See Aquinas, *In* IV *metaphys.*, lec. 6, commenting on *Metaphysica* 3.3 (éd. Didot).

9 [Trans. note: The text reads "*IV Met.*, text. 9."]

10 E.g.: John Duns Scotus *In* IV *metaphys.*, q. 3; Thomas de Vio Cajetan, *In de ente et essentia*, praemium, q. 1; Fonseca, *In* IV *meataphys.*, c. 3, q. 1, sec. 3 [Trans. note: almost certainly Pedro de Fonseca, S.J. (1528–1599)]; Francisco Suárez, *Disputatieones metaphysicae*, disp. 3, sec. 3, no. 9; John of St. Thomas, *Cursus philosphicus*, q. 25, a. 2; Goudin (1860 ed.), vol. 4, p. 254 [Trans. note: presumably *Philosophia juxta inconcussa, tutissimaque divi Thomæ dogmata quatuor tomis comprehensa*]; Joseph Kleutgen, *Phil. scol.*, no. 293–94; Tommaso Maria Zigliara, *Ontologia*, p .236, and *De la lumière intellectuelle*, vol. 3, p. 255; Delmas, *Ontologia*, p. 642 [Trans. note: almost certainly Charles Delmas, S.J., a late-nineteenth- and early-twentieth-century Jesuit].

diction,[11] "one and the same thing cannot be and not be" (or, from the logical perspective, "the same thing cannot be affirmed and denied of the same thing"), or would it not be, rather, the affirmative principle of the excluded middle [*du tiers exclu*], often cited by Aristotle—"It necessary that something be or not be"—or the simplest affirmative formulation, "Every being is a being."[12]

§2. How Saint Thomas Establishes That There Is an Ultimate Principle

Aristotle does not explicitly prove that there must be an ultimate principle. He is content with determining the conditions for it. We find this proof set forth in Saint Thomas's commentary. In the fourth book of the *Metaphysics* (*lectio* 6 of Saint Thomas's commentary), Aristotle first shows that it belongs to the metaphysician, who studies being inasmuch as it is being, to treat the most universal principles, which are concerned not with a specific modality of being, but rather with everything that can be known. He then enumerates the conditions that the most certain principle, *bebaiotatē archē* [Gk.], must fulfill: (1) this must be a principle about which every kind of error is impossible, for one commits errors only about those things which one does not know ["car c'est sur les choses qu'on ne connaît pas qu'on se trompe"]; (2) it must not presuppose any prior truth, since it is necessary for knowing whatever there is; (3) it must be naturally in us, prior to every investigation by the mind, since such investigation presupposes it. What is the principle that fulfills these conditions? It is, says Aristotle, the principle that "it is impossible that the same attribute belong and not belong to the same subject at the same time in the same respect." Indeed, (1) it is not possible that anyone ever conceive that the same thing at the same time exists and does not exist. This would be to posit an affirmation that denies itself. Heraclitus is of another opinion according to some; however, one need not think everything that one happens to say. (2) This principle does not presuppose another principle. (3)

---

[11] [Trans. note: As noted in previous chapters, Fr. Garrigou-Lagrange most often uses "principle of contradiction" for what is most commonly referred to now as the "principle of non-contradiction." Thus, on the rarer occasions when he does use "principle of non-contradiction" for the same, I mark those instances with "[*sic*]" to signal that he means the same thing as in most places he means by "principle of contradiction" (and we now commonly mean by "principle of non-contradiction").]

[12] See Suárez, *Disp. met.*, disp. 3, sec. 3, no. 9.

Our intellect possesses it from the time that it conceives being, prior to all investigations. "It is therefore to this principle that all demonstrations are ultimately reduced: of its nature, it is the principle of all the other axioms," *physei gar archē kai tōn allōn axiōmatōn autē pantō* [Gk.].

In order to render this doctrine of Aristotle more evident, Saint Thomas, in his commentary, establishes that there must be an ultimate principle. For this, he compares the first two operations of the mind: conception and judgment. By means of the first operation, "which is called the understanding of indivisibles," we conceive what a thing is (*quod quid est*), and by the second, we affirm at least that a thing is or that a thing is such (*an sit*). One does not go back infinitely in the series of concepts; the analysis of the most comprehensive concepts leads us, by degrees, to the most simple and universal concept of all, the concept of being, that which is or can be; without this very first idea, the intellect cannot conceive anything. "Being is the focal point where all the rays that are reflected by all the intelligibles are concentrated and whence they radiate forth";[13] it is that by which the intellect attains anything whatsoever, it is its formal object,[14] just as the formal object of sight is color and that of hearing sound. If there is a first in the series of concepts, the same must hold true in the series of judgments. And the simplest and most universal first judgment must depend upon the first idea; it must have as a subject *being* and as its predicate that which necessarily agrees with being. This first judgment, prior to all the others, must command all the others; it must be, along with the idea that it implies, the first objective light of our ontological [acts of] knowledge [*connaissances*].

"It seems arbitrary," we are told, "to decree *a priori* that there cannot be many independent principles without suppressing the unity of knowledge.... We must seek out, through analysis of this thought such as it presents itself to us through experience, the principles upon which it depends. If this analysis reveals only one such principle, it will be said that there is only one, and if such analysis reveals many of them, it will be said that there are many of them."[15]

The partially *a priori* determination made by Aristotle and given precision by Saint Thomas is not arbitrary. The analysis of our ideas shows in an incontestable manner that the very first idea implied in all the others

---

[13] Zigliara, *De la lumière intellectuelle*, 3:201.

[14] The intelligible center of every concept, being will also be the link of every judgment (the verb "to be") and of all reasoning.

[15] Bouyssonie, "De la réduction," 122.

THE PRINCIPLE OF *RAISON D'ÊTRE* AND THE PRINCIPLE OF IDENTITY

is the idea of being; from there one legitimately deduces that the very first judgment must have being for its subject and what first agrees with being as its predicate; by itself, this judgment must be implied in all the others. And since being is not a genus determined by extrinsic differences, but instead a transcendental that permeates the ultimate differences of things, we can already see that the ultimate principle is also a transcendental and that no modality of being can escape it. What we still must show *a posteriori* and in detail is how the other principles are connected to it; however, we already know that they necessarily depend upon it. Similarly, when through analysis of a finite being we have demonstrated that it has as the cause of its being *Self-Subsistent Being*, we can then deduce that the *Being Itself* is the cause of all beings that are other than it, whatever they may be.

Saint Thomas reasons *a priori* in a similar manner so as to establish that man has only one ultimate end.[16]

§3. What Is the Exact Formulation of the Ultimate Principle?

We have held as certain up to now that the ultimate principle must have being for its subject and what first agrees with being as its predicate. What will be its exact formulation? Aristotle says, from the perspective of logic, "it is impossible that the same attribute belong and not belong to the same subject at the same time in the same respect," or, from that of metaphysics: "One and the same being cannot be and not be at the same time in the same respect." Bouyssonie, who accepts this formulation of the principle of contradiction, notes that we must first of all to avoid employing the ideas of possibility and impossibility, of relation and time, and content ourselves with the ideas of being and of non-being: "Being is not non-being, that which is is not that which is not." Indeed, it is in function of new

---

[16] *ST* I-II, q. 1, a. 5: "Just as in the process of reasoning the principle is that which is naturally known, so too in the process of the rational appetite, which is the will, there must be a principle that is naturally desired. Now, this must be one, for nature tends only to one thing. However, the principle in the process of the rational appetite is the ultimate end. Whence, that to which the will tends from the perspective of the ultimate end must be one." [Trans. note: This needs to be read in light of what Fr. Garrigou-Lagrange says elsewhere concerning the distinction between man's natural end and his supernatural end, along with the subordination of the former to the latter. See Reginald Garrigou-Lagrange, "Immutabilité des vérités définies et la surnaturel," *Angelicum* 25 (1948): 285–98.]

experiential data (of unity and multiplicity, of change and of permanence) that the principle of contradiction takes on new determinations.

If we consider it in its simplest formulation—"that which is is not that which is not"—the principle of contradiction appears as being a negative formulation derived from the positive principle that "that which is is; that which is not is that which is not," a common formulation of the principle of identity. And just as every denial is founded upon an affirmation, *in itself* the ultimate principle is the principle of identity.[17]

To speak truly, this common formulation of the principle of identity, even though we ourselves have often employed it, does not seem to us to be completely exact. Antonius Andreas proposed it in the form "every being is a being."[18] This is generally rejected by the Scholastics. Suarez wrote, "that proposition is identical and nugatory";[19] it is a tautology that, through the addition of a predicate does not manifest anything new to the mind concerning the subject. Similarly, if I say, "A is A," I know just as much about it through the simple apprehension of A as I do in judging that A is A.[20] As Aristotle saw,[21] by means of the verb "to be," every affirmative judgment expresses the identity that there is between the being the subject signifies and the being the predicate signifies. However, this identity is not logical; it is objective and real.[22] Logically, a judgment is composed of

---

[17] Like Suárez, Cardinal Zigliara more faithfully follows the letter of Aristotle's text by according primacy to the principle of contradiction, but he adds: "[The principle of contradiction] does not, however, [have primacy] with regard to the nature of the principles *in themselves*. Rather, [it has primacy] from the perspective of our [human] way of proceeding and on account of the great weakness of the human intellect" (*De lumière Intellectuelle*, 3:255). Suárez says: "The mind, in the assent that it gives to the first principles such as they are in themselves, is aided and sustained by arguing to impossibility [Fr.: *allant à l'impossible*; Lat.: *deducendo ad impossibile*]" (*Disp. met.*, disp. 3, sect. 3, no. 9). [Trans. note: Fr. Garrigou-Lagrange's French translation of this text slightly changes it, though it does not run counter to the meaning of the original Latin in Suárez.]

[18] Antonius Andreas, *In IV metaphys.*, q. 5. [Trans. note: Andreas (ca.1380–1420) was a student of John Duns Scotus and an important figure in the early interpretation of the Subtle Doctor.]

[19] See Suárez, *Disp. met.*, disp. 3, sect. 3, no. 9.

[20] See *Summa contra gentiles* [*SCG*] I, ch. 58, no. 2: "Those things that are divided and composed by the intellect are of such a nature to be considered separately by it, for there would be no work by way of composition and division if in apprehending what a thing is [i.e., in apprehending its quiddity] one fully knew what belonged to it and what did not belong to it."

[21] This is what Kant misunderstood. See below, near the end of §4.

[22] See Aristotle *Metaphysica* 4.7 (éd. Didot): "There is no difference between these propositions 'the man *is* standing' and 'the man stands,' or between these: 'the man *is* walking,

---

two distinct parts, the subject and the predicate, which the mind unites by means of the copula so as to express that the being designated from one perspective by the subject is (or is the same as) the being designated from another perspective by the predicate. An affirmative judgment thus re-links what abstractive conception separated. To say that man is free is to say that the being that is man is a being that is free. To say, "this wall is white," is to say, "this thing that is this wall is a white thing." The principle of identity, all the while expressing an objective identity, indeed the very first, must therefore grasp something for us. To that end, as Tomasso Maria Zigliara remarks,[23] the predicate, instead of being wholly distinct from the subject, must be logically distinct from it. It must add something to being by expressing a modality that is not expressed by the very term "being."[24] But it must express a mode that agrees primarily with being, "a mode generally following upon all beings,"[25] indeed, to being considered in itself and not in relation with another thing. Now, Saint Thomas says,[26] we find two modes that agree with every being considered in itself, the one is positive, the other negative.

The positive mode consists in the fact that each being is *something determined*: "However, the only thing that can be affirmatively said to belong to every being is *its essence*, in accord with which it is said to be; thus, is this name, *thing*, imposed, which, as Avicenna says in the beginning of his *Metaphysics*, differs from *being* on account of the fact that *being* is taken from the act of existing, whereas the name *thing* expresses the quiddity or essence of the being." The term "thing" (*res*) expresses a formality that is distinct from being in that "being" designates above all the act of existing and, by this, that which exists or can exist, whereas "thing" is first and foremost concerned with the essence or *quiddity* of that which is. The ultimate judgment that must affirm what first agrees with being therefore has as its formulation: "Every being is something determined, having a

---

advancing' and 'the man walks, advances.' The same holds true for other cases." For, the copula "is" affirms that the being that is man *is* (is the same as) the being that is standing. See Charles Sentroul, *L'Objet de la Métaphysique selon Kant et Aristote*, 2nd ed. (Louvain: Institute Supérieur de Philosophie, 1913), 187 and 303 (123 and 223 in 1st ed.).

[23] Zigliara, *De lumière intellectuelle*, 3:255.

[24] *De veritate*, q. 1 a. 1: "Something is said to add to being inasmuch as it expresses a mode of it, one which is not expressed by the term being itself." [Trans. note: For more details regarding the account of truth presupposed here, see the texts cited in note 48 of the first chapter of the first part above.]

[25] *De veritate*, q. 1 a. 1.

[26] *De veritate*, q. 1 a. 1.

determinate nature that properly constitutes it." This is how we can say, without merely stating a tautology: God is God, the creature is a creature; flesh is flesh, spirit is spirit. Thus, Christ said, "est est, non non." This can be symbolized as: A is A. If one gives "being" as the subject of the proposition, it must express in the predicate the nature of being, that which defines it, and not say, "being is being," but, "being is that which is or can be." And as it is obvious that this first predicate agrees with the first subject *by itself*, we can give precision to the formula and say: "Every being is, and is by itself, of a determinate nature that properly constitutes it." This formulation is no longer a tautology. There is even a philosophy that denies the truth of it: the philosophy of becoming, captivated by the sensible appearances,[27] a philosophy that denies that there are *things* so as to acknowledge only *actions*,[28] a philosophy that defines reality not by that which is but by that which ceaselessly becomes, a philosophy that consequently refuses to see real distinctions between "a glass of water, water, sugar, and the process of dissolution of sugar in the water."[29]

The negative mode that agrees with every being considered in itself is *unity*, which is opposed to multiplicity, as identity is opposed to diversity. "However, the negation that follows upon every being absolutely is lack of division. The term 'one' expresses this, for 'the one' is nothing other than an undivided being."[30] If every being is of a determined nature, which properly constitutes it, it follows that, as such, it is not divided. If it were, it would be and not be in the same respect that which properly constitutes it. If it is simple, it is not only undivided but indivisible; if it is composed, it ceases to be when it is divided.[31] As Saint Thomas remarks, following Aristotle, given that unity is a property of being, it varies with it. Indeed, being is said first of substance, then of quantity, quality, and so on, of the different accidents that are indeed something real. Likewise, unity has multiple corresponding acceptations: *identity* is the unity of essence or of substance; *equality* is the unity of quantity; *likeness* is unity of quality.[32] Therefore, the fundamental identity of every being with itself is what is expressed by the principle "every being is one and the same."[33]

---

[27] See Aristotle, *Metaphysica* 4, and Aquinas, *In* IV *metaphys.*, lecs. 10–17.
[28] Henri Bergson, *L'évolution créatrice*, 270. [Trans. note: Fr. Garrigou-Lagrange does not mention the edition. In other books, his pagination slightly differs.]
[29] Bergson, *L'évolution créatrice*, 10 and 366.
[30] Aquinas, *De veritate*, q. 1, a. 1.
[31] Aquinas, *Summa theologiae* [*ST*] I, q. 11, a. 1.
[32] See Aristotle, *Metaphysica* 4.2, and Aquinas, *In* IV *metaphys.*, lec. 2.
[33] We have shown elsewhere how the formulation of the ultimate principle becomes in-

§4. In What Manner Are Principles Connected to the Ultimate Principle?

Having thus formulated the ultimate principle, how are we to connect the other principles to it? The School responds: not by a direct (*ostensive*) demonstration, but rather by means of an indirect demonstration (*deducendo ad impossibile*).

In order for a proposition to be susceptible to direct demonstration, it is necessary (1) that it be concerned with a necessary matter, and (2) that it not be immediately evident, or, self-evident, but that in it the predicate be united to a subject by the intermediary of a middle term (for example, the human soul is incorruptible because it is a simple, subsisting form). A first principle, because it is a proposition that is immediate and self-evident after a simple explanation of the terms (*propositio immediate et per se nota*), is not susceptible to direct demonstration.

Indirect demonstration, or *reductio ad absurdum*, by contrast, is in no way opposed to the immediate connection of the subject and the predicate. Indeed, it does not show the intrinsic truth of the proposition that one wants to acknowledge. It only presupposes that one denies this proposition but concedes another, and based on the denial raised in opposition, it infers the denial of the point that is conceded; or, based on the doubt that the opponent claims to have, it infers doubt concerning what that person affirms as being certain. Thus, it leads one's adversary to contradict himself. To demonstrate a first principle by means a *reductio ad absurdum* is to establish

creasingly explicit: (1) Being is being, non-being is non-being or, being is not non-being; (2) Every being has an essence or a nature; (3) Every being is one and the same; (4) Every being is something distinct from others (*aliquid, aliud quid*) (*God: His Existence and His Nature*, trans. Bede Rose [St. Louis, MO: B. Herder 1949], 1:159ff). This follows the order used by St. Thomas when he presents, in *De veritate*, q. 1, a. 1, the terms "being" (*ens*), "thing" or "reality" (*res*), "one" (*unum*), "something" (*aliquid*), which precede the "true" (*verum*) and the "good" (*bonum*), these last being relative to the intellect and the will. [Trans. note: As regards the transcendentals *good* and *true*, Fr. Garrigou-Lagrange is only partly correct here. He is following the letter of St. Thomas's text, but in order to explain the fully transcendental-analogical scope of these terms, one must add precisions like those found in the following authors, all of whom lie in Fr. Garrigou-Lagrange's own intellectual lineage: Austin Woodbury, *Ontology*, chs. 48–49, nos. 892–917 (John N. Deely and Anthony Russell Collection, Latimer Family Library, St. Vincent College, Latrobe, PA); Joseph Gredt, *Elementa Philosophia Aristotelica-Thomisticae*, vol. 2, ed. Eucharius Zenzen, 13th ed. (Freiburg im Breisgau: Herder, 1961), nos. 634–41; F.-X. Maquart, *Elementa Philosophiae* (Paris: Andreas Blot, 1938), 114–23.]

that he who denies it thereby denies the principle of contradiction.[34]

Leibniz said, "It is necessary to demonstrate up to the axioms." In saying this, he only repeated the doctrine of the School. "Since human genius," said Suarez, "does not immediately comprehend the rest of the first principles as they are in themselves; most are aided and confirmed in assenting to them by deducing to an impossibility, which in these other principles can be done only through this first principle: it is impossible that one and the same thing both be and not be."[35]

By means of this *reductio ad absurdum*, we do not claim to identify the principle of *raison d'être* with the principle of identity, but rather, only to show that the former depends on the latter, such that the principle of *raison d'être* cannot be denied without leading to the denial of the other. Bouyssonie justly contrasts "being connected to" and "being reduced to." He says: "Union is the unity of the multiple and diverse. This definition immediately shows that these two notions, however close they may be, are irreducible. Just as denial is connected to affirmation but is not reduced to it, so too union is connected with unity and is distinguished from it."[36] The same holds, according to us, for the principle of *raison d'être*[37] in regard to the principle of identity. If we have come to speak of reduction instead of connection, we mean this in the sense of a *reductio ad absurdum*.[38]

---

[34] If every demonstration by *reductio ad absurdum* rests on the principle of contradiction, every direct demonstration rests upon the principle of identity, for it presupposes as a point of departure the immobility or identity of a subject. As regards the very form of the syllogism, it is founded also, in the final analysis, upon the principle of identity: "Those things that are the same as some third thing are the same as each other," the real identity of two extreme terms with a middle term shows that these two extreme terms are really identical, as is expressed by the verb "to be," despite their logical diversity. [Trans. note: See the text from Hugon cited above in note 51 in pt. 1, ch. 1 of the present volume. Also see note 6 above.]

[35] Suárez, *Disp. met.*, disp. 3, sect. 3, no. 9.

[36] Bouyssonie, "De la réduction," 113.

[37] [Trans. note: Reading "principe de raison d'être", whereas the text seems to have, incorrectly, "principe de raison."]

[38] I concede, however, that in the analysis that Bouyssonie critiques, I did express myself in an inexact manner when I said: we thus arrive at this third formulation of the principle of contradiction, "The union or unconditional and immediate identification of the diverse is impossible"; however, this is also a form of the principle of *raison d'être*: "Every being has its *raison d'être* in itself or in another, in itself when it is one and the same, in another when it is the union of diverse [things]." We must recognize, with Bouyssonie, that the principle of contradiction does not indicate of any condition. It is obvious that the two principles are distinct, and the preceding wording is faulty in that it seems to present the principle of *raison d'être* as though it were a mere determination

Let us now discuss this connection in detail.[39] There is the principle of identity: every being is that which properly constitutes it. Indeed, more precisely: every being is by itself that which properly constitutes it. Whence, we have the principle of contradiction: one and the same being cannot at one and the same time be what it is and not be what it is (for example, to be round and to be not round). This formulation leads us to a second: one and the same being cannot at one and the same time and in the same respect be determined in two different manners (for example, to be round and to be square), for if it were, then, at one and the same time and in the same respect, it would be and it would not be what it is. (For example, the square inasmuch as it is square is opposed to the round, and is naturally not-round.) This second formulation is nothing other than the principle of contraries or of disparate things [*disparates*] that are necessarily excluded from the same subject. From this, we are led to a third formulation. If it is contradictory to say, "the square is round," there is no longer a contradiction in saying, "the square is red,"[40] since the relation of attribution is no longer the same. To speak of the square is to consider things from the perspective of the form; to speak of that which is red is consider things from the perspective of color. The square can be red without ceasing to be square. However, it is still contradictory to say, "the square by itself and as such (that is to say, by that which properly constitutes it) is red," for what makes the square a square is *other* than what makes red red. The square cannot be red *by itself.* Thus, we arrive at a third formulation: "Everything that belongs to a being, though not according to what properly constitutes it, does not belong to it by itself or immediately" ("Omne quod alicui convenit non secundum quod ipsum est, non convenit ei per

---

of the principle of identity. This is perhaps the position held by Auguste Penjon, whose formulation I reproduced; however, it is not that of the School.

[39] It was by reading Afrikan Spir that we were enabled to thus order the following formulations that are found in a scattered state in Aristotle and St. Thomas; see Spir, *Pensée et réalité* [trans. Augste Penjon], 140.

[40] I am told, in objection, that I unconsciously pass from the general to the particular and that am I thinking the propositions "*this* square thing is red" or "*a* square is red" when I write, "the square is red." This is not at all correct; I leave the subject in its generality, as if to say: it is contradictory to say, "man is an angel"; it is no longer contradictory to say, "man is good" or "man is black," since the relation of attribution is no longer the same and since man can be good or black without ceasing to be a man. Thus, the square can be red without ceasing to be square; therefore, it is not contradictory to say, "the square is red." Moreover, this unconscious passage from the general to the particular would not matter much for the problem to be resolved here.

se et immediate").[41] Or, in order to better place in relief the diversity that is opposed to identity: "Elements that of themselves are diverse are not, of themselves, something one"[42] ("Quae secundum se diversa sunt, non per se convenient in aliquod unum"[43]).

As we will see, we needed to obtain this third, negative formulation derived from the principle of identity in order to reduce to impossibility those who deny the most developed formulation of the principle of *raison d'être*, which speaks of an *extrinsic raison d'être*.

Take the principle of *raison d'être* or of sufficient reason in its simple form: "Everything that is has its *raison d'être*," or, "Everything has a sufficient reason," and consequently, "every being is intelligible." Let us explain the terms: the *raison d'être* of a thing is that by which a thing is of a given nature with given properties, or, again, that *in virtue of* which it exists, or, again, that *for which* it exists—consequently, that by which it is intelligible.[44] The words "*sufficient* reason" are added, that is to say, that each thing

---

[41] This formulation is drawn from that offered by St. Thomas in *SCG* II, ch. 15, no. 2, in which there is added the idea of a reason or a cause: "Omne quod alicui convenit, non secundum quod ipsum est, per aliquam causam ei convenit, nam quod causam non habet primum et immediatum est."

[42] In the critiqued analysis, I had written, "the diverse cannot in themselves and as such be one and the same," which is a negative formulation of the principle of identity. It has been objected to me that the term "one" is imprecise because the diverse can be one by a unity of union, though not that of simplicity. I respond that it suffices that there be the unity of union that exists between the subject and an accidental predicate (Socrates is a musician, Socrates exists), expressing a real identity: the being that is Socrates is the same that is a musician, that which is existing. The diverse cannot *by itself* and as such be one with this kind of unity. It would suffice that there be a unity of successive union, as in becoming. For example: a green object becomes red; it unites two different qualities indeed, different from the same point of view, though by doing so successively. That which is green does not become red by itself and as such. It would suffice even that there be a unity of likeness, as St. Thomas remarks (*De potentia*, q. 3, a. 5): "If some one thing [si aliquid unum] is found in common in many things, . . . it cannot be the case that the common thing belong to each thing of its very self, since each, according to what it is, is distinguished from the other." In these three cases—Socrates exists; Socrates grows; Socrates is a man—the predicate does not belong to the subject *per se primo* (*kath' hauto kai hē auto* [Gk.]), according to what properly constitutes it. And if it is an exaggeration to say that, so explained, the formulation "the diverse cannot in themselves and as such be one and the same" is a negative formulation of the principle of identity, it is at least obvious that it is a formulation derived from it. [Trans. note: Regarding the language of "unity of union" and "unity of simplicity" used above, see note 67 in pt. 1, ch. 1 above.]

[43] This formulation is drawn from St. Thomas, *ST* I q. 3, a. 7: "Quae secundum se diversa sunt non conveniunt in aliquod unum, nisi per aliquam causam adunantem ipsa."

[44] St. Thomas, *In de divinis nominibus*, ch. 7, lec. 5: "By means of the term 'reason' [*ratio*;

---

has what is strictly necessary in order to be a given determined nature, or, again, what is strictly necessary in order to exist. For example: that by which man is man is rationality, and it is, along with animality, what suffices for a being to be a man. His essential *raison d'être* is found in this. At the same time, it is the *extrinsic raison d'être* of his properties (freedom, morality, speech, sociability, religion), properties that are all deduced from the specific difference, which thus appears to the intellect as being their *raison d'être*, that which renders them intelligible.[45] Likewise, from the perspective of existence, we say contingent beings have their (efficient and final) *raison d'être* in Being-through-Itself. These examples show that the *raison d'être* is either intrinsic or extrinsic. If we thus wish to provide precision to the formulation of the principle of *raison d'être*, we will say: "Every being has, in itself or in another, the *raison d'être* of what belongs to it: in itself, if it belongs to it by what properly constitutes it; in another, if it does not belong to it by what properly constitutes it."

Considered in its simple formulation, as in its developed formulation, this principle is self-evident, *per se notum*. However, it can be demonstrated by a *reductio ad absurdum*.

First, let us take the simple formulation: "That which is has that by what it is, that which it needs in order to be, and that which does not have what it needs in order to be is not." Whatever Bouyssonie may say about it, not only *unintelligibility* but also *contradiction* is involved in denying it.[46]

Indeed, to say, "that which is does not have that by which it is, that which it needs in order to exist," is to identify that which is with that which is not. Likewise, to say that the square does not have that by which it is a square with such-and-such properties, rather than a circle with such-and-such other properties, is to say that a square can be a circle. Finally, to say that the contingent (that which is, without existing by itself) does not have that by which it is, is to identify it with that which is not. This

---

logos], four things are understood: (1) a certain knowing [*cognoscitiva*] power; . . . (2) a cause, as when one says, 'For what reason was this done?,' that is, 'by what cause,' and thus God is called a reason . . . or cause of all; . . . (3) a calculation; . . . (4) *something simple abstracted* from many things, namely an essence."

[45] *The idea* differs from the *image* [Trans. note: i.e., phantasm produced by an internal sense] inasmuch as by it the object is rendered *intelligible*, which presupposes that it contains the *raison d'être* of what it represents, whereas the common image contains only juxtaposed common notes.
[Trans. note: Note that, in more strictly technical Thomist language, "idea" is used for the practical spiritual "models" involved in practico-techincal knowledge, whereby the artisan forms an idea as the measure for his work.]
[46] This point has been treated very well by Delmas, *Ontologia*, 645.

comes down to saying that everything is intelligible because everything that is, all the way to its last fibrils and its individual characteristics, is still something belonging to the domain of being and must have that by which it is. Indeed, being is not a genus. One does not add to it an extrinsic difference, as rationality is added to animality. Being is a transcendental that penetrates all the way to the ultimate differences of things. They are still something belonging to the domain of being.

Let us take the developed formula: "Every being has, in itself or in another, the *raison d'être* of what belongs to it: in itself, if it belongs to it by what properly constitutes it; in another, if it does not belong to it by what properly constitutes it." The *reductio ad absurdum* is established easily if one denies the first part of the formula (I avoid on purpose the use of the word "reason" or the words "to cause" or "to do/make"). To deny that every being has, *in itself,* that by which it is *such,* when, by itself and by what properly constitutes it, it is *such*—this is obviously to deny the principle of identity. It is to deny that the red be the red by itself. (According to this principle, a being will have, in itself, that by which it *exists* when existence belongs to it according to what properly constitutes it, when it will be existence itself, *Ipsum Esse.*)

On the other hand, every being has, *in another,* the *raison d'être* of what belongs to it, if this does not belong to it by what properly constitutes it.[47] First of all, it is obvious that "all that belongs to a being, but not according to what properly constitutes it, does *not* belong to it *by itself* (or, immediately)." To deny this would be to deny our third formula derived from the principle of identity. However, the principle of *raison d'être* affirms more here: "That which is, though not by itself, is *by another*" ("quod est tale, non per se est *ab alio* quod est tale per se"). Or, "The uncaused union of diverse things is impossible" ("quae secundum se diversa sunt non conveniunt in aliquod unum nisi per aliam causam adunantem ipsa"). It is precisely here that the objection is raised to us: it is not a *contradiction* to deny this relation of dependence *ab alio,* but only a case of *unintelligibility,* "for this relation does not express an identity, but rather, belongs to the principle of sufficient reason: everything is intelligible."[48]

To this, we must respond that the copula "is" always expresses an iden-

---

[47] See *SCG* II, ch. 15, no. 2: "Everything that belongs to something, though not according to what it is, belongs to it through some cause, for that which does not have a cause is first and immediate." See also *ST* I, q. 3, a. 7: "Those things that are, of themselves, diverse (the elements of every composite, of every becoming) do not belong in some one thing except through some cause uniting them."

[48] Bouyssonie, "De la réduction," 121.

tity that is not logical, but instead, real. When we say, "that which is such, though not by itself, *is* dependent on another," the subject and predicate designate the same being from two different perspectives; to deny this identity is indirectly to contradict oneself *if*, in affirming the subject, one indirectly affirms the predicate, or vice versa.

However, it is insisted, this condition is not verified, since, in the proposition in question, the predicate is not contained in the subject. "However much you analyze an idea, you will not find *in it* the relations that it can have with others, for the relation is not *in it*,"[49] but instead, between it and the other ideas. As Father de San has noted,[50] this objection had been formulated nearly in the same terms by Saint Thomas when he asked himself in *ST* I, q. 44, a. 1, "whether it is necessary that every being be created by God." The first objection is formulated thus:

> It seems that it is not necessary that every being be created by God, for nothing prevents a thing from being found without that which does not belong to its essence [*non est de ratione rei*], just as man can be found without whiteness. Now, *a relation of caused to cause does not seem to be of the essence of beings*, because without this some beings can be understood. Therefore, without this they can be. Thus, nothing prevents some beings from being not created by God.

St. Thomas responds:

> Although the relation to a cause does not enter into the definition of a being that is caused, nevertheless it follows upon those things that are essential to it [*de eius ratione*], for precisely because something is a being by participation (or, not *per se*), it follows that it is caused by another. Whence, a being of this sort cannot be except by being caused: just as a man cannot be without being capable of laughter. However, because to be caused is not of the essence of being, *simpliciter*, therefore there is a given being that is not caused.

Contingent being, says Saint Thomas, cannot not be *from another*; this involves impossibility, a contradiction. Indeed, to deny this relation

---

[49] Bouyssonie, "De la réduction," 121.
[50] [Trans. note: It seems that Fr. Garrigou-Lagrange is noting Ludovico De San, *De Deo Uno* (Paris: Victor Lecoffre, 1894), no. 33. He cites only the text name and number.]

of dependence *ab alio* is to be led to deny the principle of contradiction; to doubt it is to be led to doubt the principle of contradiction. To deny that contingent being is conditioned or relative is to affirm that it is non-conditioned, non-relative—that is to say, absolute—and this is to be led to say: that which is, without itself being by itself, is by itself. In summary: *to deny that the being that is, without however being by itself, has a raison d'être (which it must have so as to be) is to identify it with that which it is not; to deny that it has an extrinsic raison d'être is to identify it with that which is by itself.* Without a doubt, the predicate that expresses this relation of dependence adds something to what is expressed by the subject; however, what is added designates the same being under a second aspect [that is] implied in such a manner in the first that one cannot[51] deny the predicate without the subject itself being denied. The same holds of the property with regard to the nature from which it is derived. To deny that the three angles of a triangle are equal to two right angles is to deny the nature of the triangle [in Euclidean geometry]. Correspondingly, to doubt the principle of *raison d'être* is to be led to doubt the principle of contradiction.

Therefore, the principle of *raison d'être* is distinct from the principle of identity, but it is connected to it by a *reductio ad absurdum*.

Bouyssonie wants there to be only unintelligibility and not contradiction involved in denying the principle of *raison d'être*. This principle, he says, is synthetic *a priori*: "And Kant can be given his due on this point without disadvantage, for the value of the principle of identity is not superior to that of the principle of sufficient reason, and one can logically lead anyone who would venture to doubt the latter to doubt the former.[52] Therefore, let the scholastics rest reassured, they who seem preoccupied with showing under the most brutally evident form the error of those who deny the principle of sufficient reason."

The Scholastics are not ready to grant Kant his due on this problem, to admit that the principle of *raison d'être* is synthetic *a priori*, above all in the Kantian sense, to see in it a blind judgment, lacking an objective motive, by which our thought would impose *raisons d'être* and intelligibility upon things. The principle of *raison d'être* is formulated as "everything that is has its *raison d'être*, and consequently, everything is intelligible,"

---

51 [Trans. note: The original French is missing a negative here, though it seems necessary, given the argument being made.]

52 It would be interesting to know by what logical procedure different from a *reductio ad absurdum*. We have taken up this analysis in *God: His Existence and His Nature* 1:185. There, we do so in order to respond to an objection raised by J. Laminne that is nearly identical to that raised by Bouyssonie.

and not "everything is intelligible; therefore everything must have, for us, a *raison d'être*." Just as the intellect knows *being* before knowing itself and is not intelligible to itself except in function of being (as a living relation to being), while being is intelligible by itself, so too does it perceive the first principles in being as laws of being before perceiving them as laws of thought, and these principles are only laws of thought (essentially relative to being) because they are first laws of being. Moreover, it is in reality and not in itself that the intellect seeks the reasons for things. When someone asks, "why is it day?," we do not respond that this is due to some intellectual necessity, but rather, say: "because the sun rises."

Granted, we can understand the notion of synthetic *a priori* judgment in a different sense than that of Kant and say that the principle of *raison d'être* is synthetic *a priori* and not analytic, because the predicate that expresses a relation adds something to the subject. However, if one considers things carefully, one will see that, in every judgment, even the principle of identity, the predicate logically adds something to what is expressed by the subject. Were this not so, the principle of identity would be a vain tautology that would not teach us anything. As we have said, in every affirmative judgment, there is a logical non-identity between the predicate and the subject, though there is a real identity, expressed by the copula, by the verb "to be." As we said above, in agreement with Charles Sentroul,[53] this is what Kant did not understand. Kant recognized identity only in what he calls analytic judgments, pure tautologies in his eyes, and not in extensive judgments that enable knowledge to advance, judgments that he calls synthetic *a priori* or *a posteriori* because they are formed, according to him, by the juxtaposition of distinct notions. It suffices to respond that, if no kind of real identity is affirmed by the verb "to be," the affirmative judgment is false.

Affirmative judgments must not be divided depending on whether or not there is an identity (there is never logical identity, though there is always a real identity). They must be divided in the way that Aristotle divided them: "depending on whether knowledge of this real identity springs solely from the analysis of notions or from the examination of existing things."[54]

When such real identity appears to a mere explanation or analysis of terms, one has a proposition *per se nota et immediata*, analytic in the Aristotelian sense of the word.

However, a subdivision must be introduced here. These self-evident or

---

53 Sentroul, *Kant et Aristote*, 303 (1st ed., 223).
54 Sentroul, *Kant et Aristote*, 305 (1st ed., 224).

immediate propositions are of two kinds, as Aristotle himself has shown.[55] A proposition is immediate either because the predicate is implied in the meaning [raison] of the subject, or because the subject is implied in the meaning [raison] of the predicate. The first case is that of definitions. For example: "Man is a rational animal." The predicate explains the subject; it was implied in it. The principle of identity falls into this category of immediate judgments. The second case is that of the attribution of an immediate property to its subject. For example: "man is capable of laughter." The capacity for laughter implies rationality and cannot even be conceived without it. However, the case is not reciprocal, for one can think of man without thinking of the ability to laugh. Nevertheless, one could not deny this property without denying the subject. Another example: "every intelligent being is free." Freedom is not conceivable without intelligence, whereas we conceives of intelligence without conceiving of freedom. Nevertheless, we cannot deny that a being is free without denying it is intelligent. Likewise, again, we can conceive of a triangle without thinking that its three angles are equal to two right angles. However, to deny that a figure with three angles has an angle-measure equal to two right angles is to deny that such a figure is a triangle. As we have seen,[56] Saint Thomas placed in this second category of immediate judgments the principle "that which is not *per se* is from another." The relation of dependence cannot not be conceived without conceiving of contingence, though we can think of contingent being without thinking of this relation. Nevertheless, we cannot deny that a being has this relation of dependence without at the same time denying its contingence, as we have established by our *reductio ad absurdum*: to deny that a being has this relation is to identify it with the absolute or with nothingness. In other words, to affirm that a contingent, *uncaused* being can exist is to affirm a relation of agreement [*convenance*] between a subject and a predicate that have nothing by means of which they can agree with each other.[57]

At bottom, what separates Aristotle and Kant is that, for Kant, basing himself on the representation, the "categories are purely logical," whereas for Aristotle, basing himself on being, "the categories are half-logical, half-ontological."[58] For him, the affirmative judgment recomposes and

---

[55] See Aristotle, *Analytica posteriora* 2.3. Aquinas, *In* I *analyt. post.*, lec. 10.
[56] *ST* I, q. 44, a. 1, ad 1.
[57] See Garrigou-Lagrange, *God: His Existence and His Nature*, 1:189.
[58] Sentroul, *Kant et Aristote*, 187 (1st ed.,123).

restores to the reality what abstractive conception separated.[59] Now, in reality, the intellect sets forth from being, which it knows by its direct act, before knowing itself by way of reflection, and before opposed itself to being as something intentional, or relative to something absolute. It is intelligible to itself only in function of being, its formal object, just as the will is intelligible only in function of the good, sight in function of color, and hearing in function of sound. The entire life of the intellect (in its three operations) is explained by its order to being. We cannot repeat the point too often: not only will he whose foundation is the subject never rejoin being, but moreover, for such a person, the intellect itself will become incomprehensible. Either such a person will deny it, like the empiricist, or he will see in it, like Kant, only a multitude of *a priori* syntheses, blind syntheses that are still imposed on it as being necessary but with a necessity for which he will no longer grasp the *reason why*.

§5. An Important Consequence of This Thesis in Natural Theology

Finally, there is a last difficulty raised by our thesis: it would supposedly lead to pantheism! "It is logical that a pantheist would wish to see only identity in the relations of Being with being. However, that a theist [*déiste*] adopts this thesis, this I do not understand."[60]

We do not, in any way, claim that there would be "only identity in the relations of Being with beings," a claim that would obviously be pantheism. We say only that there is identity in the relation of a contingent being to what properly belongs to it: to be dependent upon another. The being that is contingent is (is the same [being] that is) dependent upon another. Under a logical diversity of subject and predicate there is a real identity such that to deny of this being the relation of dependence is to deny its contingency and, precisely, to identify it with Being by itself, just as to deny that it has a *raison d'être* is to identify it with nothingness.

In other, more general terms, we do not claim that the principle of identity is *the only* law of reality. We say only that it is the *fundamental* and *transcendental law* of reality. It is not the only one. The existence of diverse beings and of becoming (a successive union of the diverse) affirms this point for us. The diverse and becoming have their proper laws that

---

[59] See *ST* I, q. 85, a. 5.
[60] Bouyssonie, "De la réduction," 120.

cannot be identified with the most universal and most profound laws of being inasmuch as it is being. The formulation that "the union of the diverse has its *raison d'être* in a one being [*un être un*]" is not identical with the principle of identity, but it is connected to it. It is connected to it not as two species are connected to a genus—the laws of the species to the laws of the genus—but as modalities of being are connected to being. Being is not a genus. We cannot add extrinsic differences to it, as rationality is added to animality. It is a transcendental notion, that is to say, a notion that is found analogically in all beings, all the way down into what differentiates these beings. Whereas the laws of animality are not found in those of rationality, the laws of being are found analogically in the least universal laws, in those of the diverse, of the multiple, of becoming, and all the way into the least of its laws. This is how it is that the laws of the red, as red, imply the laws of being, for the red, all the way into its ultimate difference, still belongs to the domain of being.

Thus, we rejoin the *a priori* reason that we gave at the beginning with Saint Thomas: as the notion of being is implied in all the other notions and is distinguished from them, so is the principle of identity implied in all affirmative judgments without, however, being confused with them (in necessary and contingent affirmative judgments, proportionally, according to the identity that they affirm).

Far from leading us to identify Being and beings and far from leading us to pantheism, this ultimate and transcendental, though not sole, principle provides the foundation for the refutation of this error. If it is found even so distantly as in the laws of the diverse and the laws of becoming, which are the most opposed to identity, the ultimate principle denounces at one and the same time the contingency of this diverse and of this becoming. To the degree that they are opposed to identity, the diverse and becoming are opposed, in fact, to being and therefore cannot be by themselves. *Being by itself* cannot have any diversity in it, nor any movement. For that reason, It is distinct from the world, which is essentially multiple and changing.

Thus, we retrieve, under a new appearance, the capital thesis that we have already set forth and that will become the principle for the refutation of the objections recently raised against the classical proofs of God's existence: the principle of identity, conceived as the fundamental, but not sole, law excludes the two extreme forms of pantheism.

To say that it is the *sole law* of reality is to admit, with Parmenides, that only one immutable Being exists. This is the position of the pantheists, who absorb the world into God and must thereby deny the world by denying all multiplicity and all becoming.

To say that the principle of identity *is not the fundamental law* of reality is to affirm that, at bottom, reality has contradiction as its law. There is no middle. Then, as Aristotle noted,[61] all beings are one single being, which is nothing other than the universal flux in which contraries are identified with each other. This is the Heraclitian and Hegelian thesis, which is taken up today, as we will see, by Henri Bergson.

The truth is found between these two extreme conceptions. If the principle of identity is, as we have shown, the *fundamental law* of reality as it is of thought, though *not the only law*, a qualification clearly affirmed by the existence of diverse and changing beings, then it follows that the fundamental reality should be in all times and places self-identical, that it is related to existence as A is to A, *Ipsum Esse*, Pure Act, consequently absolutely one and immutable and, by the same fact, transcendent: essentially distinct from the world, which *itself* is what is essentially made up of multiplicity and becoming.

Such is the proof to which all the Thomist proofs of God's existence are reduced.[62] The proofs by *movement* and by *efficient causality* [*causes efficientes*] come down to saying: becoming, because it is a union of that which is diverse (of potency and of act), does not have its *raison d'être* in itself and requires a cause of itself that is forever in act, meaning that it is immobile and self-identical. The proof by *contingency* is reduced to the affirmation that corruptible things, which are without existing by themselves, can only have their *raison d'être* in the being that is by itself. The proof by *the degrees of being* is that multiplicity (a plurality of beings possessing a common formality in diverse degrees) does not have its *raison d'être* in itself any more than does becoming. Each of the hierarchized beings is similar to the others from one perspective and distinct from others from another perspective; therefore, it is not similar to the others by what properly constitutes it and, consequently, cannot account, by itself, for its likeness with the others: "multitudo non redit rationem unitatis (etiam unitatis similitudinis)".[63] Therefore there must be an absolutely *one* cause that accounts for the formality participated to various degrees, a cause that is this very formality in its pure and absolute state.[64] Finally, the proof *by*

---

[61] Aristotle, *Metaphysica* 4.4., and Aquinas, *In* IV *metaphys.*, lec. 8.

[62] See *ST* I, q. 2, a. 3.

[63] St. Thomas, *De potentia,* q. 3, a. 5 (second reason).

[64] Reginald Garrigou-Lagrange, "Note sur la preuve de Dieu par les degrés des être chez saint Thomas," *Revue thomiste* 12 (1904): 363–81.

the order of the world comes down to saying that a means can be ordered to an end as to its *raison d'être* only by an intellect, for only an intellect can grasp this relation of *raison d'être* and connect the means and the end in a unity by one and the same conception. Now, the world is a system of means and ends, and even the least action of an unknowing being can no more take place without a final *raison d'être* than it can without an efficient *raison d'être*.[65] It therefore requires an organizing intellect for the world, an ultimate reason for the *raisons d'être* that we note. All these proofs have for their general form [the proposition that] that which does not exist by itself exists by another that exists by itself. And all of them are brought to a completion in this affirmation: only Being Itself exists by itself.[66] If there were the least absence of identity in it, we would need, in virtue of the principle of identity, to go higher up again and declare that this being (a union of the diverse) is not yet being by itself. Finally, the divine attributes are deduced from *Being Itself*: infinity, absolute perfection, sovereign goodness, omniscience, absolute freedom in relation to created realities, and perfect beatitude.[67]

---

[65] See pt. 1, ch. 2, §6, of the present volume concerning the analyticity of the principle of finality

[66] *ST* I, q. 3, a. 4.

[67] *ST* I, qq. 1–26. Concerning this deduction of the attributes, see pt. 3, ch. 2, §2, of the present volume. We fail to understand the remark made on the subject of this chapter [*article*] in the *Revue de philosophie* on February 1, 1909 ("recension des revues," 239). We read in it:

> Fr. Garrigou-Lagrange combats the conclusions of Bouyssonic concerning the principle of *raison d'être*. He declares that the idea of being is the foundation for all of them and that the principle of contradiction dominates all, with the aid of the notions of identity and of unity; the other principles are demonstrated by a *reductio ad absurdum* by resting upon the principle of contradiction.
>
> We believe, with Bouyssonie, that there is, in the idea of cause, something irreducible to the simple notion of being and that we must draw it from experience. Was this not the thought of St. Thomas, according to this text cited by Fr. Garrigou-Lagrange himself: "Habitudo ad causam non intrat in definitionem entis, tamen sequitur ad ea quae sunt de eius ratione." [Trans. note: The Latin is not exactly the same as what Fr. Garrigou-Lagrange cites.]

The author summarizes our conclusion exactly; however, we do not see in what way the reflection that is added to it is opposed to what we said. In the preceding pages, have we denied, even a single time, the distinction of the idea of cause and the idea of being, or the necessity of drawing the idea of cause from experience? If we had held this simplistic thesis, which even borders on the absurd, it would not be necessary even to cite a text from St. Thomas to convince us that our thought has no relation to his. The idea of cause comes from experience (as does, moreover, the idea of being), but what St.

The intellect that understands the full sense and scope of the principle of identity will thus see, *quasi a simultaneo*, that the fundamental reality, the Absolute, is not this multiple and changing universe (a union of the diverse) but rather the *Ipsum Esse Subsistens*, transcendent by his Absolute Identity and Immutability.[68]

Thomas affirms is that the idea of being is implied in all the others, not as a genus but as a transcendental, which permeates the ultimate differences of things. Consequently, the principle of identity, which affirms what belongs first to being, is implied in all affirmative necessary or contingent judgments, proportionally in accord with the real identity that they express under the logical diversity of subject and predicate. Therefore, the principle of identity is *transcendentally* implied in the principle of *raison d'être*, and this is the metaphysical foundation for the possibility of the demonstration of this latter by a *reductio ad absurdum*, a reduction admitted, as we have seen, not only by Aristotle, St. Thomas, and the Thomists, but by all Scholastics.

[68] This does not involve the ontological argument, which illegitimately passes from the ideal to reality. Rather, it is the general proof by contingence, arising from the opposition that is presented by the reality that we experience with the first rational principle. After having completed this article, we just read a response to Bouyssonie in F. Chovet, "Les principes de la raison sont-ils réductibles à l'unité," *Revue de philosophie* 13 (1908): 269–74. We are fully in agreement with him on this point.

Chapter 2

———————— ᴄᴏᴏᴏ ————————

The Modernist Critique
of the Thomist Proofs of
God's Existence

The examination that we have undertaken concerning Éduouard Le Roy's nominalist theory of common sense will enable us to judge the value of the objections that he has raised against the Thomist proofs of God's existence. And the study that we just undertook concerning the relations between the principle of *raison d'être* and the principle of identity, by permitting us to respond to these objections, will enable us to grasp more fully the pantheistic consequences of the "new philosophy."

§1. Three Objections against These Proofs

If one studies "the reasons that," for Le Roy, "render obsolete" today the classical arguments for the existence of God, one sees that they are reduced to the following three.[1]

(1) The proofs by movement, contingence, final causality [*par la cause finale*], and the degrees of beings all rest on the *postulate of fragmentation*—the world of bodies is an aggregate of radically distinct individuals—a postulate that is henceforth unacceptable. "The distinction between the mover and the mobile, between movement and its subject,

---

[1] Édouard Le Roy, "Comment se pose le problème de Dieu," *Revue de métaphysique et de morale* 15 (March 1907): 129–70. I have added the italic emphases to the text. [Trans. note: A second article followed in July 1907 in the same periodical, 470–513. He cites this latter without explicitly noting the connection of the two articles.]

THE MODERNIST CRITIQUE OF THE THOMIST PROOFS OF GOD'S EXISTENCE

and the affirmation of the primacy of act over potency, are all based on the same postulate of common thought. . . . Now, criticism shows that matter thus fragmented is only the product of a mental elaboration carried out in view of practical utility and of discourse. . . . If the world is an immense continuity of incessant transformations, we no longer must imagine this spread out and enumerable cascade that would necessarily call for a first source. . . . To affirm the primacy of act is again to imply the same postulates. If causality is only a kind of pouring from a full into a void, a communication to a receptive terminus from what another term possesses, in a word, the anthropomorphic work of an agent, then so be it! But what is the value of these idols of the practical imagination? *Why not simply identify being with becoming*?" "Given that things are movement, there is no longer any need to ask how they receive the latter."

Ferdinand Canning Scott Schiller[2] says equivalently: "The proofs *ex motu, ex causis*, are possible only on a mechanist hypothesis of the world. In a dynamist philosophy, they have no value."[3]

(2) How can we prove that a being truly is contingent? Is this not solely an appearance that really belongs only to what we have abstracted from the continuous whole? And supposing that each being, taken on its own, were contingent, we would need to show the contingence of the whole. Will we conclude that the world is really contingent because it is imperfect or because it is not contradictory to speak of its non-existence? One thus comes back to *Saint Anselm's argument* that concludes at the real existence of God based simply on the fact that His non-existence is a contradiction in terms. This objection, common form the time of Kant, is also very widespread among the English pragmatists.

(3) If there must be a necessary cause, why not hold that it is an immanent cause? None of Saint Thomas's proofs establish a *transcendent* first cause. Schiller says almost equivalently: why not stick to a finite cause?

Such are the three objections of Le Roy: (1) the abuse of the postulate

---

[2]   [Trans. note: Schiller was an Oxford philosopher from the late nineteenth and early twentieth centuries.]

[3]   See C. Dessoulavy, "Le dieu fini: quelques considérations sur l'infini catégorématique," *Revue de philosophie* 6 (1906): 652. In this article, Dessoulavy sets forth the objections of Schiller against the classical theses of natural theology, and his arguments in favor of a finite God. We have responded to these objections and refuted these arguments in Reginald Garrigou-Lagrange, "Le Dieu fini du pragmatisme," *Revue des sciences philosophiques et théologiques* 1 (1907): 252. [Trans. note: The quote is taken from Dessoulavy's review, not directly from Schiller. Fr. Garrigou-Lagrange has implicitly ellipsed portions of it without distorting the meaning. Also, he incorrectly cites 653.]

THE FIRST OF THESE OBJECTIONS

of fragmentation; (2) recourse to the ontological argument; (3) transcendence is not proven.

§2. The First of These Objections Presupposes the Truth of Absolute Nominalism and of Subjectivism

The first of these objections, if it were true, would be the definitive ruin of the whole of traditional philosophy and would make it impossible for us to respond to the following two. "Why not simply identify *being* with *becoming*? . . . The distinction of act and potency and the primacy of act rest on the postulate of fragmentation, a postulate of common thought or of the practical imagination."

This objection is made in the name of results acquired from the critique of the sciences first and then in the name of nominalist philosophy.

What Le Roy presents to us on this point as a conclusion of the critique of the sciences is far from being imposed so rigorously. A good number of scientists refuse to deny the existence of separated bodies or the existence of quantity or of extension so as no longer to admit anything but qualitative variations without any subject. All that Le Roy, like Henri Poincaré and Pierre Duhem, has clearly established is that positive science does not exceed the phenomena and their relatively constant relations, their approximated laws. It can only provisionally classify these approximated laws by means of representative theories and not by means of explanatory ones. Henceforth, science need not pose to itself (and therefore need not resolve) the problem concerning the very substance of things, concerning the *subject* of these qualitative variations. That is a problem located above the phenomenal order, a metaphysical problem.

However, the objection is based, in addition, upon a philosophical system: Bergsonian nominalism. Henri Bergson says:

There is *more* in movement than in the successive positions attributed to the mobile, *more* in becoming than in the forms traversed in turn, *more* in the evolution of the form than in the forms realized one after another. Therefore, philosophy will be able draw terms of the second kind from the first but not the first from the second. Speculation must take its point of departure from the first. However, the intellect reverses the order of the two terms, and on this point ancient philosophy proceeds along the path traveled by the intellect. It installs itself in the immutable. It gives itself only the *Ideas* . . . and passes on to becoming by way of attenuation and diminution.[4]

A perpetuity of mobility is possible only if it is appended to an eternity of immutability that it unrolls in a chain without beginning or end. Such is the final word of Greek philosophy. . . . It is connected by invisible strands to all the fibers of the ancient soul. One would wish in vain to deduce it from a simple principle. However, if we eliminate from it everything that came from poetry, religion, of social life, as well as from a still-rudimentary physics and biology, thus setting aside from our gaze the friable materials entering into the construction of this immense edifice, a solid frame remains, and this frame sketches out the broad lines of a metaphysics that is, we believe, the natural metaphysics of the human intellect.[5]

(Bergson continues:) One ends up at a philosophy of this kind as soon as one follows the cinematographic tendency of perception and thought all the way to its end. In place of the continuity of evolutionary [*évolutive*] change, our perception and our thought begin by substituting a series of stable forms that would be turn by turn strung up in passing, like the rings that children unhook with their little stick as they go around on the merry-go-round. In what, then, will the passage itself consist and on what will the forms be strung? Since one has obtained stable forms by extracting from change everything definite that could be found in it, only a negative attribute is necessary in order to characterize the instability on which the forms are posited: it will be indetermination itself. Such is the first step of our thought. . . . And such is also the essential operation of *language*. The forms are all that it is capable of expressing. *Thus arises a philosophy that holds as legitimate the dissociation thus effectuated by thought and language.* What will it do if not objectify the distinction with more force, push it all the way to its last, ultimate consequences, reducing it into a system? Therefore, it will compose the real with definite forms or immutable elements on the one hand and, on the other, a principle of mobility that, being the negation of form, will

---

4 Bergson, *L'évolution créatrice*, 2nd ed., 341, 342.
5 Bergson, *L'évolution créatrice*, 352.

escape by hypothesis from every definition and will be pure in-determination, . . . a quasi nothingness, Platonic "non-being" or Aristotelian "matter."[6]

According to Bergson, this would have been the genesis of ancient philosophy. Situated within a system of postulates of common sense, one can therefore call it "the natural metaphysics of the human intellect."

The page that we have cited is perhaps the most remarkable one that a consistent nominalist has written and could write concerning the realist conceptualism of Plato and Aristotle. But it presupposes the truth of a nominalism that Bergson is content with affirming when he reduces every *concept* to an *averaged-out image* accompanied by a *name*: "When the successive images do not differ much from one another, we consider them all as being an increase or decrease of a single *averaged-out image*, or as the distortion of this image in different ways. And this average is what we think of when we speak about the *essence* of a thing or about the thing itself."[7] And again: "That which is not determinable is not representable. I have only a *verbal knowledge* of becoming 'in general.'"[8]

From this nominalist perspective, the realist conceptualism of Plato and Aristotle, the philosophy of forms, obviously can be only a systematic reduction of the dissociation effectuated upon reality by *the practical imagination and language.*

Such is the philosophy undergirding Le Roy's first objection against the classical proofs of God's existence. This philosophy presents itself as being the utter opposite of "the natural metaphysics of the human intellect" by rejecting the *ideas*, not only as Plato conceives them, but even such as common sense conceives them, with Aristotle and classical philosophy. Hence, it claims to base itself on movement in order in order to explain the immobile, and not upon the immobile to explain movement.

Therefore, Benjamin Jacob had a clear sight of things when, in 1898, he presented this new philosophy as being the system most radically "opposed to the rationalism of Plato, Aristotle, Descartes, Leibniz": "What rises up to the surface is ancient matter, suppressing the idea."[9] Louis Couturat did not exaggerate at all when he wrote, with regard to Bergsonism:

---

6 Bergson, *L'évolution créatrice*, 354.
7 Bergson, *L'évolution créatrice*, 327.
8 Bergson, *L'évolution créatrice*, 332 (emphasis added).
9 Benjamin Jacob, "La philosophie d'hier et celle d'aujourd'hui," *Revue de métaphysique et de morale* 6 (1898): 170–201, at 177.

"Under the subtle and refined metaphysics that disguises it, we can easily recognize the old sensualism and nominalism of Condillac."[10]

Nominalism has perhaps never been presented in so radical a form: substance and cause, potency and act, essence and existence, being and nothingness, words, words, *voces et verba praetereaque nihil*, pseudo problems. In reality, there is only becoming, without fixed points and without laws, where thought can be posited only by a negation of reality, by a process of *fragmentation* that is required by the necessities of practical life and of *language*. Human thought is wholly verbal; the sciences are only well-constructed languages.

Therefore, Le Roy's first objection presupposes the truth of the most outrageous nominalism: "Behold the office of philosophy: to retrieve the sensible under the deceitful intelligible that covers and masks it, and not, as was said in past days, to retrieve the intelligible under the sensible that hides it."[11]

Moreover, Le Roy holds that the *sensible reality* to which he has reduced the *intelligible* must itself be reduced to the *image*. Thus, he adopts a subjectivist or idealist sensualism: "Every ontological realism is absurd and ruinous."[12] "Something outside, something beyond thought is by definition something absolutely unthinkable. Never can we get beyond this objection, and we must conclude with modern philosophy that a kind of idealism is necessary."[13] The fragmentation that separates the subject and the object is illusory, like all the others. Nominalism (or sensualism) and subjectivism are like two peas in a pod. Both deny that the object of the intellect is *being*. Nominalism denies *being* as an intelligible object distinct from the object of sensation or from internal experience; subjectivism denies *being* as subsisting independently from the representation.

§3. If There Is an Absurd and Ruinous Doctrine, It Is Subjectivist Nominalism, Not Ontological Realism

To respond to this first objection against the proofs of God's Existence, we will show, first, that ontological realism is necessary. Next, we will es-

---

[10] Louis Couturat, "Contre le nominalisme de M. Le Roy," *Revue de métaphysique et de morale* 8 (1900): 93.

[11] Jacob, "La philosophie d'hier et celle d'aujourd'hui," 177.

[12] Le Roy, "Comment se pose le problème de Dieu," 495.

[13] Le Roy, "Comment se pose le problème de Dieu," 488.

tablish that the distinctions of potency and act, the mover and the mobile, and movement and its subject all represent the absolutely necessary
fragmentation of *being* or of the *intelligible,* not the more-or-less useful
fragmentation of the sensible continuum, as the neo-nominalists believe.

Every ontological realism would be absurd, "because something outside, something beyond thought is by definition something absolutely
unthinkable." The new philosophy that constantly reproaches traditional
metaphysics with not getting beyond spatial imagination here falls precisely into this defect by the way it speaks of an *outside* in relation to
thought. This is a wholly *quantitative* and *material* conception of the
representation. The intellect (and even already the sense power), like
the representation by which it knows, is essentially *intentional;* it is a
quality essentially or transcendentally *relative* to something other than
itself. This is its *quid proprium:* "The knower as such differs from the
non-knower inasmuch *it becomes the other* inasmuch as it is other, and this
presupposes *immateriality,*" Saint Thomas says in substance.[14] For him as
for Aristotle,[15] this is a fact against which no theory can prevail: already,
the animal, by sensation, can in a certain manner *become other things* that
surround it, for to see and to hear these beings is in a sense to become
them. Whereas the plant is enclosed in itself, the animal, by its senses, is
open to the entire sensible world. It, so to speak, passes out from itself,
from the limits that its body occupies.[16] However this passing outward,
far from belonging to the *spatial order,* presupposes, on the contrary, a
kind of independence from extended matter; that is to say, it presupposes
a kind of spirituality. The representation that is in the animal is already
of an order that is superior to the material bodies that it represents. However, because it is the act of an *animated organ,*[17] it can give birth to the
impression made by these bodies. It is a *quality* that is essentially *relative*
to them, somewhat like the image of an object that is formed in a mirror,

---

[14] Aquinas, *Summa theologia* [*ST*] I, q. 14, a. 1.
[15] See Aristotle, *De anima* 2.12 (Aquinas, *In* II *de anima,* lec. 24) and 3.8 (Aquinas, *In* III
de anima, lec. 13).; See also *ST* I, q. 78, a. 3.
[16] [Trans. note: For a longer discussion of this topic, see Reginald Garrigou-Lagrange,
"*Cognoscens quodammodo fit vel est aliud a se* (On the Nature of Knowledge as Union
with the Other as Other)," in *Philosophizing in Faith: Essays on the Beginning and End
of Wisdom,* ed. and trans. Matthew K. Minerd (Providence, RI: Cluny Media, 2019),
63–78.]
[17] The notion of an *animated organ* (matter and form, potency and act) enables us to avoid,
at one and the same time, both idealism and materialism. See above in pt. 1, ch. 2, §4.

with this difference that the eye is a mirror that sees.[18]

To speak of an *outside* in Le Roy's sense is to speak like a geometer who cannot think without space: "Certain things are common conceptions of the soul and *per se nota* among the wise only, such as, 'incorporeal things do not exist in a place,' as Boethius says in the *De hebdomadibus.*"[19]

If one wished to give to the word *outside* an analogical sense, above the spatial sense, the idealist objection would come down to the one registered by Saint Thomas[20] in *Summa theologiae* [*ST*] I, q. 85, a. 2, obj. 1:[21] "The object, inasmuch as it is known, is in the intellect, for it is nothing other than the intellect in act, whereas the *thing* to be known cannot be present in the soul,[22] above all if it is material. It is *outside the soul.*"[23] We will find the objection elsewhere in this other form: "The intellectual act is an immanent and not a transitive act; therefore, the representation must be the terminus of knowledge and not its means."

Saint Thomas responds that the known *thing* is within the intellect by the likeness that it has impressed within it, and this likeness, which is essentially relative to the *thing*, is not *what* is known, but *that by which* the thing is known.[24] Due to its essentially *relative* or *intentional* nature, the

---

[18]   [Trans. note: On this language of mirrors as used by certain commentators like John of St. Thomas (perhaps behind Fr. Garrigou-Lagrange's language here), see the remarks in John Deely, "How to Go Nowhere with Language: Remarks on John O'Callaghan, Thomist Realism and the Linguistic Turn," *American Catholic Philosophical Quarterly* 82, no. 2 (2008): 337–59 (esp. 348–53). Due to Deely's negative evaluation of O'Callaghan, out of fairness, the latter's response should be cited here as well; see John O'Callaghan, "Concepts, Mirrors, and Signification: Response to Deely," *American Catholic Philosophical Quarterly* 84, no. 1 (2010): 133–62.]

[19]   *ST* I, q. 2, a. 1.

[20]   Whatever may be said by some, St. Thomas was not unaware of the arguments of idealism. He was aware of Protagoras and Gorgias, if only by the fourth book of the *Metaphysics*, and the pyrrhonists and the New Academy, if only by St. Augustine *Contra academicos* and *De Trinitate*.

[21]   [Trans. note: As will be seen, this quote is really a combination of two objections. In the following two notes attaching to the quote by Fr. Garrigou-Largange, I have translated the Latin he himself provided originally in those notes.]

[22]   *ST* I, q. 85, a. 2, obj. 1. "The understood thing in act is in the knower, for the understood thing in act is the very intellect in act. However, the only thing concerning the understood thing that is in the intellect which is actually understanding is the abstracted intelligible *species*. Therefore, a species of this kind is the very understood thing in act."

[23]   *ST* I, q. 85, a. 2, obj. 2 "The understood thing [*intellectum*] in act must be in something, otherwise it would be nothing. But it is not in the material thing [*in re*], which is *outside the soul*, because, since the thing [*res*], which is outside the soul, is material, nothing that is in it can be understood in act."

[24]   *ST* I, q. 85, a. 2, ad 1: "The understood thing is in him who is understanding through

representation cannot be known first; in the direct act, it enables one to know without itself being known. It is not closed, but rather open upon the terminus to which it is essentially relative; it conducts us immediately to this terminus and determines the faculty of knowing in the manner of an optical focusing point [*foyer virtuel*] that is referred essentially to the luminous object or to the source of the heat that produces it. No other explanation will ever be possible for what already takes place in the simple sense knowledge had by animals: the spontaneous passage from the self to the non-self, even to an illusory non-self. To say that every sensation has a tendency to be objectified in a similar manner to what we note in the hallucination is to explain a *primitive fact* by a *derivative fact*.[25] "One might as well explain sound by echo."[26] Furthermore, this tendency to objectify would only be a fact that would need to be rendered intelligible.

---

its likeness. And in this way, it is said that the understood thing is the intellect in act, inasmuch as the likeness of the understood thing is the form of the intellect, just as the likeness of the sensible thing is the form of the sense in act. Whence, it does not follow that the abstracted intelligible species is *that which* is known in act, but that it is its likeness."

[Trans. note: However, for important remarks concerning the distinction between the *species intellecta impressa* and the *species intellecta expressa*, see note 86 in pt. 1, ch. 2, §14 of the present volume.]

[25] Illusory perceptions are only ever concerned with things borrowed from true perceptions. The person born blind never has visual hallucinations; the person deaf from birth never has auditory hallucinations. [Trans. note: For further remarks on this position, see Reginald Garrigou-Lagrange, "There Cannot Be Genuine Sensation without a Real Sensed Thing," trans. Thomas DePauw and E. M. Macierowski in Minerd, *Philosophizing in Faith*, 101–19.]

[26] Paul Janet [*sic*]. Very recently, Evander Bradley McGilvary, in "The Physiological Argument against Realism," *Journal of Philosophy, Psychology, and Scientific Method* 4 (1907): 589–601, thus refutes the principal argument of idealists—the psychological argument. Based on the fact that, according to science and common sense, the organs of sense and the nervous system are the intermediaries required for sensation, it has generally been concluded that we perceive only our own modifications and not the qualities of independent objects. But, if this were how matters stood, the perception of the brain would be wholly as subjective just as is that of the exterior world, and thus the physiological argument would disappear. Indeed, when we have the sensation of a quality, we are not aware of the cerebral phenomenon that one supposes to be its condition; therefore, this cerebral phenomenon does not exist precisely in the virtue of the idealist outlook, which holds that "to be" is "to be perceived." If one wishes to escape this conclusion, one must acknowledge that the cerebral phenomenon is real without being perceived, and in this case, the principle of the idealist is definitively ruined. (Cited from the summary given in A. Blanche, "Bulletin de philosophie," *Revue des sciences philosophiques et theologiques* 2 [1908]: 111.)

When, later by way of an act of reflection, we attempt to know the representation itself, we will find it absolutely impossible to define it in any other way than as being a *relation* to that which is represented. What would be a thought that was not a thought of something, an expression that would be the expression of nothing? To say that the representation refers to nothing is to say that *it is at one and the same time and in one and the same respect something relative and something non-relative*; it is to destroy the very concept of representation, of the expression of an idea, just as denying the transcendental relation of the intellect to being would be to destroy the concept of the intellect.

Indeed, the intellect becomes intelligible to itself only in function of being, as relative to being. In its very first apprehension, it knows being, *to on* [Gk.], the something that is, before knowing itself. How would it know itself to be empty when it is still the understanding of nothing? Hence, in its first apprehension, it knows being without *conceiving* it precisely as the non-self; then, by a reflection upon this direct act, it knows itself as relative to being, intentional; then, it judges being as distinct from it, as the non-self.[27] It is the very first fragmentation of intelligible being into object and subject. This judgment concerning the non-self as such is obviously an act of the intellect and cannot exist in animals. In them, there is only a spontaneous passage to the non-self, which is not known precisely as such. Next, the intellect sees that its three operations (conception, judgment, and reasoning) have a meaning only in function of being: the idea differs from the image[28] because it contains the *raison d'être* of what it represents (*quod quid est*); judgment differs from the simple association or juxtaposition by the verb "to be"; reasoning differs from empirical successions because it shows the *raison d'être* of the less known in the more known. The intellect concludes: my formal object is being, just as the formal object of the will is the good, the formal object of sight color, and the formal object of hearing sound. Nothing is intelligible except in function of being, just as nothing is visible except in function of color.

The first fragmenting of being into object and subject, into absolute being and intentional being, is necessary, therefore, on pain of rendering the intellect unintelligible to itself. Far from ontological realism being "absurd," idealism is what, on the contrary, is absolutely unthinkable: a

---

[27] See Aquinas, *De veritate*, q. 1, aa. 1 and 9. [Trans. note: See Reginald Garrigou-Lagrange, "Whether the Mind Knows Itself through its Essence or through Some Species," in Minerd, *Philosophizing in Faith*, 79–100.]

[28] See pt. 1, ch. 1, B, §2, of the present volume.

representation that would be the representation of *nothing* would be, at one and the same time and in the same respect, a relative and a non-relative. This is so clearly absurd that Johann Gottlieb Fichte himself never contested the existence of other men; therefore he acknowledged a double existence for them: one real and absolute, independent of the representation that he made of them, and the other ideal, intentional, that was only the representation itself. Can I doubt that the representation that I have of Le Roy corresponds to an exterior, independent reality? Can I believe that Le Roy ceases to exist merely because that I cease to think about him? Would he become at this moment "a mere permanent possibility of sensations?" This permanence still calls for an explanation, something that that idealism does not provide.

Idealism, it goes without saying, is no less ruinous than it is absurd. It encloses man in himself and must go so far as to forbid him awareness of his own action. It annihilates consciousness. Indeed, however great be the distance that separates the skeptics of antiquity from modern idealism, it is true to say what Aristotle said of the skeptic: "What differentiates such a man from a plant?"[29] The plant can have only its own form. It is enclosed in itself. It does not become other beings ("non fit aliud in quantum aliud"). It is the property of the knowing being to be able, by its form, which is more-or-less independent from matter, to become other beings. The animal sees and hears. It is open to the entire sensible world; the intellectual being is open upon all things—"anima intellective potest omina fieri." Finite by his nature, man is *infinite intentionally*.[30] What is one to say about the idealist, who denies precisely the intentional being of the *idea*, who denies *the idea inasmuch as it is an idea* so as to preserve only its entitative being, by which the idea is a modification of the thinking subject, as color is a modification of the plant? The idealist, like the plant, is solipsistically closed up within himself. Of him we must say what Baruch Spinoza said

---

[29] Aristotle, *Metaphysica*, 4.4.

[30] Aquinas, *De veritate*, q. 2, a. 2: "The perfection of each given thing considered in itself is imperfect, as a part of the whole perfection of the universe, which arises from the individual perfections of things gathered together. Whence, *so that there may be some remedy for this imperfection*, another mode of perfection is found in created things inasmuch as the perfection that is proper to one thing is found in another. And this is the perfection of the knower inasmuch as it is a knower, for on account of the fact that something is known by a knower, that very known thing in some manner is in the presence of the knower, and therefore in *De anima* 3 it is said that the *soul in some manner is all things*, for it is of such a nature as to know all things. And in this way is it possible that the perfection of the entire universe may exist in one thing."

of the skeptic: "His true role is to remain silent." The only other option would be for the idealist to claim that his thought, like the divine thought, is identical with himself; but then, he has forever been omniscient, and every mystery fades away for him.[31] God or plant: you must make your choice.

With its wholly materialist conception of the idea, idealism not only forbids man to pass out from himself. It must go so far as to forbid him awareness of his own action. According to his own principles, the idealist does not know the *reality of his action*, but instead only the representation he fashions of it. He cannot even say, "Cogito." The reality of the act of thinking and of willing is no more imposed for him than is the correspondence of the *impossible* with the *unthinkable*, that is to say, than the objectivity of the principle of contradiction.[32] If reality can be contradictory at bottom, what assures me that the action that I hold to be real really is such?

We must conclude that idealism is "manifestly absurd and ruinous."[33] The object of the intellect is *being*, independent of the representation (contrary to subjectivism)—indeed *intelligible* being, distinct from the object of sensation or from internal experience (contrary to sensualist nominalism). However, we still must show that the distinction of potency and act is a necessary division of being and not a utilitarian fragmentation of the sensible continuum.

---

[31] See *ST* I, q. 79, a. 2.

[32] [Trans. note: As noted in previous chapters, Fr. Garrigou-Lagrange most often uses "principle of contradiction" for what is most commonly referred to now as the "principle of non-contradiction." Thus, on the rarer occasions when he does use "principle of non-contradiction" for the same, I mark those instances with "[*sic*]" to signal that he means the same thing as in most places he means by "principle of contradiction" (and we now commonly mean by "principle of non-contradiction").]

[33] No more was St. Thomas unaware of the idealist objection [*instance*] presented by Le Roy in "Comment se pose le problème de Dieu," 495: "It is impossible to attribute to matter a foundation of existence that is radically exterior, heterogeneous, irreducible to thought, ... since one cannot say anything that does not presuppose or imply the mind." St. Thomas equivalently objects to himself in *ST* I, q. 85, a. 2, obj. 2: How can what is known by the intellect be the thing itself, since what is known is abstract and universal, whereas the things placed outside [the soul] are material, concrete, and singular? He responds by means of the theory of abstraction such as the moderate realists conceive it, by distinguishing the known object and the abstract and universal *manner* that the object takes on for the intellect.

§4. The Distinctions between Potency and Act, the Mover and the Mobile, and Movement and Its Subject—All Represent the Fragmentation of Intelligible Being and Not That of the Sensible Continuum

The distinction between potency and act is the only possible response to the arguments of Parmenides if we must admit with him, against Heraclitus, that there is intelligibility only in function of *being* and of the principle of identity immediately implied in the idea of being. Parmenides denied becoming and multiplicity in the name of the principle of identity: "Being is, non-being is not; there is no way to part from this thought." Heraclitus denied being and the principle of identity in the name of becoming, which he held was the fundamental reality. Aristotle maintained being and the principle of identity and explained becoming and multiplicity by potency.

The arguments by which Parmenides denied *becoming* and *multiplicity* in the name of the principle of identity can be presented in the following form.

If something becomes, this comes from being or from non-being; there is no middle. But both hypotheses are impossible: indeed, nothing can come from being—"ex ente non fit ens"— because being is already that which is, whereas that which becomes, before becoming, is not. On the other hand, nothing comes from nothing: "ex nihilo nihil fit." Therefore, becoming is contradictory. It would be necessary to assign as its origin a real non-being; it would be necessary to say that non-being is. "Now, being is; non-being is not. There is no way to part from this thought."[34]

The principle of identity (being is; non-being is not) also requires, Parmenides said, the denial of multiplicity. Everything that is outside of being (i.e., *other* than being) is non-being, and everything that is non-being is nothingness. However, being is one, for we can conceive of nothing that is added to the notion of being so as to introduce a differentiation into it. This very thing would belong to the domain of being. Put another way: if there were two beings, they would be distinguished from one another by something *other* than being; and that which is *other* than being is non-being. "Now, being is; non-being is not. There is no way to part from this thought." Therefore, multiplicity is contradictory and, consequently, illusory, like becoming.

---

[34] See: Aristotle, *Metaphysica* 1.5 (Aquinas, *In* I *metaphys.*, lec. 9); Aristotle, *Physica* 1.8 (Aquinas, *In* I *phys.*, lec. 14).

Heraclitus, like Hegel much later and Bergson today, denied the principle of identity (or, of contradiction) in order to safeguard becoming: everything that becomes, he said,[35] before becoming is not; therefore, becoming does not proceed from being; on the other hand, nothing comes from nothing. Will we deny becoming? In no way. Rather, to the contrary, being is what must be denied: to speak truly, "nothing is, everything becomes,"—*panta rhei kai ouden menei*[Gk.]. Nominalism will say, "Being is only an abstraction, a word." Stability is only an illusion of the senses or of the constructive imagination. In reality, "each thing, at one and the same time, is and is not; everything flows [Gk. *rhei*], everything moves, nothing halts." This denial of being implies the skepticism professed by Cratylus, the most well-known of Heraclitus's disciples. It even implies, as Hegel saw, the denial of the objective value of the principle of identity (or, of the principle of non-contradiction [*sic*]), which ceases to be the law of reality so as to no longer be anything except a law of abstract and discursive thought. If, indeed, reality is essentially becoming, if *becoming is self-explanatory*, that which is violet by itself and as such (unconditionally) becomes red, even though inasmuch as it is violet it is not red. One is thus led to say that *the unconditional union of the diverse is possible*, that *the diverse, of itself, is one and the same*, "ea quae *secundum se* diversa sunt *per se* convenient in aliquod unum." Becoming, which is self-explanatory, is a realized contradiction. This is the same conclusion arrived at today by Bergson when he holds that "there is *more* in movement than in the immobile," and that the fundamental reality is becoming. Based on the fact that there is *more* in movement than in the successive positions attributed to the mobile, than in the immobilities taken by the *senses* concerning becoming, Bergson concludes, in an absolute fashion: "There is *more* in movement than in the immobile." This is indeed still true of the immobile such as the *senses* grasp it—that is to say, of what *is in rest*. However, the immobile to the eyes of the *intellect* is *that which is* in opposition to that which *becomes*, just as the immutable is that which is and cannot not be. Hence, to say absolutely, "There is *more* in movement than in the immobile," is to say, "There is *more* in what becomes and does not yet exist than in that which is"—an absurd claim. As something self-explanatory, becoming is a realized contradiction.

Plato and Aristotle maintain with Parmenides against Heraclitus, Cratylus, and the skeptics that intelligibility exists only in function of being and that the principle of identity is the fundamental law of reality. Despite this, they strive to explain the becoming and multiplicity that are

---

[35] See Aristotle, *Metaphysica* 10.5.

imposed as facts; multiplicity is also a given based on the plurality of concepts. In the *Sophist*,[36] Plato, in order to explain the multiple, "at the risk of appearing to be a patricide," did not fear "to lay hand upon Parmenides's formula," and to affirm that "*non-being is*, a middle between being and pure nothingness, a limit of being." In virtue of the very principle of identity, given that objects that we know have being as a common element, they cannot differ from one another by this common element. Therefore, we must say that they differ by something other than being. Now, that which is *other* than being is non-being. Therefore, we must affirm that non-being is, [that it is] a middle between being and pure nothingness, a limit of being. Aristotle adds this precision: the distinction of many individuals in one and the same species is explained only if one acknowledges *real non-being*—or, *matter*—as a subject or limit of the form common to these individuals; matter (inasmuch as it requires one given quantity instead of another) is the principle of individuation and suffices to distinguish two individuals, which, considering only their form and their qualities, would be indiscernible, like two drops of water. Following along these lines, Saint Thomas will provide even more precision: the multiplicity or distinction of beings in general is explained only if one acknowledges in each of them *real non-being* or *essence* as a subject and limit of *the act of existing* that is common to all these beings. This will be the thesis concerning the real distinction between essence and existence in all beings that are not *Being Itself*. And the principle of identity, which requires one to distinguish, in each thing, non-being and being, equally will require one to connect them all to *Being Itself*, which alone is self-explanatory because it is pure identity.

This non-being, which Aristotle called "potency," is therefore necessary for rendering *multiplicity* intelligible in function of being.

It is no less necessary for rendering *becoming* intelligible. We must concede to Parmenides that what becomes did not come from determined being: "ex ente non fit est ens, quia iam est ens." We also must concede that nothing comes from nothing: "ex nihilo nihil." And, nevertheless, becoming exists. In order to admit becoming, must we deny being, the principle of all intelligibility, and say that becoming is self-explanatory? In no way, for becoming is the passage of undetermined being to determined being,

---

[36] Plato, *Sophist* 241d, 257a, and 259e. Plato strives to establish that non-being exists in some manner. In this way is the communication or *participation* of the ideas with each other rendered possible, and consequently, the existence of the world, the possibility of affirmative judgments, and the possibility of error. This represents one of the master ideas of Platonism. See Victor Brochard, *De l'erreur*, 2nd ed. (Paris: Félix Alcan, 1897).

such as from the real capacity for knowing to acquired science, from the embryo to the constituted being, from the seed to the plant, and so on. We call such undetermined being, an intermediary between determined being and pure nothingness, "potency." We call the determination that it can receive "act." Potency is a *non-being that is*, if you wish, but there is no contradiction involved in this. It is called *non-being* in relation to act (non-act), and it is called *being* in opposition to nothingness, which is not only non-being relative to act, but rather absolute non-being. This potency, given that it is not act, cannot by itself pass into act. It must be reduced to act by a prior act ("ens in potentia non reducitur in actum nisi per aliquod est in actu"), by an active potency. In virtue of the same principle, this potency needs to be pre-moved and, in the final analysis, pre-moved by an ultimate active potency that does not need premotion, an ultimate active potency that *is its own activity and, in this sense, immobile.* Now, the only thing that can *act by itself* is that which *exists by itself* ("operari sequitur esse et modus operandi modum essendi"). In other words, he alone who *exists by himself* can account, by himself, for the *being* of his action. And we will show, in response to the second objection, that *that which exists by itself* must be *Being Itself,* without any limit of essence, *Pure Act,* without any mixture of potentiality. Thus, the principle of contradiction is saved, and becoming, far from being denied, is explained.

Therefore, the distinction of being into potency and act is absolutely necessary for rendering multiplicity and becoming intelligible in function of being and the principle of identity. Therefore, it does not represent, as Bergson and Le Roy claim, the more-or-less utilitarian fragmentation of the sensible continuum, but instead represents an absolutely necessary fragmentation of being. It is false to say that Aristotle was content with reducing into a system the dissociations effected by the imagination and language. In reality, he rendered becoming intelligible in function of the formal object of the intellect, *being,* and in function of the first principle that it implies.

But would it not be simpler, asks Le Roy, "To identify being with becoming"? Impossible! For the very good reason that, unlike being, becoming is not intelligible by itself. Becoming is the successive union of the diverse; this union cannot be unconditional, for the diverse, of itself and as such, cannot be *one*: "quae secundum se diversa sunt non conveniunt *per se* in aliquod unum."

If the distinction between potency and act represents the fragmentation of intelligible being and not of the sensible continuum, the same holds true for the distinction between the mover and the mobile, as well as for that between movement and its subject. We showed above[37] how the division of being into substance and accident (being and mode [*manière*] of being) is effectuated and how the principle of substance is nothing other than a determination of the principle of identity.

Hence, we now clearly see the value of the first objection raised by Le Roy against the proofs of existence of God: "Given that things are movement, there is no longer any need to ask how they receive the latter."

Schiller equivalently said: "The proofs *ex motu* and *ex causis* are possible only on a mechanist hypothesis concerning the world. In a dynamist philosophy, they have no value." Were Aristotle and Saint Thomas therefore mechanists? Would the argument concerning the first mover have only a meaning like that found in Descartes? Would it lead us only to admit a divine flicking of the switch in the past at the moment of creation? These objections prove only a profound ignorance of Aristotelianism and of Thomism. The proof *ex motu* is taken from movement defined not *mechanically*, as Descartes did, in function of *rest*, but *metaphysically*, in function of *being*. Thus, the proof indifferently has as its point of departure a local movement or a qualitative movement, a movement of a body or a movement of the spirit.[38] Let us take a movement of will. This appearance of something new, this *becoming*, presupposes an active potency [*puissance*] that was not its activity, which even did not produce this act but merely was able to produce it. How is the will reduced to the act that it did not have; how can it render account of this new being? This cannot be by itself, since potency, by itself, is not act. Therefore, it was reduced to act by a superior active potency that must itself be *its very activity and, in this sense, immobile*. This first mover can only be *Being by Itself*, for it alone, which *is by itself*, can *act by itself* ("operari sequitur esse"). He alone who exists by himself can render account of the being of his action and of the being produced with each new operation of finite things.[39] This truth, which is obvious for the metaphysician, who views things from the formal perspective of being, will become fully evident for all at the moment when the soul and the body are separated, *in terimino viae*. At this instant, when it is raised to a quasi-angelic knowledge, the soul of Gerontius said to itself:

Another marvel; someone has me fast
Within his ample palm; 'tis not a grasp
Such as they use on earth, but all around

---

[37] See pt. 1, ch. 1, B, §2.
[38] *ST* I, q. 79, a. 4; q. 105, a. 5; I-II, q. 9, a. 4.
[39] See pt. 1, ch. 1, B, §2.

Over the surface of my subtle being,
As though I were a sphere, and capable
To be accosted thus,[40] a uniform
And gentle pressure tells me I am not
Self-moving, but borne forward on my way.[41]

Hence, we can understand, as Father Marc de Munnynck has noted, the portion of truth that is concealed within Bergsonism: "Reality continuously gushes forth in the universe. . . . Each modification, each movement, even the least, introduces us into the fertile abysses of Being."[42]

The proof by movement, if we fully gasp its meaning, therefore, preserves its full weight. It in no way is bound up with a mechanistic conception of matter. The all-sufficient cause of a given a form of energy (heat) cannot be the antecedent form (mechanical work), for the transitory being of this antecedent form is also indigent and needs, just as much, an explanation. In the final accounting, we must admit the existence of a non-transitory cause, *immota in se permanens*, not at the beginning of the series of transformations of energy (it is not absolutely necessary that this series would have begun, for the eternity of the world and of movement is not obviously contradictory[43]), but rather in an order that is superior to this movement. This all-sufficient cause cannot be matter, even if one supposes it to be endowed with energy, with essential primitive forces. Here, indeed, we have a question that is not physical but, instead, metaphysical: is this matter, which is endowed with energy, an agent that can by itself render account of its own action's *being*, an agent whose power of acting is its very activity, *per se primo agens*? Impossible! For, such an agent cannot have becoming in it; such an agent, as we will see, is Pure Act and Being Itself. But it goes without saying that this argument has no efficacy for the sensualist who denies the qualitative distinction separating the senses from the intellect and who removes all meaning from the verb "to be."

---

[40] An imperfect image, since the divine motion, which is more intimate to us than ourselves, is exercised *ab intus*. [Trans. note: The French reads "capable of being touched thus."]

[41] John Henry Newman, "The Dream of Gerontius." [Trans. note: Fr. Garrigou-Lagrange does not cite a particular edition of the poem; it can be found as quoted here in Newman, *Prayers, Verses, and Devotions* (San Francisco: Ignatius Press, 1989), 699.]

[42] A. Blanche and Marc de Munnynck, "Bulletin philosophique," *Revue des sciences philosophiques et théologiques* 2 (1908): 141.

[43] See *ST* I, q. 46.

§5. The Thomist Proofs Do Not Imply Any Recourse to the Ontological Argument

Secondly, like the English pragmatists, Le Roy moreover reproduces the Kantian objection: when one concludes that the world is really contingent based on the fact that it is imperfect or because its non-existence is not contradictory, does one not thereby return to the argument given by Saint Anselm, who concluded that God must really exist merely based on the fact that his non-existence is a contradiction in terms?

It is easy to respond to this objection. Those who, in setting forth the proof *ex contingentia*, wish to conclude that the world is really contingent, based on the fact that its non-existence is not contradictory, do not in any way pass from the ideal order to the real order as Saint Anselm did. All that Saint Anselm can conlude, basing himself on the purely nominal definition of God, is that the most perfect being that can be conceived implies existence in its very definition, as an *essential* predicate; that is to say, it exists necessarily by itself and not by another, *that it is its own existence, if it exists.* This hypothetical proposition is rigorously true, but it is only a hypothetical proposition. Saint Anselm's error is to have wished to make it into an absolute or categorical proposition.

By contrast, the definition of any given finite being, that of a plant, an animal, matter, or a spirit, in no way implies existence in its comprehension.[44] Each of these beings belongs to a determinate genus and species, is defined by this genus and this species, abstraction being made from existence. In no way does its specific difference imply all perfections, and especially not the ultimate perfection, the principle of all the others, *essential existence*, aseity. The essence of this being is conceived without essential existence, and one thus formulates hypothetically: *if this being is*, it is not by itself that it exists. This is a truth of the ideal order or of essence, like that to which Saint Anselm ought to have confined himself concerning this matter.

Moreover, the proof by contingency in Saint Thomas is simpler. It comes down to this: if a necessary being does not exist, nothing exists. Now, something is, indeed, something contingent—for example, the beings whose generation and corruption we experience. Therefore, the necessary exists, indeed, distinct from these contingent beings. It suffices that this proof lead to the existence of a necessary being, without providing any further specification.

---

[44] [Trans. note: That is, in its intelligible content.]

However, Le Roy objects, following Kant: when one then passes from necessary being to the infinitely perfect being, one thus is content with returning to the argument of Saint Anselm, who passed from the infinitely perfect being to necessary being. This is not so. Saint Anselm concluded: the perfect being necessarily exists *in fact*. He ought to have said only that the perfect being exists by itself *if it exists*. He could have said, as well: if a being exists by itself, it is sovereignly perfect, for *essential* existence implies all perfections. Now, we already know by means of the proof by contingence that a necessary being *in fact* exists. Equivalences between concepts that are necessarily linked by their very definition (*necessary* and *infinitely perfect*) are legitimate for those who, against Kant, admit that real necessities correspond to necessities of thought, that *the impossible* corresponds to the *unthinkable*.

Saint Thomas shows that the necessary being (the existence of which is *in fact* proven) is infinite, by establishing that in it there cannot be a distinction between essence and existence, that it must be *Being Itself*[45] and that *Being Itself* is infinitely perfect.[46]

The proof comes down to the following. Each thing is called *perfect* when nothing that is befitting to its nature is lacking to it, when all of its potentiality is fully *actualized*. (E.g., a perfect man would be he who would realize the full development of his hierarchized faculties, complete knowledge of the truth, along with an ever-efficacious love of the good). Now, in all things, existence is *the ultimate actuality—maxime formale omnium*. Therefore, the necessary being, which must be its own existence, is *pure actuality* and, by that very fact, *infinitely perfect* without any mixture of non-being, limitation, or imperfection.

The principle of this proof is the definition of existence: *actuality* of essence. "*Existence* is the actuality of every form or nature, for goodness or humanity are not spoken of in act except as we speak of them as existing. Therefore, existence itself must be compared to essence, which is something other than it, as act to potency."[47]

Every essence is a possibility for existing, *quid capax existendi*, indeed all the more perfect as it is a less-restrained possibility of existence, as it is susceptible to a greater participation in existence. The mineral and the plant participate in it within the limits of matter and their extension. The animal, by sense knowledge, participates in it in a less restricted manner.

---

[45] *ST* I, q. 3, a. 4.
[46] *ST* I, q. 4, aa. 1 and 2; q. 7, a. 1.
[47] *ST* I, q. 3, a. 4.

Man, by his spiritual soul endowed with a kind of infinity in the order of knowledge and desire, exceeds the limits of matter and of extension. The pure created spirit participates in existence solely within the limits of the pure immaterial form that is its nature. However, it remains finite as regards its susceptibility to exist. Its essence still has the sense of being a potency, a limit with regard to existence, the ultimate actuality. Only *Being Itself*,[48] if it exists, is in no way a mixture of potency and act; it is Pure Act, sovereignly determined and, for that reason, Infinite Perfection. *Every finitude in the order of essence would posit in it a composition of that which is susceptible to existing and of existence*; its essence could be conceived without existence, which from that moment would belong to it only *as a contingent predicate*. Now, existence must belong to the *necessary being* as an *essential predicate* if it exists, and it has been demonstrated by the proof *ex contigentia* that a necessary being in fact does exist.

Therefore, the necessary being, or Being by Itself, must be Pure Being, or Pure Act. It must be related to being as A is to A, and for that reason, infinite perfection.

Without being in doubt of it, Le Roy recognizes the principle of this demonstration when, in his criticism of the ontological proof, he affirms, following Kant: "Existence is not one perfection that can be juxtaposed next to other perfections, something susceptible to being added to them. It does not enrich essence, but instead, simply *actualizes* it."[49] It is certainly the case that existence is not a perfection that enriches the essence of contingent things when it only belongs to them as a contingent (or *de facto*) predicate and not as an essential predicate. It in no way enters into their definition. However, how is one to deny that existence, considered in its formal notion as *ultimate actuality*, is a perfection? Every perfection susceptible to existing is only a modality of being, having the character of potency in relation to existence. If it is true that act takes precedence over potency, existence is therefore a perfection in it, that which completes all the others, *maxime formale omnium*; therefore, every perfection must be eminently pre-contained in *that which exists by itself* and can only be *Existence Itself*. But Le Roy, as we know, rejects the primacy of act over potency, which according to him would rest only on the utilitarian fragmentation of the sensible continuum.

---

[48] The Self-Subsistent Existence, *ipsum Esse subsistens*, of which St. Thomas speaks in *ST* I, q. 3, a. 4, and q. 7, a. 1.

[49] [Trans. note: Fr. Garrigou-Lagrange does not cite the article explicitly. See Le Roy, "Comment se pose le problème de Dieu," 164.]

§6. The Thomist Proofs Establish the Existence of a First, Transcendent Cause

Finally, Le Roy objects: if there must be a necessary cause, why not hold that it is an immanent cause? None of the Thomist proofs establish the existence of a transcendent first cause. Schiller says nearly equivalently: why not hold that it is a finite cause?

To this objection, we must respond that, by his five proofs, as Thomas de Vio Cajetan notes, Saint Thomas does not intend to establish *explicitly* the transcendence of the First Cause. He elevates himself only to the five divine predicates (first immobile mover, first maker, the first necessary thing, the greatest being, first governing being),[50] and he reserves the question concerning how they are united into one and the same subject for the following question, *De simplicitate Dei*, where he asks himself: "Whether God is a body, is composed of matter and form, is his deity, *is his existence*, can have an accident, is entirely simple, *comes into composition with others?*" To speak truly, the five proofs of God's existence come to their completion only when it is shown that the five predicates to which they lead can belong only *to Being Itself.*[51] Transcendence is proven afterward[52] and is immediately deduced from the simplicity and absolute immutability of *Self-Subsistent Being.*

The Thomist proof for [God's] transcendence can be reduced to the following syllogism:

There can be neither *multiplicity* nor *becoming* at the heart of the Absolute (or, of God).
Now, the world is essentially multiple and changing.
Therefore, God is essentially distinct from the world.

This is the proof for [God's] transcendence given by the [First] Vatican Council: "As (God) is one, unique, and spiritual substance, entirely simple and unchangeable, we must proclaim him distinct from the world in existence and essence . . . and ineffably exalted above all things that exist or can be conceived besides him."[53]

The whole of this proof, once again, rests on the concept of potency,

---

[50]   See Cajetan commentary on *ST* I, q. 1, a. 3.
[51]   See *ST* I, q. 3, a. 4.
[52]   See *ST* I, q. 3, a. 6.
[53]   [First] Vatican Council, *Dei filius*, ch. 1 (Denzinger, no. 3001).

which is necessary for rendering multiplicity and becoming intelligible in function of being and of the principle of identity.

We cannot, with Parmenides, deny becoming in the name of being and the principle of identity. We cannot, with Heraclitus, deny being and the principle of identity in the name of becoming. All that remains is to say, with Aristotle: the becoming seen in the world presupposes *potency*. Given that, of itself, potency is not act, it cannot of itself pass into act. (This would be a violation of the principle of identity.) Therefore, it must be determined by an active potency, and ultimately by an active power [*puissance*] that does not need to be pre-moved, which is its very own activity. This First Mover can be its activity, activity by itself, only if it exists by itself ("operari sequitur esse"), and consequently only if it is related to being as A is to A, Pure Being or Pure Act. Therefore, on account of the principle of identity, there can be no becoming in it.[54]

The transcendence [of God] also is established by taking as our point of departure the multiplicity that exists in the world.

We cannot deny, with Parmenides, this multiplicity in the name of the principle of identity (on the pretext that two beings could differ only by something *other* than being—that is to say, by non-being, which is not). No more can we deny the principle of identity by asserting that two beings are really distinct from one another by the very thing that is common to them: existence. Therefore, to render multiplicity intelligible in function of being, we must admit that in different beings there is a real potency distinct from existence, as matter is distinct from the form that it receives and multiplies. This real potency, a limit of existence—this non-being that is—is essence. Now, this union of potency and act (no longer dynamic, but static), of essence and existence, cannot be unconditional if the principle of identity is the law of reality. "Those things that, of themselves, are diverse do not belong in some one thing except through some cause uniting them."[55] The diverse, of itself and as such, cannot be one and the same. *The unconditional union of the diverse is impossible.* Therefore, the diverse must be connected to the identical, the multiple must be connected to the one, as non-being to being. This is the profound meaning of Saint Thomas's fourth way, which Le Roy has again critiqued from the nominalist or sensualist perspective. The Absolute must be absolutely simple, wholly and

---

[54] St. Thomas equivalently says that *Being Itself* cannot receive *any addition* since, by its very essence, it is every perfection (*ST* I, q. 3, a. 4, ad 1; q. 3, a. 6). This is how he refutes neo-Platonic pantheism in *De potentia*, q. 7, a. 2, ad 6.

[55] *ST* I, q. 3, a. 7.

entirely self-identical. It must be related to being as A is to A, *Ipsum Esse*, Pure Act and, for that very reason, distinct from the essentially composed and multiple world.[56]

"As (God) is one, unique, and spiritual substance, *entirely simple and unchangeable*, we must proclaim him distinct from the world in existence and essence."[57]

Bergson objects:

> Let us suppose a principle upon which all things rest and that all things manifest, an existence of the same nature as that of the definition of a circle or as that of the axiom "A = A." If we do, the mystery of existence vanishes, for the being at the foundation of all things thus posits itself in eternity, as logic itself does. It is true that it will exact from us a rather great sacrifice: if the principle of all things exists after the manner of a logical axiom or a mathematical definition, things themselves will need to be founded on this principle like the applications of an axiom or the consequences of a definition, and there will no longer be a place either in things or in their principle for efficacious causality understood in the sense of free choice. Such are precisely the conclusions of a doctrine like that of Spinoza or even that of Leibniz for example. Indeed, such was the genesis of it.[58]

Therefore, our thesis would represent the suppression of the *divine life* and of the *divine freedom*.

This would be true if metaphysics were reduced to logic or to mathematics, as Spinoza (and also, in a certain manner, Leibniz) wished to be the case. Spinoza wanted to make the mathematical method the universal method for all knowledge, and for this reason rejected both efficient and

---

[56] See *ST* I, q. 3, a. 8, third reason adduced, as well as the whole of a. 7. The *per se primo* cause, immediately required and *wholly sufficient* for a given effect necessarily belongs to an order superior to this effect, as St. Thomas says elsewhere (*ST* I, q. 104, a. 1), since it has *by itself* and in a pure state that which the effect possesses only by participation. H. Pinard, in the *Dictionnaire théologique*, in the article "Création," critiques us incidentally for returning, by this assertion, to the neo-Platonic conception holding that every begotten being is necessarily inferior to the principle that begets it (p. 2086). Our affirmation, translated from St. Thomas, is nothing other than the metaphysical formulation of the principle of causality, a principle poorly utilized by the neo-Platonists through their needless multiplication of *per se primo* causes.

[57] [First] Vatican Council, *Dei filius*, ch. 1 (Denzinger, no. 3001).

[58] Bergson, *L'évolution créatrice*, 301.

final causality in order to preserve, as in geometry, nothing other than formal causality and the relations of a property to an essence. As for Leibniz, he misunderstood the concept of potency, for which he substituted the concept of force. This was to return to immobilism. This force is a kind of act: monads cannot act upon one another. Having misunderstood the concept of potency, *this non-being that is*, a quasi restriction to the principle of identity, he misunderstood, by way of consequence, the contingency proper to free choice whose motive is a "sufficient reason that does not suffice," a sufficient reason from one perspective but not absolutely, as potency is a non-being that is.

If, on the contrary, metaphysics is distinct from logic—if thought is reduced to being and not being to thought—then *Ipsum Esse* or *Pure Act* is not an axiom. It is the fullness of being, and this fullness is rich enough to correspond to our concept of *life* and that of *freedom*.

As we will explain below,[59] *Self-Subsistent Being* is intelligent to the degree that it is immaterial. Given that it is independent not only from every material and spatial limit but also from every limit of essence, not only is it sovereignly intelligent, but its intellect is intellection itself, being in the state of supreme and ever-actual intelligibility. Pure Being is Pure Thought, just as Pure Good ever-actually loved is Pure Love. This immobile contemplation, because it is ever-actual or eternal, of the supreme intelligible, this eternal love of the supreme desirable, is *Life* itself, as well as the most absolute *Freedom* in relation to every created thing.

Indeed, the superior form of life does not include movement; movement, which presupposes imperfection and potentiality, is an imperfection belonging only to created life, which cannot immediately possess the fullness that it should to have, above all in the case of material life, which ceaselessly changes only because it constantly dies (through a movement of assimilation and dis-assimilation). What is absolutely essential to life, Saint Thomas says,[60] is the immanence of action, and the more a being is elevated toward God, the more does this immanence grow. The stone is not living, for it does not have in itself the principle of its action.[61] The plant

---

59 See pt. 3, ch. 2, §2.
60 *ST* I, q. 18, aa. 1 and 3.
61 [Trans. note: That is, it has a nature indeed, but only such as to be the principle and not the terminus of *its own* action. It is the principle of action *in other* beings, but is the term of actuality *in itself* only by the action of other beings. In contrast, living beings are not only the principle but also, in some way, the terminus of their own action or actuality. See F. X. Maquart, *Elementa Philosophiae*, vol. 2 (Paris: André Blot, 1937), 180–97. Also, the researcher should consult Austin M. Woodbury, *Natural Philosophy: Psychol-*

lives because it moves itself inasmuch as it nourishes itself, develops itself, and reproduces itself, though it determines for itself neither the form nor the end of these movements. This form and end are imposed upon it by the author of its nature. The animal has a superior form of life because it perceives by its senses the various objects toward which it can move itself. Indeed, the more perfect the animal's senses, the more it is living, for it can all the better vary its action. Man has a life which is superior still, for he not only knows the objects capable of specifying his various movements, but even knows the notion of an end. He can propose to himself an end and see in this end the *raison d'être* of certain means that he himself determines. Thus, he is the master of his action inasmuch as he determines it from the perspective of its form and its end. However, the human intellect needs to be moved objectively by an external truth, for it is not being. The human will has an ultimate external end, for it is not the good. And both of them, in the order of efficiency, need to be pre-moved by the First Cause. *Being Itself* is what is sovereignly living, for it possesses so well in itself all the principles of its action—formal, final, and efficient—that this action is itself. It is not adherence to an external truth; it is Truth itself in the state of ever-actual, ever-living Thought, the Good in the state of eternal love. Therefore, God is not only living; he is Life, *zōon aidion ariston* [Gk.].[62]

Therefore, the principle that we place at the summit of all things is not an axiom. When we say that God is immutable, we do not wish to say that he is inert. On the contrary, we affirm that, as the fullness of being or pure act, he is, by his very essence, his own activity and does not need to pass into act in order to act. How does the action, of itself eternal, by which God acts *ad extra* have its effect only in time? This represents, at once, the mystery of the coexistence of eternity and time and the secret of the Divine Freedom. Indeed, so great a mystery is involved here that, according to Saint Thomas,[63] only revelation can enable us to know whether the world started instead of being created *ab aeterno*. However, nothing in this mystery requires us to deny the principle of identity as the fundamental law of reality, nor to deny the super-eminent immutability of God. On the contrary, it leads us to affirm it.

As regards the divine freedom, it is founded on the sovereign indepen-

---

 ogy, nos. 473–88 (The John N. Deely and Anthony F. Russell Collection, St. Vincent College, Latrobe, PA).]

[62] See Aristotle, *Metaphysica* 12.7.

[63] See *ST* I, q. 46.

dence of *Being Itself* in relation to every created thing. It is nothing other than the *dominating indifference* of being in relation to what can exist but has no right to exist, the dominating indifference of Eternal Love of the Absolute and Infinite Good in relation to finite goods that cannot bring any new perfection to it.

Greek thought, which had little sympathy for the obscure idea of freedom, sought in vain to explain the passage from God to the world, from the One to the multiple. It "postulated," Bergson says, "a kind of metaphysical necessity,"[64] holding that immutable and pure perfection must be translated into an infinite number of imperfect and instable beings that are like pocket change in comparison.[65] This postulate is obviously not imposed from the fact that one admits Pure Act. To be convinced of this, one merely needs to meditate on *ST* I, q. 19, a. 3 ("Whether God wills whatever he wills out of necessity"): "Since God's goodness is perfect and can exist without others, since no perfection is added to him from others, it follows that his willing of things other than himself is not necessary." There is no greater perfection after creation. However, God did have a sufficient reason for creating, one that is not infallibly determining: it is fitting that the Sovereign Good would communicate what is in it and communicate it with the most absolute freedom. This is the sufficient reason for a free choice.

Such is the metaphysical proof of the divine transcendence. The way we have just established it shows us that only three positions are possible:

(1) *To acknowledge the primacy of being over becoming and deny potency.* Then, like it or not, one must return to Parmenides: multiplicity and becoming are illusory. Still, one must explain the illusion. This is the position held by those pantheists who absorb the world into God. In this way, they must arrive at acosmism, denying the world by denying all multiplicity and all becoming.

(2) *To acknowledge the primacy of being and acknowledge potency as well.* Then, with Aristotle, one must affirm the divine transcendence implied in the concept of Pure, Immutable, and Simple Act (*kechōrismenon ti kai auto kath' auto* [Gk.]).[66]

(3) *To deny the primacy of being and affirm that of becoming,* with

---

[64] Bergson, *L'évolution créatrice,* 354.

[65] [Trans. note: The expression is taken from comparisons that Bergson makes between the "gold" of pure perfection and the mutable beings that are like change or currency made from the former.]

[66] Aristotle, *Metaphysica* 12.10.

Heraclitus. And this is to deny, with Hegel, the objective value of the principle of identity, the fundamental law of thought, and to place contradiction at the root of all things. It is the position of the pantheists who absorb God into the world and must come to deny God's existence. By denying the primacy of act, "reducing being to becoming," Le Roy seems, to our eyes, necessarily to end up at this third position. Does not the encyclical *Pascendi Dominici Gregis* see in atheism the rigorous consequence of the evolutionist and agnostic immanentism of the modernists?

Chapter 3

───────── ⚬⟨⟨⟨⟩⟩⟩⚬ ─────────

The Pantheism of the New Philosophy

On the pretext that there is "*more* in a movement than in the successive positions attributed to the mobile," Henri Bergson formulates the absolute principle that "there is *more* in movement than in the immobile"; philosophy could draw immobility from movement, but not movement from immobility. As we have seen,[1] from this essentially sensualist point of departure, Bergson concludes that, *in place of the idea of being, the principle of identity, and its derivatives* (the principle of substance, of *raison d'être*, of causality, and of finality), we should substitute as our guide "the primitive intuition of the profound depths of life, the flux of duration aware of itself." As in Maine de Biran, this represents a primacy of consciousness over reason. And with this consciousness appearing like an incessant flux of becoming, every concept and every category is only a superficial view taken of the universal flux, a view that awkwardly reifies *reality in the midst of becoming* by considering it as though it were a *reality that has already become what it is*. Therefore, we must return to pure nominalism, saying—like Thomas Hobbes, Étienne Bonnot de Condillac, John Stuart Mill, Herbert Spencer, and Hippolyte Taine—that the abstract concept is residue that is poorer than the concrete and living images from which it

───────────

[1] It is necessary to respond to Bergson in the same way that Spencer has been responded to. See Émile Boutroux, *Études d'histoire de la philosophie*, 3rd ed. (Paris: Felix Alcan, 1908), 202: "Evolutionism is the truth from the perspective of the *senses*, but from the perspective of the *intellect*, it remains true that the imperfect exists and is determined only *in view* of the more perfect. . . . Moreover, the intellect insists on saying with Aristotle: everything has its reason, and the first principle must be the supreme reason of things. Now, to explain is to determine, and the supreme reason of things can only be entirely determined being."

arises, that there are neither *substances* nor *things*, that these are only *verbal entities*, since experience presents us only with phenomena and becoming.

With this principle of general metaphysics and this theory of knowledge, how can one fail to end up at evolutionist pantheism?

§1. Evolutionist Pantheism in Bergson

If there is more in movement than in immobility, in becoming than in being, what will be the fundamental reality? How should we conceive of God and creation? As an incessant becoming. We will find the image of this becoming in us,—not in immobile and rigid concepts, in Plato's Idea of the Good, in St. Augustine's eternal truths, but rather in consciousness of our life and of our interior movement.

Bergson says:

> Everything is obscure in the idea of creation, if one thinks of *things* that would be created and of a *thing* that creates, as one usually does, indeed, as our understanding cannot resist doing. This illusion is natural to our intellect, an essentially practical function, made for representing to us things and states rather than changes and acts. "However, things and states are nothing more than the way that our mind must conceive of becoming." Things do not exist; only actions do.[2]

From this perspective, God must be conceived as,

> a center from which worlds gush forth like the stars of a bursting firework—provided, however, that I do not present this center as being a *thing*, but rather, as being a continuous outpouring. God thus defined has done nothing; he is incessant life, action, freedom. Creation so conceived is not a mystery: we experience it in ourselves as soon as we act freely. Without a doubt, it is absurd to say that new things can be added to things that exist, since the *thing* results from a solidification effected by our understanding and since there are never other things than those that the understanding has constituted. . . . But what each of us notices when he

---

[2] Henri Bergson, *L'évolution créatrice,*, 269. [Trans. note: Fr. Garrigou-Lagrange does not mention the edition. In other books, his pagination slightly differs.]

looks upon his action is that action grows as it advances, that it creates for as long as it progresses.[3]

One wonders how, in such a system, *the existence of God before creation could possibly be conceived* and, nevertheless, if God is free, he could have existed without creating. Revelation even tells us that he did not create *ab aeterno*, but in time. Now, Bergson defines God as "a continuous outpouring" and later as "a need for creation."[4] Therefore, what would this God be without the world?

This is the first step toward pantheism: God can exist only if he creates; he is not distinguished from creation itself.

Not only can God no longer be conceived without the world, but he is absorbed by the world. Indeed, how will one name this principle of all reality and all life? "Lacking a better name," Bergson says, "we have called it consciousness. However, we are not speaking of this diminished consciousness that functions in each of us."[5] "Consciousness or supra-consciousness is the rocket whose lifeless fragments fall back into matter; consciousness, again, is what subsists of the rocket itself, traversing the fragments and illuminating them in organisms. However, this consciousness, which is a *need for creation*, is manifested to itself only where creation is possible. It is dormant when life is condemned to automatism; it awakens as soon as the possibility of a choice is reborn."[6] God is the *élan vital*, the free, vital activity that is opposed to *matter*, which is essentially the interruption of life: automatism, sleep, inertia. The creative *élan vital* is opposed also to *reason*, which, like matter, is automatism, immobility, and death.[7] The fundamental reality "is a reality that makes itself through that which unmakes itself."[8]

Not only is God absorbed in the world, but as Clodius Piat has noted, He seems to need to increasingly fade away:

By this very fact, it is clear what sort of notion of God one must have in light of such an outlook. God is not. He is made when he triumphs over materiality. He is unmade when he finds in it

---

[3] Bergson, *L'évolution créatrice*, 270.
[4] Bergson, *L'évolution créatrice*, 283.
[5] Bergson, *L'évolution créatrice*, 258.
[6] Bergson, *L'évolution créatrice*, 283.
[7] Like the mechanical necessity that rules the movements of bodies, the rational necessity of principles arises in us from habits that are like the dead residue of action.
[8] Bergson, *L'évolution créatrice*, 269.

an insurmountable obstacle to his action. He is equally unmade in another sense: to the degree that he sets his work in order, he withdraws from it, and automatism gains upon consciousness. It was above all at the beginning that God was. He will increasingly fade away, indeed, to the degree that the harmony of the world may suffice for strengthening itself on its own.[9]

The Bergsonian anti-intellectualism and the absolute intellectualism of Hegel thus reconnect in a common, evolutionist monism. And, on the whole, is not the intellectualistic pantheism of Hegel incontestably superior to the sensualist pantheism that seems inevitably to lead us to a philosophy that is hostile to the idea, a philosophy for which truth no longer has any meaning that rises above pure and simple experience? Hegel, as we said above, reduced reality to the rational: that which is to that which must be, fact to right, freedom to necessity. "The new philosophy" does the opposite. It reduces the rational to lived reality: what must be to what is, right to the accomplished fact, morality to success, necessity to freedom, indeed a freedom without understanding and without law, a freedom that, at base, is only spontaneity. The two extreme systems were destined to meet one another by their common denial of the objective value of the principles of identity and of non-contradiction [sic].[10]

§2. The Proof That Le Roy Substitutes for the Traditional Proofs Leads to Pantheism

Éduouard Le Roy accepts the Bergsonian point of departure—"There is more in movement than in the immobile"—and he is naturally led to the same conclusions as his master.

The traditional proofs now in ruins, behold how he orders "the dialectical series from which the affirmation of God will come forth." This is the

---

[9] Clodius Piat, *Revue pratique d'apologétique* (September 1907): 782. [Trans. note: The full details of this reference are not readily available.]

[10] [Trans. note: As noted in previous chapters, Fr. Garrigou-Lagrange most often uses "principle of contradiction" for what is most commonly referred to now as the "principle of non-contradiction." Thus, on the rarer occasions when he does use "principle of non-contradiction" for the same, I mark those instances with "[sic]" to signal that he means the same thing as in most places he means by "principle of contradiction" (and we now commonly mean by "principle of non-contradiction").]

argument called upon henceforth to replace the classical proofs.

(1) *Reality is becoming*, generative effort, or—as Bergson says—a dynamic outpouring, an élan of life, a thrust of incessant creation. Everything in nature indicates this, and we feel it better yet in ourselves, in the being that we are, and where we find under the species of lived duration the liveliest intuition of the reality in its profound depths, that is to say, of this spiritual activity from which emanates the relative immobilities that one calls matter or pure reason.

(2) *Cosmic becoming is oriented in a definite direction*. Not that the series that it unfolds tends toward an exterior limit; rather, it acknowledges an internal character of convergence. The universal reality is progress, that is to say, growth, ascent toward what is more and better, that is to say, finally, a march toward perfection. Again, everything bears witness to it in nature, notably biological evolution; everything bears witness to it also in us, and history and psychology testify to it just as well. In sum, existence itself is an effort of growth, a work of ascending realization. Thus, the *moral* appears at the foundation of being."

(3) *Spirit is freedom*, since it is creative action and even, in a certain sense, self-generating action. In other words, spirit's freedom is its action's very characteristic of being the first principle in the order of matter, as well as in that of rational legislation, in such a way that this action, presupposed by all *things*, could not in its own turn, without falling into a vicious circle, be explained by anything *physical* or *abstract*. Freedom of spirit is not wholly sovereign. . . . Three elements limit its independence, all while respecting its autonomy: (A) an obstacle to overcome, [and] this is the germ of matter; (B) an obligation of unity, [and] this is the germ of reason; (C) an orientation toward the perfect, the principle of growth that is, literally, an inspiration. Behold, in abbreviated form, what we call *moral reality*. By its very place at the summit, or, rather, at the source of existence, moral reality, spirit of our spirit, is radically irreducible to every other form of reality. Therefore, we must affirm its *primacy*, and this affirmation is what constitutes the *affirmation of God*.[11]

---

[11] Éduouard Le Roy, "Comment se pose le problème de Dieu," *Revue de métaphysique et de morale* 15 (July 1907): 470–513, at 498.

Such is the new proof of the existence of God, one that no longer has any fear of modern criticism but that, on the contrary, is built upon the most certain results of this criticism.

We can easily show that this proof rests on postulates that are far more objectionable than that of the fragmentation of being into potency and act and that, far from establishing the divine transcendence, it leads to pantheism.

This proof does not rest on any certain principle. How can one claim to replace the principles of the traditional proofs (principle of identity, of *raison d'être*, of causality): (1) by an assertion that would destroy every science ("the reality, which is essentially unstable, is becoming");[12] (2) by this poor law of physical and, above all, moral progress that is so often contradicted by the facts; and (3) by this gratuitous affirmation of a contradictory freedom, prior to reason, creating rational legislation and the first principle of morality. Far from being the affirmation of the *primacy of moral reality*, this doctrine ought to end up in *de facto amoralism*, as Jean Weber has shown.[13] Le Roy will need to say with Ockham that God could have given us as the first precept the command that we hate him. If freedom creates the principles of the moral order, why should this not be the case?

If this is what Le Roy offers us as a replacement for the traditional proofs [for God's existence], I understand the judgment that Benjamin Jacob bore upon this new philosophy ten years ago:

> It destroys and does not create; it attributes our categories to practical needs whose source we do not know, nor how the utilitarian perspective that they arouse can be maintained in conflict with the intellectual point of view of the truth. Nowhere does it bring a new clarity, and nearly everywhere does it introduce new obscurities. Nevertheless, it achieves great success, due in part to the marvelous talent of its most original interpreter, but above all to its agreement with some of the deepest aspirations of contemporary society . . . mysticism and impressionism.[14]

---

[12] Cratylus's skepticism necessarily derives from this Heraclitian perspective.

[13] Jean Weber, "Une étude réaliste de l'acte et ses conséquences morale," *Revue de métaphysique et de morale* 2 (1894): 549–60. [Trans. note: Fr. Garrigou-Lagrange here directs the reader to pt. 1, ch. 1, B, §4, where note 86 of that chapter includes a lengthy quote from Weber covering the topic.]

[14] Benjamin Jacob, "La philosophie d'hier et celle d'aujourd'hui," 201. [Trans. note: I have added the ellipsis, as Fr. Garrigou-Lagrange cites this as though it were one passage. In

Yes, indeed, an unintelligent mysticism that can lead I know not where.

This new proof, a fabric of postulates and of contradictions, leads, moreover, to pantheism. "This moral reality, spirit of our spirit," whose primacy Le Roy affirms, and "the affirmation of which constitutes the affirmation of God"—is it transcendent, distinct from the world? Can it exist without us?

Le Roy responds:

> The two opposed conceptions, God immanent and God transcendent, are equally false from a static perspective. But dynamically, a reconciliation becomes possible. We are not achieved and closed-up "natures," thus able to evolve only by explications of latent riches. On the contrary, our life is incessant creation. This is why *immanence and transcendence are not contradictory; they correspond to two distinct moments of duration: immanence to what has become, transcendence to becoming. If we declare God immanent, this is because we consider of him what has become in us and in the world; but for the world and for us, he remains forever an infinity of becoming, an infinity that will be creation, properly speaking, not a simple development, and from this perspective God appears as being transcendent.* And in our relations with him, in accord with what we have recognized with regard to the divine personality, we must treat him as transcendent.[15]

For such a conception, God cannot exist without the world. For Le Roy, as for Bergson, God is not a substance, a thing, but rather "a continuous outpouring"; what would be this continuous outpouring if God had not created? Now, it is *de fide* that [1] God could have not created and that [2] he did not create *ab aeterno*. Le Roy's God is no longer conceived without the world; the *moral reality* for which he forms the ontological foundation [*fond de l'être*] cannot be conceived, as [Le Roy] himself says, without an obstacle to overcome (germ of matter), without an obligation of unity (germ of reason), and without an orientation toward what is better [*le mieux*].

In this system, it is not only the case that God cannot exist without creation. He does not even exist after it. As Bergson says, he is "a reality

---

fact, in the original, the very closing is about half a page distant from the main body of the quote.]

15 Le Roy, "Comment se pose le problème de Dieu," 512. I have added emphasis.

that makes itself through that which unmakes itself."[16] Since he is identified with the moral reality that forms the ontological foundation [*fond de
l'être*], he is like an ascent toward the better, a march toward the perfect.

Moreover, he is such not only inasmuch as he is immanent within us,
but also inasmuch as he is transcendent, and "in our relations with him .
. . we must treat him as transcendent." From the perspective of his transcendence, God is still for Le Roy only *"an infinity of becoming,* an infinity
that will be creation, properly speaking: . . . immanence and transcendence
correspond to two distinct moments of duration." In other words, God
is becoming in the process of becoming, and we are becoming that has
already become—which is the dynamic transposition of the pantheistic
expressions *natura naturans* and *natura naturata*.[17] In other words, this
is like the case of Ernest Renan, who responded, "not yet," when he was
asked, "does God exist?" And it will always be true to say, "not yet." Unless one acknowledges that the rational order and automatism manage,
through their development, to become self-sufficient, and then, we would
need to say, as Piat notes, that "it was above all at the beginning that God
existed and that he will decreasingly exist."

This does not prevent Le Roy from admitting that God is personal in
the pragmatic sense:

> To affirm the divine personality is first of all to affirm that God *is
> not impersonal,* that it would be impossible for us to give ourselves
> to him sincerely if we judge him to be less than us in the order of
> reality, to find in him the foundation of our personal existence if
> we think of him under a form inferior to personality: a logical cat-
> egory, an abstract principle, a vague, universal subject or diffused
> cosmic force. To affirm that God is personal still has a *positive,
> pragmatic sense*: it is that we are to give ourselves to him, that is to
> say, to comport yourself in relation to him as toward a person, to
> seek in him our own personality.[18]

This divine personality in the pragmatic sense does not imply in

---

[16] Bergson, *L'évolution créatrice*, 270.
[17] [Trans. note: Fr. Garrigou-Lagrange has the French *nature naturante* and *nature naturée*.
The reference is to Baruch Spinoza, so I have chosen to use the more well-known Latin.
For example, see Baruch Spinoza, *Ethics*, trans. Samuel Shirley, ed., Seymour Feldman
(Indianapolis, IN: Hackett, 1982), I prop. 29 schol. (pp. 51–52). They likely can be viewed
as corrupted forms of the Scholastic categories "active creation" and "passive creation."]
[18] Le Roy, "Comment se pose le problème de Dieu," 498.

any way the metaphysical transcendence defined by the [First] Vatican Council. The Council defines a doctrine that is absolutely contradicted by Bersgonism:

> The holy, catholic, apostolic Roman Church believes and confesses there is one God, true and living, Creator..., infinite in his intellect and will and in all perfection. As he is one, unique and spiritual substance, *entirely simple* and *unchangeable*, we must proclaim him *distinct from the world in existence and essence*, all blissful in himself and from himself, ineffably exalted above all things that exist or an be conceived besides him.[19]

The Council further condemns different forms of pantheism, in particular evolutionist pantheism: God conceived as an ideal that tends toward being realized, but who could never be realized.[20] Finally, it affirms once again creation *ex nihilo*, formally denied by the author of *L'évolution créatrice*.[21]

Does not the pragmatist symbol of the divine personality cover over a pantheistic metaphysics? In the "new philosophy," God is no longer, as for Aristotle, the Unmoved Mover. Rather, he seems to be, as he was for the Stoics, the first mobile, *to prōton kinēton, pneuma dia pantōn dielēlythos* [Gk.]. Would not Cleanthes and Chrysippus have admitted the same terms as Bergson and Le Roy, with the exception of the word "freedom"? And did they not also reconcile with this pantheism a kind of notion of the divine personality that responded to a need of their religious sentiment and their piety? Recall Cleanthes' *Hymn to Zeus*: "Oh! The most glorious of the immortals, ... a being that is adored under a thousand names; ... it is the duty of every mortal to pray to you."[22] Did this not involve making room for pragmatist symbolism next to speculative conceptions? These philosophers were, nevertheless, also nominalists who subordinated metaphysics to morality; however, metaphysics always takes its revenge,

---

[19] [First] Vatican Council, *Dei Filius*, ch. 1 (Denzinger, no. 3001).

[20] [First] Vatican Council, *Dei Filius*, can. 1.4: "If anyone says that finite beings, the corporeal as well as the spiritual, or at least the spiritual ones, have emanated from the divine substance; or that the divine essence becomes all things by self-manifestation or self-evolution; or lastly that God is the universal or indefinite being which, by self-determination, constitutes the universality of beings, differentiated in genera, species, and individuals, let him be anathema" (Denzinger, no. 3024).

[21] Bergson, *L'évolution créatrice*, 270 and 299, 322.

[22] See the text in Friedich Ueberwegs, *Grundriss der Geschichte der Philosophie*, 9th ed., vol. 1 (Berlin: 1898), 299.

and in the moralists themselves, it is what wishes to have the last word.

Le Roy holds that the "dogma of the divine personality, like every dogma, by itself and in itself, has only a practical meaning."[23] But he adds: "After this, I grant, without reservation, that one possesses the right, indeed, even the duty (if one wishes to think through his faith philosophically) to construct, to the degree that one can, an ontological theory of the fact. . . . It is only in a kind of juridical point of view, not in the order of concrete life, that one can abstain from every speculative thought in regard to pragmatically grasped facts."[24] Unfortunately, it turns out that, far from aiding us in "thinking philosophically upon the dogma of the divine personality," the Bergsonian theory of the divine transcendence destroys it, and it is formally opposed to the [First] Vatican Council, as well as to what Bergson calls "the natural metaphysics of the human intellect."

The mobility that we observe in this world "is only possible if it is supported by an eternity of immutability." "Such is," Bergson justly says, "the final word of Greek philosophy, whose frame sketches out the broad lines of a metaphysics that is, we believe, the natural metaphysics of the human intellect."[25] However, it is false to say that one arrives at a philosophy of this kind simply by systematizing the dissociations effectuated by practical thought and language.[26] It is not "by invisible strands that this philosophy is attached to all the fibers of the ancient soul," and to what provides the foundation of the human intellect. It is false to say that one could not "deduce it from a simple principle."[27] It is attached to the intellect by the very principle of identity, implied in the idea that provides the basis for all our ideas, assuring their objectivity, intelligibility, and immateriality—namely, the idea of being. To affirm the existence of *Pure Act* or of *Ipsum Esse Subsistens*, which is related to being as A is to A, is to affirm that the principle of identity is the fundamental law of thought and of reality. If this principle of identity has an objective value, must we not say that the fundamental reality is one and the same, completely and entirely self-identical, Pure Act, *Ipsum Esse*? Given the multiplicity and becoming that are ubiquitously found within the world, the latter cannot have its own *raison d'être* within itself, for becoming, like the multiple, is *a union of the diverse*. No, *the unconditional union of the diverse is impossible*: by itself, and

---

[23] Édouard Le Roy, *Dogme et critique* (Paris: Bloud, 1907), 33.
[24] Le Roy, *Dogme et critique*, 256.
[25] Bergson, *L'évolution Évolution créatrice*, 352.
[26] See Bergson, *L'évolution créatrice*, 353.
[27] Bergson, *L'évolution créatrice*, 352.

as such, the diverse cannot be one and the same; "quae *secundum se* diversa sunt non conveniunt *per se* in aliquod unum." What this world says to us, by the multiplicity and becoming that exist in it, is, as Plato and Aristotle understood, that *non-being is*; however, if non-being is, it nevertheless cannot exist by itself. The world is a quasi violation of the principle of identity. The intellect that would understand the full meaning and the scope of this principle would, like an angel, see *quasi a simultaneo* that the fundamental reality, the Absolute, is not this multiple and changing universe, but rather a reality that is one and immutable, and by that very fact, transcendent, *Ipsum Esse, Being Itself, Pure Act.*

Such is the profound sense of Greek philosophy. Such is the reason why it ought to be called "the natural metaphysics of the human intellect." Bergson notes that "an irresistible attraction brings the intellect back to its natural movement, the metaphysics of the moderns to Greek metaphysics."[28] He says: "Forever admirable artists, the Greeks created a type of supra-sensible truth, as of sensible beauty, whose attraction is difficult to resist. As soon as one inclines to make metaphysics into a systematization of science, one slides in the direction of Plato and Aristotle. . . . And once one has entered into the zone of attraction where the Greek philosophers traveled, one is drawn into their orbit."[29]

However, whence comes, therefore, this attractive force that brings the human intellect back to the metaphysics of the Greeks? Would this be because the intellect, a wholly practical faculty, has for its object *solid bodies*, as Bergson claims?[30] Would it not rather be because it has for its formal object *being*, the intelligible foundation of all its ideas, the bond of all its judgments and reasoning, as Plato and Aristotle saw so well?

Bergson, who in our days ultimately places himself in utter opposition to this natural metaphysics, is led to say that the last word of modern philosophy, inasmuch as it is opposed to ancient philosophy, consists in affirming that *the fundamental reality is becoming.* Now, this comes down to

---

[28] Bergson, *L'évolution créatrice*, 355.

[29] Bergson, *L'évolution créatrice*, 375.

[30] Bergson, *L'évolution créatrice*, 1: "Our intellect, in the narrow sense of the word, is destined to assure the perfect insertion of our body into its surroundings, to represent to itself the relations between exterior things, and, at last, to think [upon] matter. . . . The intellect feels at home inasmuch as it is left to be among inert objects, most especially among solids, where our action finds its fulcrum and our industry finds its instruments for work; our concepts have been formed upon the image of solids, our logic is above all a logic of solids, and by that fact our intellect triumphs in geometry, where the kinship of logical thought with inert matter is revealed."

saying, as Hegel recognized, that the *intimate nature of things is a realized contradiction*. To deny that the principle of identity is the fundamental law of reality is obviously to affirm that contradiction is at the heart of reality, since the principle of non-contradiction [*sic*] is only the negative formulation of the principle of identity. *To suppress the Pure Act who is related to being as A is to A, to suppress the divine transcendence, is to place absurdity at the foundation of everything.* Bergson's anti-intellectualism is only an inverted form of Hegelianism. These two extreme systems connect back to each other in a common, evolutionist monism; if they did not exist, we would need to invent them, for they constitute the most remarkable *proofs by absurdity* for the existence of the transcendent God, who is absolutely one and immutable. We will never set aside this objection.

Therefore, we were right to say that there are only three [mutually exclusive] positions that can possibly be held in metaphysics and natural theology:

(1) *To acknowledge the primacy of being over becoming and deny potency*, and then, like it or not, one must return to Parmenides: multiplicity and becoming are illusory. Still, one must explain the illusion. This represents the position held by pantheists who absorb the world into God and must come to *deny the world* by denying all multiplicity and all becoming.

(2) *To acknowledge the primacy of being and acknowledge potency as well*. Then, with Aristotle, one must *affirm the divine transcendence* implied in the concept of Pure Act.

(3) *To deny the primacy of being, to affirm that of becoming*, with Heraclitus. And this is to deny, with Hegel, the objective value of the principle of identity, the fundamental law of thought, and to place absurdity at the very heart of reality. This is the position of the pantheists who absorb God into the world and must come to *deny God*.[31]

---

[31] We regret to read in the latest edition of the *Dictionnaire apologétique de la Foi catholique*, col. 1326, the following paragraph: "The enterprise is seductive, to wish to destroy the pantheistic assertion by showing not only that it is *false* but that it is *absurd* in itself and from every perspective. It appears that by stopping pantheism in the name of metaphysics, instead of stopping it in the name of experience, one triumphs over it more completely, and that it is better pulverized if one proves that it stands in contradiction to reason than if one only had proven that it stands in contradiction to facts. This gives birth to a manner of refuting it that consists in showing the *contradiction* into which one falls when one identifies the infinite and the finite, the perfect and

Indeed, in the end, there are but two possible options: God or radical absurdity.[32]

---

the imperfect. This manner of refuting pantheism is excellent *against a certain kind of pantheism*, the only kind that the Middle Ages knew of, and this refutation must be maintained. However, directed against the subtler form of pantheism, which we have called, by referring to the moderns, *the pantheism of the philosophers*, this refutation, without losing its value, finds itself to have lost its object. We have seen that Spinoza expressly distinguishes uncreated nature and created nature, the 'attributes' of God and his 'modes.' Similar remarks ought to be made with regard to Fichte and even Hegel. Indeed, for the latter, let it be understood once and for all that he never sustained the identity of contradictories."

Certainly, the wording of this paragraph is unfortunate, and the author doubtlessly would be quite upset that he has been interpreted as claiming that *it is impossible to refute pantheism a priori*. He could invoke what he wrote in the notes to cols. 1313–314 and 1325, where he said clearly: "That God is found *subject to the necessity of creating the finite*, and in the necessity of assuming it, under pain, for himself, of not being himself—behold what, according to us, obviously makes the infinite finite, subordinates the perfect to the imperfect, taints pure act with potency." Therefore, the pantheism of Spinoza, that of Fichte, of Hegel, and every pantheism in general that will attempt to prove itself, is *absurd*, for [such] a proof will always be an effort in connecting the world to God by a necessary link, which comes down to denying God and positing the absurd as the principle of everything.

Here, see pt. 1, ch. 2, §17 of the present volume, concerning what one must think of this assertion that Hegel had never denied the objectivity of the principle of contradiction or of identity. It is clear that he posited at the principle of all things a *becoming* that is self-explanatory; now, this is manifestly to deny the *principle of identity*, which is verified in the first place in him who has said, "I am He who is," and not, "I am He who *becomes* and never will be."

[32] [Trans. note: For more extended reflections on this, see Reginald Garrigou-Lagrange, "Conclusion: The True God or Radical Absurdity," in *God: His Existence and His Nature*, trans. Bede Rose (St. Louis, MO: B. Herder, 1936), 436–46.]

Chapter 4

THE FUNDAMENTAL TRUTH OF
THE PHILOSOPHY OF BEING

Éduouard Le Roy's objections have required us to reflect more deeply on the principle of traditional philosophy, which has appeared to us as being a philosophy of *being* radically opposed to the philosophy of *phenomena* and to that of *becoming*. It is easy now to bring into the open the fundamental truth of this philosophy.

In his treatise *De veritate philosophiae christianae*,[1] Father Norbert del Prado has shown that, in the synthetic order (*in via iudicii, non in via inventionis*),[2] the fundamental truth of Christian philosophy is that in God essence and existence are identical, whereas in creatures, they are really distinct. (The first truths of the order of discovery are the first rational principles and the primitive facts to which we apply them. The fundamental truth in the synthetic order, *in via iudicii*, is the ultimate reason that responds to our final question, "Why?," concerning God and the world: "Why is there only one uncreated, immutable, infinite, absolutely perfect, sovereignly good, omniscient, freely creating, and so on being? Why have all other beings needed to receive from him all that they are, and why do they await from him all that they desire and can be?") By employing the expression "Christian Philosophy," the author obviously does not claim to

---

[1] Norbert del Prado, *De veritate fundamentali philosophiae christianae* (Fribourg, Switzerland: Imprimerie S. Paul, 1911). In his magisterial work *De gratia et libero aribitrio*, 3 vols. (Fribourg, Switzerland: Imprimerie S. Paul, 1907), the same author has connected St. Thomas's treatise on grace to this fundamental truth.

[2] [Trans. note: See Reginald Garrigou-Lagrange, "On the Twofold *Via inventionis* and the Twofold *Via iudicii* according to St. Thomas," in *Philosophizing in Faith: Essays on the Beginning and End of Wisdom*, ed. and trans. Matthew K. Minerd (Providence, RI: Cluny Media, 2019), 11–20.]

say that this doctrine of the real distinction, which was rejected by Suarez, is a defined doctrine. He affirms only that in full metaphysical rigor, we [can] deduce from it the principle truths that must be admitted by every Christian philosophy concerning God, creatures in general, and the human soul in particular. From this ultimate truth, he deduces, in addition, many properly Thomistic doctrines. "Once that truth is known, the particular truths of Christian Philosophy spring up and flow forth; hereafter, the first truth in the way of judging, thus among the higher causes of scientific cognition, it appears as holding the highest place."[3] This is also the sentiment of Cardinal [Zeferino] González, of Cardinal [Benedetto] Lorenzelli, and of Father Matteo Liberatore, who affirms that, if one removes this doctrine from the Thomist synthesis, "All the others waver." The first book of [Father del Prado's *De veritate philosophiae christianae*] connects to this fundamental truth the five proofs of God's existence, the divine attributes, the doctrine of creation, that of the conservation of contingent beings, the doctrines of the real distinctions between created natures and their operative powers and between operative powers and their acts, the doctrine of physical premotion (that whose essence is from another requires that its power and operation be from another), and in natural philosophy,[4] the unity of existence in composites of matter and form. Thomist theologians have also shown how the thesis of the real distinction enables one to explain that the Hypostatic Union is the most intimate of unions. (It leads one to acknowledge in Christ only one existence for the two natures.) Also, it is no stranger to the solution of the most difficult objections [*instances*] raised against the mystery of the Holy Trinity[5] and that of the Beatific Vision.[6]—The second book sets forth the proofs for the

---

[3] Del Prado, *De veritate fundamentali philosophiae christianae*, xliv.

[4] [Trans. note: He has *cosmologie*. As with the problematic term "theodicy," I am translating according to language that is less Wolffian in tone. See note 40 in pt. 1, ch. 1 of the present volume.]

[5] See two remarkable articles by A. Martin, "Suarez métaphysicien: commentateur de Saint Thomas," *Science catholique*, 1898, pp. 29–59, 686–702, and 819–37, and "Suarez théologien," *Science catholique*, 1899, pp.865–85. Also, see the article "Essence et Existence" in the *Dictonnaire de théologie catholique*.

[6] It is clear what an infinite abyss separates us from empiricists akin to William James, who writes the following on the subject of the traditional proofs: "I will not discuss these arguments technically. The bare fact that all idealists since Kant have felt entitled either to scout or to neglect them shows that they are not solid enough to serve as religion's all-sufficient foundation. Absolutely impersonal reasons would be in duty bound to show more general convincingness. Causation is indeed too obscure a principle to bear the weight of the whole structure of theology. As for the argument from design, see

real distinction between essence and existence in creatures given by Saint Thomas. These proofs are reduced by him to this fundamental argument: "In created things, essence and existence are not the same, for otherwise all things would be one."[7]

It is easy, after all that we have said, to connect this argument to what is, according to us, the fundamental truth of the philosophy of being in the way of discovery [*in via inventionis*], the principle of identity.

To refuse to acknowledge that essence is a real potency distinct from existence, as matter is a real potency distinct from form, ultimately makes

---

how Darwinian ideas have revolutionized it. Conceived as we now conceive them, as so many fortunate escapes from almost limitless processes of destruction, the benevolent adaptations which we find in Nature suggest a deity very different from the one who figured in the earlier versions of the argument" (*The Varieties of Religious Experience* [New York: Longmans, Green, and Co., 1905], 437). Of the divine attributes, metaphysical attributes are meaningless: "Our conception of [the] practical consequences is for us the whole of our conception of the object, so far as that conception has positive significance at all" (445).

[Further:] "Take God's aseity, for example; or his necessariness; his immateriality; his 'simplicity' or superiority to the kind of inner variety and succession which we find in finite beings, his indivisibility, and lack of the inner distinctions of being and activity, substance and accident, potentiality and actuality, and the rest; his repudiation of inclusion in a genus; his actualized infinity; his 'personality,' apart from the moral qualities which it may comport; his relations to evil being permissive and not positive; his self-sufficiency, self-love, and absolute felicity in himself—candidly speaking, how do such qualities as these make any definite connection with our life? And if they severally call for no distinctive adaptations of our conduct, what vital difference can it possibly make to a man's religion whether they be true or false? . . . One feels that, in the theologians' hands, they are only a set of titles obtained by a mechanical manipulation of synonyms; verbality has stepped into the place of vision, professionalism into that of life. Instead of bread we have a stone; instead of a fish, a serpent" (445–46).

Are we far enough from the act of love that God has for himself? James even believes that a philosophy of religion must give more attention than it has up to now to the pluralist or polytheistic hypothesis (see 526). As a good utilitarian materialist who fails to go beyond the limitations of his senses, James sees only *words* and Scholastic jargon in every assertion of a purely intelligible order; this unreal, purely verbal *divine aseity*, without any interest for man, has nevertheless become the principle upon which the saints have built their entire lives. The whole of St. Catherine of Siena's life was founded upon these words of God: "I am He Who Is; you are she who is not."

[Trans. note: Fr. Garrigou-Lagrange cites a French translation that takes some liberties with the text, though the sense is not wholly altered. I have taken the citations from the original English. Fr. Garrigou cites, respectively, William James, *L'expérience religieuse: Essai de psychologie descriptive*, trans. Frank Abauzit (Paris: Alcan, 1906), 369, 375, 376, 436.]

7 See *Summa contra gentiles* II, ch. 52.

it impossible to provide an explanation for the *multiplicity* of beings. Either one must, with Parmenides, deny this multiplicity, or one must deny the principle of identity by affirming that two beings *really are distinct from one another* by the very thing that is *common* to them, by an essence that [for this latter claim] is absolutely the same reality as the existence common to both.[8] As Plato had understood, to explain the multiplicity and differentiation of beings, we must affirm that *non-being* is, [that it is] a middle between being and pure nothingness, a limit of being.

This union of essence and existence in any given finite being cannot be unconditional. Therefore, there must be a being in which essence and existence are identical, pure being, without a mixture with potentiality, without limits, [a being] that would be related to being as A is related to A, in which the principle of identity is realized in all its purity, a being that *is* Being, instead of only *having* being: "I am He Who Is."

At the two poles of our intellectual life, we thus find two absolute and first truths that correspond to one another like two foci, the one real and the other virtual. At the intellectual life's point of departure, in the child, we have the idea of being and the abstract principle of identity, not yet formulated: "Being is that which is and cannot be that which is not." At the terminus of the intellectual life, already in the philosopher but above all in the blessed elevated to the intuitive[9] vision of the divine essence, there

---

[8] We develop this argument more fully in pt. 3, ch. 3, §2 of the present volume. This real distinction is denied by true nominalists, as well as by those who have nominalist tendencies (such as Durandus of Saint Pourçain and Gabriel Vasquez), who have not understood that the intellect, a living relation to being, perceives through conceptual irreducibilities (the irreducibility of two concepts to each other and to one and the same third thing) real or ontological irreducibilities. Francisco Suarez also misunderstood this principle of realist conceptualism.

[9] [Trans. note: The distinction between intuitive and abstractive cognition was at best inchoate in the works of St. Thomas. By the time of Bl. Duns Scotus, it begins to play a pivotal role, one that would have significant outcomes in all of the *scholae* of the later Middle Ages and beyond, especially in nominalism. According to the position accepted by Fr. Garrigou-Lagrange, the distinction between abstractive and intuitive cognition can be simply understood as pertaining to the distinction between knowing something without or with the physical presence of that which is known. It is one thing to know intellectually a tree's essence; it is another for a tree to be present *here and now*. Intuitive cognition adds no quidditative note to what is known, only attention to the existential presence of what is known. In our current state, such presence is known only through our senses. Indeed, this is what makes the external sense powers unique, namely that they form no expressed concepts, something that *is* required for the imagination, memory, estimative/cogitative power, and the intellect. Thus, short of the Beatific Vision (which is possible only with the light of glory elevating our intellects), we have no *strictly in-*

is this concrete truth, the reason for all the others: "God is he who is and cannot not be." The last foundation for reality, like the first principle of thought, is the identity of being with itself.

Intellectual life consists essentially in passing from the idea of *being in general* and from the principle of identity, the norm of all the other principles, to the idea of *Being Itself,* the final reason for all things. Without our elevation to the supernatural order, this ultimate knowledge would remain purely analogical. However, faith tells us that our life must find its fulfillment in the immediate and eternal intuition of *Being Itself,* and this intuitive vision of God can proceed from the super-elevated vitality of our human intellect because it is an intellect. Inasmuch as it is *human,* or united to the body, our intellect has for its proper object the essence of *sensible things* and knows nothing except in function of these things. However, inasmuch as it is an *intellect* (that is to say, insofar as it dominates the body), it has for its formal and adequate object *being without restriction* and knows nothing except in function of being, for *the intellect as an intellect* (whether we are speaking of the human, angelic, or divine intellect) *is nothing other than being itself in the relative, or intentional, state.*[10] In God, who must always be intelligible in act and actual understanding, intentional being and the absolute being are identical;[11] every created intellect, whether angelic or human, remains an essential relation to being and, by that, indirectly a relation to God.[12]

The principle of identity thus appears as being the fundamental truth of the philosophy of being in the analytical order (or, the way of discovery) inasmuch as it is the first judgment implied in our first idea, the idea of being, as well as in the synthetic order, *in via iudicii,* inasmuch as it is in

---

tuitive knowledge of God. For an introduction to this topic according to the Thomist school, see John of St. Thomas, *The Material Logic of John of St. Thomas: Basic Treatises,* q. 23, a. 1, trans. Yves R. Simon, John J. Glanville, and G. Donald Hollenhorst (Chicago: University of Chicago Press, 1955), 405–21.]

[10] See *ST* I, q. 12, a. 4, corp. and ad 3.

[11] [Trans. note: That is, the being of that which is known is the deity itself in its ever-actual, unmediated self-presence.]

[12] This idea was recently highlighted well in the book of Pierre Rousselot, *L'intellectualisme de saint Thomas* (Paris: Alcan, 1908). [Trans. note: An English translation from the 3rd edition of 1936 is available as Pierre Rousselot, *Intelligence: Sense of Being, Faculty of God,* ed. and trans. Andrew Tallon (Marquette, WI: Marquette University Press, 1998).]

God, the ultimate reason of the last "why" that every intellect poses, the first object[13] of God's contemplation and that of his elect.

---

[13] Inasmuch as the divine essence common to the three Persons and the first object of essential intellection corresponds to the analogical representation that the human intellect forms of it and that every created intellect must fashion concerning it. [Trans. note: To understand this claim aright, the reader should consult Reginald Garrigou-Lagrange, *The Sense of Mystery*, trans. Matthew K. Minerd (Steubenville, OH: Emmaus Academic, 2017), 141–98.]

Appendix 1 to Part 2

———————— ⚬⚭⚬ ————————

THE PHILOSOPHY OF BEING
AND ONTOLOGISM

In its January 1909 issue, *Rivista Rosminiana*, after having summarized and fully approved one of our articles on "common sense, the philosophy of being, and dogmatic formulas,"[1] which appeared in *Revue thomiste* in July 1908, identified our thesis with that of Antonio Rosmini and opposed it to a "neo-Scholasticism that is decrepit and undermined by everything that it contains of sensualism and of subjectivism":

> In reading this article by Father Garrigou-Lagrange, one can perceive how much the outpouring of truth presses toward gushing irresistibly through every opposition and obstacle; one perceives how the philosophy of being, which is naught but the *philosophia perennis* that Leibniz commended, but which in modern times would have to take its name from *Rosmini*, is close to triumphing through the need to oppose modern errors, to whose strength a decrepit neo-Scholasticism can counterpose nothing vital, thoroughly corroded and tarnished as it is by a latent subjectivism and a philosophical outlook that reduces intellectual knowledge to sense knowledge [*sensismo*]. And we can sincerely thank the author and the periodical of the Dominical School for having, with this publication, supported our work with such authority.[2]

---

[1] Reginald Garrigigou-Lagrange, "Le sens commun, la philosophie de l'être et les formules dogmatiques," *Revue Thomiste* 16 (1908): 259–300.

[2] [Trans. note: Aid with this Italian quote was provided by Sr. Mary-Veronica Sabelli, R.S.M. The principal translator of this volume takes responsibility for its final form.]

We greatly fear that this neo-Scholasticism, so mistreated, is wholly and simply the Aristotelian and Thomist doctrine that holds that all our ideas, including among them the idea of *being*, come from the senses thanks to the *sui generis* action of this intellectual light called the *agent intellect*, which actualizes the intelligible that is in potency in the sensible, as the light of the sun renders colors actually visible.

As is well known, Rosmini rejects this explanation for the origin of ideas and substitutes for the agent intellect the idea of *being*, which he declares is innate.[3] We had no reason to address this question in our articles, and nothing that we have written suggests that we acknowledge this Rosminian thesis. It even seems to us that, in place of the obscurities involved [in] the theory of the agent intellect, this thesis substitutes contradictions when it claims to explain the formation of determinate ideas. We fail to conceive how the intellect can apply the universal idea of being to sensible things, which it supposedly does not yet know. No more do we see how this simple application of the idea of being would enable one to extricate the *quod quid est*, the essence of different things. This *quod quid est*, according to us, is placed in relief by the light of the agent intellect, which spontaneously actualizes the intelligible. However, this is only an as-yet *vague* intelligible; it will become *distinct* only to the degree that the intellect manages to define it, to determine its comprehension, and to connect it to the very first intelligible, *being* itself, the formal object of the intellect, as color is the formal object of sight, or sound the formal object of hearing. In this sense alone is being the first objective light of our ontological knowledge [*connaissances*], as was established by Cardinal Tommaso Zigliara in his remarkable work *De la lumière intellectuelle et de l'ontologisme*.

Our constant preoccupation with connecting the principal metaphysical, moral, and religious ideas to being has given to our thesis an appearance that differs somewhat from that of Scholastic works, which focus more on the details of questions and do not always elevate themselves to an overall view of things. The synthesis that we have sketched out can call to mind that of Rosmini to the degree that Rosmini followed Saint Thomas. We must admit that the two doctrines are alike on a number of points, despite notable differences that separate them concerning the origin of the idea of being, its role in the elaboration of intellectual knowledge, and also concerning the object that it enables us to know. So much is this the case that Cardinal González was able to write in his *Estudios sobre la filosofía de Santo Tomás*[4]

---

3 Antonio Rosmini-Serbati, *Nouvel essai sur l'origine des idées*, pt. 1, no. 4, ch. 1, aa. 13–23.
4 Zeferino González and Díaz Tuñón, *Estudios sobre la Filosofía de Santo Tomás* (Manila,

that, in many of its important parts, Rosmini's theory of *being* can be regarded as a commentary on St. Thomas. The dissimilarities disappear all the more as one considers in Thomism only the general lines by which it is the same as this *philosophia perennis* that justifies common sense.

What most separates Rosmini from Saint Thomas is the content that he assigns to the idea of *being*. According to Rosmini, the *being* represented by this idea is not an analogue in the classical sense; instead, it presupposes a minimal univocity between God and the creature. And this is precisely the error that motivated the 1887 condemnation of the first sixteen Rosminian propositions.

Rosmini did not see how an *analogue* differs essentially from a supreme *genus*. For him, being ultimately is only the most elevated genus, and like every genus, it is something one in itself, diversified only by extrinsic differences. This is the error contained in the sixth–eighth and tenth Rosminian propositions. "In the being that prescinds from creatures and from God, which is *indeterminate being*, and *in God*, not indeterminate but absolute being, *the essence is the same*."[5] According to Saint Thomas, an analogue cannot be perfectly abstracted from its analogates because it does not designate in each of them absolutely the same thing, but rather something proportionally similar.[6] God is *in his manner*; the creature is *in its manner*. Given that the formal notion of being [*raison d'être*] is not differentiated by something extrinsic, we cannot perfectly abstract it from its differences.

On this point, Rosmini is much closer to John Duns Scotus than to Saint Thomas. Scotus held that, in a certain sense, being and the absolute perfections are univocal; by this, he also came to hold that there is a *formal–real* distinction between the divine attributes. The Thomists see in this thesis a return to the excessive realism of Gilbert de la Porrée.[7]

At the opposite extreme, Maimonides refused to formally attribute

---

1864), vol. 1, bk. 2, ch. 2

[5] Leo XIII, Decree of the Holy Office *Post Obitum* (December 14, 1887), Against the Errors of Antonio Rosmini-Serbati, §6 (Denzinger, no. 3206).

[6] [Trans. note: This is even more so the position of Thomas da Vio Cajetan in *The Analogy of Names, and the Concept of Being*, trans. Edward A. Bushinski and Henry J. Koren (Eugene, OR: Wipf and Stock, 2009), 36–45, and John of St. Thomas in *Material Logic*, q. 13, a. 5 (p. 167–83). Also see: Yves R. Simon, "On Order in Analogical Sets," in *Philosopher at Work*, ed. Anthony O. Simon (Lanham, MD: Roman & Littlefield, 1999), 135–71; Reginald Garrigou-Lagrange, *God: His Existence and His Nature*, vol. 2, trans. Bede Rose (St. Louis, MO: B. Herder, 1949), 203–25.]

[7] See Charles René Billuart, *Summa sancti thomae*, vol. 1, diss. 2, a. 3, §2 (pp. 51–62).

the absolute perfections to God,[8] and the nominalists held that all the divine names are synonyms, on the pretext that the divine reality designated by them does not entail distinctions.[9]

These two extreme opinions both result from the fact that the analogue is conceived of univocally. Hence, if it is formally in God, it posits in him a formal-real distinction (Scotus), or if it does not posit this distinction in God, this is because it is not formally in him (Maimonides).

Saint Thomas takes an intermediate position because he sees precisely in what way the analogue differs essentially from a genus. Merely because the absolute perfections are identical in God, it does not follow that they do not formally exist in him (*formally eminently*), for we see that they require *ex propriiis*[10] that they be identified precisely by being purified of all potentiality. This purification is possible without doing harm to the formal notion itself because this formal notion is analogical and not univocal, that is to say, because it is susceptible to being realized in two very diverse modes. In truth, we do not grasp the superior analogate such as it is in itself. We directly attain only the inferior analogate (the creature) and the analogue (imperfectly abstracted). Our concept of being thus remains distinct from that of intellection for example; however, we nevertheless see that, at the limit, pure intellection must be pure being actually known and vice-versa.[11] We even see that the absolute perfections, far from not being able to be formally attributed to God, are pure only in him, but thereby cease to be distinct from one another. Thus, in God, existence is intellection, love, and providence, whereas in the creature, existence is only the ultimate actuality that posits the created essence outside of nothingness and of its causes. The minimal univocity sought by Rosmini does not exit.

---

[8] See *Summa theologiae* [*ST*] I, q. 13, a. 2.

[9] See *ST* I, q. 13, a. 4, and Billuart, *Summa sancti thomae.*, vol. 1, diss. 2, a. 3, §2 (p. 52).

[10] [Trans. note: That is, by each of their own, proper requirements.]

[11] See also pt. 3, ch. 2, §2, of the present volume. [Trans. note: See Reginald Garrigou-Lagrange, "On the Eminence of the Deity: In What Sense the Divine Perfections Are 'Formally and Eminently' in God," in Minderd, *Philosophizing in Faith*, 341–60.]

Appendix 2 to Part 2

⎯⎯⎯⎯⎯⎯ ∞◊◊◊◊◊∞ ⎯⎯⎯⎯⎯⎯

THE NATURAL AFFIRMATION
OF BEING IS NOT A POSTULATE

The following has been written concerning the preceding studies, as well as the more developed ones found in our book *God: His Existence and His Nature*:

> This is a clear and complete exposition of the Thomist doctrine that makes it possible to compare it with others and to see its dazzling superiority. Thus, we can grasp all the better the defect of the modernist theories, under the seductive appearances of their sometimes-profound insights. It also makes clear how various idealistic and agnostic systems are to be refuted. However, in Aristotelian realism, as in Euclid's geometry, there is a *postulate*. It is reasonable to admit this postulate on account of the absurd and above all unreal consequences [to which] its rejection leads. However, the postulate nonetheless exists, and just as Lobatschewski and others after him were able to build various geometries by replacing Euclid's postulate (concerning the parallel) by another, so too can one substitute a different hypothesis for the Aristotelian postulate.
>
> This postulate consists precisely in acknowledging that the intellect *attains* being. Aristotelianism does indeed establish that being is the very object of the intellect, but it does not demonstrate that it attains it; and the proof that it is possible for it not to attain it is that it is subject to error. Without a doubt, realism responds that *error cannot be produced in the intellect's immediate apprehensions*. However precisely, in these immediate apprehensions, the intellect *does not face being as an object placed before a*

subject, but it is but one with its act, in which subject and object are identical. Nothing guarantees that, in this immediate apprehension, the intellect passes out of itself and that it does not itself create this being, which is the object of its thought.

In order to escape from embarrassment, it is necessary to recognize that being has its meaning and content only in function of the intellect, such that, if in order to think it is necessary to be, without thought being would not be distinguished from nothingness, and in this sense *act* takes precedence over being and thought. And this furnishes an immediate demonstration of the existence of God, in whom being and understanding are identified in the act of thought.[1]

* * *

To this, we respond: (1) The admission that the intellect not only has being for its object but that it attains it *is not a postulate*, for a postulate is something freely posited. On the contrary, this is our intellect's *natural* and *necessary affirmation*. It is the primordial affirmation spoken of at the very end of the objection itself, with regard to the *act* of thought.

St. Thomas has shown that this first affirmation is *natural* and not *free* like the affirmation of a postulate, doing so by establishing that our adherence to the first principles of reason and of being is founded on the very nature of our intellect which, having being for its object, attains it first and attains nothing except by it.[2]

One cannot substitute another affirmation for this first, natural affirmation, nor can one prefer another proposition to the principle of contradiction,[3] even in the purely conceptual sphere. One can only substitute for the *symbol* representing the principle of contradiction (or, of identity),

---

[1] [Trans. note: Fr. Garrigou-Lagrange does not cite the source, and it has not been readily found while translating this edition.]

[2] See *Summa theologia* [*ST*] I-II, q. 51, a. 1. The *object* of a faculty is precisely what it *attains* first of all and that by which it attains all the rest; thus, the object of sight is the colored, that of hearing sound, that of the will the good. See *ST* I, q. 1, a. 8.

[3] [Trans. note: As noted in previous chapters, Fr. Garrigou-Lagrange most often uses "principle of contradiction" for what is most commonly referred to now as the "principle of non-contradiction." Thus, on the rarer occasions when he does use "principle of non-contradiction" for the same, I mark those instances with "[*sic*]" to signal that he means the same thing as in most places he means by "principle of contradiction" (and we now commonly mean by "principle of non-contradiction").]

A is A, another conventional symbol, a pure sign, just as after having symbolized the three dimensions of space, one can write the symbol of the fourth, of the fifth, of the sixth, and so on dimensions without even truly conceiving them.

(2) When we necessarily affirm the principle of contradiction as a law of being, the intellect *already faces being as an object placed before subject.* Indeed, we naturally affirm that the absurd (e.g., a square circle) is not only *unthinkable* but *really impossible,* unrealizable even by Almighty God, or by an evil genius, if he exists. To realize the absurd would be to do violence to the first law of being. This is what Descartes should have maintained at the start of the *Discourse on Method* instead of conceding to the skeptic that one can doubt it. He did not see that, once this doubt has been admitted, even *ad hominem,* the *cogito* no longer is certain. Indeed, if there can be a square circle outside of thought, there can also be a thought that is a non-thought, an existence that is a non-existence, an *I* that is lost in the universal and absolutely impersonal flux, if there still is any flux or the least reality concerning which one can say, "It *is.*"

Traditional realism is not content to affirm being and its opposition to nothingness; it also says what being is: not a genus that would be diversified by *extrinsic* differences (for nothing can be extrinsic to being), but rather an analogue that is said very differently of the Necessary Being and of contingent being, of the substance of the latter and of its accidents.

Thus conceived, being has a priority over thought, which can only be relative to it, as to its object. And if human thought does not attain this object, how could it ever *demonstrate* the existence of God, the First Being and Supreme Thought?

Finally, if our intellect itself creates this being that is the object of its thought, it would be omniscient; it would know all being. Now, it is an incontestable fact that it runs into mystery everywhere. This is a proof that being exceeds it, above all the First Being, who alone is omniscient, because he is wisdom itself.

Part 3

———————— ∽∞∞∞ ————————

Common Sense and the Understanding of Dogmatic Formulas

The State of the Question

This study strives to take up anew the problem concerning the value of dogmatic formulas, taking it up from where it was left off by the discussions in 1907 provoked by Éduouard Le Roy and the modernists.

The formulas of faith, we are told, must be interpreted as being written in the language of common sense, not in the technical language of any philosophy. We read in *Revue du clergé français*:[1]

> This point appears definitively attained after the learned discussions of Bernard Allo and Sertillanges, and Lebreton admits it without reservation when he writes, "We have arrived together at this conclusion, that dogma was independent from human systems and that the positive formula that states it must not be interpreted as being written in a philosophical language, but rather, in a common [*vulgaire*] language. . . . This independence from human systems is required by the most essential characteristics of dogmatic truth: it is immutable and cannot allow its fate to be connected with the fate of human philosophies; it is universal and cannot be reserved to a school of thinkers; it is penetrated more profoundly by those who have purer souls, are more detached from the world, and more united to Christ, not by those whose

---

[1] See F. Dubois, "Chronique du mouvement théologique en france," *Revue du clergé français* 51 (August 15, 1907): 377.

minds are more penetrating and more cultivated."[2]

Later on, we read:

In reality, contemporary theologians, by granting that *dogmatic formulas, even when expressed in scientific or philosophical language, have no other meaning than what common sense can give to them,* warn us by this very fact that we must not press too hard on the technical or scientific meaning of the terms employed and must see only the real sense which is accessible to the common man [*au vulgaire*], the sense that alone remains invariable.[3]

At the beginning of this work, we already reported the response made by Le Roy from the Bergsonian perspective:

The formulas of faith must be understood in their *obvious* sense and not in a *learned* one. We agree with all of this, and it is certainly not a negligible affair. But, all this, however, to a certain extent—here is what should be noted—constitutes perhaps less a solution to the problem than the statement thereof. Indeed, what is the precise scope of common language? To what level of thought does it belong? In what specific way and in which aspects can the affirmations of common sense be said to be wholly independent from theoretical philosophy?. . . Here, we have a fundamental problem whose resolution is not as simple as one might think at first glance. . . . Each person will be naturally inclined to hold that the primary foundation of common sense is that of his own theoretical tendencies, with which he effortlessly sympathizes. . . . *Therefore, will we need to assign the task of defining the "system" of common sense to uncritical minds [esprits], to those unlearned people who are incapable of disentangling the influences that they undergo?*

We know already how, according to the Bergsonian doctrine, Le Roy sought to define common sense. It appeared to him, as he says,

---

[2] J. Lebreton, "Dogme et critique," *Revue pratique d'apologétique* 4 (May 15, 1907): 197.
[3] F. Dubois, "Réplique de M. Dubois à M. Le Roy," *Revue du clergé français* 52 (October 15, 1907): 222. I have added emphasis.

as a utilitarian organization of thought from the practical point of view. . . . The proper language of common sense is the language of habitual perception, therefore, a *language relative to action*, made for expressing action, modeled upon action, . . . an action that obviously enough implies thought since we are speaking of the action of a rational being, though one that thus encapsulates only a *wholly practical thought* itself.

(Therefore,) the reality that constitutes the object of faith is made known to us as a fact under the various species of vital reaction that correspond to it in us. It is defined by the attitude and conduct that it requires of us.[4]

And it is rather difficult to see how this conclusion drawn by Le Roy differs from the twenty-sixth proposition condemned by the decree *Lamentabili* of July 3, 1907: "The dogmas of faith are to be held only according to their practical sense, that is to say, as preceptive norms of conduct and not as norms of believing."[5] The Holy Office sees a pragmatism that actually exists, and not a chimerical pragmatism that would make no room for the intellect in this *sensum practicum* rule of action.

At the beginning of the first part of this work, the examination of this pragmatist theory of common sense revealed to us a none-too-new application of the most radical of empirical nominalism. As we have demonstrated, this nominalism ultimately reduces intellectual knowledge to sense knowledge and must inevitably lead to the denial of the ontological value of dogmas. It tells us: one must comport oneself in relation to Jesus as though he were God, without daring, however, to affirm that Jesus is really God.

Thus, we can clearly see the problems that we still must resolve: Do dogmatic formulas, even when expressed in scientific or philosophical language, have any other meaning than what common sense can give for them?

Let us first show how, in fact, dogmatic formulas, expressed originally in terms of common sense, often are given precision in philosophical terms.

Next, we will see that, having received this kind of precision, dogmatic formulas remain accessible, to a degree, to common sense if, as we established above, the latter is the philosophy of being in a rudimentary state.

Finally, we will show that such formulas that have been given preci-

---

4 Dubois, "Réplique de M. Dubois à M. Le Roy," 212–14. I have added emphasis.
5 Pius X, Decree of the Holy Office *Lamentabili*, §26 (Denzinger, no. 3426).

sion in this manner go beyond the strict limits of common sense, but that it remains in its prolongation and does not render dogma subservient to any "system," properly speaking.

* * *

Before starting, it is not useless to prevent a potential misunderstanding.

Some may perhaps reproach us for having too little concern in the theological part of this work for the real needs of contemporary souls, for having been less preoccupied with saving souls than with saving the truth revealed for them. We have already been accused of responding only with an unqualified rejection in answer to objections derived from the modern principle of the autonomy of the mind [*esprit*].

In order to understand the nature of dogma, what we need to study is dogma itself, not the present needs of souls. And by studying it, we will be enabled to discover and arouse in souls far more profound and interesting aspirations than the contemporary needs that are brought up in objection to us. In the midst of the complications that encumber it, a kind of immanentism sometimes seems to forget the first line of the catechism, which summarizes all our duties: contemporary souls, like those living in other eras, were created and placed in the world in order to know and love, more than themselves and above everything, this Divine Truth that is the object of faith prior to being the object of vision; they are created in order subordinate themselves to this Truth and not to subordinate him to their real or artificial needs. We must "serve God" and not make God serve us.

William James finds it wholly natural to write today:

Take God's aseity, for example; or his necessariness; his immateriality; his 'simplicity' or superiority to the kind of inner variety and succession which we find in finite beings, his indivisibility, and lack of the inner distinctions of being and activity, substance and accident, potentiality and actuality, and the rest; his repudiation of inclusion in a genus; his actualized infinity; his 'personality,' apart from the moral qualities which it may comport; his relations to evil being permissive and not positive; his self-sufficiency, self-love, and absolute felicity in himself—*candidly speaking, how do such qualities as these make any definite connection with our life?* And if they severally call for no distinctive adaptations of our conduct, what vital difference can it possibly make to a man's religion whether they be true or false?[6]

Without going so far, obviously, Le Roy[7] tells us that if, as is admitted commonly by most Catholics,[8] dogmas first have an intellectual sense and only then a practical and moral sense:

> The least reproach that one could register against them is that of seeming useless, of being pointless and fruitless, quite a grave reproach in an age wherein we perceive with increasing clarity that value of a truth is measured before all else by the services that it renders, by the new results that it suggests, by the consequences with which it is pregnant, in short, by the vivifying influence that it exercises upon the whole body of knowledge.[9]

This objection presupposes that God does not merit being known for himself, independent of the consequences that can be deduced from his existence, from his nature, and from his action. It presupposes, in addition, that if the Divine Truth is revealed to our intellects, this is more so in order to be assimilated by them than to assimilate them [to him]. It is to apply to divine things that are infinitely superior to us what is true only of material things. It is to affirm of what is an end in itself and the ultimate end what is true only of a means, whose sole value is its utility in view of something else. Infinitely above utility, though fruitful as a cause and an ultimate end, the First Truth never ceases to say to us, as he did once upon a time to Saint Augustine: "I am the bread of the strong, grow and you will eat me. And you will not change me into you, as you do with

---

6 William James, *The Varieties of Religious Experience* (New York: Longmans, Green, and Co., 1905]), 445. [Trans. note: As in ch. 4 of pt. 2, I have used and cited the English edition, which slightly differs from the translation by Abauzit cited by Fr. Garrigou-Lagrange.]

7 In relating this objection and the following, we do not aim in any way at the personal thought of Le Roy. He has informed us that, in formulating them, he wished only to reveal to us "the state of mind in contemporary philosophers that is opposed to the understanding of Christian truth, . . . to state it with frankness and brutality even (if this is necessary for making it be fully understood), . . . for which precise reasons the unbelieving philosophers of today fight off the truth that is brought to them, and for which legitimate causes (agreeing on this point with believing philosophers themselves) they are not satisfied by the explanations that are furnished to them" (Le Roy, *Dogme et critique*, 2). [Trans. note: Fr. Garrigou-Lagrange here cites the 4th edition of the work.]

8 Le Roy, *Dogme et critique*, 15 ("Qu'est-ce qu'un dogme?" ["What is a Dogma?"]).

9 Le Roy, *Dogme et critique*, 12.

the food for your flesh, but it is you who will be changed into me."[10] God demands that we grow. When he reveals himself to us, he seeks, in a way, to divinize us and not to be annihilated within us. When he gives himself, he is not content with providing for our needs: with assuring our moral life, with satisfying our religious sentiment, with suggesting new results to our intellect, with aiding us in developing our own personality. He loves us above everything that we can conceive and desire, to the point of willing to associate us with his *intimate life*, to lead us, little by little, to *see him as he sees himself* and to *love him as he loves himself*. His goal is not to exercise a vivifying influence over the entire body of knowledge. His aims are infinitely higher. If we choose not to take up this supernatural perspective concerning God, preferring to halt at the contemporary needs of a number of souls, then we in reality will thereby wish to understand nothing about the meaning or scope of revelation.

On the contrary, if we wish to seek to know God as he deserves and as he ordains, *for his own sake*, then this knowledge will appear fruitful to us, not like a useful means but like an ultimate cause and ultimate end. The works of someone like Saint Augustine and like Saint Thomas tell us to what extent dogma can be intellectually fruitful. One merely needs to browse the *Summa theologiae* in order to see what influence it has exercised over all the parts of philosophy: on general metaphysics by the affirmation of creation and of creation in time; on natural theology[11] through what it tells us about our natural knowledge of God and of all the divine attributes; on rational psychology by the doctrine concerning the creation of the soul, its spirituality, its freedom, and its immortality. One needs merely to examine the progress of these sciences from Aristotle to Saint Thomas. The principal cause of this progress is incontestably the influence of revealed dogmas, which orient and finalize its investigations.[12] Such influence is not least in moral philosophy: the treatises on ultimate beatitude, on the divine and natural law, on conscience, on human acts, on the virtues, on sin, on grace. The dogmas of the Trinity and the Incarna-

---

[10] Augustine, *Confessions* 8.10: "Cibus sum grandium: cresce et manducabis me. Nec tu me in te mutabis, sicut cibum carnis tuae, set tu mutaberis in me."

[11] [Trans. note: The original reads *théodicée*. See note 40 in pt. 1, ch. 1, of the present volume.]

[12] [Trans. note: As regards Fr. Garrigou-Lagrange's position in the famed "Christian philosophy" debates in France, see Reginald Garrigou-Lagrange, "On the Relationship between Philosophy and Religion," in *Philosophizing in Faith: Essays on the Beginning and End of Wisdom*, ed. and trans. Matthew K. Minerd (Providence, RI: Cluny Media, 2019), 361–98.]

tion have enabled us to deepen, as could never have been the case without them, the notion of personality, and the dogma of transubstantiation [has deepened] the notion of substance.

This influence of dogma on the entire body of knowledge seems even to have been too profound, according to Le Roy, since it is so difficult to-day to separate it from traditional philosophy. Whose fault is it if modern philosophy loses interest in these problems, if along with the notions of creation, providence, and immortality, it every day increasingly loses the notions of the final end, obligation, sin, punishment, penitence, repentance, humility, and love of God? Plato, in the *Gorgias*, was infinitely in advance of the philosophy of our age, and yet another infinite distance separates Plato from Catholic theology. This theology is misunderstood, just like the profound and supernatural meaning of the Gospel. Simple, contemplative souls live it, but wise men, who have become too prudent [in a worldly sense] no longer live by it. "I thank thee, Father, Lord of heaven and earth, that thou hast hidden these things from the wise and understanding and revealed them to babes; yea, Father, for such was thy gracious will" (Matt 11:25-26). These words of Jesus express his love of God, and turning himself toward souls, he immediately adds: "Come to me, all who labor and are heavy laden, and I will give you rest" (Matt 11:28).

Therefore, we must study, as much as is possible, dogma in itself and not in function of contemporary needs. Moreover, if these needs became the norm of our affirmations, what would remain of the revealed Truth? The Church is asked today to purify the word of God of that which is too intransigent in its tone when it makes its affirmations, of that which is too sublime in the excessive love that it expresses (the needs of the modern soul do not reach that high), of that which is too tragic in the justices that it announces. One would like to render it accessible to a number of souls who are less enamored with truth than with intellectual freedom, less enamored with supernatural perfection than with a human ideal, less enamored with the rights of God than with their own rights. The Church will always have infinite charity for the weak; she does not forget our Savior's words to his disciples: "I have yet many things to say to you, but you cannot bear them now" (John 16:12). She exhorts her ministers to explain the most profound mysteries only to "those who are advanced enough in the knowledge of the holy truths, because, for those who are still weak in the faith, it would be feared that they would be overwhelmed by the weight of so lofty a truth."[13] In this supernatural school of Charity, Boanerges like

---

[13] See the *Catechism of the Council of Trent* with regard to the mode according to which

Saint John become gentle and know how to say but one thing: "Love one another." Nothing is more true, but nevertheless, this love of souls, solely by the fact that it is essentially founded on the love of God, can never lead the Church to commit that very fault that the world does not always perceive but that nonetheless offends God very gravely: to diminish his Glory, to more-or-less-consciously subordinate his ideas to ours, his infinitely holy will to our momentary whims.

As regards the principle of autonomy, in the absolute form that it has been presented, it goes without saying that the only thing we can do is reject it. "If it is necessary to hold," we are told, "as being secondary and derived the practical and moral sense of dogma, and to place its intellectual sense in the first place,[14]. . . a given dogma then appears to be a form of enslavement, a limitation upon the rights of thought, like a menace of intellectual tyranny, an obstacle and a restriction, externally imposed on the freedom of inquiry: all things radically opposed to the very life of the mind, to its need for autonomy and sincerity, to its generative and fundamental principle, which is the principle of immanence."[15] "Is not the undisputed first principle of method, from the time of Descartes, the fact that one must hold as being true only what one has clearly seen to be such?"[16] To the objection so formulated, our only response can be an absolute rejection: Presupposing that the first sense of dogma is intellectual, the refusal to adhere intellectually to a dogma thus revealed by God constitutes, for all theologians and for every Catholic, not the legitimate claiming of a right, but the formal sin of infidelity. The first duty of every created thought is to be submitted to the First Thought. "Since man is totally dependent upon God, as upon his Creator and Lord, and since created reason is absolutely subject to Uncreated Truth, we are bound to yield by faith the full homage of intellect and will to the God who reveals, . . . (believing supernaturally) *not because of the intrinsic truth of things,* . . . but *because of the authority of God himself who reveals.*"[17] "If anyone says that human reason is so independent that faith cannot be enjoined upon it by God, let him be anathema."[18] The principle of autonomy, expressed in this radical form, has been studied by theologians in relation to its exemplary realization, the sin of the angel: "The (fallen) angel willed to imitate God in a

---

transubstantiation takes place.
[14] Le Roy, *Dogme et critique,* 15.
[15] Le Roy, *Dogme et critique,* 9.
[16] Le Roy, *Dogme et critique,* 7.
[17] [First] Vatican Council, *De Filius,* ch. 3 (Denzinger, no. 3008).
[18] [First] Vatican Council, *De Filius,* canon 3.1 (Denzinger, no. 3031).

perverse manner by desiring as his ultimate end or beatitude *what he could attain only by the powers of his nature*, and by turning himself away from *supernatural beatitude*, which he could attain only by *God's grace*."[19] What the modern soul no longer knows well enough, what it is gravely culpable of no longer knowing, is that God is God and that, by ourselves, we are only nothingness.

As was true in the past, God forever remains he who is and we remain those who without him are nothing. If in claiming our rights we forget the glory of God, he nonetheless does not cease to think upon it, nor to will to make it ours by assimilating us to him, for he wills us for himself—in his manner, not ours. He watches over his Sacred Word, and the Church cannot obscure its tone. She cannot change one iota of it, "Heaven and earth will pass away, but my words will not pass away" (Matt 23:35); "folly to those who are perishing, but to us who are being saved it is the power of God" (1 Cor 1:18). For the same reason, God watches over his science, theology, forbidding that it be too human, defending it in relation to ideas that are in vogue, from a kind of respect that would be, in the scriptural sense of the word, only *stultitia*, "folly" or human respect. He forever brings it back to its principles. He alone naturally has evidential knowledge [*a l'évidence*] of them, and our life in eternity will be found in intuitive knowledge of these principles. Faced with the alterations of dogma, the theologian today must preserve the absolute frankness of the Fathers and the ancient theologians. Looking on the ardor expressed in the proclamation of the principle autonomy, he cannot fail to see what is called, in its true name, not always intellectual pride but [nonetheless] fear of the supernatural. We fear no longer belonging to ourselves if God becomes completely our master. We are not able to understand that our only true deliverance is found to the degree that God exists in us and reigns in us. Only the saint who abdicates all autonomy before God is fully free. Just as intrinsically efficacious grace, far from doing violence to us, makes us free, in the sense that Saint Thomas teaches,[20] so too revelation dissipates obscurities and doubts in the speculative intellect itself, if we wish to receive it not only in half but in full, with this ardent passion for the truth that tears us away from ourselves so as to lose ourselves in God. Only then do we grasp the multiple relations that exist among things; only then can

---

[19] *Summa theologiae* [*ST*] I, q. 63, a. 3. [Trans. note: I have translated from Fr. Garrigou-Lagrange's French to capture his nuance in the flow of the text. He does not distort St. Thomas's original meaning.]

[20] See *ST* I, q. 83, a. 1, ad 3.

we unite *truths* among themselves without doing violence to them. The counter-point makes all of this sound forth more clearly:

The man separated from *the Truth*, because he fears it, composes a satanic parody of unity. Not having wished to unite what is united, to reconcile what is reconcilable, he tries to unite what is necessarily and eternally contradictory. . . . He falls insensibly into this frigid, placid, and tolerant indifference, which is indignant at nothing because it loves nothing, and which believes itself to be meek because it is dead. Having become neutral between truth and error, he believes that he *dominates* both of them.[21]

This is utterly different from the intellectual freedom of the saints, of the great contemplatives. It is an absolute autonomy that prepares, like that of the prodigal son, for the worst servitudes and final degradations. It has for its supreme formula: "Immutable truth does not exist; it would be contrary to the freedom of the mind. Nothing is, everything becomes, and in this becoming contradictories are identified, being and non-being, good and evil."[22] This wise philosophy and this sweet tolerance reproduce in their own way the calm of charity. They sympathize with all religions.[23] However, when Christ comes to say, "I have come into the world, to bear witness to the truth. Everyone who is of the truth hears my voice," they find, like Pilate, only one small phrase said in response: "What is truth?" (John 18:38). Thus, man comes to no longer know even the sense of the verb implied in every judgment, "est est, non non" (Matt 5:37); he no longer sees in what way affirmation and denial are opposed to each other. "It is written," says Saint Paul, "The Lord knows that the thoughts of the wise are futile. . . . He catches the wise in their craftiness" (1 Cor 3:18–19). Without always denying the absolute character of the truth, certain people say to us: "What is important is not to know whether *God exists*, but whether the examination of the problem of God is truly free. For this, one

---

[21] Ernest Hello, *L'Homme: La vie, la science, l'art*, 3rd ed. (Paris: Perrin, 1894), 257. [Trans. note: Fr. Garrigou-Lagrange has slightly truncated the text without marking it.]

[22] Is this not the incessant leitmotiv of the "new philosophy" that wishes to substitute *becoming for Being*? Henri Bergson, like Hegel before him, is only a performer. The score was written long ago, and it is necessary to have or have had supernatural faith in order to grasp its full depths.

[23] See Pius X, *Pascendi Dominici Gregis*, no. 14. [Trans. note: Fr. Garrigou-Lagrange cites Denzinger, no. 2082. This passage no longer is in Denzinger; it falls between Denzinger, nos. 3484 and 3485 in the new edition.]

must be as *sincerely* disposed to do without God if he is not encountered, as one is to accept Him if He is encountered." The same must obviously hold too for the examination of the existence of *duty*. We know what this independence in reality is: "He who is not with me is against me" (Matt 12:30). Without going so far, we come to prefer the search for the truth to the truth itself. As Pascal remarks, "One loves to see in disputes the combat of opinions, but not at all to contemplate the truth when found, . . . (like those) who pass the whole day chasing after a hare which they would not have desired to buy."[24] This frivolous attitude sometimes tells us that the divine truth is useless and without interest, that if God were to give it to us "readymade," we would [still] like to find it ourselves. This is, in particular, the vice of subjectivism, which is radically unable to elevate itself to the *objectivity of charity*, to the love of God *for His own sake* and not *for ours*.

Such is the reason for our absolute rejection. Perhaps one will find it to be un-scientific in the modern sense of the word. Nonetheless, it is *real and theological*, and that suffices.

As for the part of the objection that deserves consideration, we believe that we have amply responded to it. To the degree that the mind's autonomy is legitimate, it too finds itself safeguarded in traditional philosophy, though in a different way from how it is [supposedly] safeguarded in the pragmatism that has been proposed to us. What is absolutely contrary to the mind's autonomy is, in the natural order, to make its most essential affirmations depend on practical expediencies and not on the objective evidence of the truth. On this point, we go even further than Descartes, who remained content with subjective evidence. In order that it be truly autonomous, objective evidence (or, evident being) is necessary for the mind. Only then can it make its assertions in full awareness of the facts, for it affirms only what it perceives in being itself. If this is how matters stand, God, in order to reveal himself to us, is above all served by the first notions of our spontaneous, speculative understanding. He has reunited these notions in a non-evident proposition.[25] He requires us to believe in it supernaturally because it came from him, and he has given us grace for this purpose. Afterward, this supernatural faith is explained in conformity with the laws of the mind's autonomy by giving precision to its first notions, through an activity directed

---

[24] [Trans. note: Fr. Garrigou-Lagrange cites pp. 389 and 392 of the 2nd edition of the *Pensées* edited by Leon Brunschvicg.]

[25] [Trans. note: That is, by means of the non-evident knowledge afforded through the theological virtue of faith.]

and sanctioned by God, one that is at once his work and our own. Only thus does the word of God preserve its objective scope. As we will see, every other explanation impoverishes and denatures it. It is not by impoverishing the word of God that souls are saved. Whether or not one so wishes, this will manage only to make them insipid and, ultimately, bring them to ruin. "If salt has lost its taste, how shall its saltiness be restored? It is no longer good for anything except to be thrown out and trodden under foot by men" (Matt 5:13).[26]

---

[26] [Trans. note: Fr. Garrigou-Lagrange cites only the Latin: "Quod si sal evanuerit, in quo salietur? Ad nihilum valet ultra, nisi ut mittatur foras et conculcetur ab hominibus."]

Chapter 1

━━━━━━━━━━ ⚬✕✕✕✕⚬ ━━━━━━━━━━

HOW DOGMATIC FORMULAS
ARE GIVEN PRECISION IN
PHILOSOPHICAL TERMS

§1. The Progressive Precision of Dogmatic Formulas

Therefore, we still must examine whether it is true to say that dogmatic formulas, even though they are expressed in a philosophical language, must be interpreted as though they were written in common [*vulgaire*] language. We will have no difficulty in acknowledging that faith *can* be expressed in the terms of common sense. (The formulation of the faith of the first faithful did not contain any technical terms.) If the notions belonging to common sense, nominal definitions (what everyone thinks when a given word is pronounced) vaguely contain a true, real definition, *quid rei*, then they can analogically translate the divine reality. However, precisely for this reason, no philosophical system that breaks with common sense, like phenomenalism or the philosophy of becoming, no system that refuses to grant an ontological scope to the first notions of being, substance, thing, and so on, can be of service for giving precision to the primitive dogmatic formula, for formulating or thinking philosophically about dogma. And if, for one reason or another, the primitive formulation made by common sense must be given precision, this can be only through recourse to this philosophy of being, which Henri Bergson calls "the natural metaphysics of the human intellect," and a philosophy that is, in reality, nothing other than the natural prolongation of spontaneous understanding. Why would this not be the metaphysics of the Councils?

This problem comes down to the question concerning the development of dogma following on the death of Christ and the apostles. All Catholic theologians define this development by saying that it does not take place in the known reality, nor in the revelation that has been made to us regarding it, but rather in the knowledge that we have of it. Moreover, they hold that our knowledge undergoes such progress by passing from the implicit to the explicit. Note, however, that Catholic theologians do not say that it takes place by passing from potency to act, nor even from the virtual to the actual, but rather by passing from the actual-implicit to the actual-explicit. The faith of the primitive Church did not have less extension than does ours; we do not know *more things*, but rather know the same things now in a more precise fashion. Various analogies have been provided for explaining this progress: that of a seed (which brings to mind, however, the passage from potency to act); that of leaven (which is perhaps less crude in certain regards). However, analogies drawn from the order of knowledge would be more fitting. Here, we could use as an example the very philosophy prepared by Socrates, developed by Plato, systematized by Aristotle, and taken up by Saint Thomas much later. However, this still provides us with an insufficient analogy. In the process of such philosophical development, there is the passage from the virtual to the actual, as takes place in the development of theology, not that of dogma. Theology deduces *new conclusions*, which were only virtually contained in the articles of faith.[1]

The true analogy that should be used for understanding the nature of the development of dogma is the progress that we noted in the knowledge we have concerning the first rational principles or, again, in the knowledge we have concerning the notions of freedom, spirituality, and so forth. Everyone possesses the first principles. They are like the very structure of reason, but the common person cannot formulate them [precisely]. Effort

---

[1] [Trans. note: There are points of development even within Fr. Garrigou-Lagrange's treatment of wisdom, which emphasize the fact that theology, precisely as a form of wisdom, also must defend and meditate upon its principles, even prior to drawing any conclusions. This point comes through quite forcefully in the beginning of Reginald Garrigou-Lagrange, "Theology and the Life of Faith," in *Philosophizing in Faith: Essays on the Beginning and End of Wisdom*, ed. and trans. Matthew K. Minerd (Providence, RI: Cluny Media, 2019), 421–43. A semi-pedagogical explanation of the Thomist doctrine concerning virtual revelation can be found in Reginald Garrigou-Lagrange, "Remarks Concerning the Metaphysical Character of St. Thomas's Moral Theology, in Particular as It Is Related to Prudence and Conscience," trans. Matthew K. Minerd, *Nova et Vetera* (English) 17, no. 1 (2019): 261–66 ("Translator's Appendix 1: Concerning the Formal Object of Acquired Theology"). For a fuller discussion of the state of this problem in the early and mid twentieth century in Catholic thought, see Matthew K. Minerd, "Wisdom Be Attentive: The Noetic Structure of Sapiential Knowledge," *Nova et Vetera* (English) 18, no. 4 (2020): 1103–46.]

had to be expended by philosophers in order for this precise formulation to be discovered, determining the ways that these different principles depend on the supreme principle, the principle of identity. Real progress does indeed take place by passing from the simple adherence of common sense to what is found in the fourth book of the *Metaphysics*, dedicated by Aristotle to the principle of contradiction.[2] However, this real progress is only a passage from the actual-implicit to the actual-explicit. Likewise, every man is aware of his free choice; he feels himself to be the master of his acts, the master of acting or of not acting. He has an idea of freedom that is not *obscure*, but rather *clear*, in the sense that it suffices for enabling him to recognize what is free and what is not. But, nonetheless, this clear idea remains, in itself, *vague [confuse]*; it will be *distinct* only when philosophical reason determines its comprehension and defines it by connecting it to being. *Self-mastery*, which everyone affirms, will then become the *dominating indifference* of the will in relation to any given partial good, an indifference founded on the knowledge of the universal good and knowledge of the infinite gulf separating it from limited goods.

This is how we must conceive of dogmatic development, at least for fundamental dogmas like the Trinity and the Incarnation that from the earliest days were an object of *explicit faith* and expressed in terms drawn from common sense. The explication of their already-clear formula was only a passage from the vague to the distinct.[3] Hence, it is to be expected

---

[2] [Trans. note: As noted in previous chapters, Fr. Garrigou-Lagrange most often uses "principle of contradiction" for what is most commonly referred to now as the "principle of non-contradiction." Thus, on the rarer occasions when he does use "principle of non-contradiction" for the same, I mark those instances with "[*sic*]" to signal that he means the same thing as in most places he means by "principle of contradiction" (and we now commonly mean by "principle of non-contradiction").]

[3] For other dogmas, like the infallibility of the pope or that of the Immaculate Conception, which were not the object of *explicit faith* from the first days, they involved passing from the *obscure* to the *distinct*, not from the *vague [confuse]* to the *distinct*. The infallibility of the pope was contained obscurely in the dogma of the infallibility of the Church and in that of the primacy of the successors of St. Peter. Likewise, the Immaculate Conception was contained in the fullness of grace attributed by the Archangel Gabriel to Mary. Thus, in the natural order, the certitude of the objectivity of our knowledge contains the certitude that the *formal object of the intellect is being*; this latter proposition is not contained clearly in the common man, but only obscurely, whereas he knows freedom clearly. Likewise, again, as Leibniz said, the common man [*vulgaire*] has an *obscure* knowledge of the various species of plants, the gardener a *clear* knowledge of them, and the botanist a *distinct* knowledge. Other examples of this development can be seen in the case of the sacraments: thus, the dogma of the three sacramental characters is an explication of the practice of the non-reiteration of three sacraments. Nothing

that this precision is brought about by a natural recourse to this philosophy of being that is the natural prolongation of common sense. From this perspective, why should the terms involved in certain propositions defined concerning the real distinction of the divine persons or concerning the Hypostatic Union be restricted within the strict limits of the domain of spontaneous understanding? Moreover, who will fix these limits exactly? Who will say exactly where common sense ends and where this natural metaphysics that is the prolongation and justification of it begins?

In order to form an exact idea of the nature of dogmatic development, we can compare the primitive formulation of the dogmas of the Trinity and of the Incarnation to the subsequent formulations destined to illuminate their meanings and to develop them in the face of the alterations proposed by the various heresies that arose. The definition of the Council of Vienne on the soul, the form of the body, and that of Trent on transubstantiation will also provide us some light concerning this process.

§2. The Dogmatic Formula of the Trinity

The confession of faith in the Trinity in its primitive simplicity is thus conceived: "Credo in unum Deum Patrem omnipotentem, et in Iesum Christum Filium eius unicum Dominum nostrum, et in Spiritum Sanctum." This was the nucleus of the creed that was required in the reception of baptism, merely reproducing the baptismal formula given by Our Savior Jesus Christ to his apostles. The heresies of the first three centuries departed from the true meaning of this formulation. They took three directions. Some, insisting too exclusively on God's unity, denied the real distinction between the Father, the Son, and the Holy Spirit; and this was the heresy of Sabellius. Others, on the contrary, insisted on the distinction of the Father, the Son, and the Holy Spirit to the point of making of the Son and the Holy Spirit into beings inferior to the true God; this was the heresy of Arius and that of Macedonianism. Finally, others, coming later, the tritheists, maintained the distinction and

---

could be more complex than a fact such as the administration of a sacrament: we can consider the sacrament in itself as a sign, in its elements, in its effects, in relation to God and to Christ, and finally, in relation to the minister and the sacrament's subject, as well as to the conditions required in each of them. In this way, by means of an explication of the content of this very complex fact, one can come to draw a host of definitions. We have treated this question of the development of dogma elsewhere, in *De revelatione*, vol. 1, pp. 18–20 and 185–90.

equality of the Father, the Son, and the Holy Spirit, though [they] did so by holding that they were in fact three gods.

The Council of Nicaea gave precision to the dogma against the Arians, not only in a *negative* manner by means of an anathema, but also in a *positive* manner, by enlarging the apostolic symbol by developing the idea of filiation or generation. The Nicene creed was thus conceived: "Et in unum Dominum, Iesum Christum Filium Dei, qui ex Patre unigenitus generatus, hoc est ex substantia Patris, Deum ex Deo, lumen ex lumine, Deum verum ex Deo vero, genitum, non factum, consubstanialem (*homoousion*) Patri, per quem omnia facta sunt, et quae in caelo et quae in terra." Next comes the anathema that rejects the idea that the Son would differ in substance from the Father, as well as the claim that he has a temporal origin.

The First Council of Constantinople gave precision to the dogma against the Macedonians in relation to the Holy Spirit. This doctrine had already been fixed against the tritheists by the dogmatic letter of Pope Dionysius and by the anathemas of Pope Damasus. The Second Council of Constantinople (553), in its first canon, excludes the three preceding heresies: "If anyone does not confess that Father, Son, and Holy Spirit are *one nature* or essence, one might and power, a *Trinity* one in being, one Godhead to be worshipped *in three hypostases or Persons*, let him be anathema."[4] It is to be noted that this anathema does not simply determine the negative sense of the dogma by condemning heresies. Beyond this, it determines what must be positively believed. The dogmatic formula now includes the abstract nouns "nature" and "substance" (*mian physin ētoi ousian* [Gk.]) and the concrete nouns *three subsistences* or *persons* (*en trisin hypostasesin ēgthon prosōpois* [Gk.]).

The so-called Athanasian Creed (likely dating from the fifth century) summarizes the entire doctrine of the Trinity by teaching that one must confuse neither the persons, (*neque confundentes personas*) nor separate the substance (*neque substantiam separantes*). The attributes of the essence belong to each person but must not be multiplied any more than the substance itself. In the patristic era, the most complete symbol of the dogma of the Trinity is that of the eleventh synod [*concile*] celebrated at Toledo in 675. "It reflects," says Matthias J. Scheeben, "the full technicality of dogma such as it developed in the fight against the heresies."[5] We no longer

---

4   Denzinger, no. 421. [Trans. note: Fr. Garrigou-Lagrange cites the original text in Latin from the 10th edition of Denzinger, no. 213.]

5   Matthias Scheeben, *La dogmatique*, vol. 2, §106; "The dogmatic formulations concerning the Trinity."

have here only the abstract nouns "nature" or "substance" and the concrete names "person" and "subsistence"; rather, what distinguishes the persons from one another are the "relations."[6] It is *de fide* that there are real relations in God. The Creed promulgated at Toledo says expressly:

> In the relative names of the Persons, the Father is related to the Son, the Son to the Father, and the Holy Spirit to both. *While they are called three Persons in view of their relations*, we believe in one nature or substance. Although we profess three Persons, we do not profess three substances, but one substance and three persons. For the Father is Father not with respect to himself but to the Son, and the Son is Son not to himself but in relation to the Father; and likewise the Holy Spirit is not referred to himself but is related to the Father and the Son, inasmuch as he is called the Spirit of the Father and the Son. So when we say, "God," this does not express a relationship to another, as of the Father to the Son or of the Son to the Father or of the Holy Spirit to the Father and the Son, but "God" refers to himself only. . . .
>
> Because *in the relationships* [*in relatione*] of the Persons there appears *number*, but in the substance of the Godhead nothing is comprised that could be counted. Therefore they imply number only insofar as they are *mutually* related, but they lack number insofar as they are *by themselves*.[7]

This doctrine, which will be reproduced by the Council of Florence, is incontestably the expression of a defined point of faith. Hereafter, the Fourth Lateran Council brought a new precision. In its definition *contra abbatem Joachim*, joined to its creed, it affirms the real identity of the divine substance with each of the divine persons, which excludes a division of substance in the different persons: "Each of the Persons is that reality, that is, that divine substance, essence or nature. . . . [And] this reality is neither generating nor generated nor proceeding, but it is the Father who generates, the Son who is generated, and the Holy Spirit who proceeds, so

---

6 St. Gregory of Nazianzus, St. Gregory of Nyssa, and St. Augustine had already shown that the unity of nature was reconcilable with the real distinction of the persons only by reducing the persons to subsistent relations. See Jansens, *De Deo Trino*, 221. [Trans. note: Fr. Garrigou-Lagrange is perhaps referring to Laurentio Janssens, *Tractatus de Deo Trino* (Fribourg, Switzerland: Herder, 1900).]

7 Denzinger, nos. 528–30.

that there be distinctions between the Persons but unity in nature."[8] Finally, the *Filioque*[9] was defined at the Councils of Lyon and of Florence; and the *Decree for the Jacobites* gives a general exposition of all the doctrine of the Trinity, which can be considered as the final expression of the dogmatic progress: (1) it gives precision to the real and indestructible distinction of the persons on the basis of their origin; (2) [and to] their absolute unity, except in that which pertains to the relations ("These three Persons are one God, not three gods, because there is one substance of the three, one essence, one nature, one Godhead, one immensity, one eternity, and everything [in them] is one where there is no opposition of relation"[10]), from which unity follows the circumincession of the persons and their equality; and (3)° the three persons are one single God and one single principle of all things. This *Decree*[11] is a solemn definition, as the first words indicate, "Sacrosancta romana Ecclesia ... firmiter credit profitetur et praedicat, et cetera." Therefore, the dogmatic formula developed henceforth includes the concepts of *nature, subsistence,* and *relation.*

In the modern age, there is little to cite except for the Church's declarations against Anton Günther. Günther recognized the divine origin of Christianity as well as the Church's infallibility, but according to him:

> Inasmuch as the progress of the human mind was not able to arrive fully at the understanding of Christianity, this infallibility could serve only to make the best possible choice among the reigning interpretations. Therefore, the interpretations infallibly proposed by the Church had been those that are most in harmony with the civilization and the needs of that given age. All the Councils' definitions thus contained a bit of the truth;

---

8 Denzinger, no. 804.
9 [Trans. note: Heeding, however, the precisions of official statements such as the Union of Brest, no. 1: "Since there is a quarrel between the Romans and Greeks about the procession of the Holy Spirit, which greatly impede unity really for no other reason than that we do not wish to understand one another—we ask that we should not be compelled to any other creed but that we should remain with that which was handed down to us in the Holy Scriptures, in the Gospel, and in the writings of the holy Greek Doctors, that is, that the Holy Spirit proceeds, not from two sources and not by a double procession, but from one origin, from the Father through the Son." See "Reunion Treaty of Brest," ewtn.com/catholicism/library/reunion-treaty-of-brest-1474.]
10 [Trans. note: The reference is unmarked but is from Denzinger, no. 1330, the Council of Florence's Bull, *Cantate Domino.*]
11 See Denzinger, no. 1330. [Trans. note: One will need to bear in mind, however, qualifications necessary surrounding the Filioque. See note 9 above, citing the Union of Brest.]

however, to the degree that the march of progress required it, they had to be replaced by others closer to the absolute truth and more conformed to reason.[12]

A modernist before the term was coined, Günther held that the philosophy of the Fathers and of the theologians was outdated. They were not able to establish, he said, the theory of knowledge that must seek its foundations in awareness of the *self.* Descartes was the one who opened the true way. From this modern point of view, personality can consist only in awareness of the *self.* Hence, our conception of Christianity's dogmas must be modified. If God has awareness of himself by his essence, there is only one person in him. If God knows himself, he therefore has such knowledge, according to Günther, through the three persons that are in him; this is so by his being opposed to himself as subject and to himself as object and by affirming at the same time the equality of this subject and this object. In this way, we have an explanation for the mystery of the Holy Trinity. The subject having awareness of himself would be the First Person. The object having awareness of himself would be the Second Person. Finally, the consciousness of the equality of this subject and of this object would constitute the Third Person. The act of self-awareness or of intellection is thus tripled in order for there to be three persons. However, the divine nature itself is thereby *tripled,* for it is identical with the divine understanding. Thus, according to Günther, there is no longer a numeric unity of nature and of understanding for the three divine persons, but only a formal, dynamic unity; the divine nature is tripled. "God is opposed to himself in himself as a real substance, or he duplicates [himself] through emanation."[13] As regards the question of explaining the preface of the Holy Trinity, "non in unius singularitate personae, sed in unius Trinitate substantiae [Not in the singularity of one person, but in the Trinity of one substance]," Günther has recourse to this exegesis: "The expression *unius* in the second place must not be taken in the same sense as in the first, but for the sake of euphony is *unius substantiae* said for *eiusdem substantiae,* for here the concern is with a *threefold, or triplicated, substance [de ternaria seu triplicate substantia].*"[14]

---

[12] Jean-Michel-Alfred Vacant, *Études théologiques sur les constitutions du Concile du Vatican d'après les actes du concile,* vol. 2 (Paris: Delhomme et Briguet, 1895), 283.

[13] Version presented in Franzelin, see *De Deo Trino,* th. 18, p. 289. [Trans. note: Likely, he is referring to some edition of *Tractatus de Deo Trino secundum personas* by Johannes Baptist Franzelin.]

[14] Anton Günther, *Propaed.,* vol. 2, p. 539. See Franzelin, *De Deo Trino,* 297.

It is on the subject of this error that Pius IX wrote his letter to the archbishop of Cologne on June 15, 1857: "We note that in the same books are found, among other things, much that is not a little at variance with the Catholic faith and with the genuine explanation of the unity of the divine substance in three distinct, eternal Persons."[15] It is also against this neo-tritheism that there were formulated the three canons that are found in the *schema* of the [First] Vatican Council concerning the dogma of the Trinity.[16]

§3. Dogmatic Formulas of the Mystery of the Incarnation

One can follow an analogous and parallel progress by comparing the successive formulas for the dogma of the Incarnation. The primitive dogmatic formula relative to the person of the Savior is the following in the Apostle's Creed received in the West: "Credo . . . in Iesum Christum Filium eius (Patris) unicum, Dominum nostrum, qui natus est de Spiritu Sancto ex Maria Virgine." In the later Western form, we read: "Qui conceptus est de Spiritu Sanctu, natus ex Maria Virgine." Four successive heresies departed from the true meaing of this formula. Arius said: "The unity of God requires us to admit that the Logos is created. This pre-existing Logos could not receive a complete human nature in Mary's womb and elevate such a nature to it, but only a human body. It seems absurd to think of uniting two created spirits in one and the same person." St. Athanathius responded: "We would not have been redeemed, divinized, if the Logos-become-flesh had not been, in his nature, the true Logos of God." And the Council of Nicaea then expanded the symbol, and after affirming therein that the *Son is consubstantial* to the Father, it adds: "Qui propter nostrum salutem descendit, incarnatus est et *homo factus est.*" Apollinaris, who took part in the battles against the Arians, did not wish to recognize anything of the created order in the spiritual nature of Christ: "If Christ," he said,

---

[15] Denzinger, no. 2828.

[16] *Collectio Lacensis*, vol. 7, p. 1637. "If one were to say, that, just as there are three persons in God, so too there are three essences or substances in him, let him be anathema. If one were to say that the divine substance is one and the same not in number but in species or in quality, let him be anathema. If one were to say that the Trinity is one God not on account of a singularity of one substance but on account of an equality of three substances and the relation of the persons to each other, let him be anathema." [Trans. note: He is almost certainly referring to the seventh volume of an edition of *Acta et decreta sacrorum conciliorum recentiorum*, originally printed in Friburg between 1870 and 1892.]

"had had a rational soul like ours, he would not have been impeccable and his merits would not have had a value sufficing to redeem us." He added that, moreover, "the divine Logos and a rational soul cannot form a single being." All that remained, was to say that Jesus, the divine Logos replaced the rational soul. Thus [in response], the sense of the symbol of Nicaea was perfectly explained in a long creed reproduced in the *Ancoratus* of Saint Epiphanius and widespread in the West around 374: "We believe in the Son of God ... who ... also was made man; that is, *he assumed the complete man, soul and body* and mind and all that is man except sin, not from the seed of man or in a man, but he formed in himself one flesh, consisting in one holy unity. . . . He became fully man."[17] Nestorius, in reaction to Apollinaris, was not content with maintaining the integrity of Christ's human nature. He makes it into a particular person alongside that of the Logos: "If Christ," says he, "is born of Mary, he is not of the divine nature; the Logos-God could not be born of a woman; he only dwells in him who was born of Mary." The Incarnation was nothing more than a mere moral union between God and of the man Jesus. The Council of Ephesus approved the twelve anathemas of Saint Cyril of Alexandria against Nestorius. The second of these anathemas was conceived thus: "If anyone does not confess that the Word from God the Father was united to the flesh hypostatically (*kath' hypostasin* [Gk.]) and that he is one sole Christ with his own flesh—namely, the same at once both God and man—let him be anathema."[18] Let us note again that this anathema does not constitute only the negative meaning of the dogma by ruling out Nestorius's error. It also determines its positive meaning. Henceforth, it is necessary to positively believe ("If anyone does not confess") in the *Hypostatic Union* of two natures. Eutychès, an adversary of Nestorius, presented himself as a defender of Saint Cyril's theology and insisted so heavily on the union

---

[17] Denzinger, no. 44. [Trans. note: Fr. Garrigou-Lagrange cites the older Denzinger numbering as 13. He also cites the text in Latin, though the Greek is the original. To be consistent with Denzinger citations, I have used the 43rd Denzinger English edition as elsewhere. The senses are close enough for this. For the sake of reference, the Latin reads: "Credimus in Filium Dei ... qui ... et homo factus est, hoc est *assumpsit perfectum hominem* (hoc est), *animam et corpus* et mentem et omne quidquid est homo, except peccato, non ex semine viri, nec ita ut in homine dumtaxat inesset, sed in seipsum effectam ilam carnem transtulit, at in unam ac sanctam singularitatem coniunxit ... homo perfectus esse voluit."]

[18] [Trans. note: Taken from Denzinger, no. 253, which is translated from the original Greek. Fr. Garrigou-Lagrange has the equivalent Latin: "Si quis non confitetur, carni *secundum subsistentiam* [*kath' hypostasin*] *unitum* Dei Patris Verbum unumque esse Christum cum propria carne, eumdem scilicet Deum simul et hominem, A.S."

(*henōsis kath' hypostasin* [Gk.]) that he came to lose sight of the duality of divine and human natures in it. According to him, after the union there was only a single divine-human nature. The Council of Chalcedon defined the distinction of the two natures and gave precision to personal or hypostatic unity thus: "One and the same Lord Jesus Christ, the only begotten Son, must be acknowledged *in two natures, without confusion*; ... the character proper to each of the two natures was preserved as they came together *in one person and one hypostasis*. He is not split or divided into two persons."[19] The fourth canon of the Council of Constantinople (653) reproduced these expressions. The Lateran Council (649) condemned the monothelites by defining that there are two wills in Christ, just as there are two natures. Henceforth, dogmatic progress can be considered as having come to its completion. The so-called Athanasian Creed illuminates the Hypostatic Union by using the very distant analogy of the union of the soul and the body. The symbol of Toledo (675) determines more exactly Christ's relations with the Trinity. The Council of Florence, in its decree for the Jacobites, summarizes all the preceding definitions with a retrospective glance over the principal heresies.

In the modern era, in the nineteenth century, Günther reckoned that the doctrine of the Council of Ephesus against Nestorius corresponded to a philosophy henceforth reduced to ruin under the blows of Kantian criticism. The modern philosophy that makes personality consist in self-consciousness requires us today, according to Günther, to recognize two persons in Christ just as there are two consciousnesses in him, one divine and the other human, though they are two very intimately united persons. According to him, there is no personal unity here, but rather a *dynamic union* of persons; Christ as man is aware of being subordinated to the Word and belonging to him, and the Word is aware of acting in Jesus. This doctrine of Günther was regarded by theologians as representing a return to Nestorianism, and Pius IX declared that it was no less false than his doctrine concerning the Trinity: "Likewise, We have found that neither better nor more accurate is what is related about the mystery of the incarnate Word and about the unity of the divine person of the Word in two natures, divine and human."[20] Also, in the schemata of the [First] Vatican Council,

---

[19] [Trans. note: Again, from Denzinger, no. 301, translated from the Greek. The Latin cited by Fr. Garrigou-Lagrange: "Unum eumdemque Christum Filium Dominum unigenitum, *in duabus naturis inconfuse*, ... salva proprietate utriusque naturae *et in unam personam atque subsistentiam* concurente, non in duas personas partitum aut divisum."

[20] Pius IX, Brief *eximiam tuam* to the Archbishop of Cologne (Denzinger, no. 2828).

we can find three canons against this error.[21]

§4. The Council of Vienne's Definition Concerning the Soul, the Form of the Body

Finally, let us cite one final definition that Günther believed could not be reconciled with modern philosophy, namely the Council of Vienne's definition concerning the rational soul, the form of the body: "In order that the truth of the pure faith may be known to all and the path of error barred, we define that from now on whoever presumes to assert, defend, or obstinately hold that the rational and intellectual soul is not of itself essentially the form of the human body is to be censured as a heretic."[22] The Fourth Council of Constantinople (869) had already defined that man has no other soul than his rational soul and condemned the Apollinarists, who distinguished in man the body, the animal soul, and the rational soul. This teaching concerning the unity of man's soul was only a corollary of the principles related to the Incarnation proclaimed by the Council of Ephesus and the Second Council of Constantinople, according to which the Word had taken on flesh animated by a rational soul. Also, Pius IX declared against Günther and Johann Baptista Baltzer that the doctrine that makes the *rational soul the principle of our bodily life* "cannot be denied without error in faith."[23] "This truth," says Jean Vacant, "was denied by two categories of adversaries: those who believed there to be many souls in man (gnostics, Manicheans, Apollinaris, Günther) and those who explain man's vegetative or sensitive life by something other than the rational soul

---

[21] *Collectio Lacensis*, vol. 7, p. 1637: "If one were to deny that the human nature of Christ is so united to God the Word such that it subsists through the latter's hypostasis and has it as its own, let him be anathema"; "If one were to understand the one subsistence or person of Jesus Christ [to] include multiple ones, and thus were to introduce two persons, divine and human, into the mystery of Christ, persons that, conjoined by an indissoluble connection henceforth from birth, make one composite person, let him be anathema"; "If one were to say there necessarily are as many persons as there are intellects and wills, or else, having rejected two persons in Christ, hold that perfection of human nature, self-awareness, and freedom must be denied, let him be anathema." [Trans. note: Fr. Garrigou-Lagrange's text has several small errors and removals. The original text is followed in this footnote, though the differences are minor.]

[22] Denzinger, no. 902.

[23] See Denzinger, no. 2828. [Trans. note: Fr. Garrigou-Lagrange cites Denzinger, no. 1655, note 1.]

(mechanists, Malebranche, Leibniz)."[24] However, the Council of Vienne was not content to say that the rational soul is the principle of our bodily life. It affirms, moreover, that *"the soul is per se and essentially the form* of the human body." And in the passage that immediately precedes the one we have cited, it says even, *"the substance* of the rational and intellectual soul is truly and of itself the form of the human body."[25] The Fifth Lateran Council repeats the same formula, "vere per se et essentialiter humani corporis forma [truly *per se* and essentially the form of the human body],"[26] and Pius IX again gives precision to it, if it is possible, by calling it a Catholic doctrine "vera, per se atque immediata corporis forma [the true, *per se*, and immediate form of the body.]"[27]

There was a great deal of discussion about forty years ago concerning the exact sense of the word *form* in this definition by the Council of Vienne. Matteo Liberatore, in his book *Du composé humain*, says:

The Church, in her decrees, does not define the vague sense of a word in order to thereby leave each person the freedom of attaching to it the meaning that happens to please him. She does not make a fool of herself in this way, and were we to say that this was what she meant, would we not thereby insult the supreme teacher [*maîtresse*] of truth? The Church defines things by means of terms and she employs them in the sense commonly received among those to whom she speaks. Consequently, in the case of scientific terms, the Church employs them in the sense admitted by contemporary doctors, and she wills that the thing defined in this sense remain immutable.[28]

In 1878, Cardinal Tomasso Zigliara published his *De mente concilii Viennensis*: "The Fathers of the Council of Vienne used the word *forma* in the strictly Scholastic sense."[29] He adds, however, that the Council took

---

[24] Vacant, *Études theologiques*, 1:246.

[25] [Trans. note: The actual passage from Denzinger no. 902 is negatively formed so as to be condemned.]

[26] Denzinger, no. 1440.

[27] Denzinger, no. 2828.

[28] Matteo Liberatore, *Du composé humain* [French edition of *Dell'Anima Umana*] (Lyon: Brinday, 1865), 306.

[29] Tommaso Maria Zigliara, *De mente Concilii Viennensis in definiendo dogmate unionis animae humanae cum corpore deque unitate formae substantialis in homine iuxta doctrinam S. Thomae praemissa theoria scholastica de corporum compositione* (Rome: Sacred

the word "form" in a sense common to Saint Thomas and to John Duns Scotus. (Saint Thomas holds that the rational soul gives the human body not only the fact that it is human and living, but also the very fact that it is a body and a determinate substance, thus holding that the rational soul is the *only* form of the body. Scotus, by contrast, acknowledges a subordinated form, called *the form of corporeity*.) Father Domenico Palmieri[30] held that, since the definition was reconcilable with Thomism and Scotism, it could also be reconciled with a *certain atomism* that makes the rational soul the principle of bodily life. He said: "The Council of Vienne meant to define the *fact* that the rational soul is what gives life to the body, not the *way* the soul gives life to the body; it indicated the way that was commonly acknowledged at the beginning of the fourtheenth century (by information), but this is not what it has principally in view." The Church respected the numerous works in which Father Palmieri's sentiment was set forth. These works were not placed on the *Index*, and a letter that Pius IX wrote on June 5, 1877, to the rector of the University of Lille even said that "Catholic schools can follow different sentiments on this point," and that "the Supreme authority of the Church never has born a judgment that favors one of these sentiments to the exclusion of the others."[31] The Church, the same letter says, requires only that one recognize the theological principle of the "substantial unity of human nature, which is composed of two partial substances, the body and the rational soul," and it has always condemned authors who have held, as did Günther, that man has some principle of life other than the rational soul.

Conclusion

These three examples of dogmatic formulas suffice for our purposes. The developed formula of the dogma of the Holy Trinity includes the concepts

---

Congregation for the Propogation of the Faith, 1878), no. 136. See no. 134: "I judge that this thesis is proven with utter clarity on a number of bases: (1) from the time when it was set forth in the aforementioned conciliar definition; (2) from the unanimous authority of Scholastic authors; (3) from Council's aim to defend the truth of man's *substantial unity* and to refute the error of *dualism* in relation to man himself."

[30] In vol. 2 of Domenico Palmieri, *Institutiones philosphiae*. [Trans. note: Fr. Garrigou-Lagrange does not cite the edition of the Jesuit manual.]

[31] Vacant, *Études theologiques*, 1:261. This letter is also cited in Zigliara, *De mente Concilii Viennensis*, no. 251.

of "nature" or "essence" or "substance," of "person" or "subsistence,"[32] and of "relation" (each divine person is a subsistent relation). The developed formula of the dogma of the Incarnation also includes the concepts of "nature" or "essence" or "substance," of "person" or "subsistence," of "Hypostatic Union"—that is, the union of two natures in one and the same person or subsistence. The Council of Vienne's definition concerning the rational soul, finally, affirms at least that the rational soul is the principle of the life of the human body.

The notion of substance, with regard to bodily substance, will be given precision again by the definitions of the Councils of Florence and Trent concerning transubstantiation:

> If anyone says that in the most holy sacrament of the Eucharist the substance of bread and wine remains together with the body and blood of our Lord Jesus Christ and denies that wonderful and unique change of the whole substance of the bread into his body and the whole substance of the wine into his blood while only the species of bread and wine remain, a change which the Catholic Church very fittingly calls transubstantiation, let him be anathema.[33]

This last definition presupposes that bodily substance is distinct from its quantity, from its extension, and from its phenomenal laws, since after the consecration, the substance of bread no longer exists, whereas its quantity remains, as also do its qualities with their natural properties.[34]

---

[32] The term *subsistentia*, which translates [the Greek] *hypostasis* in the Councils, is the equivalent of the concrete term "person." It is only later on, in theological language, that it will become the equivalent of the abstract term "personality." See De Regnon, *Études sur la Sainte Trinité*, vol. 1, pp. 243 and 265. [Trans. note: He does not cite the edition, though one can consult Théodore de Regnon, *Études de théologie positive sur la Sainte Trinité*, vol. 1 (Paris: Victor Retaux, 1892)].

[33] Trent, *Canons on the Most Holy Sacrament of the Eucharist*, can. 2 (Denzinger, no. 1652).

[34] This is the common teaching of the theologians against certain Cartesians: "The physical reality of the accidents *is at least theologically certain, nay rather, it seems to pertain to faith.*"

Chapter 2

⸻ ∾⟨⟨⟨⟩⟩⟩∾ ⸻

Do Dogmatic Formulas, Thus Given Precision, Remain Accessible to Common Sense?

Are dogmatic formulas thus given precision accessible to common sense? Yes, to a degree, if common sense is indeed what we have said it to be: the philosophy of being in a rudimentary state. No, however, if it is only "a utilitarian organization of thought in view of practical life."

§1. Dogmatic Formulas, Thus Given Precision, Are Inaccessible to Common Sense if the Latter Is Only a Utilitarian Organization of Thought in View of Practical Life

If, as Éduouard Le Roy wishes, "the notions of substance, cause, relation, and subject" are only "reifications and symbols"[1] of spontaneous understanding in view of action, if the *substance* or *thing* is only a *verbal entity* by which common sense reifies and immobilizes the universal flux of phenomena or of qualitative images, it goes without saying that the dogmatic formulas that contain these notions do not enable us to know the divine reality directly, but rather "make it known to us only under the species of vital reaction that correspond to it in us."[2] "To say that God

---

[1] Éduouard Le Roy, "Science et philosophie," *Revue de métaphysique et de morale* 7 (1899): 375–425, at 392.

[2] See Éduouard Le Roy and F. Dubois, "Dogme et vérité," *Revue du clergé français* 52

is personal means to say: comport yourself in your relations with God as in your relations with a human person."[3] "Dogmatic formula encapsulates only a wholly practical thought, and it contains the divine reality only, in one form or another, so as to justify the prescribed conduct as reasonable or salutary."[4] The positive meaning of a dogma has only a practical value fundamentally fixed by the attitude that it can enable in relation to God, instead of being fixed by the divine reality itself.

Now, this is not the meaning that the Church gives to her dogmatic formulas in which her dogmas are expressed. To those who doubt this, she just recalled this fact by condemning, in the decree *Lamentabili* on July 3, 1907, this twenty-sixth proposition: "The dogmas of the faith are to be held only according to their *practical sense*; that is to say, as preceptive norms of *conduct* and not as norms of *believing*."[5] The Holy Office cannot here have in mind a chimerical pragmatism that would deny any correspondence between this "practical sense" and the divine reality; no, it aims at an actually existing pragmatism that sought to give nothing more than a practical sense to the most speculative of dogmas.

For the Church, Jesus *is* God; the verb "to be" here, as elsewhere, has an objective scope. If the Church had not believed in the ontological value of the terms of revelation, how could she have had recourse to metaphysical terms for giving them precision? How, "for the sake of these metaphysical terms, could she have resisted to the point of blood, how would she have resigned herself to the most dolorous of schisms, how could she have gone so far as to anathametize the memory of one of her pontiffs,[6] holding him

---

(October, 15, 1907): 210–25, at 212–14.

3   See Édouard Le Roy, "Qu'est-ce qu'un dogme?" *Quinzaine* (1905).

4   Le Roy, "Dogme et vérité," [Trans. note: Fr. Garrigou-Lagrange does not cite the page number. The exact text is difficult to find in the article, though the beginning of the quote can basically be found on page 214.]

5   [Trans. note: I have taken this from Denzinger, no. 3426.]

6   The Third Ecumenical Council of Constantinople condemned the late Pope Honorius I for having favored the monothelite heresy. Pope St. Leo II, as well as the seventh and eight ecumenical councils, repeated this condemnation. The author of the monthelite heresy, Sergius, the patriarch of Constantinople, had written to Honorius that it would be harsh to reduce millions of Christians to apostasy about a single word, "*a single operation in Christ*"; he added that the best thing to do was "not to speak of one or of two operations." Pope Honorius ceded to this counsel. He saw in the opposition made to Sergius, in the name of tradition, only a useless dispute over words, and forbade the speaking either of one or of two operations. This act by Pope Honorius had the sad result of favoring monothelitism. The heresy of Sergius did not go so far as to confuse the two natures in Christ, to admitting only a divine-human operation, but he so sub-

culpable only of not having been sufficiently clear concerning a point of Christological speculation that would appear quite secondary to the symbolists of our days?"[7] There were enough opportunists among her children so as to counsel her to remain silent concerning the doctrine of Sabellius, concerning those of the Semi-Arians [or] those of Eutychès or of Sergius. Sabellius, like Kant later on, wanted to admit only a *distinction of reason* between the divine persons and to see in them only three functions or three roles of God in relation to humanity. What is the good of defining the *real distinction* if dogma does not enable us to know the divine reality? Why should the Fathers and Doctors have written so many treatises whose sole aim was to establish that this real distinction posits *no imperfection in God*? Why so many similar works on the Hypostatic Union? What is the use of having recourse to the concept of "relation" and defining that there are real relations in God in order to avoid the evident contradiction into which Sabellius wanted to corner the orthodox? Why have all the Scholastic theologians treated of the metaphysical foundation of the analogy of the divine names? Why all of these lengthy works on the similarity and dissimilarity that exists between the divine relations and relation inasmuch as it exists as an accident in creatures? Why would the Council of Reims have condemned Gilbert de la Porrée, who admitted a real distinction between the divine essence and the relations? Why condemn Anton Günther later? Finally, why would the [First] Vatican Council, having defined the object of faith, write:

The perpetual common belief of the Catholic Church has held and holds also this: there is a *twofold order of knowledge*, distinct not only in its principle but also in its object: in its *principle* because in the one we know by natural reason, in the other by divine faith; in its *object* because, apart from what natural reason can attain, *there are proposed to our belief mysteries that are hidden in God* that can never be known unless they are revealed by God.[8]

Our faith has as its object these truths hidden in God, truths that can be known only if God reveals them and that the Holy Spirit has revealed to us.

---

ordinated Christ's human will to his divine will that the first no longer retained any particular activity. This was contrary to the very word of Christ: "Not as I will, but as thou wilt" (Matt 26:39).

7   B. Allo, "Trois conceptions philosophiques du dogme chrétien," *Revue thomiste* 13 (1905): 263.

8   [Trand. note: Although not given a citation by Fr. Garrigou-Lagrange, this is *Dei Filius*, ch. 4 (Denzinger, no. 3015). The emphases are based on Fr. Garrigou-Lagrange's text.]

"For the Spirit searches everything, even the *depths* of God" (1 Cor 2:10), recalls the Council. It is this very same truth, it says again, that we will intuitively see in heaven, the truth that "God decreed before the ages for our glorification" (1 Cor 2:7). It remains enveloped as though in a kind of cloud for as long as we are distant from God in this mortal life, "shrouded as it were, in darkness as long as in this mortal life, 'we are away from the Lord; for we walk by faith, not by sight.'"[9] If dogma has only a practical sense, how could the same Council say that "reason, illuminated by faith, acquires by God's gift *some very fruitful understanding* of the mysteries, as much by *analogy* with the things that it knows naturally as by the connection of the mysteries with one another and with man's final end"?[10]

Let us recall that Christ, during his mortal life, had the Beatific Vision. It would at least be rash to deny this. How can one claim that the truth that he taught us was devoid of ontological value? Let us no more forget the most elevated phenomena of mystical contemplation, the intellectual visions of the Holy Trinity spoken of by Saint Theresa on several occasions, visions that enabled her to grasp the real distinction of the divine persons and their circumincession in a more profound manner than is possible for speculative theology. As the saint says: "On the day of Saint Augustine, at the moment when I came to communicate, I understood, I could nearly say *I saw*—I could not explain how, I know only that it was something intellectual and very rapid—how the three persons of the Holy Trinity, whom I carry engraved in my soul, are one and the same thing. . . . The Lord enabled me to understand how the three persons, being only one and the same thing, are nevertheless distinct."[11]

§2. Why Le Roy's Objections against the Thomist Doctrine of Analogy Do Not Hold; the Foundation of This Doctrine

To these arguments from authority against the pragmatist, nominalist,

---

[9] *Dei Filius*, ch. 4 (Denzinger, no. 3017).

[10] [Trans. note: Fr. Garrigou-Lagrange cites the text in French, changing it very slightly from the Latin original to fit the context. See Denzinger, no. 3016.]

[11] *Oeuvres completes de saint Thérèse*, new Carmelite ed. (Paris: 1907). This is taken from her communication with her confessors found in vol., 2, pp. 262 and 235. In another passage (p. 304), St. Theresa, describing this intellectual vision, says: "I see a distinction between the Divine Persons, and see this as clearly as I saw a distinction yesterday between you, my father, and the provincial when you spoke with him, except, however, I neither saw nor heard anything, as I have already told you." Also, see p. 312.

or empiricist conception of dogma, there is added the rational argument that founds the *analogical value of the divine names* or of the concepts that express *simpliciter simplices* perfections, whose formal notion implies no trace of imperfection. Le Roy contests the value of this proof in the pages he has written about the Thomist notion of analogy,[12] but the objections that he raises show that he is content with a very rapid reading of *Summa theologiae* [*ST*] I, q. 13, and some corresponding passages of the *Summa contra gentes*, ignoring the foundation of this doctrine of Saint Thomas.[13] This foundation, as Father Ambroise Gardeil has established,[14] is realist conceptualism. Before asking whether our concepts of the metaphysical and moral order (of the third degree of abstraction) have an analogical value in relation to God, we obviously must know what is their value with regard to the *being* that they represent immediately. Now, for the fervent nominalist that Le Roy is, we find that the concept is only an "average,"[15] a common image, an impoverished residue of experience. It does not translate the fundamental being of things that, for a realist conceptualist, constitutes the object of the intellect's abstractive intuition. Hence, according to Le Roy, who ceaselessly makes this point, recourse to concepts in religious knowledge can be nothing other than recourse to the imagination, a naïve anthropomorphism. Himself a nominalist, Le Roy is in disagreement with us concerning the proper object of the human intellect, an object that belongs to it inasmuch as it is *human* (the essence of sensible things), so *a fortiori* he does not see what we mean by the formal and adequate object of the human intellect, the object that belongs to it inasmuch as it is an *intellect*. This latter object is *being* in all its universality. This is precisely what founds the possibility (the non-contradictory character) of our elevation to the supernatural order (or, the order of the Beatific Vision).[16] It is also what founds, here-below, the possibility of having analogical knowledge that truly attains the being of God.

In fact, the Aristotelian and Thomist doctrine of analogy is nothing other than the doctrine of being conceived of as a transcendental and not as a genus. The detail of this doctrine of analogy has been exposited many times

---

[12] Éduouard Le Roy, *Dogme et critique* (Paris: Bloud, 1907), 96–99 and 138–47.

[13] Likewise, B. Desbuts in his article, "La notion d'analogie d'après saint Thomas d'Aquin," *Annales de philosophie chrétienne*, January 1906, pp. 377–85.

[14] Ambroise Gardeil, "La relativité des formules dogmatiques," *Revue thomiste* 12 (1904): 62.

[15] See Bergson, *L'évolution créatrice*, 327. [Trans. note: Fr. Garrigou-Lagrange does not mention the edition. In other books, his pagination slightly differs.]

[16] See Aquinas, *Summa theologiar, ST* I, q. 12, a. 4.

without sufficiently indicating its essential element, already found in Aristotle. *"Being* and *unity,"* the Stagirite said, "are not genera to which extrinsic specific differences are added (as rationality is added to animality). Indeed, it is wholly necessary that the difference *be* and that it be *one.*"[17] Therefore, being and unity permeates even that which differentiates beings and belongs to different beings *kath' analogia* [Gk.] / *secundum proportionem.*[18] Each participates in being *in its own manner.* The same holds for the good and[19] the true, transcendental properties of being that accompany all the categories. Being, unity, truth, and goodness are attributed to substance, quantity, quality, action, and so on. We speak of a good fruit, a good citizen, a good size, a good quality, a good action, and so on. Therefore, being is not a common nucleus to which are added the difference proper to substance and that proper to accident. Since these differences are again something belonging to the domain of being, the word "being" does not designate absolutely the same thing in the cases of substance and accident, but instead things that are proportionally similar. Substance is to its being as accident is to its being, each *is in its own manner.* Such is the analogy of being in finite things. Now, the fundamental law of being and of our thought, the principle *of identity,* requires us to affirm that the fundamental, self-sufficient reality is not the *multiple and changing* world, but instead a reality that is wholly and entirely self-identical, which is related to being as A is to A, *Ipsum Esse,* Pure Being or Pure Act.

Through the first principle that it implies, the concept of being itself postulates *Ipsum Esse* and is therefore applied analogically to it. The likeness between the two is proportional: as *Ipsum Esse* is to its existence, so too is the creature to its existence. In short: each *exists in its own manner.* In the creature, existence is the act of a potency (or, an essence) capable of existing (created mode); in God, existence is pure, unreceived act (uncreated mode). It is clear that the formal notion of existence in no way implies, of itself, its created mode, in which potentiality or imperfection are intermingled with act. Therefore, far from being unknowable, *Ipsum Esse* is as Aristotle said, the first intelligible [thing] (*to prōton noēon* [Gk.]).[20] It is sovereignly good (*to agathon kai to ariston* [Gk.]) because, given that it is the fullness of being, it is the first desirable [thing] (*to prōton orekton*

---

[17] See Aristotle, *Metaphysica* 10.1 (Aquinas, *In* X *metaphys.,* lec. 1 to end); *Metaphysica* 4 (Aquinas, *In* IV *metaphys.,* lec. 1); *Metaphysica* 12.4 (Aquinas, *In* XII *metaphys.,* lec., 4); etc.

[18] See Aristotle, *Analytica posteriora* 2.13–14.

[19] See Aristotle, *Ethica nicomachea* 1.6 (*In* I *eth.,* lec. 6–7).

[20] See Aristotle, *Metaphysica* 12.7.

[Gk.]), capable of attracting all things to itself.[21] It is infinite because it is pure being without limit of essence.[22]

To *Ipsum Esse* there must be attributed analogically all the perfections whose formal notions imply no imperfection. These perfections are, in fact, those that are defined by *an immediate relation to being* or to one of the transcendentals (the intellect in relation to being, the will in relation to the good, similarly the attributes of the intellect and of the will). Therefore, they must be transcendentals or analogues like being itself, susceptible like it to being purified of all potentiality and to being applied formally (*formaliter eminenter* [formally and in an eminent manner]) to God. Moreover, like being, they are in a *pure state* only in God. It is in the creature that they are, so to speak, soiled by the mixture of potentiality or imperfection.[23]

Ipsum Esse must be *intelligent* in its own manner, as man is in his own. Man is intelligent to the degree that he is immaterial, to the degree that his form—which dominates matter, space, and time—enables him to know not only a given particular and contingent being, but *being* [itself]. And as man is not being itself, his intellect is only a power relative to being, intentional. It is an accident in the category of quality, and human intellection is only an accidental act of this potency. *Ipsum Esse* is also intelligent to the degree that it is immaterial and given that, by definition, it is independent not only of every material and spatial limit, but also of every limit of essence. Not only is it sovereignly intelligent, but moreover, its intellect is intellection itself; that is to say, [it is] being itself in the state of ultimate intelligibility, forever actually known, a pure, eternally subsistent, intellectual flash. Here, we do not look for the duality of subject and object. This arises, says Saint Thomas, only from the potentiality of subject and object.[24] Already in our own actual intellection are our intellect and its object (inasmuch as it is known) identical:[25] in our act of reflection

---

[21] See *ST* I, q. 5.

[22] See *ST* I, q. 7, a. 1.

[23] [Trans. note: See Reginald Garrigou-Lagrange, "On the Eminence of the Deity: In What Sense the Divine Perfections Are 'Formally and Eminently' in God," in *Philosophizing in Faith: Essays on the Beginning and End of Wisdom*, ed. and trans. Matthew K. Minerd (Providence, RI: Cluny Media, 2019), 341–60.]

[24] See *ST* I, q. 14, a. 2: "According to this alone is the sense or the intellect other from the sensible or the intelligible, because each is in potency."

[25] Indeed, the intellect knows the object only insofar as it intentionally *becomes* this object; "*fit aliud in quantum aliud.*" St. Thomas and Thomas de Vio Cajetan often recall the expression of Averroes "from the intellect and what is known there is made something that is more united than what is made from matter and form." Matter does not

are the knowing intellect and known intellect identical, and in God, pure intellection and the pure being that he thinks are identical. This is no less evident if we begin by considering *Ipsum Esse* as the first intelligible and no longer as the first knower. To be purified of act from every perspective, it must be forever intelligible, not only in potency but in act and even understood in act (*intellectum in actu*). Now, the ever-actual intelligible is nothing other than eternal intellection. *Estin hē nosis noēseōs noēsis* [Gk.].[26] All this is more certain than the most absolute certitudes of the positive sciences, for the quite excellent reason that our intellect perceives it immediately in being, its formal object. It is seen in this pure intellectual light. This analogical attribution of intellect to God is true with utter strictness: just as the formal notion of existence is independent of a created mode (limited by essence, mixed with potentiality), so too the formal notion of intellection is independent of the created mode that makes intellection the accidental mode of a potency and situates it in a category, the category of "quality," distinct from the category of "substance." In God, intellection is God's very nature, that is to say, being itself.[27] Therefore, not only is this identification of being and intellection required by a proof *ex communibus* (because there cannot be duality or multiplicity in the Absolute), but it is required *ex propriis*, by the formal notion of each of these two perfections. Pure being must be forever intelligible in act, and pure thought must be pure being actually known.[28]

Ipsum Esse is sovereignly *living*, for he possesses the most *immanent*, and consequently the most living, action of all: intellection. And this action proceeds so much so from him and from him alone that it is himself. He is not a kind of adherence to an external truth. No, he is Truth Itself in the state of ever-actual, ever-living thought. Therefore, God is not only

---

become the form, but only *receives* it. See Cajetan, commentary on *ST* I, q. 79, a. 2, no. 19: "The soul, as Averroes most excellently said in *De anima*, bk. 3, comm. 5, does not thus receive the knowable such as to make a knowing *composite* from them [i.e. from the soul and the intelligible]; rather, the soul itself is made to be the intelligible itself, and thus made to be in act, acts." [Trans. note: See note 23 of pt. 1, ch. 2 of the present volume.]

[26] See Aristotle, *Metaphysica* 12.9.

[27] See *ST* I, q. 14, aa. 2 and 4.

[28] Everywhere else, intellection is something imperfect that is accompanied with a kind of lack of satisfaction: the intellect would like to touch being immediately without having to ask about the value of the representation by which it attains it. This lack of satisfaction common to every created intellect will only disappear in the Beatific Vision (*ST* I, q. 12, a. 2); it never has existed for God, for in him alone is the intellect in a pure state.

living, but is Life:[29]

> What God enjoys in this felicity we know only in instants. Life is
> in him, for the action of the intellect is a form of life, and God is
> the very actuality of the intellect. This actuality, taken in itself,
> is his perfect and eternal life. We also call God an eternal, perfect
> living thing, *zōon aidion ariston* [Gk.]. Therefore, eternal life be-
> longs to God, for it is God himself.[30]

To *Ipsum Esse* there must be attributed *will*, specified by another transcendental, the good. The will has for its object the good inasmuch as it is
known. Therefore, it follows the intellect, just as the unknowing natural
inclination follows the very form, the very nature of beings that do not
have knowledge. In God, will is no more a potency than is intellect; it is
the very Act of love of the Good or the Good Itself, forever actually loved.[31]
Each of these concepts is analogous, like the good, which is a property of
being. *Ipsum Esse* is *free* with regard to all the created order, for, being by
himself and by himself alone the fullness of being, creation adds nothing
to his perfection; nevertheless, it is fitting that the Sovereign Good would
communicate himself with the most absolute freedom.[32]

Ipsum Esse is *provident* because his exterior action that extends to all
beings and to all the fibers of created beings is essentially that of an intelligent agent. Now, the intelligent agent acts for a known end that is
the *raison d'être* of all the means that it employs. Therefore, God orders
all things to an ultimate end, which is himself. Providence, *ratio oridinis
rerum in finem*, is again a pure perfection that is defined by a relation to
the notion of being.[33]

Ipsum Esse is *just* because, as intelligent and good, he owes it to himself to give to each being everything that is necessary for it to attain the
end to which he calls it.[34] Necessarily loving the Good above all, he owes
it to himself also to enforce its imprescriptible rights and to punish the
violation of them.[35]

Ipsum Esse is *merciful* because it is proper to the all-powerful and in-

---

[29] See *ST* I, q. 18, a. 2.
[30] Aristotle, *Metaphysica* 12.7. [Trans. note: Taken from the French.]
[31] See *ST* I, q. 19, a. 1.
[32] See *ST* I, q. 19, a. 3.
[33] See *ST* I, q. 22, a. 1.
[34] See *ST* I, q. 21, a. 1.
[35] See *ST* I-II, q. 87, aa. 1 and 3.

finitely good being to give to others, to come to their aid, to relieve them of their misery, not only to make something out of nothing but also to draw good from evil, repentance and love from sin, indeed a love all the more intense as the sin was all the more profound. In this is found the triumph of God and the reason that attracts "the supreme richness toward the supreme poverty." "It pertains to mercy that it overflows to others and, what is more, that it lightens the defects of others. And this *is maximally superior.* Whence also to be merciful is posited as being proper to God."[36] It would require as many specific articles to precisely establish the analogical value of each of these concepts, doing so through a reduction to being. What we have just said suffices to show that these absolutely simple perfections, by their immediate relation to pure being, imply no potentiality in their formal notion and [imperfectly] abstract from their created modalities. *At the limit,* they are realized in full purity from all potentiality and are identical, *ex propriis* and not only *ex communibus,* with Pure Act.

In recent debates, endless remarks have been made about the transposition of our categories to God. In reality, what is transposed to God are not the categories or supreme genera, which are univocal, but instead transcendentals or analogues that dominate all the genera. This is clear for being, the one, the true, and the good; it is no less clear for intellect, will, and freedom, as well as for the intellectual and voluntary perfections whose formal notions are not in a category (substance or quality) but, instead, are defined by an immediate relation to being.[37] "God," Saint Thomas says, "is not in the genus of *substance,* for the word 'substance' does not mean only that which exists by itself, but moreover the essence that must exist by itself and not in another, without however being existence itself."[38] As regards *relation,* it is not an accident in God, and the most difficult objections against the mystery of the Holy Trinity are resolved by showing that the *esse in* of the relation in God is substantial.[39]

---

[36] *ST* II-II, q. 30, a. 4; see also I, q. 21, a. 3.

[37] If our intellect and our will are in the *category of quality,* this is inasmuch as they are faculties, on account of their created modality and not inasmuch as they are an intellect and will.

[38] *ST* I, q. 3, a. 5, ad 1. [Trans. note: I have followed Fr. Garrigou-Lagrange's French, which is made to fit the sentence, though without adulterating the original sense in the Latin. Note also that he incorrectly cites ST I, q. 3, a. 6, ad 1.]

[39] [Trans. note: That is, while maintaining the unique *esse ad* proper to relation, the Divine Persons do not share the same sort of accidental inherence that is found in predicamental relations. Instead of being accidental relations, distinct from the created

We do not conceive of God as a *man* whose proportions would be carried to infinity, but as *Being Itself.* And we recognize for him only those attributes that necessarily follow upon the notion of *Ipsum Esse.* This does not involve anthropomorphism. We do not conceive of God in the image of man. Man is the one who is made in the image of God, inasmuch as he has received an intellect that has as its object being and its absolute laws: "signatum est super nos lumen vultus tui Domine" (Ps 4:7).

Le Roy objects that the proportion established by analogy does not illuminate the divine reality, for a proportion is illuminating and definable only if three of the four terms are known independently of the proportion. However, we here have two unknowns: God and his attribute. Moreover, these two unknowns are but one objectively, since in God, all is one. Therefore, the true formula for the proportion would be, for example, this: "God is to God what personality is to man." Once again, the pretense of grasping God such as he is in himself would lead to agnosticism.[40]

Without making the Deity known such as it is in itself, as the blessed see him, the analogy of proportionality—"God is personal (that is to say, subsistent, intelligent, and free) *in his manner* as man is *in his*"—expresses to us something concerning the divine reality. It is false to say that there would be two absolutely unknown terms involved in the proportions thus established. When, in virtue of the principle of identity and of the principle of *raison d'être*, we affirm the existence of *Ipsum Esse*, God is known, insofar as that which is without being by itself does not suffice so as to exist, insofar as that which exists without being by itself must have a likeness with what exists by itself, so long as we correct the dissimilarity by affirming necessarily that existence in God is pure existence, unreceived. All these affirmations have an *ontological* value, since they are all asserted in order to render reality intelligible in function of being, since they are all required by the very concept of being. When we thereafter establish the proportion that *Ipsum Esse* is X in his manner just as man is intelligent in his manner, in the four members of the proportion, there are two immediately known [terms] (man and intelligence) and one analogically known (*Ipsum Esse*), and our right to affirm the proportional likeness rests on the evidence of the immediate relation that binds together the formal notion of intelligence with that of being. We grasp this latter relation not only *a*

---

substance in which they inhere (*esse in*), the Divine Persons are subsistent relations, identical with the Deity, introducing no distinction into the Deity other than their opposition as relations.]

[40] Le Roy, *Dogme et Critique*, 146.

posteriori in experience, as Le Roy says, but *a priori* in being itself, and just as being is necessarily analogous, intelligence must be analogous as well. Then, thus knowing the divine intelligence analogically, we pass on to the will, and so on.

It is objected, however, that these different formal notions, stripped of their created modality, are identical in the eminence of the Deity. However, far from weakening the analogical value of the concepts involved, this is affirmed *ex propriis* by these very concepts precisely inasmuch as they are analogues and purified of all potentiality: Pure Being must be Pure Intellection and not intelligible in potency; likewise, Pure Intellection must be Pure Being and not an intentional reproduction, and by that, a potential reproduction of pure being [*potentielle de l'être pur*]. Le Roy does not understand this *crossing of the limits* because he does not see that absolutely simple perfections have an immediate relation to being and that, when we pass beyond all limitation, being is unreceived *Ipsum Esse*, in virtue of the principle of identity.

However if, instead of admitting realist conceptualism, one remains confined to nominalist sensualism, if from the instability of sensible appearances, now asserted as the sole reality, one infers that the principle of identity and of non-contradiction [*sic*][41] is a merely logical law and not a law of reality, the fundamental reality is no longer anything but becoming, a realized contradiction. On this account, obviously, analogical conceptual knowledge of God is vain. By contrast, once we have admitted that the principle of identity is the foundational law of reality, we will say with Saint Thomas: "These names (being, goodness, wisdom, and so on) as regards *the thing signified* by the name *are said primarily of God*, then of creatures, because perfections of these kinds flow forth from God. However, as regards *the imposition of the name, they are primarily applied by us to creatures*, which we know first."[42] Maimonides denied this ontological priority; for him, the words "God is good" signified only, "God is the cause of the goodness of creatures." In response, Saint Thomas[43] asked: why not say just as much, "God is an animal," inasmuch as he is the cause of animality, "corporeal" inasmuch as he is the cause of corpore-

---

[41] [Trans. note: As noted in previous chapters, Fr. Garrigou-Lagrange most often uses "principle of contradiction" for what is most commonly referred to now as the "principle of non-contradiction." Thus, on the rarer occasions when he does use "principle of non-contradiction" for the same, I mark those instances with "[*sic*]" to signal that he means the same thing as in most places he means by "principle of contradiction" (and we now commonly mean by "principle of non-contradiction").]

[42] *ST* I, q. 13, a. 6.

[43] See *ST* I, q. 13, a. 2.

ity? Maimonides did not understand the way that goodness, which is a transcendental, differs from a genus. There is only one manner of being a body and of being an animal. These are genera to which *extrinsic* differences are added. However, there are many ways of being good, being true, being one, of being a being, for these transcendentals permeate the very thing that differentiates beings. It is true to say: this fruit is *good* in its own manner (physically, from the point of view of taste); this virtuous man is *good* in his manner (morally); God is *good* in his manner (that is, absolutely). In this, for all the Schools [*pour tout l'École*], there is a *denomination* that is not *extrinsic*, but rather, *intrinsic*. The attribution is formal. Only the *mode* of the attribution is what is human, based on the fact that it implies the imposition of a subject and of a predicate. This is so true that Our Lord went so far as to say, "No one is good but God alone" (Luke 18:19). God is good by himself and without limits, although we, by ourselves, are that which is not, that which holds itself back rather than gives itself, what is weak and returns to nothingness. Likewise, as Saint Thomas notes here, Saint Paul says of God the Father, that he is the one "from whom every family in heaven and on earth is named" (Eph 3:15).

We cannot hold that the sentiments of Saint Thomas and Maimonides differ "only as regards their manners of speaking."[44] Scholastic thinkers [*l'École*] have always held that they are wholly opposed to each other.[45] It suffices to cite *ST* I, q. 13, a. 2:

> Therefore, when it is said God is good, the sense is not that God is the cause of goodness or that God is not evil, but rather: what we call goodness in creatures pre-exists in God, indeed, according to a loftier mode. Hence, from this it does not follow that God is good inasmuch as he causes goodness, but rather, vice-versa, because he is good, he pours out goodness into things.

Meister Eckhart later fell into an error that is very close to that of Maimonides, as is proven by the condemned proposition: "God is not good or better or best; whenever I call God good, I am just as wrong as if I were to call white black."[46]

In these agnostic days, this fact cannot be repeated often enough: *in a sense, we know God much better than we know the men with whom we most*

---

[44] A.-D. Sertillanges, "Agnosticisme ou anthropomorphisme," *Revue de philosphie* 9 (1906): 164.

[45] See M. Chossat, "Agnosticisme," *Dictionnaire apologétique de la foi catholique*, 4th ed., p.41.

[46] John XXII, *In Agro Dominico* (Denzinger, no. 978).

intimately live. The man who holds his hand out to me perhaps decides at the same moment to betray me. Perhaps his gesture is a lie. I can doubt his speech, his virtue, his goodness. By contrast, I know with an absolutely certain knowledge [*science*], even by reason alone, that God cannot lie, that he is infinitely good, infinitely just, infinitely holy. Of all beings, it is he, in a sense, that I know the best, when I recite the *Our Father* in meditation, as it is by him that I am best known. We are more certain of the rectitude of his intentions than we are of the righteousness of our own heart.

Moreover, in a sense, we know the divine nature better than human nature, and above all better than we know animal or plant natures: a Thomist who has commented one or two times on the treatise *De Deo uno* of Saint Thomas should be able to connect to *Ipsum Esse* all the divine attributes and to show the interdependence of all its theses with this fundamental proposition: "In God alone are essence and existence one and the same." It is certainly more difficult to connect the entire treatise on man to the definition of *reason.* Did not Aristotle say that "divine things are more knowable, more intelligible *in themselves* than all the others ('maxime scibilia sunt ipsa prima et causae [the most knowable things are the very principles and causes]') *but relative to us,* they are difficult to know ('quia a sensibus sunt remotissima [because they are most distant from the senses]')"?[47]

In the case of the concepts that express the Trinity, like the concept of relation, reason could not establish their analogical value; however, God having made use of it for revealing himself to us, it suffices that theology establish that relation does not posit an evident imperfection in God.

Such is the rational refutation of the pragmatist conception of dogma. In the latter system, the *criterion* of truth is no longer evident being, but instead is the relation of an action commanded or counseled to what is innate to us [*nos innéités*], our deep needs. But what are these innate needs [*ces innéités*] worth in a system that cannot admit the immutablity of our nature and its ontological and fixed relationship with God? They are the eddies of the unconscious.

§3. Dogmatic Formulas Expressed in Philosophical Language Remain to a Degree Accessible to Common Sense if the Latter Is a Rudimentary Ontology

Therefore, it seems evident to us that dogmatic formulas are inaccessible

---

[47] Aristotle *Metaphysica* 1.2 (Aquinas, *In* I *metaphys.,* lec. 2).

to common sense if one wishes for it to be nothing more than a "utilitarian organization of thought in view of practice." Things are wholly different if common sense is, as we have defined it, the *philosophy of being* in a rudimentary state. What we have said suffices to establish this in general, but it is important to give precision to our thesis by means of an example and to prove it negatively by showing how every other philosophy is incompatible with dogma.

Outside the philosophy of *being*, one conceives, in general metaphysics, only a philosophy of *phenomena* and a philosophy of *becoming*. The encyclical *Pascendi Dominici Gregis* condemns phenomenalism using the name "agnosticism," and the philosophy of becoming using the name of "evolutionism." The [First] Vatican Council had already condemned Hegelian evolutionism and all forms of pantheism.[48] As regards phenomenalism, it was already reached, according to Jean Vacant,[49] by the same Council, which had defined, by repeating the formula of the Fourth Lateran Council, that three classes of creatures (material, spiritual, and human) have been produced by God *ex nihilo, secundum totam substantiam* [according to their entire substance].[50] Nicolas Malebranche himself had understood that he had to admit the existence of bodily substances because revelation tells us that God created them. Again, phenomenalism is irreconcilable with the dogma of transubstantiation. Among other arguments in favor of this system, Charles Renouvier said to those who wished to listen to him: "If you admit substance, you will be given the Trinity, the Hypostatic Union, and all the rest."

To draw an example from among the dogmatic formulas whose development we indicated earlier, let us consider the notion of personality that empiricist phenomenalism presents to us, that which rational phenomenalism gives us, and finally that which is required by the philosophy of becoming.[51] Far from enabling us to think philosophically about the Hypostatic Union, these three conceptions destroy it; in contrast, this dogma is accessible to the rudimentary ontology of common sense.

---

[48] See the [First] Vatican Council, *Dei Filius,* can, 1.4 (Denzinger, no. 3024). We have already shown how the pantheism of the new philosophy of Bergon and Le Roy falls under these condemnations. See pt. 2, ch. 3, §1 and §2.

[49] Jean-Michel-Alfred Vacant, *Études théologiques sur les constitutions du Concile du Vatican d'après les actes du concile*, vol. 1, p. 223.

[50] See [First] Vatican Council, *Dei Filius*, ch. 1 and can. 1.5 (Denzinger, nos. 3002 and 3025).

[51] See Charles Jeanmarie, *L'idée de personnalité dans la psychologie moderne* (Paris: Alcan). [Trans. note: A date for this Alcan edition is not readily available. Editions were published in Toulouse and Paris in 1882.]

A. The Phenomenalistic or Purely Dynamistic Notions of Personality Are Irreconcilable with the Dogma of the Incarnation

For empiricist phenomenalists (David Hume, John Stuart Mill, Hippolyte Taine), we attain only states of consciousness and in no way an I-substance. Personality is a series or aggregate of conscious phenomena reunited by the laws of the association of ideas. Like every mental or organic composite, the self has its normal form. However, if the elements are altered or the work of the composite disturbed, the form deviates and the final work is monstrous. This is how split personalities are produced, and even sometimes, in madness, a person believes himself completely to have become another person and acts in conformity with his belief.[52]

According to the rationalist phenomenalists (Renouvier), personality is an *a priori* form of our thought, the most elevated of the categories. It contains all the others, since it is in the representative activity that is proper to it that the other categories find their center and their application. Persons are not things in themselves. There is nothing real except for phenomena. Personality is a general, complex, and durable phenomenon that is the synthesis and law of other phenomena, a representation embracing the others. Our existence is nothing other than what is represented; outside our real or possible representations, there is nothing for us.[53]

For a partisan of the philosophy of becoming, the person or self is neither an aggregate of phenomena nor a category. It is a free and vital *élan* that successively takes on the various forms that we call states of consciousness. This is the thesis developed at length and defended today by Henri Bergson.

For the philosophy of being, "the natural metaphysics of the human intellect," personality is something more profound than the phenomena and their empirical or *a priori* laws, more profound than the underlying becoming. It is a metaphysical entity. There is such a thing as *ontological* personality (a subsistence intrinsically independent of matter), the foundation of what one could call *psychological* personality (self-consciousness) and *moral* personality (freedom and self-mastery). As we will come to see, this classical conception of personality is only the explication of common sense's notion.

---

[52] See Hippolyte Taine, *De l'Intelligence*, vol. 2, p. 231. [Trans. note: Fr. Garrigou-Lagrange does not indicate the edition. An edition matching this pagination is not easily retrievable.]

[53] Charles Renouvier, *Logique*, vol. 2, p. 493. [Trans. note: This pagination is difficult to find. The relevant text might be found in Charles Renouvier, *Essais de critique générale: premier essai: Traité de logique générale et de logique formelle*, vol. 2 (Paris: Librarie Armand Colin, 1912), 177–84.]

First, let us show that the phenomenalist or purely dynamist notions of personality cannot in any way be reconciled with the definition of the Hypostatic Union.

According to this definition, the human nature and divine nature in Jesus Christ are united in the divine personality of the Word in such a way that he does not have a human personality. Now, one obviously cannot say that the person of the Word is a collection of phenomena grouped together by an empirical law or by an *a priori* form. These phenomenalist conceptions of personality obviously do not express a *simpliciter simplex* perfection. There is no possible analogy since, according to the Councils, this divine personality of the Word is not really distinct from the Absolute, from the divine nature, and therefore cannot, in any manner, be a phenomenon or a law of phenomena.

No more can it be said that the divine person of the Word is a becoming, a free and vital *élan*, and not a *thing*, for this person is God himself. And the [First] Vatican Council defines, against Hegel,[54] that God is an *absolutely simple and immutable* spiritual substance, really and essentially distinct from the world, which is composed and changing. "As he is one, unique, and *spiritual substance, entirely simple and unchangeable*, we must proclaim him distinct from the world in existence and essence."

Does one wish to attempt to give precision to the nature of this becoming and define personality from the psychological perspective by making it consist formally in *self-consciousness*? In that case, one will then fall into Günther's error, and inevitably returning to Nestorius's position, one must admit in Christ, with the two divine and human natures, *two consciousnesses*, and consequently, [on this account,] two persons. One will fall into the same heresy if one defines personality from the moral perspective by *freedom*, for there are *two free wills* in Christ, just as there are two natures. If one wishes to escape Nestorianism and save the unicity of the person by admitting only one free will, one will thereby fall into the monothelite heresy and, consequently, into the monophysitism of Eutychès.

B. Common Sense Possesses an Ontological Notion of Personality, the Foundation of Psychological Personality and Moral Personality

However, it is a much more profound notion of personality, a notion that is no longer only psychological or moral, but ontological. It is that of common sense, given precision by the philosophy of being. It is also that of the Councils.

---

[54] See [First] Vatican Council, *Dei Filius*, ch. 1 and can. 1.4 (Denzinger, nos. 3001 and 3024).

Common sense uses the name "person" for certain beings that it distinguishes from those that it simply calls "things." The person is a rational and free being, the master of his acts, independent, *sui iurus*, as opposed to the animal, the plant, and the mineral. Roman law even distinguished the person from the slave: the slave juridically is not a person, "non est sui iurus." Therefore, what characterizes the person, to the eyes of common sense, is indeed freedom, mastery of self. However, for this same common sense, freedom presupposes the intellect, which deliberates, and self-consciousness; and, in turn, self-consciousness indeed presupposes the *self*, which is, properly speaking, the person. This is clear. Therefore, the person or the self is conceived by everyone, in the same way as are things, as being a substance, for prior to phenomena and to becoming, there is the *being* that appears and changes appearance. However, it is a substance of an order that is more elevated than others, a substance endowed with reason and, consequently, with freedom. The definition of person given by Boethius only translates this common-sense notion: "A person is an individual substance of a rational nature"; nobody, remarks Boethius, has ever said that a stone or a cow is a person.

However, common sense goes further. It distinguishes, in a certain manner, *person* and *nature*. Everyone says, "my arm, my body, my soul, my intellect, my will, my resolution," meaning thereby: "the arm that is *mine*, the soul and body that are *mine*." Everyone says, again, "*I* run, *I* think." In this way, we contrast to a *self*, to one and the same self, everything that we attribute to it: our spiritual and bodily nature, our existence, our faculties, our acts. The self is already, for common sense, *the first subject of attribution* that cannot itself be attributed. It is said that the rational nature (soul and body) belongs to it, but it is not said that it belongs to this nature. It possesses the nature as an essential part, just as it possesses its activities [*opérations*] as transitory, accidental parts. Therefore, the person is a *whole* composed of essential and permanent elements, as well as passing elements, and it is to this whole and not to its parts that we attributes existence and action. What exists is Peter and not his human nature; similarly, Peter is the one who acts and who wills by his will. His will is not what wills. This insight by common sense is translated in the [philosophical] formula: "*A person is a whole, essentially [*per se*] existing separately, *that which* exists and acts while, by contrast, *the nature* is *that by which* it is such—for instance, is a man. The intellect is *that by which* he knows. Existence is *that by which* he exists."[55] The person is a whole existing or subsisting separate-

---

[55] See the exposition of this natural metaphysics in *ST* I, q. 29, a. 1 ("On the definition of

ly, *that which* exists, *that which* acts, whereas, the nature is *that by which* this whole is essentially constituted, the intellect *that by which* it emits acts of knowledge, and so on.

In truth, a "thing" is already a whole existing or subsisting separately, but the person has a unique sort of subsistence that earns for it a special name, a subsistence that is intrinsically independent from matter (or, a spiritual subsistence), as the philosophy of being will say, a subsistence that precisely, hence, is the foundation for reason (the principle of universal knowledge that dominates matter, space, and time) and for the possibility of reflection or self-consciousness, a consciousness that, in turn, is the foundation for freedom. Man's properties are deduced from his rational soul conceived of as being a subsistent form.

The philosophy of being will also study what is required in reality for verifying the judgments of common sense and the opposition that it makes in these judgments between person and nature, between the first subject of attribution and its attributes. It will ask itself what can constitute the *subject* as a *subject* (that by which something is a *quod*), what can constitute this *whole* as a *whole*. It is in this way that the metaphysical concept of *subsistence, hypostasis,* will be given precision, which will need to be studied in its relations with the two first divisions of being—*essence* (potency) and *existence* (act)—in order to connect it to *being,* the intellect's first conception and the formal object of metaphysics.

However, this work of analysis is in no way necessary for giving a *clear* meaning to the words "person" and "nature." (Note that we do not say a "distinct" sense.) Common sense admits without difficulty that one and the same person, one and the same self, can have, and in fact has, a spiritual nature and a bodily nature, a soul and a body, spiritual acts and bodily acts.

C. This Ontological Notion of Personality Enables Common Sense to Understand the Mysteries of the Hypostatic Union and of the Trinity

Behold a man, Jesus, to whom are attributed bodily actions, spiritual human actions, and moreover, properly divine activities [*opérations*]. He says: "*I* who speak to you. . . . *I* and the Father are one" (John 10:30). He declares *himself* to be greater than David (Mark 12:36; Matt 22:44; Luke 20:42), greater than Moses and Elijah (Matt 17; Mark 9; Luke 9:28), superior to the angels, who are his angels, his ministers (Mark 1:13; 13:27; Matt 4:11;

---

person"), and in *ST* III, q. 2, a. 2 ("Whether the union of the Incarnate Word was made in a person").

13:41; 16:27; 24:31). He requires faith, obedience, and love with respect to *his own person* to the point of renouncing every created affection that would be contrary to him, to the point of sacrificing one's life: "He who loves his father and his mother more than *me* is not worthy of *me*" (Mark 8:34; Matt 10:32; 16:24; Luke. 9:23; 14:26; 18:29). He makes himself equal to the divine lawgiver of Sinai: "You have heard that it was said to the men of old, 'You shall not kill; and whoever kills shall be liable to judgment.' But I say to you that everyone who is angry with his brother shall be liable to judgment" (Matt 5:22–44). He is attributed the power of "refashioning / refreshing" [*refaire*] souls, of remitting them their sins: "Come to *me*, . . . and *I* will give you rest" (Matt 11:28). He claims the no-less-exorbitant right to one day be the judge of the living and the dead (Mark 8:38, 13:26, 14:62; Matt 14:27; Luke 9:26; 12:9); he declares he will send the Holy Spirit: "*I* will send the promise of my Father upon you*" (Luke 24:49; John 15:26). He gives eternal life: "My sheep hear my voice, and I know them, . . . and I give them eternal life" (John 10:27–28); "The Father and *I* are one" (John 10:30); "No one knows the Son except the Father, and no one knows the Father except the Son and any one to whom the Son chooses to reveal him" (Matt 11:27). His disciples say of him: "We know that the Son of God has come and has given us understanding, to know him who is true; and we are in him who is true, in his Son Jesus Christ. This is the true God and eternal life (Hic est verus Deus et vita aeterna)" (1 John 5:20).

This colossal *self* is at one and the same time divine and human. To this same *subject* we must attribute what belongs to God and what belongs to man. This is a person who possess not only a body and a soul but also a human nature and a divine nature, and consequently, a divine intellect and a human intellect and a divine freedom and a human freedom. Common sense, illuminated by the light of faith, suffices for affirming all this, following upon Jesus's declarations.

As Father Théodore de Regnon has shown,[56] this simple common-sense notion even sufficed for refuting the principal heresies. Against Sabellius it is proven that God is not one and the same person playing three different roles, but that there are three persons in him because Scripture affirms three distinct subjects of attribution, three "selves." It is said of the Son that He is begotten by the Father, sent by His Father, that He became incarnate. It is said of the Holy Spirit that he proceeds from the Father,

---

[56] Théodore de Regnon, *Études sur la Saint Trinité*, vol. 1, p. 64 [Trans. note: He does not cite the edition, though one can consult Théodore de Regnon, *Études de théologie positive sur la Sainte Trinité*, vol. 1 (Paris: Victor Retaux, 1892)].

that he is sent by the Father and the Son. Against Arius, it is shown that a son is of the same nature as his father, that moreover the Son is declared the eternal, omnipotent creator. Against Nestorius, it is established that, according to the Gospel, it is indeed to one and the same *self* that the divine attributes and human acts of Christ belong. Against Eutychès and the monothelites, one invokes the texts that clearly distinguish the two natures and the two wills. Against the tritheists, it suffices that one recall the dogma of the unity of God that is required by natural reason itself.

In truth, the Councils contrasted Christ's two natures to his one person much better than common sense alone, illuminated by faith, could do. However, the most developed dogmatic formulas remain accessible, to a certain degree, to the intellect that lacks philosophical cultivation. The Council of Chalcedon defines that "Christ is one and the same being because there are indeed two distinct natures in him, each with its properties; nevertheless, there is one subsistence or person, that of the Word." The term *subsistentia*, which in the Councils translates *hypostasis*, is the equivalent of the concrete term "person"; later, in theological language, it will become the equivalent of the abstract term "personality."[57] Even in this latter sense, this term is not inaccessible to common sense. If, for everyone, a person is already a whole that subsists separately, it is easy to see that what constitutes the person (that is to say, personality) can be translated by the abstract word "subsistence." If Christ, the God-Man, is one and the same subsistent being, He can have only one subsistence in him.[58] Common sense does not realize that this abstract notion is necessary for rendering personality intelligible in function of being. It does not grasp the metaphysical relations of subsistence with nature or essence, on the one hand, and with existence, on the other. However, this is in no way necessary. The Hypostatic Union, such as it is explicitly defined, is not meaningless for common sense, although common sense does not fully understand it.

The same holds for the developed formulas of the Trinity. Common sense understands why the term "person" can be applied to God. It suffices to say with Saint Thomas: "The term 'person' designates a subsistent being endowed with intelligence and freedom. Now, subsistence, intelligence, and freedom are absolutely simple perfections that imply no imperfection. Therefore, they must be attributed to God, who, by definition, is the ultimate perfection. Personality belongs to God, though, it goes without say-

---

[57] De Regnon, *Études sur la Saint Trinité*, 1:243 and 1:265.
[58] See *ST* I, q. 29, a. 2 ("Whether person is the same as hypostasis and subsistence").

ing, in a supereminent degree."[59] As Scripture affirms the existence in God of three distinct "selves," three subjects of attribution, common sense understands the formula "three persons." Even the formula "three subsistences," common in the language of theology, is not unintelligible to its eyes.

D. By the Preaching of "Elevations," the Profound Meaning of the Mysteries of the Incarnation and the Trinity Can Be Made Accessible to Common Sense

It is not impossible to place within the reach of an ordinary listener, of whatever era, the same elevation concerning the mystery of the Hypostatic Union. It will be composed easily with three articles drawn by Saint Thomas: *ST* I, q. 29, a. 1 ("On the definition of person"); a. 2 (Whether the term "person" can be applied to God"); and *ST* III, q. 2, a. 2 ("Whether the union of the Incarnate Word was brought about in the person [of the Word]"). Subsistence and, consequently, personality appear increasingly perfect to it by ascending the scale of beings. At the limit, one will have the divine personality. Let us indicate briefly the degrees of this ascent.

According to Saint Thomas, what gives the person his dignity is the fact that he exists by himself separately, *per se separatim existere*, being independent in his existence and, consequently, being self-reliant in the order of action, *per se agere sequitur ad per se esse*. Without a doubt, an individual of any species—an animal, vegetable, or even mineral—is already a subsisting whole, undivided in itself and distinct from every other. However, how imperfect is such subsistence and independence? The stone of itself can only fall; it cannot even stop itself in its fall. Of itself, the plant can only nourish itself, grow, and reproduce, and all this inevitably, in a dependence on an appropriate environment, such that, if this environment is lacking, the plant ceases to subsist. The animal also is led inevitably by its instinct. It cannot not react under the attraction of the sensible good that is fitting to its nature. All these beings are as little subsistent and independent as possible. Imprisoned within the determinism that rules the bodily world, they are like pieces of the world, automata. They are not, properly speaking, sources of action. They are rather acted upon than act, and are content to transmit the action.[60] Man, by contrast, because he is

---

[59] See *ST* I, q. 29, a. 3 ("Whether the name of 'person' may be said of God").

[60] [Trans. note: Fr. Garrigou-Lagrange obviously is simplifying matters. Elsewhere, he does note the role of the estimative sense in animals. Nonetheless, the gulf between such animals and man remains infinite. This is the point he is trying to emphasize here.]

endowed with reason, which is elevated above the sensible phenomena so as to attain being and pass beyond the material world, can return to his own acts, to his judgment, can judge this very judgment and free himself from the suggestions made by his sensibility, can discover superior motives and introduce into the world a series of facts that do not result necessarily from antecedent ones [*posés*]. Man, if he knows how to will, can play a role in the world; he is a person.[61] His freedom draws from his knowledge of the universal good a dominating indifference with regard to all particular goods; he dominates all the influences of the physical world and remains the master of his acts, *sui iuris*. This independence from matter in the order of willing presupposes independence from matter in the order of knowledge, and the latter, in turn, presupposes independence from matter in *being* itself, *operari sequitur esse*. This is true *subsistence*, that which is not reached by bodily corruption, that which provides the metaphysical foundation for our natural desire to live *forever*.

But man will fully be a *person*, a *per se subsistens* and a *per se operans*, only to the extent that the life of reason and freedom dominate the life of the senses and passions in him. Without this, he will remain like the animal, a mere *individual*, the slave of events and circumstances, forever pulled along in the tow of something else, incapable of directing himself. He will be only a part, without being able to claim he is a whole. The *individuality* that distinguishes us from beings of the same species comes from the body, from the matter that occupies a given portion of space that is distinct from that occupied by another man. By our individuality, we are essentially dependent upon a given environment, a given climate, a given heredity—Greeks, Latins, or Saxons. Christ was Jewish. *Personality*, by contrast, comes from the soul. It is the very subsistence of the soul independent from the body. To develop one's individuality is to live the egoistic life of the passions, to make oneself the center of all things and, in the end, to allow oneself to be enslaved by a thousand passing goods that bring

---

[61] Such is precisely the etymology of the word "person": "This word," says Boethius, "First refers to the mask that the actors in comedies and tragedies used. *Persona* comes from *personare*. If the accent is placed on the ante-penultimate, its relation to *sonus* will be clear, for the sound, by rolling in the concavity of the mask, becomes stronger. But, given that these masks represented the individuals of whom the actors played the role (Medea, Simon, Chremes), one became accustomed to likewise using the term 'person' for other men, who are recognized and distinguished by their particular appearance" and who act in the world like the theater character does upon the stage (*De persona et duabus naturis* 3). [Trans. note: The text here is taken from Fr. Garrigou-Lagrange's French, with slight emendations.]

us a paltry, momentary joy. Personality, by contrast, grows to the degree the soul elevates itself above the sensible world, attaches itself more closely by the intellect and the will to that which makes for the life of the spirit. The philosophers have glimpsed, though the saints above all have understood, that the full development of our poor personality consists in losing it, in some manner, in God, who alone possesses personality in the perfect sense of this word, for he alone is absolutely independent in his being and in his action. He alone who is *Being Itself* has an existence that is not only independent from matter, but also independent from all that is not it. His understanding of things is omniscient; his freedom is the most absolute dominating indifference in relation to every created thing. The elements that constitute personality (subsistence, intelligence, freedom) designate as many perfections whose formal notion implies no imperfection. Therefore, we must affirm that they are realized eminently in him who is the supreme perfection, that God is consequently the exemplar and source of every personality deserving of the name.[62]

This is why, in the order of knowledge and love, the saints have endeavored to substitute, in some manner, God's personality for their own, to "die to themselves" so that God may reign in them. They are armed with a holy hatred of their own *self.* They have sought to place God at the principle of all their acts, by acting no longer according to the maxims of the world or according to their own judgments, but according to the ideas and maxims of God received by faith. They have sought to substitute for their own will God's will, to act not for themselves but for God, to love this God not only as another *self,* but infinitely more than themselves and above all else. They have understood that God must become another self for them, more intimate to them than is their own self, that God was more themselves than they themselves because he is eminently a self. They have thus sought to renounce all personality or independence in relation to God; they have sought to make themselves something of God, *quid Dei.* Thus have they acquired the most powerful personality that can be conceived of; they have acquired, in a sense, what God possesses by nature: independence in relation to every created thing, no longer only independence in relation to the world of bodies, but even independence in relation to intelligences. As Pascal said so admirably in his *Pensées*: "The saints have their dominion, their radiance, their victory, their luster, and have no need of *fleshly* or *spiritual* grandeurs, for which they have no affinity, for these neither add nor take away from them. They are seen of God and the

---

[62] See *ST* I, q. 29, a. 3.

angels and not of the body, nor of the curious mind. God alone suffices for them." The saint, having succeeded at substituting God's personality for his own, can exclaim with Saint Paul: "I have been crucified with Christ; it is *no longer I* who live, but Christ who lives in me" (Gal 2:20). Is it indeed he who lives or God who lives in Him? In the order of *activity* [*opération*], that of knowledge and love, the saint has indeed, so to speak, substituted the divine self for his own self, but in the order of *being*, he remains a self, distinct from God. Christ, the God-Man, emerges as the terminus toward which holiness strives in vain.

At the limit, it is no longer in the order of *activity* [*opération*] that the human self gives way to a divine person. It is in the very order of *being*, the root of activity, so that it is literally true to say that Jesus's personality is the very personality of the Word and that he subsists with the subsistence of the Word, with which his makes only one and the same being. Such is the ultimate reason for this prodigious personality, never before seen in history, nor ever again. Such is the final reason for the infinite majesty of this *I* that belongs only to Christ: "*I* am the way, the truth, and the life" (John 14:6); "Come to *me*, all who labor and are heavy laden, and I will give you rest" (Matt 11:28); "If anyone thirst, let him come to *me* and drink" (John 7:37); "He who believes in *me*, as the Scripture has said, 'Out of his heart shall flow rivers of living water'" (John 7:38); "It will become in him a spring of water welling up to eternal life" (John 4:14); "And *I* will raise him up at the last day" (John 6:44); This is already the terrible personality of God, the just judge: "Which of you convicts me of sin? (John 8:46); "Woe to you scribes and Pharisees, woe to you blind guides, woe to you who are full, woe to you who now laugh" (Matt 23:13ff; Luke 11:42). Our ultimate end in person is the one who says to us: "He who is not *with me* is against *me*" (Matt 12:30).

There is a category of men for whom so colossal a personality is a scandal, as it likewise is an egoistic monstrosity. "The powerful caste of the mediocre feel fear and horror before saints and men of genius. It finds them to be exaggerated. Fierce enemy of all that which is great,"[63] it takes pleasure in confusing the two extremes, the individual and the person, the most culpable excesses of individualism with the ultimate development of personality: it crucifies Christ between two thieves. But Christ has arisen, and his disciples recall what he had said before dying: "Be of good cheer, I have overcome the world" (John 16:33). Just one of his acts drew from his

---

[63] Ernest Hello, *L'homme*, 59 (chapter on "The Mediocre Man"). [Trans. note: Fr. Garrigou-Lagrange has taken some small liberties with the quote without altering the sense.]

divine personality an infinite meritorious and satisfactory value.

Such is the profound meaning of the Hypostatic Union. It is understood by the great contemplatives and the great theologians, by someone like Saint Augustine, like Saint Anselm, and like Saint Thomas Aquinas, as well as by the little ones whom God is pleased to illuminate. Common sense, with its rudimentary metaphysics, can understand it. In the midst of the men of genius whose minds have a profound kinship with the absolute and the humble, there is a certain "intellectual bourgeoisie" that today seeks a middle between Immanuel Kant and Auguste Comte, who has tasted Ernst Renan and reads Adolf von Harnack. Its eyes can stand only what is mediocre like it. It is essentially modest. Not long ago "it believed itself inferior to the dullest imbeciles of the eighteenth century, but mocked St. Theresa."[64] "The enormous makes it fearful." The theological virtues unnerve it. Moral virtues suffice for it. "It has eyes for not seeing and ears for not hearing." It voluntarily encloses itself within the world of phenomena. Imprisoned within time and becoming, the immobility of eternal life seems like death to its eyes. It goes on repeating its dogma concerning the *autonomy of the mind*, which forbids God to reveal anything of himself. It calls this "self-respecting pride [*fierté*]," just as it calls "humility" the sensualist agnosticism that debases it to the level of the animals. Theology responds: in terms of autonomy, out of all the intellects, the human intellect is the last. As *pure potency*, it can ask only to receive; its humility is found in that fact. However, this is a pure potency of an order infinitely superior to the senses. It is a participation, in us, of the uncreated light of God; "signatum est super nos lumen vultus tui Domine" (Ps 4:6). This is what gives it all its grandeur. "I thank thee, Father, Lord of heaven and earth, that thou hast hidden these things from the wise and understanding and revealed them to babes" (Matt 11:25).

* * *

What we have just said concerning the developed formulas of the dogma of the Incarnation apply as well to those of the dogma of the Trinity. As we have shown, common sense understands that one can apply the term "person" to God. As Scripture affirms the existence in God of three distinct "selves," three subjects of attribution, common sense understands the formula "three persons" and even "three subsistences." The Council of Florence affirmed that "in God everything is absolutely one and identical

---

[64] Hello, *L'homme*, 62 ("The Mediocre Man").

where there is no opposition of relation," which is generally translated in the School[65] by saying that the three distinct divine personalities are subsistent relations or relative subsistences. Here, the formula is no longer accessible except to the theologians. However, common sense vaguely grasps that the name "Father" and, similarly, that of "Son" express opposed relations, that the divine nature cannot be tripled without there being three gods, and consequently that the Father must not have anything that is incommunicable except for his paternity, the Son except for his filiation, that the entire personality of the Father consists in his paternity, and all of the Son's in his filiation.

To follow an elevation[66] on the mystery of the Holy Trinity, there is no need for a technical philosophy. It is easy to make one see, by ascending the scale of beings, that the good is essentially self-diffusive, that, to the degree a being is more elevated, it communicates itself more perfectly and what proceeds from it remains more intimately united to it.[67] The plant and the animal beget, outside of themselves, a new being distinct from themselves, which can leave them. The doctor communicates his science externally to his disciples. If he is truly a master, a cause in the intellectual order, he communicates to them something most fundamental, his mind. And through this profound and intimate action, his disciples remain united to him. The friend would like to give his friend all that he possesses, to place in his service everything that he has, to give himself, no longer retaining anything for himself so that he may be one and the same being with his friend, having one and the same intellect, one and the same will. *At the limit, he who is the Sovereign Good communicates himself as fully and as intimately as possible.* He does not give only his ideas, his will, and his love. He gives his very *nature* in the ineffable mystery of his divine paternity: "You are my son. Today I have begotten you" (Ps 2:7). God begets, but he does not beget like man, by producing outside of himself a new being distinct from himself. He does not beget by multiplying his nature, as happens in material generation (which multiplies the form). God is pure spirit, and in the order of Spirit, he communicates his nature without losing it, without dividing it, without multiplying it. What He gives to his Son is in-

---

[65] See: Charles Billuart, *Summa sancti thomae*, vol. 2, p. 96; *ST* I, q. 29, a. 2 ("Whether the name of 'person' in God signifies a relation or substance"); *ST* I, q. 40, a. 1 ("Whether the relation is the same as the person").

[66] [Trans. note: That is, preaching after the manner, for example, of Jacques-Bénigne Bossuet.]

[67] *Summa contra gentiles* IV, ch. 11: "The loftier some nature is, the more that which emanates from it is more intimate to it."

deed all of himself, by reserving for himself only his relation of paternity. This is the most absolute self-diffusion, in the most intimate communion. *The more a being is perfect, the more fully it communicates itself and the more what proceeds from it remains intimately united to it.*

It is also easy to follow the Augustinian analogies that show us in the divine relations the supreme type of the life of the intellect and of the life of charity, the exemplar of all supernatural life: three "selves" living the same truth by one and the same act of intellection, likewise good by one and the same act of love. Thus, it is given to every soul to understand that the entire personality of the Father, "the entire self-ness [*egoïsme*] of the Father, consists in being related to his Son, in communicating his nature to the Son; the entire self-ness [*egoïsme*] of this Son, in being relation to his Father."[68] The entire self-ness [*egoïsme*] of the Holy Spirit is to render to the first two persons all that he has received from them. By the very thing that distinguishes them, the divine persons are related to the others by being opposed: "In Deo omnia sunt unum et idem ubi non obviate relationis oppositio."[69] Christ had said in very simple terms: "All mine are thine, and thine are mine" (John 17:10).

* * *

It is not even the case that the doctrine defined concerning the rational soul, the principle of bodily life, cannot be rendered accessible to common sense. Everyone distinguishes in man three degrees of life: the vegetative life that exists already in the plant, the sense life that exists in the animal, and rational life. Must one destroy the natural unity of the human composite by admitting three souls therein?[70] Moreover, is not man aware that he has within himself a single radical principle of intellection and of sensation, so that one and the same man experiences and perceives that *he himself* understands and *he himself* senses?[71] If the rational soul and the sensitive soul were really distinct, one self would perceive its sensations and another self its thoughts. However, given that sensation is an act of an animated organ (of the eye, of the ear), it must proceed from a root principle that determines or informs and animates the body. Therefore, the rational soul must give sense life to the body. It must give it vegetative life

---

[68] De Regnon, *Études sur la Sainte Trinité*, 1:69.
[69] [Trans. note: See Council of Florence, *Cantate domino* (Denzinger, no. 1330).]
[70] As Aristotle often repeats: "A *per se* unity is not made from act and act."
[71] See *ST* I, q. 76, a. 1 ("Whether the intellectual principle is united to the body as form").

also. The unity of the composite requires this, and in fact, the functions of sensibility being intrinsically inherent to the living organs, the principle that animates the body and imparts the power of sensation to it must also impart life to it.

[To draw one last example:] to explain for the faithful the mode of the Real Presence, one will say with the *Catechism of the Council of Trent*:

> Our Savior Jesus Christ is not in the Eucharist as in a place. Things are in a place only inasmuch as they have some kind of extension. Now, when we say that Jesus Christ is in the Eucharist, we do not give attention to the more or less great extension of his Body, but to the substance itself, considered independent from its extension. For the substance of bread is changed into the substance and not into the quantity, nor into the magnitude, of the Body of Jesus Christ. Now, nobody doubts that a substance can be equally contained in a small space as well as in a large [space]. Thus, the substance of air is as entire in a small part of air as in a large one; the nature (or the substance) of water is not less entire in a small vessel than in a large one. And as the Body of Our Lord replaces the substance of the bread in the Eucharist, one is required to agree that he is in the Sacrament in the same manner as the substance of bread was in it before the consecration. Now, the substance of bread is likewise and just as entirely in the smallest part as in the whole. This is not even debated.[72]

---

[72] [Trans. note: I have taken this from Fr. Garrigou-Lagrange's French. Without differing greatly from other English translations, slight nuances that he clearly wants to make would be absent were the Latin text used. Also, the text is this abrupt in the original French.]

Chapter 3

THE DOGMATIC FORMULAS EXPRESSED IN PHILOSOPHICAL LANGUAGE EXCEED COMMON SENSE BY THEIR PRECISION, BUT THEY DO NOT RENDER DOGMA SUBSERVIENT TO ANY SYSTEM

Therefore, dogmatic formulas developed and expressed in philosophical language remain accessible, to a degree, to common sense. Must we conclude that they do not exceed its strict limits? We do not think so. All that we must affirm is that they remain within the normal prolongation of common sense and do not make dogma subservient to any system, properly speaking. This is what we still must establish.

§1. These Formulas Exceed Common Sense by Their Precision

The notion of "subsistence," employed in dogmatic definitions as an equivalent for the notion of "person," is opposed in these same definitions to the notion of "nature" or of "substance" much better than simple common sense illuminated by faith provides for. Common sense only implicitly distinguishes these notions by formulating propositions in which a subject and predicates are related to each other. Here, by contrast, "subsistence" and "nature" are already very explicitly distinguished. It suffices to reread attentively the twelve anathemas of Saint Cyril of Alexandria against Nestorius, approved by the Council of Ephesus ("If anyone does not confess that the Word from God the Father was united to the flesh hypostatically (*kath' hypostasis* [Gk.]"[1]), the definition of the Council of Chalcedon against Eutychès ("In two natures, without confusion . . . and in one Person and one hypostasis"[2]), the fourteen canons of the Second Council of Constantinople that reproduce and explain this expression,[3] the twenty canons of the Lateran Council against the monothelites,[4] the Creed of Toledo[5] and the Decree for the Jacobites issued by the Council of Florence.[6]

The terms of the definition of the Second Council of Constantinople are so explicit that Saint Thomas does not fear to accuse with heresy two opinions emerging later, one of which admits in Christ only one person and two hypostases, and the other of which admits only an accidental union of the two natures: "These must not be called opinions, but instead, heresies condemned by the Church in the Councils."[7]

As Saint Thomas sufficiently indicates in the same article, by the conciliar definitions, under pain of error in faith and falling into the heresy of Nestorius or into that of Eutychès, it is necessary to admit the objective value of the metaphysical notion of *subsistence*, designating ontological personality, the foundation for what one can call psychological personality (self-consciousness) and moral personality (freedom). As we have said, to wish, with Anton Günther, if one contents oneself with a psychological or moral definition of personality, one will inevitably be led to hold, with Nestorius, that there are two persons in Christ, since there are two consciousnesses and two freedoms in him, unless one holds that there is only one consciousness and freedom [in Christ], which is the heresy of Eutychès and of the monothelites.

This notion of "subsistence," thus given precision, is obviously already an explication of the rudimentary metaphysics that common sense pro-

---

[1] Denzinger, no. 253. [Trans. note: Fr. Garrigou-Lagrange cites the text in Latin, including the original Greek for "hypostatically." His text reads, "Si quis non confitetur, carni secundum subsistentiam (*kath' hypostasis*) unitum Dei Patris verbum . . ."]

[2] Denzinger, no. 302. [Trans. note: Again, in the Latin, "hypostasis" is *subsistentiam*.]

[3] See Denzinger, nos. 421–38.

[4] See Denzinger, nos. 501–22.

[5] See Denzinger, no. 534.

[6] See Denzinger, no. 1337.

[7] Aquinas, *Summa theologiae* [*ST*] III, q. 2, a. 6.

fesses (*in actu exercito*), without reflecting upon it. Common sense uses *subjects* and *predicates* without noting (*in actu signato*) what constitutes the subject as subject. It employs the verb *subsister*, applying it to the persons and to things and not to their parts, but it does not ask why. Someone like Aristotle will need to come and write chapter 8 of the fifth book of the *Metaphysics* in order to extricate the metaphysics of *first substance* implicitly contained in the least phrase composed of a concrete subject, the verb "to be," and a predicate. Everyone uses the principle of contradiction,[8] but Aristotle needed to write the fourth book of the *Metaphysics* in order for it to be abstractly and rigorously formulated in a way susceptible to being applied to all beings. The same was true for the notion of "subsistence." As an explication of a vague datum of common sense, it is accessible to a degree to the latter, though it [also] exceeds it to a degree by its rigor and its precision. Were not quite lengthy debates between the Greeks and the Latins, between Saint Basil and Pope Saint Damasus, necessary before the formula "three persons" was admitted by the Greeks and that of "three subsistences" by the Latins? Were one to deny that the philosophical terms employed by developed dogmatic definitions exceed the strict limits of common sense, would this not be to wish to deny progress in our knowledge of dogma such as it is universally defined by Catholic theologians? Between the merely common-sense notion that the primitive Church had concerning the God-Man and the definition of the Second Council of Constantinople concerning the Hypostatic Union, there is an all-too-obvious passage from the implicit to the explicit.

Likewise, as it is found in the Council of Florence applied to the Trinity, the notion of "relation" also exceeds the limits of what we have called common sense. To exposit this definition in common [*vulgaire*] terms, without committing eight or ten heresies per sermon, one must elevate oneself above the simple data of common sense. Jacques-Bénigne Bossuet obviously could never have written his *Élevations sur les mystères* if he had not, for years, deepened his knowledge of theology. It is even precisely because he deeply possessed it that he succeeded at making it understood without using Scholastic terminology and, without altering it, succeeded in plunging it deep into the living sources of faith and our primitive intellectu-

---

8 [Trans. note: As noted in previous chapters, Fr. Garrigou-Lagrange most often uses "principle of contradiction" for what is most commonly referred to now as the "principle of non-contradiction." Thus, on the rarer occasions when he does use "principle of non-contradiction" for the same, I mark those instances with "[*sic*]" to signal that he means the same thing as in most places he means by "principle of contradiction" (and we now commonly mean by "principle of non-contradiction").]

al intuitions. Likewise, Aristotle came to compare his metaphysics with the spontaneous intuitions of the peasant, thus comparing reflection to nature. The same is the case for speculative thought as for art. Did not Molière read his plays to his servant?

The same holds true for the Council of Vienne's definition concerning the soul as the form of the body, and that of Trent concerning transubstantiation. "Substance" must be conceived of as distinct from quantity and from the law of phenomena, since only these latter remain in the consecrated bread. This precision obviously exceeds common sense.

§2. The Dogmatic Formula Expressed in Philosophical Language Remains within the Prolongation of Common Sense and Does Not Render Dogma Subservient to Any System, Properly Speaking; Theological Systems

Nevertheless, the dogmatic formula thus given precision does not render dogma *subservient* to any philosophical system, properly speaking. What is a philosophical system? It is a body of doctrine in which all the truths are ordered under a fundamental principle, or at least under a small number of general principles that one does not despair of reducing to unity. Thus, in general metaphysics, we have: (empirical or rational) *phenomenalism* or idealism, which reduces all of reality to our representations or ideas; the *philosophy of becoming* (empirical or rational), which reduces all the real to an evolutive movement underlying the phenomena; *substantialism*, which is subdivided into materialism, spiritualism, and dualism, depending on whether it reduces everything to matter or to spirit, or whether it admits both. These very systems take on more precise names when we consider their repercussions in natural theology, natural philosophy, and [philosophical] psychology, and in morality. In natural theology, we have: pantheism, atheism, dualism, deism, theism, pessimism, absolute optimism, and relative optimism. In natural philosophy: dynamism, mechanism, hylomorphism. In psychology: empiricism and rationalism; determinism and freedom. In morality: hedonism, utilitarianism, and rational[istic] morality. It is clear that dogma, as well as common sense, is radically opposed to a number of these very explicitly condemned systems. It is no less clear that many others are the expression of what the Church calls the *praeambula fidei*: the existence of one God, the first creative cause, distinct from the world; providence; the spirituality and the immortality of the soul; duty; freedom. We have even said that, of the three systems that can be conceived in general metaphysics, two are irreconcilable with dogma. But when, in order to express oneself in a more explicit manner, dogma borrows from a metaphysical system a notion like that of *subsistence*, or of *relation*, it does not need to understand it with its full systematic value, which arises from the relations that it has with the other parts of the system and, in particular, with the first principles or the first principle of the body of doctrine.

This is easy to show for the notion of subsistence. It arrives at the degree of explication necessary for science if one can connect it to being and to the first divisions of being: essence and existence or potency and act. And we find that Catholic theologians are not always in agreement when it comes to this work of analysis and of reduction to being. There are at least three theories of subsistence: that of the Thomists, that of John Duns Scotus, and that of Francisco Suárez. Likewise, the Suárezian notion of relation in the treatise on the Trinity notably differs, as is well-known, from the Thomist notion.

To know what personality or subsistence is, Saint Thomas studies what is required *a parte rei*[9] in order to verify the judgments of common sense that oppose the self *who* is a man to the nature *by which* he is a man, the self *who* exists to the existence *by which* he exists, the self *who* acts to the faculty *by which* he acts and to the acts that belong to him. Saint Thomas, in this analysis, is not content, as Henri Bergson claims, to "reduce into a system the dissociations effectuated upon reality by common thought and language."[10] Instead, he seeks to render the judgments of common sense *intelligible in function of being*. Following Aristotle's methodology, language helps him to distinguish the concepts expressed in words;[11] and to concepts that are mutually irreducible and irreducible to a third, in virtue of the objectivity of the intellect, there must correspond irreducible realities.[12] The criterion for these conceptual and real irreducibilities is not language. It is *being*, the formal object of the intellect. The criterion is the relation that the various concepts have with the first concept of all.

---

9 That is to say, from the perspective of the thing outside the mind, in extramental reality.
10 Henri Bergson, *L'évolution créatrice*, 353. [Trans. note: Fr. Garrigou-Lagrange does not mention the edition. In other books, his pagination slightly differs.]
11 See *ST* I, q. 13, a. 1: "According to the Philosopher (*De enterpretatione* 1.1), expressions are signs of understandings, and understandings are likenesses of things."
12 [Trans. note: Fr. Garrigou-Lagrange has *Quodlibet* II, q. 2, a. 4, ad 1, which does not exist in the most current edition. He may be referring to *Quodlibet* II, q. 2, a. 1, ad 1, though that text is not quite what one expects here regarding the principle mentioned in the body of the text above.]

Let us make an application of this methodology so that we might show how it is that one comes to know what personality or subsistence is. Everyone says, "this man *is* good; this man *is* reasonable." However, we do not say, "this man is goodness; this man is rationality." Why? Because the verb "to be" claims to express the *identity*—not merely logical, but instead *real* identity—of the subject and the predicate. Now, this man's goodness or rationality is only one of his characteristics. It is not he himself. On the other hand, on the pretext that the verb "to be" should express a real identity, one cannot refuse with the Sophists to admit the truth of the proposition "This man is good." One cannot be content with saying, "man is man," "good is good," or with Parmenides, "being is, non-being is not." One cannot deny, said Plato, the possibility of judgment.[13]

What we need to explain is merely what founds its truth *a parte rei*. Whence comes it that we can say, "this man is good, this man is existing, this man is acting, and so on"? We can do so because, under multiple formalities—goodness, existence, and action—there is one and the same subject who is good, who exists, and who acts. Indeed, to say, "this man is good," is to say, "this being that is a man is (the same [thing] that is) good; this being that is a man is (the same [thing] that is) acting." Under these multiple formalities (that *by which* he is good, that *by which* he is man, that *by which* he exists, that *by which* he acts), there must be a real identity (that by which he is *a that*, or, that by which he is *a subject*) that constitutes the subject as a subject, the whole as a whole. If our judgments are *true*, verified by reality, just as there is (from the logical perspective) a subject of attribution that itself cannot be attributed to anything (this man), so too there must be (from the metaphysical perspective, *a parte rei*) a subject to which belongs everything that is in him (nature, existence, activity [*opération*]) and that itself belongs only to him, one and the same subject who is a man by his specific form, who exists by the act of existing, self-conscious by reflection, acting by his will, but who is one and the same subject by something distinct from nature, from existence, from operations. Such is the profound meaning of the affirmative judgment and of the verb 'to be' that is the soul of this judgment. By this second operation of the intellect [*esprit*], we restore to reality what we have taken away by abstraction. After having abstracted two notions from the same being, by reuniting (*componendo*) them, we affirm that they express one and the same being under two aspects.

---

[13] [Trans. note: Among applicable texts, Plato's *Sophist* is almost certainly in Fr. Garrigou-Lagrange's mind on this point, where this topic comes up, even using similar examples. See *Sophist* 251a–d, and 261a–263e.]

This is what Kant did not understand, as we said above. He saw identity only in analytical judgments, pure tautologies in his eyes, whereas, in point of fact, every affirmative judgment, whether necessary or contingent, expresses by means of the verb "to be" an identity that is real, not merely logical. This is the foundation for the Thomist theory of the "supposit" or of the person, of subsistence or of personality. This can be realized by meditating on, along with the aforementioned articles from *Summa theologiae* [*ST*] I and III, the article where Saint Thomas asks himself "whether it is true to say, 'God is man'?"[14] In this text, one will see clearly expressed the claim that the truth of every affirmative judgment presupposes the identity of the *supposit* under the logical diversity of predicate and subject. In this way can this judgment be verified in Christ: "God is man."

But we do not thus have a *distinct* metaphysical notion of subsistence yet. *That by which* the subject remains one and the same subject under the multiplicity of formalities that are attributable to it (essence, existence, action), sustains the ontological relations with essence and existence that represent the first divisions of being. What are these relations? The solution to this problem depends on that given to the problem of the relations between essence and existence, as is clear upon reading the article in which Saint Thomas examines "whether there is one existence in Christ,"[15] along with the classical commentaries on this article.

Saint Thomas admits the real distinction of essence and existence in creatures.[16] The fundamental proof for this comes down to the following. An act can be multiple and limited only by a real potency, really distinct from act. Now, existence in creatures is an ultimate act multiplied and limited, in fact, by the essence of different creatures (stones, plants, animals, men, angels). Therefore, essence in creatures is a real potency that is really distinct from the act of existence. The minor premise of this argument contains the definition of existence and the affirmation of a fact. Existence is conceived only as the ultimate determination of what exists, that by which everything that is susceptible to existing is posited outside the state of possibility, outside of nothingness and [outside] of its causes. For each thing, for each activity [*opération*], for everything that can be, *to exist* is the final achievement. If some perfection is lacking in a being, this is because something in it has not arrived at existence. Moreover, in fact,

---

14 *ST* III, q. 16, a. 1.
15 ST III, q. 17, a. 2.
16 *ST* I, q. 3, a. 4; q. 7, a. 1; q. 54, a. 2. See also *Summa contra gentiles* II, ch. 52, and *De ente et essentia*, ch. 5.

existence is not unique. There is that of stones, of plants, of men, and so on. How are we to explain this *multiplicity* of existences? The major premise of our proof furnishes the response to this problem, which Parmenides denied because he could not resolve it. Parmenides denied *multiplicity*, just as he denied *movement*. And his denial of multiplicity posed the fundamental metaphysical problem as clearly as possible—namely, that of the relations between essence and existence. "What differs from non-being is being," said Parmenides, "and non-being is not. Now, two beings could be distinguished only by something other than being, that is to say, by non-being, which is not. Therefore, the multiplicity of beings is impossible and their distinction illusory."[17] He likewise had said, "Everything which is not being is nothingness. However, from being nothing can come, for being already is. On the other hand, from nothingness, nothing can arise. Therefore, becoming is not." Aristotle responds to the latter argument by distinguishing potency and act: "Nothing can come from already-determined being, for determined being already is. However, between this determined being and pure nothingness, there is room for a middle, real potency, a relative *non-being* that is." Saint Thomas understood that the same division of being suffices to resolve Parmenides's argument against the multiple: what differs from determined being is not determined being (*ens simpliciter*), but instead can be *undetermined being or potency* (*ens secundum quid*). Now, two distinct beings can be distinguished neither by the determined existence that is common to them nor by nothingness. Therefore, they are distinct by undetermined and potential being, by the real essence under existence, as matter is real under the form that determines it.

And this is not a purely conceptual distinction. These two concepts of potency and act are mutually irreducible because they are opposed. They are irreducible to some same, third thing. This third thing could be only *being*, and it is precisely the division of *being* into potency and act that is required *a parte rei* in order to render intelligible the multiplicity and becoming that exist *a parte rei*. If the intellect has an objective value, a real irreducibility must therefore correspond to this conceptual irreducibility. Essence and existence in the creature are really and ontologically distinct. Were we to deny this distinction, we would suppress the distinction between the uncreated and the created and return with Parmenides to acosmism by denying the multiple, or indeed, we would deny the objective

---

[17] Aquinas, *In* I *metaphya.*, lec. 9. [Trans. note: I have here followed the French, given that the text appears to be slightly altered by Fr. Garrigou-Lagrange.]

value of the principle of identity by affirming that beings are really differentiated without there being between them any real principle of differentiation that explains how existence is multiplied.

If such is the case, what will subsistence be? What constitutes a whole, separate subsistent as *a whole* as a subject that exists as *a subject* must be an element that "terminates" by uniting the nature or essence and the other parts of this whole. Moreover, this element is presupposed for existence (ultimate actuality), since the whole is what exists; it is to this whole, already presupposed as being constituted as such, that we attribute existence. Subsistence henceforth appears as an intermediary between the individuated nature and existence. It is that by which the whole is constituted an immediate subject of existence. "Existence follows upon nature not as upon that which has existence, but as upon *that by which* something is, but it follows upon the hypostasis or person as upon that which has existence."[18]

---

[18] *ST* III, q. 17, a. 2. [Trans. note: Fr. Garrigou-Lagrange's text is slightly problematic. It is very close to *ST* III, q. 17, a. 2, ad 1.]

Following in this matter the greatest Thomist theologians, we cannot admit that, according to St. Thomas, personality or subsistence is formally constituted by existence itself. He says very clearly in the text that we have cited, *ST* III, q. 17, a. 2: "*Existence follows upon* the supposit as upon that which has existence." Therefore, existence (*esse*) is not what formally constitutes the supposit as such. If it were to constitute it formally, the supposit or created person, instead of *having* existence, would *be* its existence, like God, and the real distinction of *what is* and of *that by which it is*, of the created essence and existence, would disappear. St. Thomas formally says, in *Quodlibet* II, q. 2, a. 2, ad 2, "Ipsum Esse (existence) non est de ratione suppositi," existence is not in the definition of man, neither in that of *Peter* nor in that of *Paul*, if one could define them, whereas personality is indeed what makes Peter be Peter, distinct from Paul, and makes him *able to exist separately* from him.

Moreover, St. Thomas says in *ST* I, q. 17, a. 2, ad 3, that there is *only one existence* in the Trinity, and he affirms elsewhere, in *ST* I, q. 29, a. 2, ad 2, that there are *three subsistences* in it. Therefore, one cannot claim that according to him subsistence is the same as existence.

Finally, in the treatise on the Incarnation, it is only after having determined what is the personality of Christ, and the Hypostatic Union, that he addresses the question "Is there only one existence in Christ?" (*ST* III, q. 17, a. 2). He treats it among the *consequences* of the Hypostatic Union: the unity of person entails the unity of existence.

See on this question Cajetan, John of St. Thomas, the theologians of Salamanca [i.e., the *Salmanticenses*], Jean Baptiste Gonet, and Charles René Billuart. [Trans. note: Fr. Garrigou-Lagrange's citation from *ST* III, q. 17, a. 2, is almost certainly that of ad 1. In this note, his vocabulary is slightly closer to the original than it is in the body of the text. Also, for his citation of the quodlibet, he uses a dated citation: *Quodlibet* II, a. 4, ad 2. This refers to the fourth overall article of the quodlibet in question: *Quodlibet* II, q. 2, a. 2, ad 2, as corrected above in this same note. Finally, the note reads near the

This is the process of which we have spoken: "*To connect to being this vague notion of common sense*, a notion that is possessed by all who give a sense to the word 'to subsist,' and who, in common parlance, contrast the self to everything that is attributable to it." Having finished this analysis, Saint Thomas concludes that in Christ the unique self is constituted by a unique subsistence, that of the Word, that Christ's human nature is deprived of the created subsistence that naturally would have needed to terminate it.[19] Finally, upon unity of subsistence there follows unity of existence. Christ's human nature exists by the same existence as the Word, and the Hypostatic Union is the most intimate of unions.[20] From this, again, one deduces that it is highly fitting that Christ had the Beatific Vision on earth so as to have clearly, by his human intellect as by his divine intellect, *self-consciousness*, consciousness of his divine self. To refuse to say that he had this Vision is to say he had only faith in his own personality. Finally, from this are deduced both Christ's impeccability and the infinite value of his merits, since the ontological personality that is the principle (*quod*) of Jesus's *divine freedom* is a divine personality. It is the very Word of God made man, who by his human freedom, offered himself, merited, and made satisfaction for us.

This notion of subsistence, thus analyzed and connected to being by the first division of being into potency and act enables us to conceive analogically the profound meaning of the dogma of the Hypostatic Union. But it is in no way necessary to give precision on this point in order to adhere to the most developed formulas of this dogma. In this work of analysis, there are even divergences among theologians. Suárez, who does not succeed at conceiving of real potency as an intermediary between act and pure nothingness, does not see the necessity of admitting a real or ontological distinction in creatures between essence and existence. Hence, he conceives of subsistence as posterior to existence and is led to admit that there are two existences in Christ. In the Thomists' eyes,[21] Suárez here commits an error in metaphysics and, in theology, compromises the intimacy of the union of the two natures in Christ. As for the Scotist conception that reduces personality to a simple negation (on the pretext that independence is a negative mode[22]), and that also admits two existences in Christ, it seems

---

end, "Ia, q.17, a. 2," instead of "IIIa, q. 17, a. 2," which Fr. Garrigou-Lagrange almost certainly means.]

[19] See *ST* III, q. 4, a. 2.

[20] See *ST* III, q. 17, a. 2.

[21] See Billuart, *Summa sancti thomae*, vol. 3, p. 45.

[22] In reality, it is a positive perfection expressed negatively, like infinity. If dependence is something positive, *a fortiori* so too is independence—that is to say, what constitutes

so little to safeguard the intimacy of the Hypostatic Union that Matthias Scheeben, following many theologians, could write: "The relation of the two natures appears from this perspective rather like an artificial juxtaposition rather than as an organic existence; . . . thus, we have the unsustainable or, in part, offensive propositions of Scotisco-nominalist theology on the formal holiness of Christ's humanity, on the diminished value of his merits, on a kind of possibility of sin."[23]

Whatever may be the dangers of these latter two theories, a certain latitude is permitted in the way theologians are permitted to conceive of subsistence, and it has never been defined that there is only one existence in Christ. Therefore, the term "subsistence" does not enter into the developed dogmatic formula with its properly systematic value that implies determined relations with other metaphysical notions.[24] As the condemnation of Günther has shown, what absolutely must be admitted, in order to avoid the heresy of Nestorius or that of Eutychès, is not only a psychological and moral notion of personality, but also an ontological one.

Therefore, the terms of the developed dogmatic formulas exceed the strict limits of common sense, but they remain within its prolongation. They remain accessible to it to a degree and do not make dogma subservient to any system, properly speaking.

§3. Far from Being Rendered Subservient to Our Concepts, Revelation Judges Them and Utilizes Them

One will not fail to object: "If the terms of these formulas exceed the limits of common sense, who guarantees for us their immutable value?" The Church herself, the instrument [organe] of Christ, who, in her infallibility, has judged the analogical value of the concepts expressed by

---

the unconditioned or the absolute as such, that which makes it to be self-explanatory, a *ratio sui.*

[23] Matthias Scheeben, *La dogmatique*, vol. 4, §416. [Trans. note: Fr. Garrigou-Lagrange does not cite the edition in question. Perhaps he is referring to M.-J. Scheeben, *La dogmatique*, vol. 4, trans. P. Belet (Paris: Victor Palmé, 1882), §416 (pp. 739–41) wherein this is treated.]

[24] The same could be said of the concept of *relation* in the Trinity. The divergences between St. Thomas and Suárez on the notion of relation have been placed in relief very well in A. Martin's article "Suárez théologien" in *Science catholique* from August 1899. [Trans. note: See note 5 in p. 2, ch. 4, of the present volume] Suárez accords a proper existence to each relation and seems not to be able to give any satisfactory response to the classic objection against the Trinity (see Suárez, *De Trinitate*, bk. 4, ch. 2, no. 7).

means of these terms. Far from *being made subservient* to these concepts, Revelation *makes use* of them. It *makes use of* them just as, in all orders, the superior *utilizes* the inferior, that is, in the philosophical sense of the word: the superior orders the inferior to the former's own end. The supernatural *makes use of* nature. Before making use of these concepts and these terms, Christ, through the Church, has judged and approved them in a wholly divine light that cannot have time as its measure, but rather the immobility of eternity. These concepts, which are obviously inadequate, can always be given precision. Nonetheless, they will never become obsolete. Dogma thus defined cannot *allow itself be assimilated* by a human thought that perpetually evolves; this assimilation would be only a corruption. On the contrary, dogma is what wishes *to assimilate* this human thought that ceaselessly changes because it dies every day; it wishes to assimilate it so as to communicate to it, already here-below, something of God's immutable life. The great believer is he whose intellect is the most profoundly passive in relation to God, who gives it life.[25]

Franzelin developed this idea in his treatise *De verbo incarnato*. In the twenty-sixth thesis on the notion of hypostasis and essence (or nature) to be refined by revealed truths, he states: "From certain truths that are revealed and known by faith and brought to completion through the history of dogmas, it is not possible for philosophy without error to claim for itself its *full autonomy* and independence from theology in constituting the notion of hypostasis and person and in determining its relation to nature and substance, at least if the notion is not solely restricted to the *connatural* mode of creatures' existence, but must be absolute and thus universal, such that it may embrace under itself the analogical notions of divine and created hypostases and of nature, and so that it may be extended not only to the mode of subsisting connatural to created substance but also to the supernatural mode of subsisting."

§4. The Principle of the Autonomy of the Mind

But what then becomes of the modern principle of the autonomy of the mind if we must receive from Christ a ready-made truth? "Dogma appears as being a form of enslavement, a limit upon the rights of thought, like a menace of intellectual tyranny, an obstacle and a restriction, externally

---

[25] In infused contemplation, the soul is more passive than active, under the action of the Holy Spirit within it.

imposed on the freedom of inquiry, all things radically opposed to the very life of the mind, to its need for autonomy and sincerity, to its generative and fundamental principle, which is the principle of immanence. . . . Is not the undisputed first principle of method, from the time of Descartes, the fact that one must only hold as being true what one has clearly seen to be such?"[26]

To this objection, already formulated by Günther[27] and by thousands of others before him, one could respond by recalling the value of the motives of credibility, the great fittingness of dogmas, their mutual harmony with each other and with the most fundamental needs of our nature. This profound, precise, in-no-way-extrinsecist apologetics is nothing other than speculative theology concerning each of the great revealed mysteries, theology of the Trinity, the Incarnation, the Sacraments, grace, and concerning the theological virtues. This apologetics shows the theologian, with ever-increasing power, that it is good—morally good and obligatory—to supernaturally believe by the speculative intellect in a testimony so divinely guaranteed (motives of credibility) that are given as a testimony of the First Truth (formal motive of faith) and the Word of eternal life (at-

---

[26] Éduouard Le Roy, *Dogme et critique* (Paris: Bloud, 1907), 9 and 7 ("Qu'est-ce qu'un dogme?" ["What is a Dogma?"]).

[27] Pius IX responded to this objection on December 21, 1863 (Letter to the Archbishop of Munich-Freising; Denzinger, nos. 2875–77), by warning the semi-rationalist Güntherians: "[We have heard . . . that some Catholics who diligently devote themselves to cultivating serious scholarship, trusting too much in the powers of the human mind (and) not at all deterred by the dangers of errors] in asserting a *false and in no way genuine liberty of science*, have been carried outside the limits beyond which the obedience due to the teaching authority of the Church, divinely appointed to preserve the integrity of all revealed truth, does not permit them to proceed" (Denzinger, no. 2875). On the subject of philosophy and the sciences, the Pope added: "For, although those natural disciplines rely *upon their own proper principles, apprehended by reason*, nevertheless, Catholics who cultivate [these disciplines] *must have divine revelation before their eyes as a guiding star*, so that with the help of its light, they may guard against shoals and errors, when they perceive in their investigations and deliberations that they could be led by them—as often happens—to bring forward what is more or less in conflict with the infallible truth of things that have been revealed by God" (Denzinger, no. 2877). [Trans. note: The text in brackets was not included by Fr. Garrigou-Lagrange but was added for the sake of readability. As regards Fr. Garrigou-Lagrange's position regarding the relationship between natural reason and revelation (framed in terms of the well-known French debates concerning "Christian philosophy"), see Reginald Garrigou-Lagrange, "On the Relationship between Philosophy and Religion," *Philosophizing in Faith: Essays on the Beginning and End of Wisdom*, ed. and trans. Matthew K. Minerd (Providence, RI: Cluny Media, 2019), 361–98.]

traction of the ultimate end). To believe by the speculative intellect[28] is to believe that what is revealed *is*—that God *is* triune and one, that Jesus *is* God—and this act of understanding can proceed only from this supernatural intellectual *habitus* that is faith itself.

However, since the objection is naturalist in its foundation and brings us back to the criterion for evidence in knowledge (by which, moreover, Descartes has only brought ruin to authority by conceiving of evidence as being subjective), and since the foundation of reality is not a first, immanent principle, but instead the transcendent and supernatural God, it suffices to respond to those whom this exterior revelation scandalizes: the agent must assimilate the patient and not let itself be assimilated by it. The plant assimilates the mineral, the animal assimilates the plant, man assimilates the animal, and God assimilates man and that by which man is man, the intellect. "All are yours; and you are Christ's; and Christ is God's" (1 Cor 3:22–23).

It is what Saint Thomas has shown in one of the most beautiful articles of the treatise on faith,[29] where he distinguishes a twofold movement in all created beings, the one that is natural to them and another that is communicated to them by a superior agent. By itself, sea water tends toward the center of the earth, but it is also moved by the moon, which produces ebb and flow in it. Thus, the human intellect, autonomous in its natural movement, through a supernatural movement must *obey* God, who wills to instruct it in supernatural things. (The first movement proceeds from a natural potency, the second from an *obediential* potency.)[30] The animal trained by man in a sense participates in human intelligence. The man instructed by God participates in the divine intelligence. [This is] servitude, if you wish, but after the manner of religious vows, a servitude that delivers from all other things, from all those things of the world, from its prejudices and its maxims, from its theories, from that of human masters so often unbearable through their vanity and pretension. Here again, it is

---

[28] [Trans. note: Though, one must remember that, according to the later Thomist school (following Thomas), while the knowledge of faith and theology are primarily speculative in character, they are technically *formally and eminently* speculative and practical. See: *ST* III, q. 3, a. 8; Garrigou-Lagrange, *The One God*, trans. Bede Rose (St. Louis, MO: B. Herder, 1943), 60–63; Garrigou-Lagrange, *De virtutibus theologicis* (Turin: Berruti, 1948), 244–45. See the Latin edition of this text, not the English translation by Herder, which is somewhat free at times with the text and its formatting.]

[29] *ST* II-II, q. 2, a. 3.

[30] [Trans. note: That is, to the created nature's non-opposition to being elevated to a higher order.]

true to say, "to serve God is to reign." A glorious servitude that above all delivers us from ourselves, from that alleged self-autonomy that is, to the eyes of the saints, the worst of servitudes, the most difficult to destroy, a servitude that God alone succeeds at annihilating in the terrible *passive* purifications of the spirit, which prepare for the loftiest contemplation. This alleged autonomy of mind [*esprit*] is true slavery because it leads us to *naturally* judge concerning *supernatural* things. It thus leads us to destroy God inasmuch as he is in us and to destroy ourselves by depriving ourselves of true life. When we forget the life of grace, we are like slaves chained by the *very limits of our created nature*. Through his revelation, God comes to break these chains and prepare us already here-below for the intuitive vision of the infinite, for the ineffable knowledge that he alone can naturally have of himself. A limit to the rights of thought, if you wish. Saint Thomas says expressly: "The understanding of the believer is said to be *captive* because *it is held by external terms* [*terminis alienis*] and *not by its own*."[31] However, this is a limitation that prevents us from wandering about, uncertain regarding all of the most important questions, a limitation that prevents us from falling back into what Pascal calls the order of minds and that of bodies, a limitation that requires us to elevate ourselves always higher in the specifically divine order.

A menace of intellectual tyranny? Perhaps, in appearance, at certain moments that the great contemplatives know, when God purifies their faith of every natural alloy. The First Truth thus acts at such depths in the created intellect, says Saint John of the Cross, that:

---

[31] Aquinas, *De veritate*, q. 14, a.1: "In faith, assent and cogitation are, as it were, on equal terms. For its assent is not caused by cogitation, but by the will, as has been said. However, because the intellect is not in this way terminated to one thing so that it is led to its proper term, which is the vision of some intelligible thing, thence is it that its motion is not yet quieted, but rather still has cogitation and inquiry concerning the things that it believes, although it most firmly assents to them: for as regards what is from [the intellect] itself, it is not satisfied by it, nor is it terminated at one thing; but it is only terminated by something extrinsic to it. And thence is it that the intellect of the believer is said to be *captive* because *it is held by external terms* [*terminis alienis*] and *not by its own*, as is said in 2 Cor 10:5, 'Bringing into captivity every understanding.'" [Trans. note: I follow the Leonine edition where there is a minor textual issue in Fr. Garrigou-Lagrange's text.]

As regards the movement of the will that commands the act of faith, it is itself commanded by this judgment: "It is good, morally good and obligatory, to believe by the speculative intellect in a testimony so divinely guaranteed (motives of credibility) that is given as a testimony of the First Truth (formal motive of faith) and a word of eternal life (attraction of the final end)."

Both the sense and the spirit, as though under an immense and dark load, undergo such agony and pain that the soul would consider death a relief. . . . Persons suffer affliction in the second manner [i.e., because of the soul's baseness and impurity] because of their *natural*, moral, and spiritual *weakness*. Since this divine contemplation assails them somewhat forcibly in order *to subdue and strengthen their soul*, they suffer so much in their weakness that they almost die, particularly at times when the light is more powerful. . . . How amazing and pitiful it is that the soul be so utterly weak and impure that the hand of God, though light and gentle, should feel so heavy and contrary. For the hand of God does not press down or weigh on the soul, but only touches it; and this mercifully, for God's aim is to grant it favors and not to chastise it.[32]

The brighter the natural light, the more does it dazzle and blind the owl; the more one looks with a fixed glance upon the sun, the more do its splendors fatigue its gaze; the more intense the divine light, the more the soul that is still powerless to bear it is plunged into the spiritual darkness. What a tremendous [*terrible*] and sweet mystery, the divine action upon created intelligence and freedom.

We refer here to these border cases in order to show the aspect of the truth found in the word "slavery" [or "servitude"][33] that scandalizes Éduouard Le Roy. Moreover, the saying is Saint Paul's, "Take every thought captive to obey Christ" (2 Cor 10:7). The apostle speaks in the name of God, *as one having power*, "The weapons of our warfare are not worldly but have divine power to destroy strongholds. We destroy arguments and every proud obstacle to the knowledge of God, and take every thought captive to obey Christ" (2 Cor 10:5–7). Would we wish to have a God who would act as

---

[32] St. John of the Cross, *Dark Night of the Soul* 2.5. Only these spiritual torments can help us to suspect what Christ must have experienced when he cried out, "My God, My God, why have you abandoned me?" [Trans. note: The translation for John of the Cross is taken from *The Collected Works of Saint John of the Cross*, trans. Kieran Kavanaugh and Otilio Rodriguez (Washington, DC: ICS, 1991). The order of Fr. Garrigou-Lagrange's text slightly differs from that of the recent English translation. There are also small differences. The particular difference of note is the fact that John of the Cross clearly wants to emphasize the moral weakness involved in this purification. The term is missing from Fr. Garrigou-Lagrange's French, which focuses on the natural infirmity of the soul and upon its "imperfection." He does not cite the edition of the French.]

[33] [Trans. note: Above, I was rhetorically loose with this translation in English, though the context makes clear the meaning and relationship between the uses.]

though he did not exist, a God who would be content with posing problems rather than resolving them? The human intellect must *obey* the First Intellect and Truth; it must obey Christ who has revealed this truth to us. Such obedience must be reasonable (motives of credibility), but it must not cease to be a form of obedience, *rationabile obsequium* (Rom 12:1; Phil 2:17).

Today, thanks to Kant and Bergson, certain philosophers believe that they *speculatively* reflect on the ultimate foundation of things more than did Christ, who would have had only a practical knowledge of reality. Their speculation would exceed him who for twenty centuries had been the master of humanity in the things of eternal life, up to the end of time, him who, when he spoke to us, had the immediate vision of the divine essence. How could the Word preach a vague religiosity to us, one that could be accommodated to all systems of thought regarding the fundamental relations between the soul and God? What a poor, fashionable philosophy that, thanks to modern progress, believes itself to have surpassed the Word of God pronouncing his priestly prayer before his own. This nonsense [*ridicule*] escapes notice precisely because of its depth; it passes by unnoticed. As for us theologians, charged with preserving, pure and exempt from every error, the truth revealed to the world, may Christ not have need to reproach us with this fault, which consists in *impoverishing the word of God* on the pretext of defending it and spreading it. The Church is asked to violate or blur dogmas in order to render them accessible to a great number of souls enamored with freedom. As regards the love of souls, the Church can know only that which is founded on the love of God, on an ardent, supernatural passion for the Truth. The rest is misery: "The reason for loving one's neighbor is *God*, for we ought to love our neighbor so that he may be in God."[34] The diminution of the truth will never serve souls. It can only make them lose their savor, instead of assimilating them to God.

There are impossible conciliations that only a Hegelian or a Bergsonian could dream up, that of falsity and truth, that of the devil and God. The reconciliation of the supernatural with the naturalist principle of the *autonomy of the mind* is of such a kind, for it may ultimately be the case that this principle would be found expressed in these words of Saint Thomas: "In this, (the angel) inordinately desired to be similar to God, because the angel desired as his final end *that to which it had been able to attain in virtue of its own nature,* turning its desire from the *supernatural* beatitude that is *from the grace of God.*"[35]

---

[34] *ST* II-II, q. 25, a. 1.
[35] *ST* I, q. 63, a. 4. [Trans. note: Unlike earlier in the work, Fr. Garrigou-Lagrange places

But how can we speak of intellectual pride? Is it not the nominalist who reconciles contradictories within becoming the most modest of philosophers? We do not claim, he will say, to diminish Christ's knowledge [*science*] or teaching; we only refuse to grant that human reason has the immutability accorded to it by theology. Christ and the Church, like it or not, have needed to make use of human concepts, and these concepts, because they are human, one day or another will be surpassed. We have sufficiently responded in advance to this objection by showing the immutability of what Bergson calls "the natural metaphysics of the human intellect," the natural prolongation and justification of common sense. For us theologians—and one need not fear saying "for the Church"—the human intellect, a living relation to being, is already, in the natural order, a participation in the immutable knowledge of God. "*The light of your face is signed upon us, Lord*; for the very intellectual light that is in us is nothing other than a kind of participated likeness in the uncreated light in which the eternal notions are contained."[36] Our concepts are *human* through the *mode* by which they enable us to know reality (because they are *abstracted* from sensible things, which constitute the object of the human intellect inasmuch as it is *human*). However, despite this human mode, our transcendental and analogical concepts (of being, unity, truth, goodness, the intellect, the will, etc.) represent to us a formal notion purified from any imperfection, an object that constitutes the object of the human intellect no longer inasmuch as it is human, but inasmuch as it is an *intellect*. Finally, history shows us that, contrary to the positive sciences, metaphysics, above all general metaphysics, develops very little. There are, fundamentally, only two possible positions: that held by those who affirm the objectivity of the idea of being and of the principle of identity (the philosophy of being) and that held by those who deny it (the philosophy of becoming and phenomenalism). In philosophy, we possess a great number of partial truths. The only thing remaining, as Afrikan Spir said,[37] is to show that all these truths are ordered under a unique principle, the principle of identity. Then, they form a whole and take on their true meaning and all their value.

---

the Latin of this passage in the body. I have translated from the Latin.]

[36] *ST* I, q. 84, a. 5.

[37] See Afrikan Spir, *Pensée et réalité*, trans. Auguste Penjon (Paris: Félix Alcan, 1896).

§5. Dogma Is Known More Explicitly in the Church by the *Maiores* Charged with Teaching Others, but It Is Penetrated More Profoundly by Those Whose Souls Are Purer

There is one last objection that could be registered against our thesis: the meaning of the terms employed in developed dogmatic formulas does not seem to need to exceed the limits of common sense. Dogmatic truth is "more profoundly penetrated by those whose soul is purer, more detached from the world, more united to Christ, not by those whose mind [*esprit*] is more penetrating and more cultivated."[38]

It is easy to respond to this objection: It is one thing "to penetrate more profoundly" and another "to know more explicitly." To use an example cited by Jules Lebreton, Napoleon's generals who lived during his lifetime knew him more profoundly than any of his historians, who, at a hundred years' distance, accumulate thousands of facts, a good number of which escaped the great man's intimate friends. A given theologian who has very mediocre faith and an interior life next to nothing is not unaware of the Church's decrees touching upon Christ. Such a man has his faith in Denzinger or tucked away in one partition of his memory, just as he has physics in another. His intellect does not live by it. One does not sense that he has what Saint Anselm calls *fides quaerens intellectum*. When he treats of the Incarnation, he does not seem to speak about something belonging to *reality*. He aligns texts and syllogisms on this subject as well as on another. He knows all the formulas very explicitly, but he scarcely has the *spirit* of the concepts, the spirit of the words and of the formulas—in this domain, the supernatural spirit, "this element that is irreducible to analy sis and that one is entitled to call synthetic, . . . this mysterious something, imperceptible to the senses and to the intellect that analyzes, intangible like the spirit, floating about things like their double, principle of their life *par excellence*, without which spoken words are only skeletons and small bones."[39] Then, this same theologian finds himself in a confessional in the presence of a poor woman who has fallen into the most heartbreaking distress. Obligated to come forth from his habitual banality for a moment, he ends up finding a word that consoles and fortifies: "Our Savior suffered

---

[38] [Trans. note: The text is originally from Jules Lebreton, "Dogme et critique," *Revue pratique d'Apologétique* 4 (May 15, 1907), 193–221, at 197. Fr. Garrigou-Lagrange does not cite it directly here.]

[39] B. Lacome, *Questions de Principes concernant l'exégèse catholique contemporaine* (Paris: Bureaux de la Revue Thomiste, 1904), 153.

even more than you for you." The Christian who loves his Christ with all his soul, more than herself and above all, then responds to him with a conviction that the theologian has never had: "This is the most exact truth." She believes more profoundly than does he in the redemptive Incarnation. Is this to say that the knowledge that the theologian has concerning dogma is of no use and that the terms employed for defining dogmatic truth must in no way exceed common sense? Saint Thomas responds to this objection when he teaches that the members of the Church are not all required to have a faith that is equally explicit: "Those of a higher degree [*maiores*] to whom it belongs to teach others are required to have a fuller knowledge concerning things to be believed and to believe more explicitly."[40] These *maiores*, in order to have a more explicit faith, do not [strictly speaking need to] have a more profound faith than this or that person from among the *minores* who is more detached from the world and more united to God.

Theology is not necessary for a given *individual*. It is necessary for the *species*, for the society that is the Church. The saints whose experiential knowledge would seem to be able to dispense with theology have expressly recognized this:

My opinion has always been, and always will be, that every Christian should try to consult some learned person, if he can, and the more learned this person, the better. Those who walk in the way of prayer have the greater need of learning; and the more spiritual they are, the greater is their need. Let us not make the mistake of saying that learned men who do not [practice] prayer are not suitable directors for those who do. I have consulted many such; and for some years past, feeling a greater need of them, I have sought them out more. I have always got on well with them; for, though some of them have no experience, they are not averse from spirituality, nor are they ignorant of its nature, for they study Holy Scripture, where the truth about it can always be found. I believe myself that, if a person who [practices] prayer consults learned men, the devil will not deceive him with illusions except by his own desire; for I think devils are very much afraid of learned men who are humble and virtuous, knowing that they will find them out and defeat them. I have said this because some people think that learned men, if they are

---

[40] *ST* II-II, q. 2, a. 6, ad 1. [Trans. note: Fr. Garrigou-Lagrange cites only the article, not the response number.]

not spiritual, are unsuitable for those who [practice] prayer. . . . I should prefer spirituality to be unaccompanied by prayer *than not to be founded upon the truth*. *Learning* is a great thing, for it teaches those of us who have little knowledge, and gives us light, so that, *when we are faced* with the truth of Holy Scripture, we act as we should. From foolish devotions may God deliver us![41]

Saint Theresa could live the mysteries of the Trinity and the Incarnation more profoundly than someone like Domingo Bañez, but she did not neglect, for this reason, the lights that this speculative theologian could bring to it; she wished to be *judged* by him. She drafted her autobiography so that three Thomistic theologians, her confessors, might know of the graces with which God favored her and the path that she followed in prayer.[42]

Saint Theresa knew that Christianity is not only a *life* but is also a *doctrine*, and that sacred doctrine is the foundation and the rule of the interior life (nothing is willed unless it is first known [*nihil volitum nisi praecognitum*]). Such obviously has been the thought of the Church from the beginning and ever. It suffices that one reflect on the insistence with which Saint Paul exhorts Titus and Timothy to know true doctrine well, to defend it with firmness despite persecution, to preach it, to conserve it intact as a "deposit," "[by avoiding] godless chatter and contradictions of what is falsely called knowledge" (1 Tim 6:20). "[The bishop] must hold firm to the sure word as taught, so that he may be able to give instruction in sound doctrine and also to confute those who contradict it" (Tit 1:9).

---

[41] *Vie de sainte Thérèse par elle-même* (new translation by the Carmelites of Paris), ch. 13 ([vol. 1,] pp. 174–75), ch. 5 (p. 78), and ch. 28 (p. 366). The words that we have emphasized show that St. Theresa admits between theology and mysticism the same relations as do theologians who are the most committed to their science. [Trans. note: Fr. Garrigou-Lagrange does not present full bibliographical details for this new translation. Based on the data provided here and in the next footnote, it is almost certainly taken from the *Oeuvres complètes*, published in Paris by Beuchesne from 1908 to 1920. The text above is taken from *The Life of Teresa of Jesus: The Autobiography of Teresa of Ávila*, ed. and trans. E. Allison Peers (New York: Image, 2004), 96–96. It is very close to the French that Fr. Garrigou-Lagrange cites, though he seems to reorder the text, reversing the order of the two sections of content. One should note that he is citing here only selections from chapter 13. As regards the emphasized expressions, the wording is a little different. The first reads "a poorly established spirituality"; the second is "doctrine," which may have a slightly different sense than "learning"; and, the sense of the final emphasized word is "supported upon".]

[42] *Vie de sainte Thérèse par elle-même*, 1:3.

Saint Augustine summarizes the entire tradition when in a classic definition of sacred science he presents it as the source of religious life *par
excellence*: "To this knowledge [*scientiae*] is attributed only those things
by which that most wholesome faith is begotten, nourished, defended, and
strengthened."[43] All orthodox mystics who have most fully lived this religious experience, which certain people today wish to confuse with faith,
distinguished, like Saint Thomas and all theology, two wisdoms that
should mutually aid each other: speculative wisdom (theology) and experiential wisdom (the gift of wisdom). "Wisdom," says Saint Thomas,

> denotes a kind of rectitude of judgment according to the divine
> reasons. *However, rectitude of judgment can take place in two man-
> ners*: in one way, *according to the perfect use of reason*; in the other
> manner, *according to a kind of connaturality with those things con-
> cerning which one must judge*. Thus, on the one hand, concerning
> those things pertaining to chastity, he who teaches moral sci-
> ence rightly judges through reason's inquiry; however through a
> kind of connaturality to chastity, he who has this virtue rightly
> judges concerning them. Accordingly, it pertains to the wisdom
> that is an intellectual virtue to have right judgment concerning
> divine things by means of reason's inquiry. However, it pertains
> to wisdom inasmuch as it is the gift of the Holy Spirit to have
> right judgment concerning them according to a kind of connat-
> urality with them; as [Pseudo-]Dionysius says in *On the Divine
> Names* 2.4, that "Hierotheus is perfect in Divine things, not only
> learning divine things but also suffering them. Now, this kind of
> sympathy, or connaturality, for divine things takes place through
> charity, which indeed unites us to God, just as said in 1 Cor 6:17:
> "He who is joined to God is one Spirit."[44]

Such is the true pragmatism that scoffs at [contemporary] pragmatism.
Not only does the will *apply* the intellect to consider divine things in preference of all others (order of exercise), but precisely because this will is
foundationally and divinely rectified, these divine things appear to it as
being conformed to the subject, *good* for it and all the more so as charity is
more intense and *true*, since they fully correspond to the most fundamentally rectified desires, by the divine light of faith. "Love passes over into

---

[43] Augustine, *De Trinitate* 14.1.
[44] *ST* II-II, q. 45, a. 2. Also, see *ST* I, q. 51, a. 3, ad 1.

the condition of an object [amor transit in conditionem obiecti]."[45]

§6. The Church Has Her Own Sense of Things, as well as Her Own Philosophy

Christianity is a *life* that is more particularly lived by those whose soul is purer and more detached from the world. However, the root of the living will that is borne toward the good is the intellect, which understands and judges this good. In order to be a *form of life* [*une vie*], Christianity must be a *doctrine*. This doctrine is more explicitly known by those whose mind is more penetrating and more cultivated. Expressed first in the terms of common sense, it is explained and gradually given precision in the dogmatic formulas that show with increasing clarity the relations of dogmas with each other, as well as with the great truths of the natural order. By this, there comes to be established what one can call, in a sense, the philosophy of the Church, or Christian philosophy. An elaboration of common sense in the light of faith, this philosophy is not a system, properly speaking. Nevertheless, it has its solutions for the principal philosophical problems—concerning sensible and intellectual knowledge, concerning God, concerning the human soul, concerning bodily substance. For the Church, sense knowledge has an objective value: the Eucharistic accidents are real and exist even when they are not actual objects of sensation in a closed tabernacle (thus, we have the denial of [*the idealistic claim that*] *esse est percipi*).[46] Intellectual knowledge, which alone attains substance directly, above

---

[45] The nature of this judgment *in the mode of a connatural inclination* has been studied at length by John of St. Thomas in his beautiful discussions concerning the gift of wisdom. See disp. 18, a. 4, on *ST* I-II, q. 58 [in the *Cursus theologicus*]. There, we find expressed, quite exactly, the true pragmatism, which is born of supernatural charity, which presupposes faith: "*Desire passes over into the state of an object* inasmuch as from such an affective experience the object is rendered more conformed, proportioned, and united to the person and more in agreement with him, and thus is the intellect borne toward it so as to have experience of, and contact with, it, and in this manner love is not related [to the intellect] precisely as moving in the manner of an *efficient* cause [*in genere causae effectivae*], but as moving in the manner of an *objective* cause [*in genere causae obiectivae*], inasmuch as through such an experience the object is variously [*diversimode*] proportioned and rendered in agreement [to the intellect]. Whence it is said in John 7:17: 'If anyone desires to do his will, he will know concerning the teaching whether it is from God.'"

[46] See, in the writings of theologians (for example, Billuart, *Summa sancti thomae*, vol. 9, p. 79) the refutation of the Cartesian opinion holding that the Eucharistic accidents are

the data of the senses, is also objective. Substance exists as really distinct from the sensible accidents; the substance of bread has been converted into that of the body of Christ. This natural intellectual knowledge enables us to affirm the existence of God with certitude.[47] This God is essentially distinct from the world, absolutely simple, immutable, eternal, infinitely perfect, omniscient, sovereignly good, absolutely free, provident, just, and merciful. He has freely created from nothing, in time,[48] spiritual substances, bodily substances, and man, composed of spirit and body. He can act outside the order of the natural laws that he has established. In man, the rational soul is also the principle of sense and vegetative life. This soul is specially created by God and not begotten by the parents. It is immortal; it will take up its body again after having been separated from it. It will be eternally rewarded or punished. It is free; the freedom needed for meriting is not only a kind of spontaneity.[49] There is such a thing as ontological personality, the root of self-awareness and of freedom. Such are the principal assertions of Christian philosophy; they largely result from the specifying of revealed data.

By developing [*évoluant*], dogma condemns systems. Do we really need to complain that error is judged to be such and that the domain illuminated by the divine light would grow? Monsignor Louis Duchesne expressed this truth quite well by comparing the development of Catholic dogma to the voyage of a ship that has sailed forth upon a ballasted voyage and is gradually loaded with goods:

> The water line rises along the hull. In other words, it sinks into the sea. A gash above the waterline at the start of the trip would not allow water to flood this ship. Now, however, it would be underwater and would sink it; and the ship would be endangered by damage

---

only subjective impressions produced by God in our senses.

[47] See the documents of the [First] Vatican Council.

[48] See John XXII, *In Agro Dominico*, the condemnation of propositions of Meister Eckhart wherein *creation ab aeterno* is affirmed [by Eckhart] (Denzinger, nos. 951–53). Also, see Denzinger, nos. 391 [old numbering; also, see notes in current Denzinger no. 745, Eugene III, Synod of Reims (started March 21, 1148)], 800 (Lateran IV), 3002 ([First] Vatican Council, *Dei Filius*, ch. 1).

[49] [Trans. note: Fr. Garrigou-Lagnrange cites Denzinger no. 1904 according to the old numbering, which corresponds to 3214 in the new, taken from the Holy Office Decree *Post Obitum* against Antonio Rosmini-Serbati. The text number does not seem to correct. It reads: "By divine abstraction, initial being is produced, the first element of finite beings; but by divine imagination the finite real (being) or all realities are produced of which the world consists."]

that, at the beginning of its voyage, would have been inconsequential. . . . Through its long voyage, the vessel of tradition has penetrated more deeply into the ocean depths; the submerged surface of the hull has become larger than at the start, although this is always the same doctrine, always the same ship. In the second or third centuries, it could be struck, with impunity, in certain places which are now under water *and must be respected for fear of jeapoardizing everything.*[50]

This is why we should not be surprised to read in the encyclical *Pascendi Dominici Gregis*, after the condemnation of agnosticism, immanentism, and evolutionism: "Further, let professors remember that they cannot set Saint Thomas aside, especially in metaphysical questions, without grave detriment."[51] Just as there is "a natural metaphysics of the human intellect,"[52] there is, in the sense that we have spoken of, a philosophy of the Church.

---

[50] Monsignor Louis Duchesne, "Les témoins anténicéens du dogme de la Trinité," *Revue des sciences ecclesiastiques*, 5th ser., 6 (December 1882).

[51] Pius X, *Pascendi Dominici Gregis*, §45.

[52] Bergson, *L'évolution créatrice*, 351.

Chapter 4

⟩⟨⟩⟨⟩

The Intellect's First
Glance and Contemplation

Si oculus tuus fuerit simplex, totum corpus tuum lucidum erit.
If thy eye be single, thy whole body shall be lightsome.
—Matt 6:22 (Douay Rheims)

Nearly thirty years after the composition of this book on *Common Sense*, we will take back up its fundamental theme in the following form, which will enable the reader to consider these things more simply and from above.

If ever there was a subject of such a nature as to interest, at once, the philosopher, the theologian, and those who are simple but who have lofty souls with great aspirations, it is that of the intellect's first glance concerning things and life.

This is what we would like to speak about here, first in the natural order then in that of grace, in order to show the value of this first glance and its virtual richness, something that is often unrecognized, along with the need to return to it, by means of a more-profound penetration, so as to free oneself from a sometimes-inextricable complexity that could potentially lead the intellect to sink into the multiple instead of dominating it and grasping its true meaning.

In particular, we would here like to note the resemblance that exists between the child's first intellectual glance and the simple contemplation experienced by the old man who has discovered the true meaning and value of life after the trials and disillusions that time brings in order to prepare us for eternity.

301

The First Intellectual Apprehension of Intelligible Being

When we speak of the intellect's first glance, we must first note that a rapid and superficial view often leads us into error because it focuses on something accidental or accessory. Thus, a first glance at a fundamentally erroneous though deceptively attractive doctrine, like that of Hegel, can lead us to adhere to it momentarily, or again, in another order, at first sight, Francis of Assisi could seem to certain people as being extravagant and nothing more. This is a deceptive first view of things. However, matters are different for the intellectual first glance that looks on the proper object of our intellect and proceeds immediately from the nature of the latter.

Our first intellectual apprehension looks precisely on the *intelligible being* of sensible things. Whereas sight attains the colored reality precisely as colored, the intellect attains this reality [precisely] as an intelligible reality. Likewise, just as hearing attains reality as sonorous and taste perceives it as more or less palatable, the intellect grasps it as *intelligible and true reality*. Thus, at its first contact with reality, it has a first, vague notion of being and the truth. Likewise, it has a vague intuition of the *first, universal, and necessary principles* that are the foundational laws of reality: "It is impossible that something at one and the same time exist and not exist, be and not be of a given nature"; "It is impossible that something would happen without a cause"; and so forth. From this moment, the intellect seeks out something that surpasses the senses and the imagination: *the raisons d'être* of things, their "why," their cause (e.g., *the raison d'être* of a clock's movement, something that no animal can ask itself about). From this first contact with intelligible reality, our intellect thus grasps that *the true* is *that which is* and that a true judgment is one that is conformed to reality.

This intellectual view of a *universal and necessary* object so inspired Plato and his disciples (and, later on, the ontologists) that they thought that they already had, in this initial view, a vague but immediate intuition of God's being and of the universal and necessary laws inscribed first and foremost within the divine essence. This represented a confusion of being in general with the divine being, which would lead to pantheism, as the doctrine of Parmenides shows (and, in the moderns, that of Baruch Spinoza).[1]

---

[1] Among the propositions of the ontologists, reported in the *Enchiridion* of Denzinger (nos. 2841–45), we read the following: "*The immediate knowledge of God*, habitual at least, is essential to the human intellect, so much so that, without it, it [the intellect] can

However, while dismissing this obvious exaggeration, it remains true to say that the first glance of the human intellect on reality vaguely contains all the truth that will ever be discovered by philosophical wisdom, which elevates itself to knowledge of the Supreme Being, the First Truth, who according to revelation is called "He Who Is." "Ego sum qui sum" (Exod 3:11–14).

Like gold that resists every sort of acid, the primordial and indestructible certitudes that resist every critique rest upon the first datum of the intellect. What is important here is to proceed methodically according to the order founded on the very nature of the mind [*esprit*] and of things.

If one denies the real value of this first datum and that of the principle of contradiction,[2] likewise wishing to resolve the critical problem by, like Descartes, establishing one's foundation on *the pure cogito*, the latter would vanish, for once the real value of the principle of contradiction has been placed into doubt, one could say: "perhaps I am me and not me"; "per-

---

know nothing, since indeed it is itself the light of understanding. *That being* which we know in all things and without which [we know] nothing is the *divine being*. Universals, *considered in their reality*, are not really distinct from God. The intimate knowledge of God, as being clear and simple, includes, in an eminent way, all other knowledge. . . . All other ideas are nothing else but modifications of the idea by which God, as clear and simple being, is known."

St. Thomas says in *Summa theologiae* [*ST*] I, q. 5, a. 2: "Being is the first thing that falls into the conception of the intellect; . . . whence, being is the proper object of the intellect and thus is the first intelligible thing, just as sound is the first audible thing." However, St. Thomas means that our intellect first grasps *the intelligible being of sensible things* and not *the being of God*. This is what profoundly separates Thomism from ontologism. See *ST* I, q. 88, a. 3: "The first thing that is known by us in the present state of life is the quiddity of material things, which is the object of our intellect, as has been said many times above (q. 84, a. 7; q. 85, a. 1; q. 87, a. 2, ad 2).

We cannot say that we first know our spirit, given that we define *spirituality* as *immateriality* (a sign that we first know matter) and speak metaphorically of the elevation, depth, breadth of our spirit, by analogy with spatial dimensions.

Moreover, if by introspection we discerned *the universal being* (attributable to everything that is and that can be) of our *individual* spiritual being in such a way that the notion of being and the principle of contradiction would have a real and universal value, why could our intellect not just as well *abstract* the universal notion of being from sensible things, known by our senses?

2 [Trans. note: As noted in previous chapters, Fr. Garrigou-Lagrange most often uses "principle of contradiction" for what is most commonly referred to now as the "principle of non-contradiction." Thus, on the rarer occasions when he does use "principle of non-contradiction" for the same, I mark those instances with "[*sic*]" to signal that he means the same thing as in most places he means by "principle of contradiction" (and we now commonly mean by "principle of non-contradiction").]

haps I think and do not think"; "perhaps I am and am not."

By contrast, if we maintain the real value of the principle of contradiction and methodically defend it against skeptics, as Aristotle does in the fourth book of the *Metaphysics*, then we will be certain that *the absurd* (e.g., the square circle) not only is *inconceivable*, but indeed is *unrealizable* outside the mind, unrealizable by any power whatsoever that there may be. When it affirms this law of reality, the mind already passes beyond itself by the *relation* that it has to extramental reality. From there, it is led to admit that "that which begins, or that which is contingent, cannot be uncaused," that "an uncaused contingent being" is not only unintelligible, but in fact, is really impossible. Likewise, it will be led to admit that every agent acts for an end, or that every conscious or unconscious action tends toward a goal.

From there, the mind [*esprit*] is also led to affirm, with absolute certitude, that there cannot be *experience*, properly speaking, without *an existing, experienced reality*, no internal experience without an existing mental reality (thus, *the cogito* is indestructible), no external experience without an existing external reality, no sensation of resistance (distinct from hallucination) without something that resists: "Feel and see [*palpate et videte*]; a spirit does not have flesh and bones," as Jesus said after his resurrection. *Videte.* One cannot truly *see* that which does not exist.[3]

A hallucination is to a true sensation what an echo is to a true, presupposed sound. The vague idea of hallucination already suffices to affirm this, and thus, *a fortiori,* does the distinct idea thereof, the result of scientific observation.

* * *

Such are the indestructible certitudes had in the order of possible reality and in that of existence. By that, we can see that, without the intellect's first glance on intelligible reality, all human, scientific, and philosophical knowledge would be impossible. And therefore, philosophy, as its development draws toward its terminus, should return, by reflection, to this first knowledge, whose true value it comes to appreciate more and more.[4] Ac-

---

3   See *ST* I, q. 51, a. 2, and on the *Palpate et videte*, see: *ST* III, q. 55, a. 6; q. 57, a .6, ad 3. [Trans. note: On this topic, see also Reginald Garrigou-Lagrange, "There Cannot Be Genuine Sensation without a Real Sensed Thing," trans. Thomas DePauw and E. M. Macierowski in *Philosophizing in Faith: Essays on the Beginning and End of Wisdom*, ed. Matthew K. Minerd (Providence, RI: Cluny Media, 2019), 101–19.]

4   See *ST* I, q. 79, a. 8: "Human reasoning, according to the way of acquisition or of discov-

cording to traditional realism, this is what makes manifest the weakness of nominalism and that of the subjectivist conceptualism of the agnostics, who, falling into the excess opposed to Platonism, think that our intellect attains only sensible phenomena and the subjective laws of logic. In the agnostic, the intellectual first glance is obscured. It has lost its penetration and stops at the surface of things. The agnostic misses the fact that, under the phenomena, the intellect attains, from its first awakening, *intelligible reality* and *the foundational laws of reality*, expressed in the first rational principles.[5]

Such is, to the eyes of traditional realism, the value of the intellect's first glance upon things, upon the intelligible being of sensible things.

---

ery, proceeds from certain things that are *understood without qualification*, which are the first principles. And, in turn, the *way of judging*, by way of resolution, *returns to the first principles*, in light of which it examines what has been found." The reason for this is, as is said in the same article, "Because motion always proceeds from the immobile and is terminated at something at rest." [Trans. note: See also the text cited in note 19 of pt. 1, ch. 2 of the present volume.]

[5] As St. Thomas shows in *ST* I, q. 85, a. 2, one cannot hold that the first object known by our intellect is *the idea of being* and not the intelligible being of sensible things. Indeed, the idea is known only by reflection. In direct intellectual knowledge, which is first, the idea is not, properly speaking, *that which* is known, but that *by which* we know the nature of things.

The idea is essentially relative to what it represents (for example, to the nature of the stone or of the plant that we know), and in order to know these extramental realities, we do not need, whatever idealism may say, *to pass out of ourselves*, as a man passes from his room; it suffices that the act of knowing and the idea be an *immanent quality that is essentially relative* to the nature of the extramental thing. This essential relation is what idealism misunderstands when it claims that we know only our ideas and not extramental reality. It would follow that the real value of the notion of being and of the principle of contradiction would remain at least doubtful.

It would also follow that our sciences, our physics, our mathematics, would have for an object not things, but our ideas, and it would be accidently that things would take place in accord with the laws discovered by science.

As we noted earlier, we could not even say, "I think, therefore I am," for given that the real value of the principle of contradiction would be in doubt, we would need to say, "Perhaps I am me and not me; perhaps I think and do not think; perhaps I am and am not."

With Descartes, it would be necessary to find a criterion of truth, to resort to the divine veracity that would have ordered our intellect; but this recourse would contain a *petitio principii*, for it would presuppose the proof of God's existence, which itself presupposes a criterion of truth.

Finally, this would be the very destruction of common sense: the criminal could say to his judges: I am the author of this assassination according to the subjective categories of your mind, but not according to a real causality, which you, in fact, do not know.

* * *

Hence, the principle of causality enables us to elevate ourselves to knowledge of the existence of God, the First Cause. This elevation is even a spontaneous movement for the child's intellect when, for example, he contemplates the firmament and the stars. He does not delay in grasping that *the heavens proclaim the glory of God*, according to the Psalmist's expression (Ps 18:2 [19:1]). As is said in Wisdom 13:1–9:

> For all men who were ignorant of God were foolish by nature; and they were unable from the good things that are seen to know him who exists, nor did they recognize the craftsman while paying heed to his works. . . . Yet again, not even they are to be excused; for if they had the power to know so much that they could investigate the world, how did they fail to find sooner the Lord of these things.

The intellect's first sight of the starry sky leads to God and reveals his grandeur. However, it often happens thereafter that this first glance is obscured when it tarries too much over the multiplicity of things and their details. This is what happens for the child when he must begin to study cosmography, to grasp the names and places of the various constellations and principal stars. Absorbed in this study of details, he sees less of the whole, which he had first grasped in a single glance full of admiration. He misses the forest for the trees. However, precisely because the study of particularities fatigues the mind, it experiences the need to return to the view that looks at things from above, one that is now richer, more penetrating, more extensive, confirmed by multiple experiences, and recorded in memory. A little science thus takes away the virtual richness of the first glance, and much science brings one back to it. The same is true in the moral order.

The First Glance of the Intellect on the Good

When the child comes to the full use of reason, he has the simple intuition of the first principle of the moral law—"The good must be done and evil avoided"—a principle that virtually contains the whole of ethics. As St. Thomas says:

> Just as the first glance of the speculative intellect is concerned

with *being*, that of the practical intellect is concerned with *the good*. Indeed, every agent acts for an end, which is a good. And therefore, the first principle of practical reason is founded on the notion of the good. It is expressed: "The good must be done and evil avoided." This is the first precept of the natural law, on which all the others rest.[6]

Many contemporary philosophers, more or less captive to the utilitarianism of the positivists or to Kantian subjectivism, no longer see the elevation of this first principle. They take no notice of it because, to their eyes, it is a banal thing, something that everyone knows.

Nevertheless, this is concerned with a truth of sovereign importance, for when we state this principle that "the good must be done and evil avoided," we are concerned not merely with the delightful or useful good, but with the *fitting, rational*, or *moral good*, to which our faculties, especially our will (the rational appetite), are ordered by the very Author of our nature.

Here, we are concerned with the *fitting good*, which must be *loved for its own sake*,[7] independent of the utility and delight that follow from it, and thus, even if we would need to die for it, we would need to sacrifice ourselves for love of this truth. *Do what you must, come what may*. Behold, the object of the practical intellect's first glance: the moral good to be loved for itself and more than ourselves.

This is what is generally misjudged both by individualism and by communism, which are opposed to each other so violently because they do not elevate themselves to this superior point of view.[8] Individualism

---

[6] [Trans. note: Here, Fr. Garrigou-Lagrange includes the Latin. I have chosen to translate his French and include the Latin here as he does. The changes in his translation are minor.] See *ST* I-II, q. 94, a. 2: "Sicut ens est primum quod cadit in apprehensionem simpliciter, ita bonum est primum, quod cadit in apprehensionem practicae rationis, quae ordinatur ad opus. Omne enim agens agit propter finem, qui habet rationem boni. Et ideo primum principium in ratione practica est quod fundatur supra rationem boni, quae est *bonum est quod omnia appetunt*. Hoc est ergo primum praeceptum legis, quod *bonum est faciendum et prosequendum et malum vitandum*, et super hoc fundatur omnia alia praecepta legis naturae."

[7] See *ST* I, q. 5, a. 6: "That which is desired *on its own account* is called the *fitting* [*honestum*]." See also *ST* II-II, q. 145, a. 3, ad 1: "That which is desired *on its own account* by the rational appetite, which tends toward that which is befitting [*conveniens*] to reason, is called the *fitting* [*honestum*]. However, the delightful [good] is desired on its own account by the sense appetite."

[8] [Trans. note: For an expansion on this topic, see Réginald Garrigou-Lagrange, "The

hardly considers anything other than the useful and delightful individual good; communism envisions only the useful and delightful common good. If they happen to consider the fitting good, they do so only to the degree that it brings us some subjective perfection, not in itself and inasmuch as it deserves to be loved for itself and more than ourselves, as the truth and end to which every intellect and every human will is ordered, in all places and at all times.[9] Sadly, this first glance is obscured in many people.

And nevertheless, is it not true that the individual is naturally inclined to love his species more than himself, as Saint Thomas says?[10] Did not our Lord deign to compare his goodness toward us to that of the *hen that gathers her little chicks under her wings*[11] in order to defend them, ready to sacrifice herself for them? The intellect should lead us to do, with full awareness, what the hen does without knowing her finality. It should (and does) lead us to love the truth and the moral good for their own sakes. This is what is openly expressed in the evangelical beatitude: "Blessed are they who hunger and thirst for justice" (Matt 5:6).

Saint Thomas has so lofty an idea of this first glance by the intellect upon the good, that according to him, if the unbaptized infant, nurtured among nonbelievers, upon arriving at the full use of reason, *efficaciously loves the fitting good for itself* and *more than himself,* he is justified. Why? Because he thus *efficaciously* loves God the Author of nature and the sovereign good, vaguely known, an EFFICACIOUS[12] love that, in the fallen state,

---

Subordination of the State to the Perfection of the Human Person According to St. Thomas," in Minerd (trans.), *Philosophizing in Faith,* 184–203.]

[9] At the beginning of the *Metaphysics* (1.1–2), Aristotle says that wisdom and truth ought to be loved for their own sakes.

[10] *ST* I, q. 60, a. 5, ad 3: "Nature reflects upon itself, not only as regards that which is singular in it, but much more with regard to what is common. Indeed, each being is inclined to conserve not only its own individual self but also its species. And much more does each being have a natural inclination toward that which is, without qualification, the universal good." In the body of the same article: "Because every creature naturally, on account of what it is, *is from God,* it likewise follows that, from a natural love, *both angels and men love God* (the Author and Conserver of nature) *more, and more principally, than themselves.* Otherwise, if by nature one were to love oneself more than God, it would follow that natural love would be *perverse,* and that it would be destroyed, not perfected, by charity."

[11] See St. Thomas's Commentary on Matt 23:37.

[12] [Trans. note: I here preserve an occasional style practice of Fr. Farrigou-Lagrange, the use of small caps for emphasis. In other supplementatary notes in the present volume and in other translations of Fr. Garrigou-Lagrange's work, I have noted the same practice by his student, Fr. Austin Woodbury, who picked up the habit from his mentor.]

is possible *only through the grace that elevates and heals.*[13] Saint Thomas expressly states the admirable boldness of genius:[14] "When he begins truly to have the use of reason, the first thing that man must do is to deliberate about himself *(deliberare de seipso).* And if he orders his life to the true end, to the true good (by efficaciously loving the fitting good more than himself), then, by grace, he receives the remission of original sin."[15] This is one of the forms of the baptism of desire: it involves a mysterious *supernatural illumination*, sufficing for an *act of supernatural faith*, and there is also the infusion of sanctifying grace and of charity, without which original sin would not be remitted.[16]

---

[13] See *ST* I-II, q. 109, a. 3: "In the state of unfallen [*integrae*] nature, man referred love of himself to the love of God as to an end, and, similarly referred the love of all other things to him as well, thus loving God more than himself and above all other things. However, *in the state of corrupted nature, man falls short of this* according to the appetite of the rational will, which on account of the corruption of nature *follows the private good unless it is healed through God's grace.*" [Trans. note: See Reginald Garrigou-Lagrange, "Whether Aversion from the Supernatural End Cannot Exist without Aversion from the Natural End," in *Grace*, trans. Dominican Nuns of Corpus Christi Monastery (St. Louis, MO: B. Herder, 1952), 504–6; Garrigou-Lagrange, "The Instability of the Acquired Moral Virtues in the State of Mortal Sin," in Minerd (trans.), *Philosophizing in Faith*, 171–82.]

[14] *ST* I-II, q. 89, a. 6: "Cum usum rationis habere incoeperit non omnino excusatur homo a culpa venialis et mortalis peccati. Sed primum, quod tunc homini cogitandum occurrit, est *deliberare de seipso*. Et *siquidem seipsum ordinaverit ad debitum finem, per gratiam consequitur remissionem originalis peccati*." [Trans. note: Because Fr. Garrigou-Lagrange has slightly changed the content of the passage, I have translated from his French and have included the Latin in this note. He includes the Latin in his original edition.]

[15] Pius IX also said: "We know as well as you that those who suffer from invincible ignorance with regard to our most holy religion, by carefully keeping the natural law and its precepts, which have been written by God in the hearts of all, by being disposed to obey God and to lead a virtuous and correct life, can, *by the power of divine light and grace, attain eternal life.* For God [who sees, examines, and knows completely the minds and souls, the thoughts and qualities of all] *will not permit, in His infinite goodness and mercy, anyone who is not guilty of a voluntary fault to suffer eternal punishment"* (*Quanto Conficiamur Moerore*; Denzinger, no. 2866).

[16] See John of St. Thomas, the Salamanca Carmelites, Jean Baptiste Gonet, and Charles Billuart on this famous article, *ST* I-II, q. 89, a. 6. Under the supernatural illumination that is thus given, there is *an act of supernatural faith*, which adheres, at least vaguely, to *the existence of God, the Author of salvation and remunerator.* This essentially supernatural act is called "implicit faith" in relation to the mysteries of Holy Trinity and of the Incarnation. We explain it in the remainder of this chapter.
[Trans. note: On this topic, also see: Édouard Hugon, *Hors de l'Eglise point de salut*, 4th ed. (Paris: Téqui, 1927), 82–127; Joseph C. Fenton, *The Catholic Church and Salvation* (Westminster, MD: Newman Press, 1958); Jacques Maritain, "The Immanent Dialectic

If Saint Thomas had not formulated this affirmation, very few theologians would dare to do so. But it shows us, according to him, what value this first glance by the intellect on the moral good (*the good must be done*) has, when, *under the movement of divine grace*, the will follows it by efficaciously loving more than ourselves the good itself and, thus, the Sovereign Good, vaguely known.

If this first glance perseveres in what follows with a greater clarity and penetration despite the multiplicity of things to be considered in the midst of the complexities of investigation and reasonings, persisting by becoming richer, more deeply lived, more profound, then it merits the name of "contemplation." Indeed, Saint Thomas defines contemplation precisely as this *simplex intuitus veritatis*, a simple, admiring consideration of the truth.[17]

Contemplation, which already exists in the natural order, is like the soul of investigation into the truth and the true good. Thus, little by little, the intellect passes from vague ideas of virtue, justice, religion, and righteousness to distinct idea of them, to the deepened and lived knowledge of these same objects, of this ideal that was at first glanced, an ideal whose grandeur imposes itself more and more. Finally, ethics, having been constituted, returns to its principle, to the first glance, which is thus richer, more penetrating, more extensive, and confirmed by the whole of life's experience. In this way, one comes to profoundly grasp the sense and scope of the principle: "The good must be done and evil avoided, no matter what the cost; do what you must, come what may." Who can measure the wisdom contained in these words that are transmitted from one generation to the next!

The virtual richness of the intellect's first glance in the natural order enables us to catch a glimpse of what is analogically similar in the order of grace.

The Supernatural First Glance

In the order of grace, infused faith enables us to adhere to the divine word and to what it expresses. It has for its motive the authority of God the Re-

---

of the First Act of Freedom," in *The Range of Reason* (New York: Charles Scribner's Sons, 1952), 66–85.]

[17] See *ST* II-II, q. 180, a. 6: "With the ceasing of discourse, the gaze (of the intellect) is fixed in contemplation of one, simple truth."

vealer, and *by adhering* to the revealed mysteries in the midst of obscurity, faith *penetrates* and *tastes them* to the degree that it is itself illuminated by the Spirit's gifts of understanding and wisdom, which are given to all the just.[18]

Thus, the supernatural first glance on the mysteries is a glance of faith. What are the principle truths with which it is first and foremost concerned? With those two primordial truths spoken of by Saint Paul when he tells us: "And without faith it is impossible to please him. *For whoever would draw near to God must believe that He exists and that He rewards those who seek him*" (Heb 11:6).

This is concerned not only with God the Author of nature, but rather with *God the Author of grace* and the Supreme Remunerator in the order of salvation. The Old Testament calls him "the God of Abraham, of Isaac, and of Jacob"; the New Testament calls him "Our Father, who art in heaven."

We see that this simple, supernatural glance on the revealed divine truth, and on the divine promises, inspired the entire lives of the patriarchs and that, at times, it took the form of an utterly lofty contemplation in them, as when Abraham, on God's order, prepared to sacrifice his son Isaac, who was, nonetheless, the son of the promise. The faith of the father of believers, a faith that was already unshakeable, became, after this ordeal, increasingly penetrating and fruitful. Similarly, says Saint Paul, "It is by faith that Moses held firm (against the persecution in Egypt), as though he saw him who is invisible" (Heb 11:27).[19]

This simple glance, which vaguely embraces all the mysteries of salvation, was also what was experienced by the shepherds who came to adore the Savior at his birth in Bethlehem. As Saint Luke relates it:

> And in that region there were shepherds out in the field, keeping watch over their flock by night. And an angel of the Lord appeared to them, and the glory of the Lord shone around them, and they were filled with fear.
> And the angel said to them, "Be not afraid; for behold, I bring you good news of a great joy which will come to all the people; *for*

---

[18] See: *ST* I-II, q. 68, a. 1, aa. 2 and 5; II-II, qq. 8 and 45.

[19] [Trans. note: Here, I have followed Fr. Garrigou-Lagrange's French, as it differs somewhat from the RSV, which reads "By faith he left Egypt, not being afraid of the anger of the king; for he endured as seeing him who is invisible." Also, he cites 9:27, but the text is a French rendering of 11:27.]

to you is born this day in the city of David a Savior, who is Christ the Lord. And this will be a sign for you: you will find a babe wrapped in swaddling cloths and lying in a manger.

And suddenly there was with the angel a multitude of the heavenly host praising God and saying, *"Glory to God in the highest, and on earth peace among men with whom he is pleased!"* (Luke 2:8–14)

The object of this glance of faith, the birth of the Savior, who is foreshadowed in all the promises of the Old Testament, contains, as though in a seed, all the mysteries that will be revealed in what follows, up to our entry into heaven.

The simple faithful and great contemplatives drink from the same well when they hear in the Christmas liturgy these words from Isaiah: "The light will shine today upon us, for the LORD is born for us, and he will be called the Wonderful, Mighty God, Prince of Peace, Father of the Future Age, whose reign will have no end" (see Isa 9:2–7).[20]

In the age when these words, "Mighty God," were pronounced, they were grasped by a *vague concept*, then later by a *distinct concept*, and then finally by a *lived concept*. It is one and the same concept, growing just as a plant develops.[21]

We find this first glance upon the divine truth in the first hearers of the Savior after the Sermon on the Mount. As is said in Matthew 7:28–29: *"And when Jesus finished these sayings, the crowds were astonished at his teaching, for he taught them as one who had authority, and not as their scribes."* This admiration was the sign of the nascent contemplation that, with charity, ought to inspire all our life.

We too should have this simple, supernatural glance, and each time that the mystery of Christmas reappears in the liturgical cycle, this glance should be more penetrating and more profound. It is concerned with the very Author of all the graces that we have received, of all those that we will receive, with the Author of life, who wills the salvation of all and who makes all things contribute to the good in the lives of those who love him and who persevere in this love. If we were to allow this glance to endure

---

[20] [Trans. note: Fr. Garrigou-Lagrnage only cites Isa 9:5, though the quote is an abbreviation of the section cited above. Given this abbreviation, the text is translated from Fr. Garrigou-Lagrange's French.]

[21] Likewise, in the development of dogma, for example that of the infallibility of Peter and of his successors, there is the passage from a *vague concept* to a *distinct concept* and, finally, to a *lived concept*.

more or less latently in the midst of our occupations and work, we would truly be contemplatives. This is realized in those who are simple and have lofty souls, in a given holy worker who was recently biographied, who each day united himself profoundly to the sacrifice of the Mass, by praying and offering himself for sinners.[22] This simple glance was particularly penetrating in the sublime beggar named Saint Benedict Joseph Labre, who so intimately lived on the Eucharist that he was transformed by it.[23]

Likewise, this first glance is often enough given to those who hear *the divine call to a higher life*. A young man who had forgotten what the Mass was entered into a church one Sunday morning while the Holy Sacrifice was being celebrated there. He had the impression that something indefinable but immensely grand was happening before him. Then, soon thereafter, he understood that he had a religious and priestly vocation. Another person who was Jewish one day had the occasion to avenge himself upon his greatest enemy, and at this very moment, he recalled this expression of the *Our Father*: "Forgive us our trespasses, as we forgive those who trespass against us." Instead of avenging himself, he pardoned [his enemy], and immediately he received faith in the entire Gospel. Soon thereafter he entered the Catholic Church and became a priest and a religious. His entire life, up to his last breath, was inspired by this first glance. Alfred de Vigny said: "A beautiful life is a youthful thought realized in mature age." More beautiful still is the life that, up to its last breath, is the realization of a divine inspiration. This is the mystery of the predestination of the saints.

Another example of the first, supernatural glance is found in the history of certain facts of divine origin, like that of Lourdes, destined to illuminate those who are simple, so as to save them. These facts, even from the outset, are easy enough to grasp for those who have pure hearts, like Bernadette Soubirous and those who defended her. They did not delay in seeing that there was a divine intervention involved here. To various degrees, they grasped its meaning and its scope. However, if one sets aside this outlook on reality, an outlook that is at once simple and superior, in order to be absorbed, with a curiosity that is more-or-less intermingled with pride, in

---

[22] See Reginald Garrigou-Lagrange, "Une sainte ouvrière, Ange de l'Eucharistie (1891–1922)," *Vie Spirituelle* 39 (1934): 268–81. [Trans. note: The footnote actually cites the article as though it was added by an editor, writing: "Cf. *Vie spirituelle*, June 1934, p. 268ff, 'Une sainte ouvrière' par R. G.-L."]

[23] See the admirable summary of St. Benedict Joseph Labre's life in Charles Grolleau, *Saint Benoît-Joseph Labre, Pèlerin Mendiant (1748–1783)* (Marseille: Publiroc, 1929). These powerful pages truly recapture the spiritual physiognomy of this great contemplative.

the study of the details of these facts materially taken, it is possible that one will no longer find anything but an indecipherable enigma in it. Thus, while learned men discourse as far as the eye can see and propose all sorts of hypotheses, God makes his work known to those whose hearts are pure. Finally, profound scientific knowledge, accompanied with humility, leads us to return to our primitive view of the whole of things seen from on high, in order to confirm it, in order to recognize God's action and the profound good done for souls.

The Darkening of the First Glance

Alas, though! Often enough, it happens that the mind's first glance comes to be weakened in those who had experienced its insight.

The natural intellect's first glance upon *intelligible reailty* and upon the truth in general is even sometimes darkened to such a point that man, led astray by false philosophy, persuades himself that he no longer attains anything but sensible phenomena or the subjective laws of thought.

The intellect's simple glance upon the *moral good* to be accomplished likewise comes to be obscured to the point of fading into utilitarianism, which preserves morality and virtue in name alone.

Likewise, the first supernatural glance upon *the Christian life* had grasped, quite profoundly, the first line of the catechism: "Why was man created and placed in the world? To know God, to love him, to serve him, and by this means to obtain eternal life."[24] Then, this first view is darkened for many people by the multiplicity and complexity of things, which they consider with a somewhat pure heart [*un coeur plus ou moins pur*]. Consequently, through the same causes, in certain chosen souls, the ideal of religious life or that of the priestly life, whose elevation they had once upon a time glimpsed, little by little fades, like a star lost in the depths of the sky.

This weakening of the mind's view results from the fact that the heart loses its purity and generosity. One begins to consider *the small aspects of great things*, seeing less and less *the great aspects of the small daily duties* that give the days and years their value. One comes to forget that the hour is made of minutes and the minute of seconds. And little by little, in place

---

[24] See *ST* II-II, q. 8, a. 3. Here, St. Thomas notes that the gift of understanding, which is like that of wisdom, at the same time speculative and practical, sometimes illuminates in a lively manner our thought concerning the ultimate end of the whole of life.

of the primitive simplicity of an already-elevated glance, one finds the supposedly-learned complexity of a knowledge that in fact slides downward into decay. Thus, thought descends with life, for if our life is not elevated to the heights of our thought, then the latter does not delay in descending to the level of our life, in virtue of the principle often cited by Saint Thomas: "As a given man is, so too does the end seem to him [Qualis unusquisque est, talis finis videtur ei]."[25] According to how our will and sensibility are well or poorly disposed, we judge well or poorly concerning the end that we must propose to ourselves. Thus, we come to replace our admiring vision of the starry sky with a material, if not materialist, study of the movement of the stars. In place of the contemplation of the ideal of a religious order, such as it was conceived by its founder and its great saints, there follows, little by little, a desiccated nomenclature, a code, or a host of laws that are considered more in their letter than in their spirit. True intellectual, moral, and religious life tends, thus, to disappear, giving way to a pointless form of mechanical observance. Thus, the spirit, encumbered as it is with a thousand useless things, needs to undergo great purification. Such was the case, in particular, for Scholasticism in its period of decline, deprived of the simple and superior insights of someone like Saint Thomas Aquinas. The spirit of systematization replaced its spirit of synthesis, and pedantry, with its fatiguing minutiae, led men to forget that the true masters of theology had been great contemplatives. The intellect lost the sense of mystery and of unity, sinking down either into the wholly material multiplicity of external facts or into a vain formalism that dwelt solely on *ens rationis*, the logical form of thought, by turning itself away from true reality and from life. The theologian ceased to be a theologian so as to become a philosopher who speculated on the faith. He even became, at times, a mere logician. The superior life of theology disappeared.

The Superior Simplicity Retrieved with Greater Experience

If superficial scientific knowledge sometimes distances us from the simplicity of the intellect's first glance, thorough scientific knowledge brings us back to it. The same must be said of the experience of life, whether superficial or profound.

   Great astronomers, through deep knowledge of the laws of the stars' movement, see in this harmony one of the most dazzling signs of the Su-

---

[25] *ST* I-II, q. 57, a. 5; q. 58, a. 5.

preme Intelligence who has ordered all things. The study of the marvels of animal instinct leads to the same result.

More striking still is the unification of knowledge in great theologians, notably in Saint Thomas. Some of his very technical works, like the disputed questions *De veritate*, *De potentia*, and *De malo*, contain an often-quite-complex exposition concerning great problems. It is not uncommon to find in these works, at the beginning of the articles, fifteen difficulties on one side of the problem followed by a dozen on the other, all prior to the search for the true solution. Then, Saint Thomas comes to the lofty simplicity of the principal articles of the *Summa theologiae*, articles that are like the great summits of a mountain range, illuminating all the others by the light reflecting off of them. This superior simplicity is utterly different from the superficial simplification of the popularizer. It is the superior simplicity of contemplation. Whereas popularization remains inferior to technical investigations, the contemplation of someone like Saint Thomas is superior to his technical writings. Thus, his language is elevated and free from technicality. Like great classics, it avoids neologisms and archaisms because it discovers the most profound meaning of received terms, which thereby lose their banality and take on an actuality that is superior to that of time. These summits of the *Summa theologiae* truly dispose us to contemplation.

Saint Thomas himself arrived at the fullness of contemplation when he became unable to dictate the end of this work, his masterpiece. He could no longer descend into the division of questions and articles, into the three objections that he had the habit of formulating for each article in order to show the difficulty of the problem. Henceforth, he dominated this complexity from far-too-lofty a height to descend again back down to that level; he contemplated the object of his treatises in a simpler and superior light. Then, the principle that he often had cited was truly realized: "Quae sunt divisim in inferioribus unite sunt in superioribus"; things that are divided in an inferior domain are united in a superior point, as the sides of a pyramid converge toward a summit.

At the end of his life, Saint Thomas entered into a superior contemplation that condemned him to silence. Something similar took place in the life of his master, Saint Albert the Great. At the end of his life, he could no longer attend to anything other than contemplation of divine things. He lived in retirement in his cell. One day, a bishop came to knock at the door in order to ask Master Albert about a question; the old theologian responded without opening it, "Albert is dead [Albertus mortuus est]." As this life was ending for him, he was preparing himself for the next.

Great contemplatives like Saint Augustine, Saint Gregory, Saint Bernard, [Blessed John van] Ruysbroeck, and Saint John of the Cross come to have an utterly lofty simplicity, full of life, charm, and meekness. As has been said with regard to Ruysbroeck: "The loftier one's contemplation, . . . to that degree is the contemplative's gaze more profound, more able to grasp human miseries in their depths: more merciful so as to encourage, milder so as to comfort, more ardent so as to love, more tender so as to bring relief. Tenderness grows with loftiness."[26] The contemplation had by these saints is "softer than the breathing of a sleeping child."[27] What could be softer and simpler than the breathing of the child Jesus, asleep in the crib of Bethlehem?

* * *

If, following along the pathway of contemplation, the unification of knowledge leads us back to the simplicity of the intellect's first glance by enabling us to discover the riches that it virtually contained, something similar must be said concerning the profound experience of life had by an elderly saint, even if he has no other knowledge than this.

The elderly man who is more and more sanctified returns, in a sense, to the simplicity of the child. The child, above all when he is raised in a very Christian environment, spontaneously believes what his father and mother tell him. He has confidence in them and loves them. Likewise, he is led by grace to believe in the word of God passed on to him by his mother, to hope in God, and to love him. He already lives the theological virtues, the acts of which he is made to perform in morning and evening prayer. He does not yet see the necessity of the moral virtues of prudence, justice, courage, and temperance.

Later, upon becoming a man, he realizes the need for these human virtues in order negotiate, as is necessary, his life with other men, and he often enough loses sight of the superior importance of the theological virtues that unite us to God. This is the complexity that follows upon simplicity. The old man who is sanctified returns to this first simplicity, but with lengthy experience in addition. Thus, he sees better and better what was virtually contained in the intellect's first glance upon things and upon life.

It has been said that there are two beings that are simple: the child that does not yet know evil and the saint who has forgotten evil by dint of

---

[26] Ernest Hello, in Jan van Rusbrock, *Rusbrock l'admirabile: oevres choisis*, ed. and trans. Ernest Hello (Paris: Librairie Poussielgue Frères, 1869), ix–x.

[27] Hello, in Rusbrock, *Rusbrock l'admirabile: oevres choisis*, , ix–x.

THE INTELLECT'S FIRST GLANCE AND CONTEMPLATION

having overcome it.

Thus, above the complications of existence, the simplicity of the first glance is retrieved through a contemplation that is penetrating and enriched by all the experience of a long life. This is what explains why the saints love children and are loved by them.

The Savior himself was once a child, and he held children closest to his heart because of their innocence and their simplicity.

Let us return time and again to the simplicity of the first glance of Christian faith such as it is expressed, for example, in the letter of Saint Paul to Titus, 3:4–7, which the second Mass of Christmas recalls:

> *Apparuit benignitas et humanitas Salvatoris nostri Dei.* But when the goodness and loving kindness of God our Savior appeared, he saved us, not because of deeds done by us in righteousness, but in virtue of his own mercy, by the washing of regeneration and renewal in the Holy Spirit, which he poured out upon us richly through Jesus Christ our Savior, so that we might be justified by his grace and become heirs in hope of eternal life.

This is the simple glance on the divine truth, accompanied by a truly right intention. When it perseveres in the mist of life's complications, then we have the fulfillment of the Master's saying: "If your eye is sound,[28] your whole body will be full of light" (Matt 6:22), your whole life will be illuminated. This perseverance of the simple glance of faith, enriched through the experience of life and becoming ever-more penetrating each day—this is what contemplation is. It is not something extraordinary like a vision, a revelation, or the stigmata. It is the fruit of an eminent grace, though one that belongs to the normal paths of sanctity. Sometimes, it has a savor of eternal life, for it is, as Saint Thomas said, like the prelude of heavenly beatitude.[29]

How marvelous it will be: the first glance of our entrance into heaven, a first glance that will no longer know any end, a glance looking upon the divine essence itself, immediately known, without the intermediary of any creature or of any created idea, however perfect it may be—a glance that will enable us to see, from on high, all things in God, as in their dawning!

---

[28] [Trans. note: This is taken from the RSV. The French presented by Fr. Garrigou-Lagrange reads, *simple*.]

[29] *ST* I-II, q. 69, a. 2: "The evangelical beatitudes . . . are a kind of beginning of eternal beatitude."

"A morning vision," said Saint Augustine, of an eternal morning![30] Then, the primitive simplicity of the natural first glance and that of the supernatural first glance will be eminently retrieved and immensely enriched. "Oculus non vidit, nec auris audivit, nec in cor hominis ascendit, quae praeparavit Deus his qui diligunt illum"—"Eye has not seen, nor has the ear heard, nor has it arisen into the heart of man, what God has prepared for those who love Him" (1 Cor 2:9).

---

[30] [Trans. note: As a place to begin concerning the Augustinian division of morning and evening knowledge, see: Aquinas, *De veritate*, q. 8, aa. 16–17; *ST* I, q. 58, aa. 6–7.]

INDEX